EXPLORING THE SWC300

David M. Addison

Other Books by
David M. Addison

A Meander in Menorca

Bananas about La Palma

Misadventures in Tuscany

An Innocent Abroad

Confessions of a Banffshire Loon

The Cuban Missus Crisis

Still Innocent Abroad

Exploring the NC500

Travels Through Time in Italy

Travels Around Sorrento

EXPLORING THE SWC300

A Cultural and Historical Companion to the South-West Coastal 300 Route

David M. Addison

EXTREMIS
publishing

Exploring the SWC300: A Cultural and Historical Companion to the South-West Coastal 300 Route by David M. Addison

First edition published in Great Britain in 2019 by Extremis Publishing Ltd., Suite 218, Castle House, 1 Baker Street, Stirling, FK8 1AL, United Kingdom. *www.extremispublishing.com*

Extremis Publishing is a Private Limited Company registered in Scotland (SC509983) whose Registered Office is Suite 218, Castle House, 1 Baker Street, Stirling, FK8 1AL, United Kingdom.

A CIP catalogue record for this book is available from the British Library.

ISBN: 978-0-9955897-8-0

Typeset in Goudy Bookletter 1911, designed by The League of Moveable Type.
Printed and bound in Great Britain by IngramSpark, Chapter House, Pitfield, Kiln Farm, Milton Keynes, MK11 3LW, United Kingdom.

Cover artwork is Copyright © Neil Mitchell at Shutterstock Inc.
Cover design and book design is Copyright © Thomas A. Christie.
Incidental vector artwork from Pixabay.

Author image and internal photographic images are Copyright © David M. Addison and Fiona J. Addison and are sourced from their private collection, unless otherwise stated.

For Fiona

Family member, friend, photographer
and much, much more,
this book is humbly dedicated in
appreciation for the time
she spent proofreading when she
could have been
pursuing her own interests.

Map of the SWC300 Route and its surroundings

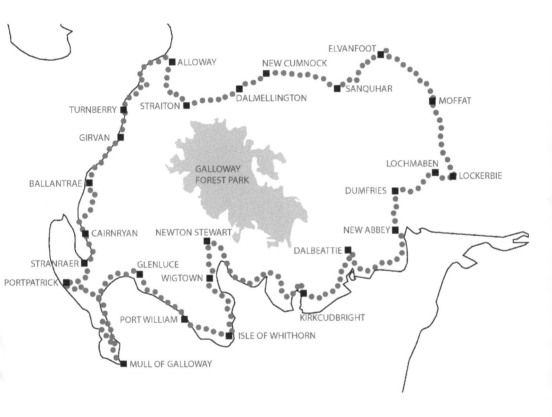

Contents

Acknowledgements

For my information on Robert Burns I am indebted to Maurice Lindsay's *Burns Encylopedia* [sic] (*robertburns.org*) for its comprehensive details about the life and work of Burns. It contains everything most people could possibly ever want to know about him.

For their assistance and information imparted, my grateful thanks to, as I encountered them:

- Ewan Maxwell of the Southpark Guest House, Locharbriggs
- Miriam Ridah of the Globe Inn, Dumfries
- Ruth Curley, Tom Hughes, Duncan MacLachlan, Carolyn Traill of the Dumfries Museum and Camera Obscura and Joanne Turner, curator
- Mhairi Hastings and Kay Yvonne Kingstone of the Savings Bank Museum, Ruthwell
- Christine McNay and Mary Ritchie of the Annan Museum
- David Heal and Robin Hall of the Devil's Porridge Museum, Eastriggs
- Joanne Dalgleish of the Visitors' Centre, Lockerbie
- Daria Zandomeneghi of the Old Bridge Museum
- Susan Neal and Paul Cowley of the Robert Burns House, Dumfries
- Heather Riley and Hazel Simpson of St Michael's Parish Church, Dumfries
- Maureen Milton, Hon. Sec. of Friends of Ellisland, and Alan Lammin.
- David Reid, Janet Lange and Charlie Ewing of the Dumfries & Galloway Aviation Museum
- Norman Wilson of the John Paul Jones Cottage Museum, Arbigland
- Howard Brown and Martin Rosendale of Threave Gardens
- Agnes Dow of the Dalbeattie Museum
- Tim and Carolyn Stephenson of the Gem Rock Museum, Creetown
- Bob Loudon, Gill Dolphin, Margaret Smith and the Trustees of the Wanlockhead Museum and Library
- Martin Hollingworth of the Leadhills and Wanlockhead Railway
- Ian McAndrew, Chairman of Visit South-West Scotland
- Angela Sloan of Gallie Craig Coffee House, Mull of Galloway
- Bob Roger of Culzean Castle
- Eileen Rainsberry, Project Manager at Visit South-West Scotland
- Michelle Andersson of Historic Environment Scotland

EXPLORING THE SWC300

A Cultural and Historical Companion to the South-West Coastal 300 Route

Chapter One

Dumfries: A Murder Most Foul

S O this is Dumfries! The Queen of the South. It sounds romantic and exciting – a very good place to begin our tour of the SWC300, Scotland's secret corner.

From our parking place on the spacious Whitesands, we can see the dark brown Nith flowing at a fair lick under Buccleuch Bridge. Downstream a little way, is the older and much more picturesque bridge named after Devorgilla, the mother of the infamous King John I of Scotland. After that, the dark brown of the river turns to white as it tumbles over the caul.

As I recall, the eponymous hero of *David Copperfield* was born with such a thing. It was advertised in the newspapers, going cheap at fifteen guineas. In case it has slipped your mind for the moment, the caul is the foetal membrane that, in rare cases, clings to the head of a newborn baby. It is considered to be very lucky and a protection against drowning. In Scots, without any nonsense of that sort, it simply means a weir.

On the other bank, the river glides silkily past what used to be the tweed mill. It was built by Thomas Frew in 1707. It served its purpose in its time but the wheels of progress grind relentlessly on and now the building has been turned into the multi-purpose Burns Centre, restaurant and film theatre.

We shall go there in due course, but first of all, as newcomers, we head for the Tourist Information Office which is at the other side of the Sands. There we pick up a disc which lets us park for two hours for free, and a street map. Thus armed, we turn to the right and head for Friars Vennel, which, like a dagger, thrusts into the heart of the town.

It's an appropriate image, because on Thursday, 10th February 1306, a man was stabbed to death in the church of Greyfriars Monastery which used to stand in the grounds now bisected by the Vennel. It was a murder that changed the course of Scottish history.

The victim was the Red Comyn and the killer was to become one of Scotland's greatest heroes, the future king, Robert the Bruce, vanquisher of

Edward II and deliverer of Scottish Independence. There was no love lost between the Comyns and the Bruces, cousins and aspirants to the throne of Scotland. The country had been plunged into a constitutional crisis when the seven-year old Maid of Norway on her way to claim the throne of Scotland, died in Orkney of severe seasickness.

The Nith, the Devorgilla Bridge and the Caul

The church was supposed to be neutral ground, a place of sanctuary, a place where the mortal enemies could meet and feel safe. Bruce had requested the meeting to propose that he and the Comyn buried the hatchet and formed an alliance against Edward I. After the murder, the Comyns were not slow to claim that their man's death was nothing short of premeditated murder, that he had been lured there under false pretences.

To give Bruce the benefit of the doubt, it is not beyond credibility, given the rivalry between the families, that what happened was simply a case of tempers flaring and hot-headed impetuousness taking over. Whatever prompted the stabbing, what happened next has passed into folklore.

Bruce, it is said, came out of the chapel and confessed to his henchmen Roger de Kirkpatrick and Sir Robert Fleming that he thought he might have killed his cousin. Kirkpatrick uttered the immortal words "I mak siccar" and drawing his dagger, hastened into the chapel to make sure that the Comyn was indeed, dead. To this day, the Kirkpatrick clan crest shows a hand holding a bloody dagger with the motto inscribed on a buckled belt below "I make sure", translated into English to make sure everyone gets the message.

Not wanting to be left out, Fleming accompanied him and came out of the chapel bearing the head of the Comyn saying, "Let the deed shaw", thus possibly trumping Kirkpatrick in deed and words. In any case, the Fleming crest shows the head of a very scary-looking goat with golden horns and Fleming's words inscribed above as the motto.

In another version of the story, it wasn't Fleming but Sir John Lindsay who accompanied Kirkpatrick and who merely stabbed the Comyn rather than decapitating him. Bruce himself was only saved by his chain mail when the Comyn's uncle attacked him with his sword. For his pains, he was cut down by

Sir Christopher Seton, Bruce's brother-in-law. After that, it was each man for himself as fighting broke out around the monastery. Bruce's men won the skirmish and made their escape to Dumfries Castle. There is nothing to be seen of that now. Their ghosts have gone long, long ago.

A mere six weeks after the murder, Bruce was crowned King of Scots. That said, it took years of guerrilla fighting against his enemies at home and battles against the English, before Scotland gained its independence from England, not to mention, according to another famous legend, the intervention of a certain persistent arachnid.

Independence did not come, as you might suppose, straight after Bannockburn, as the new king, Edward II (his father had died in 1307), stubbornly refused to give up his claim to sovereignty. It was not until the Treaty of Edinburgh-Northampton, in 1328, that he finally renounced all claims to the throne of Scotland. At the same time, Pope John XXII gave his blessing to Scotland becoming an independent nation as well as rescinding Bruce's excommunication which had been put in place by his predecessor, Clement V, for the murder of the Red Comyn.

Sadly, the place where that dastardly deed took place is altered beyond all recognition. It is, in its way, a sign of the times. It was a shop, once; a discount shop, actually. Now a sign says "To Let", a familiar sight in towns and cities throughout the land. Happily, however, there is a bronze plaque on a pillar outside which tells passers-by, or those waiting for a bus (for it is outside the bus station), that this unlikely-looking place is indeed a site of historical significance.

The plaque is not very obvious – you could easily pass it without noticing it but if you do notice it as countless bus passengers must have, it provides a very valuable service (like the buses). Without it, it would not unduly surprise me if even the native *Doonhamers* as they are known, to say nothing of visitors, might assume that the murder took place in the impressive neo-Gothic red sandstone Greyfriars Kirk just a couple of hundred yards away on the other side of the street. No chance. It's a mere youngster, dating from 1868 to be precise, and on our visit was as impenetrable as a fortress.

The monastery for the Franciscan order of Grey Friars, in whose chapel the Comyn was slain, was founded by the splendidly-named Devorgilla (c.1210-1290). She could afford it since she was a rich heiress (along with her two older sisters), her father being Alan, Lord of Galloway. Her mother, Margaret of Huntingdon, was the daughter of David, the grandson of David I (reigned 1124-1153) whose two older brothers had been king before him. Thus the blood in Devorgilla's veins was most decidedly a hue of blue.

• • •

Indeed, although well stricken in years, she might have been a queen herself, had she not predeceased only by a matter of months, the Maid of Norway. In what was known as the "Grand Cause", the matter of who should succeed to the throne was settled by Edward I, who out of fourteen candidates, chose Devorgilla's son, John Balliol. He was Edward's puppet and mockingly known as *Toom Tabard,* or empty coat.

Devorgilla's husband was also named John (c.1208-68) and believe it or not, he was the Sheriff of Nottingham from 1261-62 – a century before the one we love to hate, Robin Hood's bitter enemy. In 1263, after a land dispute with the Bishop of Durham, Balliol was forced to pay a penance by founding a college for the poor at Oxford. After his death, Devorgilla picked up the tab, thus ensuring its existence to this very day.

As far as being a *Doonhamer* is concerned, it is the equivalent of being a Falkirk *Bairn* or a Paisley *Buddy.* It's not difficult to work out the reason for the nickname, even if you have no knowledge of Scots, given Dumfries's southerly location and the major centres of employment, Glasgow and Edinburgh, being to the north. In the 19th century, if you were lucky enough to have some time off, you might announce to your new friends and workmates, "Ah'm ga'n doon hame" – but only if you came from Dumfries, of course.

Incidentally, the *Doonhamers* is also the nickname of Dumfries's football club, aka *Queen of the South.* Both the town and the club acquired this soubriquet in 1857 when a local poet, David Dunbar, who was standing for parliament, called it so in one of his election speeches. Regardless of how it distinguishes itself on the football field of battle, or not, it's one of the very few teams, perhaps the only one, to have the honour of being mentioned in the Bible: *The Queen of the South shall rise up at the judgement with the men of this generation and condemn them.* Luke 11:31.

Look it up for yourself if you don't believe me.

Chapter Two

Dumfries: A Walk Down the High Street

THE Carrara marble of statue of Robert Burns sits on a plinth of grey sandstone marooned by Buccleuch Street, Church Place and Castle Street. Burns himself sits on a tree stump with his back to Greyfriars Kirk (also known as the Burgh Church) with his face towards the High Street. At his feet is his *bunnet* and his faithful hound, Luath.

Luath was a collie and this member of the canine race doesn't look in the least like a collie, more like the lion from the *Wizard of Oz.* Designed by Amelia Hill (1820-1904), it was carved by Italian craftsmen and if you get a sense of *déja-vu* when you see it, put your hand in your pocket and should you happen to a have a fiver in it, you will see why.

Incidentally, Luath was supposedly responsible for introducing Burns to the greatest love of his life, his wife, Jean Armour, when he sent the dog home from a dance saying he wished he could get a lass as faithful as him. A couple of days later, Jean and he happened to meet and she asked him if he had found his lass yet. Two years later in 1786 (a bit slow for Burns), she gave birth to his twins, a boy and a girl. Sadly, the girl, who was named Jean, died the following year. The son, Robert, went on to have a long life, dying in 1857. Such is the lottery of life. It was nothing he did; he was just one of life's winners.

Luath, however, was a loser. One day he went a-wandering and was found dead the next day, having been killed by a person or persons unknown. The following day, Burns's

Statue of Robert Burns, Dumfries

Hole i' the Wa' Inn, Dumfries

father died. Perhaps only dog lovers and owners can understand what a double whammy that was. Lady Bracknell would no doubt have unsympathetically described such losses as "carelessness".

High on his pedestal, Burns is determined not to lose the posy of flowers he has clamped in his left fist. It's a wise precaution: the daisy he daintily holds between finger and thumb in his statue on Union Terrace in Aberdeen is always being nicked.

The statue was unveiled in 1882 by the Earl of Roseberry whose parents cruelly named him "Archibald Primrose". Nevertheless, despite this early setback in life, he rose (pardon the pun) to become Gladstone's successor as Prime Minister in 1894. He only lasted for a little over a year, however.

The memorial marks the start of our Burns Trail as we set off up the High Street. The first connection comes in the form of one of Burns's watering holes. A sign bearing his portrait and the legend "Hole i' the Wa' Inn Est. 1620" hangs high above a narrow alleyway. Incredible to think that by the time Burns had his first pint here, they had been pulling them for nearly two centuries!

A pair of cross-eyed lions above our heads snarl at us as we enter the close. At the top on the left, is a *trompe de l'oeil* street scene painted on the brickwork. I'm not sure what period it's meant to be, but a couple of gas lamps cast a golden glow over the scene, while a pair of parallel lines, presumably the tracks of carriage wheels have left their imprint on what appears to be sand – only it must have been drawn by a phantom horse as there is no sign of any hoof marks. In the distance stands a red sandstone church, probably meant to be Greyfriars Kirk. It certainly opens the close up but to be honest, it looks rather just too clean and tidy to be lifelike and is spoiled somewhat by a drainpipe running down the right-hand side.

On the wall to the right of the doorway into the bar is a framed quotation from *Ae Fond Kiss* written in 1791 to "Clarinda", aka Mrs McLehose. Born in the same year as Burns, she entered into a loveless marriage with her husband. Whilst pregnant with her fourth child to him, she ran home to daddy while her husband hied him hence to Jamaica.

After her father's death, she moved to Edinburgh, where in December 1787 she met Burns. There was a mutual attraction from the first. She was an aspiring poet herself. Under the pseudonyms of Sylvester and Clarinda, the letters flew back and forth between them, face-to-face meetings not being so easy. Apart from the slight matter of impropriety, Jean being his common-law wife, he had dislocated his kneecap after being thrown out of a carriage in an alleged drink-driving accident. Later it was to give him grief as it led to rheumatoid arthritis which got worse as he got older.

The relationship was never consummated, but guess what – Jenny Clowd, Clarinda's maid who played postie, hand-delivering the letters, delivered something else nine months later, in November 1788. Meanwhile, the long-suffering Jean, who was pregnant with twins for the second time, delivered *them* on 3rd March 1788. Sad to say, they died soon after birth. In November, Jenny gave birth to a healthy son. As ever, Burns wanted to do the right thing, but Jenny decided to keep the child herself.

As for Clarinda, after twelve years of being parted from her husband and in what seems an astonishing decision, perhaps to get over Burns and his affair with Jenny, she took ship to Jamaica to join her husband. Ironically, the *Roselle* was the very same vessel Burns had been on the point of taking to the same destination, only he changed his mind after word came to him that the critic and minor poet, Dr Blacklock, had told a friend he thought Burns should publish a 2nd edition of his *Poems and Songs* and was convinced it would be a success. Three thousand copies were printed (compared to six-hundred of the Kilmarnock edition). Blacklock was right. Burns was on his way, not to Jamaica, but literary success.

For poor Clarinda, however, her voyage was a big mistake. She found her husband happily ensconced with a black slave and mistress and found herself surplus to requirements. There was nothing else for it but to return to Scotland where she died a good many years later, in 1841. Happily for us we have the poem, and it was one Mrs McLehose treasured until her dying day. It's utterly poignant, a sort of latter-day *Brief Encounter*, except Coward's lovers never even got so far as exchanging a kiss, let alone consummating the relationship.

Inside the surprisingly spacious premises, in the public bar, are more framed lines from Burn's poems and a wall dedicated to QoS footballers of the past, but what intrigues me is an old black and white photograph of a street scene taken outside the premises. A crowd has gathered to watch a dancing grizzly bear, eight-foot high at least, muzzled, and at the end of a lead being held by a man armed with a long pole. You would have thought with one swipe of a mighty paw he could have dispatched his keeper if he had a mind to. In its own way that is a very poignant scene too.

The next point of interest as we continue our progress up the pedestrianised High Street is a column and a very badly-worn memorial to the Duke of Queensberry whose "exalted virtues rendered him the ornament of Society and whose numerous acts of public beneficence and private charity endeared him to his country". You could say they rather liked him. He died in 1778, aged 80.

Charles Douglas by name, he was Lord of the Bedchamber to George I, Vice Admiral of Scotland and Privy Councillor from 1721-29, and in 1763 and 1778, was respectively, Keeper of the Great Seal of Scotland and Lord Justice-General in the reign of George III. He did not serve under George II because of a spat between his wife and the monarch over his refusal to license John Gay's opera *Polly*, which satirised Sir Robert Walpole.

Resuming our walk, we come to the Mid Steeple in the middle of the High Street. Three storeys high, with a clock tower, it was built in 1708 and replaced the merkat cross as the Town House or administrative centre. Since then it has seen service variously as a jail-house, court house, weigh house and guard house, and in 1796 – a funeral parlour. Here it was that Burns's body lay in state and from where a lengthy procession left for St Michael's cemetery. Despite his dying wish to his friend William Gibson not to let the "awkward squad" fire over him, as a member of the Dumfries Volunteers, he was nevertheless given a military funeral and three volleys were fired over the grave. You don't always get what you wish for in life and you don't in death either, so it seems.

On one wall of the building, look for the Scots measure of an ell, 37 inches, as well as the distances to various places, including London. You can also see a bronze relief map of the town as it was in Burns's day and also the Royal Arms of Scotland and St Michael, the patron saint of the town who is standing on a dragon. They have been brightly painted. You can't miss them. The ell is a vertical iron rod and much harder to spot.

Not much further down the street is something else that has been brightly painted – or had been once. Actually "gaudy" would be a more apposite word. It's an ornamental fountain dating from 1882 and stands on the site of an earlier one to celebrate the

Sun Foundry Fountain, Dumfries

arrival of piped drinking water into the town in 1850. It was made by the Sun Foundry of Glasgow and it's just like those we saw on our tour of the NC500. You can spot them a mile away. Not the best choice of colours in my view – a deep maroon which looks as if the fountain had once gushed not water, but arterial blood, dowsing angelic cherubs from head to toe in gore – apart from certain items of jewellery they are wearing, and what I took at first to be fish, but actually are baby crocodiles. Somehow they have escaped the bloodbath and gleam with an undiminished golden lustre.

I know the Greeks painted their statues and in such vivid colours even a blind man could see them. We are accustomed to seeing them unpainted and I have to say, I much prefer them that way. I suppose there is a need for painting the fountain, it being iron, but more muted pastel colours for the plaster cherubs would have been better.

Across the street, on the wall of Waterstones, formerly the Commercial Hotel, a plaque announces that this was Bonnie Prince Charlie's HQ on his march north from Derby where, unlike Dick Whittington, he was forced to turn his back on London and ultimately face his date with destiny at Culloden. What it doesn't tell you is that the good people of Dumfries were put into a state of fear and alarm when they heard the news that he and his army of 4,000 men were advancing, nor that they were heartily glad to see the back of him. You would never have heard the strains of *Will Ye No' Come Back Again?* resonating through the streets of Dumfries – more likely cries of "Good riddance to bad rubbish" – if they were brave enough to risk having a dirk stuck between their ribs by a zealous Jacobite.

They were right to be worried. The Young Pretender arrived in Dumfries in late December 1745, demanding money with menaces – £2000, and 1,000 pairs of shoes, to be delivered within 24 hours. As a journal of the time put it: "They were most rude in the town – pillaged some shops – pulled shoes off gentlemen's feet in the streets." By the deadline of 8pm, £1,195 had been raised but only 255 pairs of shoes. What their would-be king did not realise is that Dumfries was not a rich town and most of the people, like his army, went shoeless.

The Prince's secretary was not amused and issued orders that the rest should be delivered as soon as possible. The impossible takes a bit longer, as secretaries never tire of reminding their bosses, but then later that evening, salvation came.

Word arrived that Cumberland's army was on the march and expected to arrive by daybreak. No time to lose. Before dawn, to the sound of a drumbeat and the beating of joyous hearts from the people of Dumfries, the Jacobites marched out of town, never to return. Had they known that for a fact, they would have hung out more flags.

With the retreating army went a couple of hostages to fortune: former provost Andrew Crosbie and one of the councillors, Walter Riddell of Glenriddell, surety against the rest of the money. By the time the Jacobites had advanced to Glasgow (another unwelcome host) somehow the money had been raised and the hostages were set free. Four months later, the Jacobite threat to the Lowlands was extinguished. Charlie and his ragged bunch of ill-shod Highlanders would never trouble the Hanoverian supporters who dwelt there again.

Chapter Three

Dumfries: In the Society of a Dead Poet

WE'RE beating a path now to another *howff*, another haunt of Burns and his favourite one – *The Globe*. It dates from 1610, making it even older than the *The Hole i' the Wa'*. In a similar fashion, it is entered through a narrow passage with Burns's portrait by Nasmyth hanging over the entrance. On one side of it, large blue letters proudly boasts that it is "Burns Howff" and on the other side, lower down, that it has a "Burns Room" and the "Poet's Chair".

I am not here to take the waters as I hasten to explain to the barmaid but to see the room and the chair aforesaid. Miriam, as I later discover her name to be, is very happy to oblige, but first of all she gives us a guided tour of the premises.

"That used to be the stables," she says, indicating a long room to our right, now filled with tables and chairs. Then, as we follow her along a short passage to our left, she indicates a small room off to the right. "This was the tack room," she tells us. A few steps further along the passage, we come to the Burns room, the present-day snug.

It is well named and all the better for that, for here, in this confined space, you don't have to exercise your imagination much to get a real sense that you are in the society of the dead poet. There's the chair on which he sat. *His* chair, right by the fire, but not the ingle neuk as there is no recess in this tiny room. Whenever he came into the bar, whoever was sitting in it got up so he could plonk his posterior on it, the place of honour – the reward for being a celebrity.

I knew beforehand that you are allowed to sit on it, just as long as you recite a verse of Burns, to which end I had been rehearsing *To a Mouse* off and on all the way up the High Street, well aware that if I failed to complete it, I would have to buy everyone a drink. (Does that include the bar staff?)

The Globe Inn, Dumfries

I let Miriam know that I am aware of the rules and ask if I may sit on the chair. She is quick to correct me. "Recite a line or two *and* buy everyone in the bar a drink."

Oh yes? When did the rules change and by whom? And which enterprising landlord made them up in the first place?

I can't help wondering about the name, *The Globe.* The theatre of that name which famously staged Shakespeare's plays was built in 1599. I don't suppose anyone would dispute that he is England's greatest playwright and poet too. What an amazing coincidence that Scotland's greatest poet/lyricist should chose this as his favourite drinking den. Maybe it was the name that attracted him.

Nevertheless, despite these associations with our National Bard, the place is hardly heaving. I can't help but think if this had been Shakespeare's drinking den, I'd bet they would charge you an entrance fee *and* charge you a fiver a pint just so you could boast that you had a drink in the same pub as him.

Fortunately that day of mass commercialism has yet to dawn in Dumfries. The locals have seen it all before. That said, there are enough of them in the place to make a poor pensioner like me not ponder for long if I really, really want to sit on that chair.

It's a curious sort of thing. I'm sure there must be a name for it. It has a curved back with arms that embrace but a square seat, so it's possible to face in two directions just as the mood takes you. In our poet's day I'm sure it would have been the most luxurious article of furniture in the room and the price of Burns's occupancy must have been to entertain the customers and by shifting his position just a little, he could ensure he could face his entire audience. That said, you couldn't get a lot of them in here.

Nothing to do with sour grapes but I decide I don't want to sit in it. For a start, that over-flowing and plump cushion looks as if it could have been made yesterday. Your arms may rest on the same place as the poet's but the seat of your pants wouldn't. No, it's just not worth the bar bill.

Miriam leads us upstairs to the bedroom where Burns slept when he was too *fu'* to totter home, leaving Jean to look after the kids. To be fair to him, being a hands-on father hadn't been thought of then.

There's the bed, not the original, although it looks the part. The mattress, however, is the original, so Miriam tells us. Surely I can touch *that*? I don't ask and have a feel at the nearest corner where it's poking out. It's light blue and feels hard and rough. Horsehair. The only way I would get to sleep on *that* would be if I were in a drunken stupor. I bet Burns slept soundly and snored the night away.

Robert Burns's House, Dumfries

The room contains some Burns memorabilia, but bed apart, the items of real interest are three window panes on which Burns has scratched some verses. It was the graffiti of its day but you couldn't just spray and run away. It must have taken ages to scratch those lines with the diamond-tipped stylus given to him by James Cunningham, 14th Earl of Glencairn. Try doing that in your local hostelry today and see where it gets you.

A notice in a frame by the window tells us these are facsimiles, that the original panes have been removed to the birthplace museum in Alloway. This is the chorus. Not one of his finest compositions, it has to be said:

O lovely Polly Stewart
O charming Polly Stewart
There's not a flower that blooms in May
That's half as fair as thou art.

My attention is drawn back to the biggest object in the room – the bed. I come armed with a little foreknowledge. Was it in this room and on that mattress that he impregnated Anne (Anna) Park, barmaid and niece of mine hostess, Mrs Hyslop? Burns was not a bad-looking loon (if Nasmyth can be trusted) and of course he had celebrity status. Along with that comes temptation, as the pop stars of today know all too well. What's a red-blooded male to do? Oscar Wilde quipped he could "resist anything except temptation". Our Rabbie could not resist a pretty face.

She inspired the poem *Anna of the Gowden Locks* (her reward, her slight claim to immortality). The first line runs: *Yestreen, I had a pint o' wine.* No wonder he needed to sleep over if that was his consumption! Still capable of fathering a child, mind you – a daughter, as it happens, Elizabeth, whom they called Betty.

Nine days after she was born, on 31st March 1791, Jean Armour presented her husband with a son, William. Prolific poet and lyricist, now prolific parent. And however incredible it may seem, Jean brought up Betty as her daughter. "Oor Robin should hae had twa wives," she is reputed to have said. You can just see her shrugging her shoulders at her husband's peccadilloes as if nothing could be done about it. That's just the way he was and life is. Boys will be boys and men will be men. You can imagine the dead feminists of the time (if there were any then) birling in their graves and those alive today spitting feathers at her forgiveness and understanding.

According to one version, Anna died giving birth to Betty, which might go some way to explaining Jean's generosity of spirit, but another tale has it she married a soldier and died giving birth to *his* child.

We are heading now to Burns Street where the poet himself died. We are following in the footsteps of those literary greats – Wordsworth, Keats and Coleridge who came here to pay their respects to the dead poet. Literally following in their footsteps, as those steps up to the front door look so worn they must be the originals.

It has often been said that the best things in life are free, and this is the proof. Unbelievable but true, it's completely *gratis* to enter the house which Burns occupied for the last two years of his life and which Jean did until she died in 1834. A long time to be a widow: longer than Burns lived. As the plaque outside testifies, the house was bought by their son, William, in 1851 and handed over to trustees to preserve the house and his father's memory. Well done, William!

The room to the left, now the reception room, is, as you would expect, filled with artefacts: a desk, a chair, original editions and some manuscripts, the tools of his exciseman's trade, as well as personal belongings which are always of special interest to me as it helps me to picture them better. But what captures my attention most is not this room but the kitchen across the passage. This would have been the hub of the house and boasts the original fireplace. I can just picture the admirable Jean at home in front of the range catering for her family with the help of a maid.

Her portrait hangs on the wall. Burns described her as his *Bonnie Jean*. Alas there are no paintings of her when she was in her prime to let us see what Burns fell in love with. This was painted when she was fifty-seven. She was no stranger to hard work and childbirth, nine in all, which tend to take their toll on a woman's face and figure. She looks back at me sternly and I can't hold her gaze. I have to look away. If Burns had been married to her looking like that then, I am sure he would have been afraid to stray.

• • •

I have been here before and call me morbid if you like but what I really want to do is revisit that room where that too, too short a life came to an end. Thirty-seven is a terribly young age to hand in your dinner pail.

At the top of the stairs, a room goes off to the left and one to the right, the death room, with a little room off that, over the stairs. That was Burns's study and office and served as the nurse's room when he lay dying next door. The main items of furniture in it are a writing desk and chair. Little brass plaques give their provenance. A notice says not to sit on the chairs for "safety's sake". That's a polite way of saying "Don't you dare!"

A little framed notice in the death room tells us that Burns composed nearly a hundred songs in this room and invites us to look for his signature which he scratched with his diamond stylus. The graffiti vandal had struck again.

And here is the bed (not the original) where he drew his last breath about five o'clock in the morning and where the drawing down of the blind in that small room announced to the watchers outside, who had got word that the end was nigh, that their worst fears were realised.

One shouted out in his grief: "Who's going to be our poet now?"

Chapter Four

Dumfries: Following in the Footsteps of a Dead Poet

ACROSS the road from the Burns House is a rose garden with a heart-shaped bed of red roses and in front of it a slate slab on which in gold lettering, the first two verses of *A Red Red Rose* are inscribed. It's a pleasant place where you can sit and reflect in tranquillity or have a stroll around it and look at the paintings on the walls or have a picnic with a tablet of the Selkirk grace conveniently placed above the table before you start. As for us, we are waiting for the eleventh hour when Paul, our guide, will take us on a guided tour to the Burns mausoleum.

At the appointed time, he emerges from the Burns house, where at the end of the street, a statue to Jean (1765-1834) has been erected. One of their sons is holding onto her right hand with both of his. I imagine by his height, it is probably meant to be Francis who was only seven when he was told his father had gone to heaven and he's clinging onto his mother for grim life lest she decides to follow him. Little did he know, and just as well, that he would join his father himself in seven short years later. Jean looks as if she might well be thirty-one, the age when her status changed from wife to widow.

Jean Armour Statue, Dumfries

We follow Paul across Brooms Road to the gates of St Michael's cemetery where outside them is what is known as the "Robert Burns Rock" which a plaque nearby tells us was gifted by the People's Project to mark the 60th Anniversary of the Queen's coronation. It features on one side, a great deal of comical-looking sheep from *Ca' the Yowes to the Knowes* and the Brig o' Doon with, on the other side, Tam o' Shanter and Maggie his mare, along with a wee *tim'rous cowerin' mousie* in the corner.

In the cemetery, a plaque lists the names of the friends of Burns who are in this earth interred. It is a taphophile's dream, as not only is there a map, but each grave is clearly marked with a little blue plaque and the name of the deceased. Very useful indeed. At No. 17 for example, lies James McClure who was with Burns when he took his last breath but the stone being flat, the letters have been invaded with moss rendering it illegible.

They are forty-four personages in all and I will not weary you with telling about each and every one but here (No. 11) lie the bones of the Rev. William Inglis, minister of Loreburn Church where Burns was a regular attender and who attended him on his deathbed. He formerly worshipped in St Michael's, where he had a family pew. We shall see where he prayed shortly, but first we shall see where he is laid.

Jesus, as everybody knows, arose from the dead. Burns didn't do that exactly, but he did arise from the grave in this obscure corner of the churchyard where Paul has led us. Wordsworth and his sister, Dorothy, had a bit of a job trying to locate the grave when they visited the cemetery in 1803. This prompted the good people of Dumfries to think they could and should do better for their dead poet.

Nevertheless, it took ten years after that before John Syme, one of the last people to see Burns alive and who had organised his funeral, to form a committee whose aim was to launch an appeal to raise the money for a more fitting monument. One of the subscribers was the Prince Regent no less, the future George IV, who contributed fifty guineas and Sir Walter Scott, who, as well as his cash, contributed his influence and connections.

After some problems with John Milligan, a local stonemason, who was contracted to build it, the mausoleum was finally completed in September 1817 to a design by Thomas Hunt at a cost of £331 8s 6d. (I wonder where the 6d. came in.)

The old grave is now occupied by the bones of Mrs Perochon. If you think that sounds French you would be right. She was Agnes Eleanor, the eldest of Burns's friend Mrs Dunlop's six daughters. She married a French royalist who fled the Revolution and originally set up as a merchant in London. She befriended Jean and in 1816, she wrote to Agnes agreeing that she might have the honour of occupying the spot where Burns was buried. She did not need it until 1825.

No need for Paul to guide us to where Burns lies now: you can't miss the mausoleum's stark whiteness amongst the red tombstones which form a guard of honour to where it stands at the end of a path of the same stone. Actually, the mausoleum is actually made of the same thing and if I objected to the gaudy paint on the fountain on the High Street, I think the brilliant-white paint rather becomes this monument to death. From a distance you might think it constructed of marble. Its elegant Greek curves and pillars make me think of a scaled-down Jefferson Memorial.

Like a jailer, Paul fits his key in the lock and we are free to enter. Beneath our feet is a trapdoor and, beneath that, is the tomb. On the wall facing us is the sculpture *The Muse of Poetry finding Burns at the Plough* by the London-based Peter Turnerelli who was of Irish-Italian extraction. Made of white marble, it showed Burns resting from his labours, gussied up in breeches and tailcoat with buckles on his shoon. He was gazing upwards in rapture at his Muse, Coila (so-named because of his origins in Kyle in Ayrshire), who was hovering above his head, her outspread cloak about to envelop him with poetic inspiration.

You will have noted my deliberate use of the past tense. What visitors today see is a copy made in 1936 by Hermon Cawthra, as the original, despite being sheltered from the elements, was showing signs of wear and tear. It's not a faithful reproduction. The renovators realised that Burns looked more like a gentleman addressing his fans in a salon in Edinburgh rather than someone about to do a hard day's graft behind the plough.

In addition, some anacronisms with regard to that implement were attended to. I suppose they might as well, since they were at it, but personally speaking, I couldn't tell my pattle from my ploughshare. And while *you* are at it, make a point of looking for the daisy and the mouse, the subject of two of Burns's most famous odes, which were added at the same time. Good idea, Hermon, if it's not a wee bit too twee.

The cupola is now copper-plated which is why a leaking roof was undoubtedly the reason why the statuary needed to be replaced. The restored cupola has been

The Burns Mausoleum, Dumfries

• • •

painted a very fetching colour of blue and studded with gold medallions of what I presume is Coila. Very tasteful.

On the floor lies a slab of red sandstone on which, inscribed in black letters, we are told that sleeping through eternity, along with our bard, are his sons, Maxwell and Francis Wallace. The former died on 29th April 1799, aged 2 years and 9 months, and who was born on his father's deathday. Francis Wallace died on 9th July 1803 aged 14 years. All were removed from their big sleep in the former grave and placed in the vault on 19th September 1815.

And then we come to this: *Also the Remains of JEAN ARMOUR, Relict of the Poet, born Feby 1763, died 26th March 1834.* Of all the names to call a poor, widowed wife, then "relict" surely must the worst. Finally we are told, in smaller letters, to make it fit in, that Robert, his eldest son, who died on 4th May 1857, aged 70, rests here too. The first shall come last.

Also sharing the mausoleum is Burns's son, Colonel William Nicol Burns (he who bought his father's house, remember) and who was born at Ellisland in 1791 and died in Cheltenham in 1872. Also entombed is another of Burns's sons, Major James Glencairn Burns, who was born in Dumfries in 1794 and who also died in in Cheltenham, in 1865.

His memorial tablet makes interesting reading. Also mentioned in dispatches, so to speak, are his first wife, Sarah Robinson, who died at Neemuch in the West Indies in 1821 aged only 24. A month later, their son, Robert Shaw, died there aged 18 months and if God had not tried him quite enough, their daughter, Jean Isabella, died at sea in 1823, aged 4 years 5 months. No wonder the poor man tried to seek some solace and happiness in a second marriage. Let's hope he did find some, but more sadness was in store when his second wife, Mary Beckett, predeceased him at the appropriately named Gravesend in Kent, 1844, aged 52 years. After he was widowed, he lived with William.

Incidentally, we couldn't help but notice on our way to the mausoleum, just how many tombstones recorded deaths in Jamaica and the West Indies. No doubt it had something to do with the East India Company of which the Burns brothers were both employees.

Before poor Jean's bones were laid to rest upon those of her husband and her unfortunate children who never had much of a life, poor sods, a plaster cast was made of Burns's skull and those clever people under the leadership of Caroline Wilkinson, Professor of Craniofacial Identification at Dundee University, have given us just about as close an idea as you can get, of what it would have been like to meet Burns face to face.

Their work was revealed to the nation, on STV, in 2013, a couple of days before Burns's birthday (a pity they didn't wait till then – it would have been like a rebirth). The University team did not base their likeness on the skull alone, but on portraits by Nasmyth and others. A certain Alexander Reid painted a miniature of Burns less than two years before his death and this is what the subject said about it: "I think he has hit by far the best likeness of what I am at this moment, that I think was ever taken of anybody." Now here's

Cholera Memorial, Dumfries

the thing. Reid's miniature is a profile. Can you work out what looks back at you in the mirror from that?

It's not for me to say if the Dundee University's team's face makes him look handsome or not. What do I know about what ladies find attractive? All I can say is judging from that, he looks nothing like as handsome as the ubiquitous Nasmyth portrait which has become *the* face of Rabbie Burns. And let's face it, whatever the real physiognomy looked like, it never held him back from the lassies-o. But then, bear in mind, never did Mick Jagger's.

Paul guides us to the exit but on the way, our attention is drawn to a large monument to the left of the path. It stands in the middle of a rectangular plot enclosed by iron railings. The date is 1832 and it makes for grim reading. "Here lie the remains of 420 victims of Asiatic cholera". The pestilence began on 13th September and remained until 27th November and "seized at least 900 individuals of whom 44 died in one day". It goes on to say that no more than 415 were reported as having recovered.

The money for the monument was raised from collections in churches in the town. They couldn't resist taking the chance to do a bit of proselytising. We are told it was erected as a "solemn warning" that the "benefit might not be lost to posterity" and at the very bottom, a quotation from Matthew XXV. 15: *Watch therefore, for ye know neither the day nor the hour.*

Covenanters' Monument, Dumfries

On our way between the first Burns grave and the mausoleum, our attention had been drawn to a tall pyramid of grey granite. It is the Martyrs' Monument. They seem to have had some doubt where to put the apostrophe and so put it on either side of the "s". One of them has to be right! It was erected in 1834, just two years after the cholera epedemic, but it commemorates a time so grim it was known as the "Killing Time" – a time of religious persecution against the Covenanters who were prepared to lay down their lives in order to prevent Charles II's best efforts to renege on his Covenant not to restore bishops and shove in Catholicism by the back door.

This impressive monument, in contrast to the one to the cholera victims, marks the remains of only two men, William Grierson and William Welsh "who suffered unto death for their adherence to the principles of the Reformation Jany 2nd 1667". The service was conducted by the Rev. Symington of Sanquhar which was a hotbed of Covenanters in those days. But that is a tale I must keep for another time, when we go there, as we shall, in due course.

The monument also commemorates the sacrifice of James Kirk who was shot on the sands of Dumfries in March 1685. This information is followed by a reference to Revelations XII, II: *...they did not cling to life even in the face of death.* It must be a great thing to go into the jaws of death without fear, even to welcome it.

And so ends our tour of the graveyard. Goodbye Paul, and thanks.

• • •

Chapter Five

St Michael's: The Anaesthetist and the Communion Tokens

NOW for the church. There's the steeple and there's the people, or at least two of them. Their names turn out to be Heather and Hazel and they have been planted *unco richt* by the entrance in order to welcome visitors. Heather takes us into the vestibule where she gives us a brief history of the church.

It's an old, old story, almost as old as time itself. Long before Christianity came to these shores, not so far away, at Whithorn (another tale for another time), they reckon this was a site of Druid worship. If there is no firm evidence to substantiate this, so what!

It is thought there was a sanctuary here for pilgrims en route to the Holy of Holies, St Ninian's *Candida Casa*, aka the *White House*, which, of course, has absolutely nothing to do with it being the official residence of the President of the United States of America.

The first church here, on this site, was mentioned in a grant from William the Lion in 1179. By the early 18th century, only the nave and chancel remained, and the decision was taken to pull them down and build a new church. It was constructed out of the local red sandstone, naturally, and completed in 1746.

In the vestibule, amongst a good many others, there is a memorial tablet to Dr James McLauchlan, senior surgeon at Dumfries Infirmary who died 1848 at the height of another cholera epidemic. He assisted his colleague, Dr William Scott, during an operation on 19th December 1846 when ether was used as an anaesthetic for the very first time in the United Kingdom. Or was it?

There were three local newspapers in Dumfries at that time and you would have thought that this ground-breaking development would have made the front page of all three journals, but the earliest reference to the operation was a month later in the *Dumfries and Galloway Courier* of Monday, 18th

January 1847. It stated: "We understand that several minor operations have been performed in the Dumfries Infirmary, when the patients were under the influence of sulphuric ether, the results of which were highly satisfactory, inasmuch as complete freedom from pain was obtained."

So there you have it. Far from shouting it from the rooftops, it almost sounds like an understatement, a matter of hardly any consequence. Was this due to modesty on the part of McLauchlan and Scott, or what? Please note the use of the word "minor". That is significant.

There is no question that an operation took place, using ether. Scott's claim was supported by no less a luminary than James Young Simpson, the discoverer of chloroform. The question is, was it really the first?

Unfortunately many of the hospital records were lost or destroyed. What does remain, however, are the annual reports of the Infirmary. In his 2004 paper *Another Look at Dumfries*, and combing through the newspapers and hospital reports, retired anaesthetist L.V.H. Martin could not pinpoint a patient who would have required a major operation on 19th December 1846. He concluded, however, that on the day in question, Scott *did* perform a minor operation using ether. Perhaps he and McLauchlan thought it was such a minor matter it was scarcely worth mentioning to the press. It does rather chime with the newspaper account above.

So minor, not major, but that still means that Dumfries Infirmary was the

St Michael's Church, Dumfries

first in the UK to use ether as an anaesthetic, doesn't it? Well, sadly, not necessarily so. On that same day, in London, a dentist named Mr Robinson extracted a molar from a Miss Lonsdale. Two days later, on December 21st 1847, Robert Liston amputated the lower leg of a Frederick Churchill at London's University College Hospital. To him must go the credit for anaesthetising a patient with ether for a major operation and Churchill being the lucky fellow, in a manner of speaking.

Before this pioneering use of ether, when speed was of the utmost to lessen the pain and to try and ensure the patient's survival, Liston was dubbed "The fastest knife in the West End".

Speed was not always a virtue however. He once amputated a leg in less than two-and-a-half minutes, but accidentally removed his assistant's fingers as well. In another leg amputation case of exactly the same length, he also removed the poor man's testicles as well. And talking of testicles, in another famous case, he removed a tumour from the scrotum of a man which was so large he had to wheel it about in a wheelbarrow. It took him four minutes to do that one, but then it was a big operation. The tumour weighed forty-five pounds.

Inside the church, Heather shows me the pew that Burns occupied when he was a member of the congregation here. It's quite near the back. Heather invites me to take a pew. Great! Now I can sit where Burns sat and not buy anyone a drink. Hurrah for that! Except you get what you pay for. It's not exactly where Burns sat at all. The original box pews were removed in 1869 when the church was restored.

"Lean your head against the pillar," says Heather. "Can you see the pulpit?"

I do and I can't.

"That's why Burns sat there," Heather explains. "He sat with his head against the pillar so the minister couldn't see him. He didn't get on with him," Heather goes on, "because of his drinking, and erm, you know what."

I do indeed know what and had I not seen the grave of the minister, William Inglis, of the Loreburn church which Burns attended to remove himself further from the sight of the incumbent here. This was, however, Jean's place of worship until her dying day, thirty-eight years later.

So, I still may not have sat exactly where Burns sat but my head has been where his has been. That seems much more satisfactory. Give me heads over bums, any day, as nature intended.

At the other side of the church is a face that Burns would have known well. It hangs on the wall and I can imagine Burns looking at it often, especially as the minister's sermon droned on and on. Yes, it is a clock. Apart from being a *well-kent face* to Burns and hexagonal, its other point of interest is that it was known as a *wag at the wa'*. Its pendulum and weights were exposed unlike a grandfather clock and not subject to tax. No wonder the wags were so popular long before footballers had them! It dates from 1758 and keeps excellent time – runs like clockwork in fact.

It is not the only Burns connection. The Robert Burns World Federation presented a white marble bust of their hero to mark the 250th anniversary of his birth. There is also a stained-glass window of Robert and Jean commemorating the year of their deaths. Birth would have been a better thing to celebrate, so it seems to me.

There is much else of interest to see in this historic church but you really need to come and see it for yourself. As a token of our visit and a souvenir, Heather very kindly gives me a communication token of 1820. They are sold in aid of church funds. I hope she doesn't get in trouble. (Worry not, ye elders, Fiona the photographer made a donation.)

The reason that tokens came about was because that 16th century Protestant firebrand, John Calvin, was worried that people who did not deserve communion were receiving the host. In order to prevent what he called "profanation of the Table" he dreamed up the token scheme. They weren't issued willy-nilly. In the week before communion, the elders would visit the members and quiz them as to their knowledge of the Bible to ensure their eligibility to participate. They were collected in again at the end of the service. In the case of St Michael's, they were collected by a couple of elders who sat inside the pair of massive pillars at the bottom of the steps. They used to be hollow, like sentry boxes.

Well that was the idea, but during the Covenanting Times, communicants retained the tokens as evidence they were bona fide members of the church and not a government spy. Some requested their token be buried with them, so when they arrived in heaven, they could flash it in front of St Peter and the Pearly Gates would swing open like an automatic door, or a contactless credit card machine at a check-out till.

Each church minted their own tokens, usually in a base metal such as lead, pewter or aluminium, though some were made from iron or brass. They were made in a plethora of shapes and designs, some with appropriate texts to the Eucharist with the church's name and the date, some with merely the minister's initials. Some people collect them, rather like postage stamps, only they are more durable, so you would think. Not so. When the church became less inquisitorial and more liberal, most of them ended up being melted down.

No doubt amongst the most traditional, there was a shaking of grizzled heads and dark mutterings about what the state of the world was coming to.

Chapter Six

Dumfries: The Theatre and the Bridges

ON the subject of tokens, the churches were not the only institutions to issue such things. We are on our way to see the Theatre Royal on Shakespeare Street – Scotland's oldest working theatre. Unfortunately it is closed which comes as no surprise at this time in the morning, far too early for a matinée, even if there were one. It would have been nice to see the inside and I suppose we could, had we tickets and time enough.

It was the brainchild of actor-manager George Stephen Sutherland, who launched a fund-raising campaign to build a theatre for the town. Those who subscribed ten guineas or more were rewarded with a silver token which allowed them free admission to the performances. Designed by local architect Thomas Boyd, with seating for an audience of 600, it cost £800 to build and opened on 29th September 1792, not long after Burns arrived in the town. Although he couldn't afford to be a subscriber, Burns contributed in other ways – by writing prologues and other pieces – and it was on his recommendation that Alexander Nasmyth, his portrait painter, was commissioned to paint the scenery. As a token of their appreciation, the owners gave Burns one of the coveted tokens.

A month after the opening of the theatre, on 30th March, Burns was involved in a scandal. After a performance of *As You Like It*, it was announced that the national anthem would be sung. This was greeted by counter-calls for the French Revolutionary song *Ça Ira*. Scuffling broke out and when *God Save the King* was sung, it was noted that Burns remained seated. Since he was a Government employee, you might consider this rather a foolhardy thing to do. To show his loyalty to the Crown, Burns joined the Dumfries Volunteers when it was founded in January 1795. In December, he wrote a poem where the title and first line run *Does haughty Gaul invasion threat?* No-one could be in doubt where his sympathies lay now.

In 1876, the theatre was renovated under the guidance of the architect Charles J. Phipps. He lowered the stage and stalls into the basement, installed

The Theatre Royal, Dumfries

boxes in a horseshoe shape and built a balcony thereby increasing the capacity of the theatre to 1,000. He also changed its outward appearance by building a new façade and that's the one we see today (apart from the 21st century expansion to the side), and very good and fresh it looks too.

The façade of the house we are standing in front of now, in Banks Street, must have changed too I imagine. The street itself surely must have, for in Burns's time it was known as the "Wee" or "Stinking Vennel". High on the wall, a little framed notice, blue plaque it is not – more like a funeral card with its black border – tells us this is where Burns first lived when he came to Dumfries in 1791. He occupied the rooms on the first floor on the right. Above the windows, another noticeboard proclaims this was once known as the "Sanghoose o' Scotland" where Burns completed over sixty songs, amongst them *Ae Fond Kiss* and *The Deil's Awa' with the Exciseman*.

Above him lived a blacksmith, which is appropriate, as one of the windows has been blanked out and painted black. There are two more, while the facings and sills of the others have also been picked out in black. If there is a more mournful house in all of Dumfries, then I'd like to see it.

The ground floor used to be the office of Burns's friend, John Syme, an estate factor by profession and who bore the title of "Collector of Stamps" for the District. It sounds very grand and had to do with Burns's new trade in the Excise. Nothing whatsoever to do with philately.

Nowadays it is home to a Burns Gift Shop and a Burns Café. Well, wouldn't you cash in on the name if you had a business to run? You'd be mad not to. That said, the sign above the café door looks as if it could do with a bit of TLC. One end has fallen off while, appropriately enough for a café, the other end bears a picture of a disembowelled haggis beneath the legend *Fair fa', your honest sonsie face*.

Regardless of what the house looked like then, I can't help wondering what Jean must have thought when he brought her to this tiny tenement flat in this not so charmingly-named little street. Some change from their whitewashed cottage at Ellisland in the midst of meadows.

We cross the river by the 200-foot span suspension bridge which was built in 1875 by J. Willett, engineer, and J. Abernethy & Co, contractors, at a cost of £1,500. I especially like the Doric columns at the ends. Linking them is a memorial arch bearing the Dumfries coat of arms and the name of the provost at the time, T. F. Smith. The bridge was principally used by mill

Burns's first house in Dumfries

workers to get to and from work. I bet they blessed the shortcut.

Visitor, please pause for a moment and think of those who trudged unwillingly to work like Shakespeare's schoolboy went to his desk. You are treading where they have trod. Feel the hand of history beneath your feet, so to speak. It became a category B listed building in 1981.

Dock Park, the former harbour, is downstream to our right. A cycle path runs through it and it must be a very pleasant stroll on a summer's evening. In the park is a sixteen-foot high obelisk that commemorates two members of the *Titanic* disaster – John (Jock) Law Hume, violinist in the band that famously "played on" and steward, Thomas Mullin.

Hume, only 21, had previously been on board the sister ship *Olympic* when she was involved in a collision with the warship *Hawk* on her maiden voyage out of Belfast. Whilst repairs were being made, Hume went back to see his family in Dumfries. His mum had a premonition and begged him not to go to sea again. Jock laughed at her and told her not to be so superstitious. He planned to marry on his return. Moral of the tale: sons should always listen to their mum's advice.

Suspension Bridge, Dumfries

We turn right at the other side of the bridge and presently come to a row of terraced houses. No. 1 was the boyhood home of John Laurie (1897-1980). He was a prolific actor on stage and screen but most people will remember him best as Sgt. Frazer in *Dad's Army*. I'm not sure if that is how *he* would

The Robert Burns Centre, Dumfries

care to be remembered since, in his day, he was a noted Shakespearean actor at the Old Vic undertaking such weighty roles as *Macbeth, Hamlet,* and *Richard III.*

He also appeared in his friend, Laurence Olivier's, Shakespearean films, *Henry V,* as well as the last two mentioned above. But long, long before that, Laurie cut his acting teeth as a member of the amateur Guild of Players, here in Dumfries, and long before they took over the Theatre Royal in 1959. He was also an acknowledged reciter of Burns's poems, which will come as no surprise.

Passing through the Mill Green, we arrive at the Burns Centre. In the evening it is converted into an arthouse cinema with a seating capacity of 69, but during the day, it houses some artefacts and manuscripts and an audio-visual display of the life and times of Dumfries. There is also a scale model of the town as it was in Burns's day. At the time of our visit, the centre was undergoing refurbishment so we missed, amongst other things, the plaster cast of Burn's skull, his burgess certificate, and some examples of Mauchline ware.

The Burgess Ticket was not, as you might have supposed, presented to him when he became a citizen of the town, but on his way back from a tour of the Borders. In June 1787, he stopped in Dumfries on his way to sign the lease at Ellisland. His fame had preceded him. The Edinburgh edition was selling like the proverbial hot cakes but unfortunately, in April, he had sold the "property" of his poems to his publisher, Creech, for 100 guineas. It was a lot of money for those days but if only he could have foreseen how well his work was going to sell and how famous he was going to become!

On the other hand, in 1793, he was able to cash in on the Burgess Certificate which entitled Robert and Francis to be educated for ten marks, Scots, instead of the normal price of eighty pounds, Scots. That's like 14p as opposed to £20. Well worth having.

Mauchline, near Burns's farm of Mossgiel, is where *Bonnie Jean* stemmed from, one of the so-called *Mauchline Belles.* Mauchline was famous for quarrying sandstone, making curling stones, clocks thanks to John 'Clockie' Brown, and box-work. Box-work was the art of producing an image on the

• • •

product, not necessarily on a box. From the 1820s until a fire unfortunately stopped production in 1933, W&A Smith produced some very collectable items bearing the Bard's image or places associated with him, on vases, jugs – and boxes, of course.

We will come back another day to see these treasures and resuming our walk along the river bank, we come to yet another museum, the Old Bridge Museum at the western end of the Devorgilla Bridge, and yes, like all the others, it's free.

From this side, as we approach it, it rises high from the river bank, an extension that was built in the 1880s, but on the other side where the entrance is, it looks like a small, single-storey dwelling. Look closely and you will see part of a window peeping over the surface of the road. That's because, over the centuries, the level of the road has been raised.

Once an inn, it is the oldest house in Dumfries, built in 1660 by James Birkmyre, a cooper or barrel maker. The Council was worried his house would obstruct the street and asked him to move it back. It was a sma' request. They also told him not to cross the bridge with heavily-laden wagons of timber, worried that the bridge could not bear the weight. Bureaucracy has a long pedigree. Note the boulders at the corners. That was a sort of buffer to stop carts banging into the walls of the house.

Legend has it that it was a meeting place for Covenanters. At some stage in its long life it became an inn, still was in Burns's day, and lasted well into the 19th century. The last resident was Granny Black, the so-called *matriarch of Maxwelltown* who provided a service to the community at both ends of life's spectrum – delivering babies and laying out the dead. She died in 1955 aged 86.

Now it is a museum of everyday life, featuring a kitchen from 1850, a parlour from 1910, a nursery with children's toys from the 1880s, a bedroom from 1870 and perhaps most intriguing of all, a dentist's surgery with a chair from 1850 and one of the earliest examples of anaesthetic equipment. There is a cabinet full of false teeth made from ivory and porcelain. Burns was no stranger to the toothache, even writing a humorous poem about it, though God knows how he could.

As for the bridge itself, it was built in 1432, with the help of an Indulgence from Pope Eugene IV. It is one of the oldest, if not *the* oldest stone bridge in Scotland, although it has seen major reconstruction over the years. It was badly damaged by a flood in 1621 when five arches were swept away. The new bridge had nine arches. Look closely at them. Can you spot something? The one nearest the house, the oldest, is slightly pointed whereas the rest are rounded. The parapets were rebuilt in 1725 and a tollhouse in the middle was

• • •

demolished in 1769 to reduce the weight. You can see it in an old print in the museum.

Actually Dumfries was a frontier town. On the western bank was Maxwelltown in the Stewartry of Kirkcudbright; on the east, Dumfries in Dumfriesshire, naturally. In 1671, five women accused of witchcraft were dragged – screaming, you imagine – across it to face trial in Kirkcudbright. Maxwelltown was not amalgamated with Dumfries until 1929. Isn't that an amazing thing!

Less than a century earlier, in 1828, land was reclaimed to extend the Whitesands and the bridge was reduced from nine arches to six. In 1961 it became an A-listed building, one up on the suspension bridge downstream, which, as I said, was built in 1875. The Buccleuch Street Bridge, just upstream, was built to Thomas Boyd's design in 1794. Over the years it has been widened and strengthened.

I'm glad to hear that. It's very busy bridge indeed. Its broad back carries the A701, the main artery into the town centre from the east.

Chapter Seven

The Museum and the Camera Obscura: Matters of Mortality

WE have arrived at the Dumfries Museum and Camera Obscura. The latter is housed in a former windmill. It was erected in 1798 and converted into an observatory and camera obscura in 1836 by architect Walter Newall (1780-1863). Unfortunately the observatory was not completed in time for the viewing of Halley's Comet in November 1835. And unless you saw the last one in 1986 (which I didn't) then you've probably missed your chance, as the next one will not be until July 2061. That for one, counts me out. On my tombstone could be writ: "Dead and never saw Halley's Comet".

The camera obscura is the oldest in the world and for that reason alone, is worth the climb up the spiral stairs to the top floor where you can soar on silent wings like an eagle over the town and its hinterland. It's quite magical. They do it by mirrors and ropes, projecting the image onto a circular white table that can be raised and lowered to adjust the focus. It's like looking through a giant telescope and although you feel within touching distance of the activity in the street far below, it is eerily silent, like an old black-and-white movie, only in living colour. Visitor and townspeople alike beware as you go about your business: Big Brother is watching you.

The Museum is on two floors and tells the story of the life and times of not just Dumfries, but Galloway as a whole. It is the largest in the Region and I will not weary you with listing all the attractions, which are many and varied. Instead I will restrict myself to what interested me most. (It's my book, after all, is it not?)

I have to say you get a fine appreciation for death here. We are looking at the plaster cast of the skull of our once-and-former king, Robert the Bruce. The eye sockets are wide, the jaws slightly apart, as if the Grim Reaper had tapped

Dumfries Museum and Camera Obscura

him on the shoulder, told him his time was up and Bruce is saying, "Who? Me? But I'm only fifty-four."

No-one actually knows what carried him off exactly, but it's unlikely it was from a surfeit of eels, as his Italian physician, Maino de Maineri, had prophesised he would be unless he kicked the habit. It's hard to see how anyone could be addicted to such a slithery thing, yea, even to the point of death. But there's no accounting for taste and if it *did* kill him, he couldn't say he hadn't been warned. We know he didn't die in battle, though the skull does show some occupational hazards of being a warrior – damage to the left eye socket and cheekbone, probably the result of a sword or axe wound.

What he actually *did* die of is unclear. Accounts of him being a leper are greatly exaggerated: there were no contemporary Scottish accounts of him being one. It's possible he might have been suffering from syphilis, which would have had a similar appearance. Whatever it was he *was* suffering from, he went to Whithorn in 1329, hoping for a miracle cure. It didn't work. He died three weeks later. Richard Neave of Manchester University has reconstructed what the face might have looked like and a photograph is on display along with the skull. Not a pretty sight. It's hard to envisage him conducting the affairs of state with a phizog like that, meeting his advisors face to face and them trying hard not to look away. I suppose it was a sight they might have got used to, but still...

Burns aficionados know how the ploughman poet accidentally condemned a mouse to death at Mossgiel farm in November 1785 when he disturbed its nest with his plough. In January 1957, another ploughman in another place, Mainsriddle Farm, near here, disturbed something much more substantial and sinister.

His cruel coulter hit a stone slab, and on lifting it up, this modern ploughman found a different sort of cell. He did not need to worry his head, like Burns did, about the inhabitant having to find somewhere to shelter from

• • •

"winter's weary blast" because he was quite dead. What he had uncovered was a body. The victim was aged about 55 and there was no obvious cause of death.

An unnatural death could not be ruled out, but had he been unlawfully killed, an enquiry would have been futile. The perpetrator would have long-since departed, not only the scene, but the planet – about 3,800 thousand years ago in fact. Furthermore, it was obvious this was no hasty burial by a killer to conceal a corpse. It was a cist burial, composed of slabs on the sides and at each end with a capstone as a lid. In this little space, the deceased had reverently and ceremoniously been laid to rest on his left side with his legs drawn up to his chest. You can understand that; a lot less digging in the days of the primitive spade.

Hopefully it was his preferred sleeping side, since he was going to have the biggest sleep of his life. A beaker was buried with him, along with a bone ring. The significance of that we cannot say for certain, but the beaker, which would have been filled with mead, was intended to sustain him on his journey to the after-life. Since the living have yet to find out how long a journey that is exactly, we hope it was enough to sustain him to the other side. It would be a terrible thing to expire (again) of thirst or hunger in the underworld and not attain the lofty heights of heaven.

His jaw is slack and reminds me very much of *Tam o' Shanter* where our inebriated hero describes the items on the *haly table*. Amongst them, as I'm sure you will recall, was *a thief, new-cutted frae a rape/wi' his last gasp his gab did gape*. His expression is harder to read than Bruce's. Is it utter joy at the delights of heaven, or abject disappointment to find he has ended up in hell? If my opinion counts for anything (and it usually doesn't), I think he's having a good laugh.

Nearly four thousand years ago is recent history compared to the age of the exhibits we are looking at now. They are the fossil footprints of reptiles which trod this earth 225 million years ago. They were found in local sandstone quarries and one of them is from the collection of the Rev. Henry Duncan (1774-1846). He was a real genius, a man o' many *pairts*. More about him later, but for the moment suffice it to say, he was a pioneer collector of fossils. In 1828, he presented a paper to the Royal Society of Edinburgh on fossil tracks that came from Cornockle Quarry near Lochmaben. The paper was subsequently published in 1831 and the tracks were called *Chelichnus duncani* in his honour. They were the first quadruped fossil tracks to be found in Britain. You can see a plaster cast of them in the National Museum in Edinburgh.

Descending to the basement, I come across something I had never seen before. There is an impressive collection of Pictish stones, gravemarkers, and

Roman altars from around the district. I've seen a good many such stones on my travels but I've never seen or heard of a suicide stone before. There are two on display here from Lowther Hill at Wanlockhead. As I expect you know, suicide victims could not be buried in consecrated ground and when it *was* allowed in the early part of the 19th century, they were kept apart from decent dead folk. According to the notice that accompanies the stones, John Brown, in *The Enterkin* (1876), explains that the hill was on the border between Lanarkshire and Dumfriesshire, and the bodies of suicides from all around were taken to this remote spot and laid to rest.

One stone has the initials "W K", the date "1767" and "E 25". Possibly it stands for "Expired age 25". Who was he (if he was a he) and did he kill himself when the love of his life rejected him for another? The other stone is arguably even more interesting. It bears the initials "C C" and "A I" with the date "1756". Was this a suicide pact, the young couple driven to this extreme measure when their parents refused them permission to see each other again? We shall never know.

And now for something a bit more cheerful after all this talk of death. Hands up who knows who invented the bicycle? If you don't, let me inform you. It was Kirkpatrick Macmillan (1812-78), born near Thornhill, about fifteen miles north of Dumfries. He was the son of a blacksmith and apprenticed to his father when he was twelve. Before Macmillan's invention, or should I say "improvement", there was the dandy horse, a two-wheeled vehicle which the rider sat astride and propelled with his feet. Macmillan's machine, the first rear-wheel, pedal-powered bicycle in the world appeared in 1839. You can see a couple of them here. Note how one has a much larger rear wheel than the front. For durability, it had iron-rimmed wheels, thereby eliminating the need to carry a pump and a puncture-repair kit. He thought of everything, even a figurehead like Jaguar cars have, only this, to my eyes, looks rather like a carnyx, the Celtic warhorn.

Actually it's not strictly true that he thought of everything. He failed to patent his machine and Gavin Dalzell of Lesmahagow brought out a very similar machine in 1846, by which time Kirkpatrick's bike had many, many miles under its wheels. Also to Mr Macmillan falls the doubtful honour of having committed the first cycling offence, when in 1842, having ridden seventy or so miles to Glasgow, he knocked over a little girl in the Gorbals. He was fined five shillings. His invention, it seems, was in need of modification – a bell. It's a pity that the carnyx, if it is one, wasn't capable of emitting a warning blast. And another thing that didn't occur to him – brakes.

Another famous Gallovidian is represented here too – John Mctaggart. (Come on, admit it, you'd never heard of him before – and neither had I.) He was born at Borgue, near Kirkcudbright, in 1791. And what was he famous for I hear you ask? The answer is his *Gallovidian Encylopaedia* which appeared in 1824.

It is a collection of curious anecdotes, sketches and eccentric characters and much else besides, including a dictionary of unusual words and phrases. You can see an extract – a panel which features a list of words connected with the weather. (Which just goes to show you that if Galloway can be said to have produced anything, apart from a lot of famous people, then it's plenty of variable weather.)

The book itself is a curiosity in more ways than one. For one thing, it must be a contender for an entry in the *Guinness Book of Records* as having the world's longest subtitle. In fact it is too wordy to repeat here. If only the book itself had lasted as half as long...

Unfortunately, the father of a certain lady known as the *Star of Dungyle* took exception to what Mactaggart had written about his daughter and demanded that the defamatory article was excised. In the event, the whole book was withdrawn. However, before that happened, the author's father, seeing the *Encyclopaedia* in a Kirkcudbright bookshop, spake to his bright spark of a son thus: "John, yer ain family kent ye were a fule, noo the hale world'll ken". Poor John, in more ways than one. But you know what Jesus said about a prophet in his own land...

Long after Mctaggart's death in 1830, a limited edition of 250 copies was printed in 1876, making both editions very rare – a collector's item in fact, and very expensive. Another (affordable) edition was published in 2017. But even better than that, you can read it online for free. I make no apologies for pointing this out if the book is of interest to you, as poor John, having turned to dust long ago, is not losing out on any royalties. And if you care to dip into the book, or are dying of curiosity to know what exactly had so angered the father of the *Star of Dungyle*, you will be relieved to know that if you search for her under "S" for "star", you will find the answer. I won't spoil the suspense for you except to say her real name was Miss H—. She seems to have been extraordinarily beautiful – a real heartbreaker.

Mctaggart was a frequent contributor to journals and periodicals both in this country and Canada where, in 1826, he went as Clerk of Works and engineer of the Rideau Canal in Ontario. After suffering a debilitating fever, he came home again and published a book entitled *Three Years in Canada*. The formula was as before. With a subtitle to match that of the *Encyclopaedia*, mainly it was a description of the state of the land but it contained anecdotes and accounts of the "queer" characters he met during his sojourn. Unfortunately he died on 7th January 1830, just a fortnight after his little book came out. No royalties again for poor John.

There are other local heroes featured in the museum. Doctors Scott and McLauchlan I have already mentioned. Another doctor, Thomas Boyle Grierson (1818-89), opened a museum in Thornhill which had such eclectic exhibits as the bones from a dodo, a fragment from Mary, Queen of Scots' velvet gown, and some wrapping from a mummy. Alas, it closed in 1965 and its exhibits were dispersed.

Robert Louis Waland (1908-99), was born in Dumfries and educated at the Academy. In 1962, he was Chief Optician at the Lunar and Planetary Department at the University of Arizona in Tucson. With his 61-inch reflecting telescope, he mapped the moon and thus was directly responsible for the moon landing in 1969. His first telescope was one he built himself from an acetylene bicycle lamp immersed in castor oil and placed between two pieces of plate glass.

Cecil (Jock) Riding MC (1913-98), grew up in the Lockerbie area and died in Dumfries. He was one of the first members of the SAS created by David Stirling in 1941. Three days after D-Day, he was parachuted into Nazi-occupied France with a carrier pigeon strapped to his chest so he could send a message back. Along with his equipment such as a compass in the shape of a button and a code "book" in the form of a silk handkerchief, he had food for the pigeon. His dangerous mission was to blow up railway lines, locomotives and stations as well as liaise with the French Resistance. Some of his colleagues were killed, including his commanding officer, and he narrowly escaped death himself on a couple of occasions.

Finally, let us not forget John Paul Jones (1747-92), the Father of the American Navy. He was born at Arbigland near Kirkbean and died in Paris. More of him later.

Arguably, the outside of the museum is just as interesting, if not more, than the interior. You can't miss the Sinclair memorial. In its Greek style, it is strongly reminiscent of Burns's mausoleum and despite its name, it actually celebrates the life of John Paterson, aka Old Mortality. This will immediately bring to mind Scott's novel of that name. To be honest, I am not a big fan of Sir Walter – too long-winded by half – but the life of Old Mortality the person, although it was long, is interesting. I will be brief, but before we come to him, it is only fitting to explain why the monument is not called the "Old Mortality Memorial".

Behind the glass screen, a noticeboard tells us that Dr John Sinclair was "beloved by all, of high promise and superior talents". He won, in a lottery, life-size figures of Old Mortality and his pony which were "conceived and executed" by a local artist, John Currie. The date was the 25th October 1840. I only mention such an apparently insignificant detail, because alas, the next day, the poor doctor was dead. Life does indeed seem to be a lottery sometimes. It could have been worse, I suppose. Imagine if he'd won a million guineas instead of a pair of statues and never got a chance to spend a penny of it.

You can tell he was young when he died because of the "high promise" mentioned on the plaque. We are also told he died a "mournful death". Actually, he was thrown from his gig and died of his injuries. He was only twenty-six. He was Assistant Surgeon on HMS *Excellent* at Portsmouth, actually the naval gunnery school, and was described as being of "superior talent". What a shame.

So much for Sinclair, but who was "Old Mortality"? Well, he was born James Paterson in Hawick in 1715. He had a long life, even by today's standards, only leaving this mortal coil in 1801. He made a living as a stonemason, and the reason Sir Walter immortalised him in one of his books is because he dedicated forty years of his life travelling around Scotland inscribing on headstones the names of the Covenanters who sacrificed their lives in what came to be called the "Killing Time" from 1680-88.

That dreadful time began with a difference of opinion on religious matters between the Scottish Presbyterians and Charles II. No sooner had the son of the executed monarch plonked his posterior on the restored throne, when he revoked the Solemn League and Covenant, agreed in 1643 by the Covenanters and the English Parliamentarians. Its purpose was two-pronged: the preservation of Protestantism and the "extirpation of popery and prelacy". As a consequence, ministers either had to accept the reintroduction of the hated bishops or give up their churches. Many refused. Others jumped before they were pushed from their pulpits, while still others defied the law by holding open-air services called "conventicles". The penalty for preaching at such a meeting was death; for attending one, a fine. There were about one hundred parsons who paid the extreme penalty.

Actually, when I said Paterson made a living by being a stonemason, I was being economical with the truth. A committed Cameronian (the hard left wing, so to speak, of the Covenanting Party), his work to ensure the Covenanters were not forgotten was more a labour of love than a way of making a living, for he died destitute. But he did not die in vain. I would say this is more *his* memorial than Sinclair's and it's not everyone who gets a book named after them, which of course, is by far the greater honour.

Through a glass screen, we see the old man lying on his left side, wearing a wide-brimmed hat that might have kept the worst of the vicissitudes of the Scottish climate at bay, travelling and working in all weathers as he did. It's a wonder he lived as long as he did and didn't perish from pneumonia. His patient pony is standing beside him and if he is envious of the patch of grass that his master is lying on, he doesn't show it, for he is standing on a barren patch. A candle is stuck into the neck of a pottery jar, so the poor stonemason could afford that at least – or perhaps it was donated by a sympathiser.

One thing we know for sure is he wouldn't have been using it to read the book named in his honour, as it was not published until 1816. Pity that. As a book at bedtime, it might have been a pretty good soporific. Only joking. *Old Mortality* is regarded as one of Scott's more readable yarns nowadays.

In 1869, nearly seventy years after the stonemason's death, Scott's publishers erected a memorial tombstone to him in the churchyard of Caerlaverock village where he died. Better late than never. It was only fitting, after what he had done for others, the same should be done for him also. And that's not all. Another pair of statues showing Paterson, again on his side and accompanied by his trusty, patient pony, was erected in Balmaclennan near New Galloway where he lived for a large part of his life and where his wife is buried. They were separated for much of their marriage on account of his self-imposed task so it's fitting they should be separated in death also. And incidentally, that tiny place of less than a thousand souls that few have heard of was once a hotbed of the Covenanting movement.

Appropriately enough, Paterson is also one of the figures on the Scott monument on Princes Street in Edinburgh. He is standing this time. Another monument featuring the trio of Scott, Old Mortality and his pony can be seen at Laurel Hill Cemetery, Philadelphia. It's a sort of poor man's Forest Lawn, which is in the Hollywood Hills part of Los Angeles. As you would expect, it makes a big production out of death with massive memorials and some not so massive, with a whole firmament of movie stars planted there. But just what our trio is doing in Forest Hill in the first place, you might well ask – and wonder.

Finally, before we leave the museum and the camera obscura behind and walk down the hill to the car, our attention is drawn to a cannon, its barrel aimed at the town below. It's a relic from the Crimean War (1854-55). I mention it because never, in the field of human conflict, did so many clothes owe so much to that war – the balaclava, the cardigan and the raglan sleeve.

Chapter Eight

Dumfries: In the Footsteps of a Dead Playwright

TALKING of famous people who are associated with Dumfries, as I was in the last chapter, Burns is indubitably the most famous but there are a good many others.

On the perimeter wall of Dumfries Academy, a plaque names some of its most famous *alumni*. Dear, dead John Laurie is one, but there is only one other whom I had heard of before, before I came to Dumfries – J.M. Barrie. This undoubtedly says more about me, and my lack of knowledge, than the extent of their fame.

I will mention in the passing, however, Sir James Anderson (1824-93), captain of the SS *Great Eastern* which laid the first lasting transatlantic telegraph cable in 1866. I suppose I had heard of Alexander S. Graham (1917-91), since I remember his cartoon creation, Fred Basset, the hound of that ilk from the *Daily Mail*. Finally, on a much more serious note, I must mention Jane Haining (1897-1944), Church of Scotland missionary to Hungary, who defied orders to leave and perished in Auschwitz.

I hope the others on the plaque will sincerely pardon me for not mentioning them, as well as a galaxy of more recent famous ex-pupils, too numerous to mention, but we are now on the trail of Sir James M. Barrie (1860-1937). Born and buried in Kirriemuir, he came to Dumfries with his two elder siblings, Alexander and Mary Ann, when he was fourteen.

They lived at 6 Victoria Terrace, a row of red sandstone Georgian mansions which you will find tucked behind the station. Some have been

Notable Alumni of Dumfries Academy

painted white, but not Barrie's former home. One of the blocks to the left of the door, engraved in block capitals, appropriately enough, in gold lettering, tells us Barrie stayed here from 1873-78 and regarded those years as amongst the happiest of his life.

Alas, there was a lot of unhappiness in it. His marriage in 1894 to the actress Mary Ansell was reputedly unconsummated and they divorced in 1909 after she began an affair. He did, however, form a very close relationship with the family of Llewelyn Davies and their five sons. Similar to the way Lewis Carroll entertained the young Alice Liddell with her adventures in Wonderland, Barrie regaled the two oldest boys, George and Jack, with the adventures of their little brother, Peter, whom he reliably informed them, could fly.

In 1910, following the deaths of both their parents, Barrie became the boys' guardian. Sadly, George was killed in action in 1915 and Michael drowned in a swimming accident in 1921. The triple whammy happened when Peter threw himself under a train in 1960. Happily, Barrie was spared knowledge of that tragedy.

Barrie himself died, or – to quote his creation, Peter – began his "awfully big adventure" in 1937. Pneumonia was the cause and he bequeathed all the rights of the *Peter Pan* series to the Great Ormond Street Hospital. Believe it or not, there are no fewer than forty-five versions of Peter and his friends' adventures, not forgetting the crocodile of course. And if you think *that* generous, then I think he did something even more so. He supported his ex-wife in her new life with her lover. Maybe he felt he was making amends for his sin of omission. Who knows? I think it was good of him all the same. He didn't need to.

There was a lot of sadness in Barrie's life but it must have been a happy day in 1924 when he came from London to be made a Freeman of Dumfries, the equivalent of a burgess in Burns's day. Barrie was not unaccustomed to honours. In 1913, George V created him a baronet and in the New Year's Honours List of 1922, he was given the Order of Merit. Having seen the Pathé News film of the Freeman celebration, Barrie looks more like a man on his way to a funeral rather than a

Home of J.M. Barrie, Dumfries

celebrant of a joyous occasion. (Curious word "funeral" that there should be so much "fun" in it.)

In the museum we had seen the silver casket, which, as the cursive writing on the front tells us, contains Barrie's freeman's "ticket" as it was called. The lid features St Michael standing on the body of the dragon he vanquished, only it doesn't look quite dead yet; the head looks ready to exhale one last jet of flame before it expired. The casket itself it looks a posh version of the sort of thing in which you might keep the ashes of your nearest and dearest to display on the mantelpiece. Always there to remind you.

The block of stone on his former home lists Barrie's works, of which *Peter Pan* is the best known. Indeed Peter was conceived here in Dumfries, Barrie himself tells us, and we're retracing our steps now to see the very place, the Georgian villa of Moat Brae, the gardens of which he described as "an enchanted land". It was there he played at pirates and other games of the imagination with the Gordon brothers, Stuart and Hal, and recorded their adventures in what he called his *Log Book*. It was their escapades there which were "the genesis of that nefarious work". He meant *Peter Pan*. (Curious word to use – "nefarious".)

J.M. recounts how he first met Stuart at the Academy: 'He came up to me and asked my name. I told him. That didn't seem to please him. He said, "I'll call you Sixteen String Jack." I asked his name and he said it was Dare Devil Dick. He asked me if I would join his pirate crew. I did.' So that is where the pirates in *Peter Pan* came from, but Peter himself has a sadder and more poignant genesis.

Barrie was the son of a weaver in Kirriemuir, as I said, and his mother was prolific. She had ten children, of whom Barrie was the ninth. Just think what the world would have missed if she had stopped at eight! He never knew two of his siblings as they died before he was born but he did know his older brother, David, next to him in age and who died two days before his fourteenth birthday, the result of an ice-skating accident. He was crashed into by a friend (some think it was J.M. himself) and died a week later of inflammation of the brain. He was his mother's favourite and little James (and he *was* short of stature) tried to comfort his mother, once wearing his dead brother's clothes and whistling in the way he used to do. (Was he trying to atone?)

In his biography of his mother, Barrie tells of going into her darkened bedroom. "Is that you?" she said. He was in no doubt that it was David she was thinking of. "No, it's no' him, it's just me," Barrie replied. Terribly sad, but in a way, although his name was David, not Peter, *he* was the boy who never grew up.

Fortunately his younger brother *did* grow up and it was at the Academy that the shaping of the future author and playwright took place. It was in the school magazine, *The Clown,* that his work appeared in print for the first time with a story called *Rekollekshuns of a Skoolmaster.* (Incidentally, the founder of the magazine was the nephew of Sir James Anderson, master of the SS *Great Britain.*)

These two enterprising pupils went on to found the Academy's Dramatic Club. Barrie was the Secretary, Anderson the Stage Manager, and the stage was the floor of the English classroom. One of the three plays performed was *Bandelero the Bandit* written by Barrie. Unbelievably, instead of praising the initiative and enterprise of their star pupils, a member of the School Board – a stuffed shirt going under the name of the Rev. D.L. Scott – objected to the club. Fortunately his objections were not heeded, and the club went on to bigger and better things. Their next production was held in March in 1878 in the Assembly Rooms where Barrie played the part of Adèle in a one-act comedy called *Awkwardly Alike, or Which is Browne?* It was his swan song as far as the Academy was concerned. That summer he left school to go to Edinburgh University.

As you can imagine, when he lived in Dumfries, the young Barrie was a fan of the Theatre Royal where his favourite place to sit was in the front row, but to the side, so he could see both the action and glimpse the goings-on off stage.

As for Moat House itself, built in 1823, it was designed by a local architect, Walter Newall, who – you will remember – was responsible for adapting the windmill to become an observatory. It was the premier house in all of Dumfries.

The house changed hands several times over the years, and in 1914 became a nursing home. In 2009, it was acquired by the Loreburn Housing Association who planned to demolish it and use the site to build affordable housing. To think that the former most desirable house in the town was nearly reduced to rubble!

Enter stage left, the Peter Pan Action Group who saved the house from destruction by a whisker – just three days before the bulldozers moved in. Now the Peter Pan Moat Brae Trust is embarked on an ambitious £5.5 million project to create a National Centre for Children's Literature and Storytelling by restoring the house and creating a Neverland Garden of Discovery which will feature such exciting things as a pirate cave and pirate ship, a skull rock, an Indian camp, a Wendy house and much, much more.

At the time of our visit, June 2018, it looked like a building under siege by the builders. It hopes to open in the Spring of 2019. It's an awfully exciting prospect!

Chapter Nine

Caerlaverock Castle: Sieges and Snakes

THIS morning we are taking the B725 to Caerlaverock Castle. On the way we stop at Glencaple.

It's astonishing to think that this tiny place was once a major shipbuilding centre operated by Messrs Thomson & Co., who employed about fifty tradesmen – from carpenters to cabinet-makers and rope-makers to sail-makers. Between 1806 and 1858, two ships were built every year. Amongst other goods, they brought tobacco from America, timber from the Baltic, tea from Ceylon, rum from the West Indies, port from Spain, lime and coal from Cumberland and groceries from Liverpool. The major export was farm produce and later, passengers shuttled to and from Liverpool, some on an excursion, some to emigrate.

Three weathered wooden benches by the roadside bear testimony to this glorious past. One lists the names of the ships that were built between those years while another tells us that enough tobacco was landed here to fill 750 million pipes and enough tea to make 14 million cups. The third tells the tragic tale of the *Duchess of Buccleuch*, a two-masted brig of 260 tons built in 1735. She was out of Bristol, bound for Havana, when she was wrecked off the coast of Cuba in 1842. All of those aboard including William Thomson, builder, owner and master, made it safely to shore only for the grim reaper to have the last laugh – a good many of them, including Thomson, died of a fever soon after. He was 69. His wife, however, survived and made it safely back home.

We move on to Caerlaverock Castle which, for my money, (and you don't need any if you are a member of Historic Environment Scotland), is

Wooden Bench, Glencaple

Caerlaverock Castle

one of the most impressive castles in Scotland, indeed the United Kingdom. Alexander II granted Caerlaverock to Sir John Maccuswell (Maxwell) who built the first castle about 1220. In 1277, Sir Herbert Maxwell completed the building of the new castle in the present location. The name means "fort of the lark" from the Brittonic *caer* meaning "fort" and Old English *laewerce* meaning "lark".

Built of red sandstone, it looks enormously impressive, not to say invincible, surrounded by its moat and the gatehouse guarded by enormous twin cotton-reel towers. It is unique – the only triangular castle in the UK. In addition to the towers at the gatehouse, there used to be a round tower at each corner, connected by a curtain wall while a further defence was achieved by a dry ditch.

The tower to the southwest is called "Murdoch's Tower" where, according to legend, Murdoch Stewart, the Duke of Albany, was held captive before his execution in 1425. Murdoch was a cousin of the future James I and was Governor of Scotland after his father's death and during James's captivity in England. In James's view, Murdoch did not desperately strive to secure his release and when James did finally return in 1424 after the payment of a massive ransom, he had Murdoch arrested in Perth and executed in Stirling along with two of his sons. Which begs the question, why would he have gone to all the trouble of imprisoning him here? The truth is Murdoch was probably never here at all.

At first sight, the castle looks remarkably well preserved and you might be forgiven for thinking that these defences had been sufficient to keep it out of the wars, seemingly being so impregnable that any would-be attacker just wouldn't bother. But if you resist the urge to wander straight into the castle over the drawbridge (Historic Environment Scotland makes it so easy nowadays), and chose to walk round it first, when you reach the southern side, you can see that it has indeed been pretty much battered about.

Over the centuries, it was built and rebuilt, modified and improved, but the ruins the visitor sees today are the result of a siege in 1640 during the Second Bishops' War. The castle, garrisoned by 200 men, held out for thirteen weeks before Robert Maxwell, the 1st Earl of Nithsdale – a loyal supporter of Charles I – was forced to surrender to the Covenanters. To prevent it from ever again being a centre of resistance, the southern curtain wall was demolished as well as the roof of the Nithsdale Lodging (which makes it sound far less grand than it actually was).

It was built in 1634 by the First Earl. You can see the date on one of the ornate typana on the façade of the Lodging. He must have been looking forward to a time of peace and prosperity, not expecting the castle to be attacked as he lightened up the rooms considerably by creating large windows in the defensive eastern curtain wall. There were three floors, each with two rooms which all had fireplaces. In what was a great advance from a potty beneath the bed, most of the rooms had an in-built closet where the deposits plopped into the moat below. This also had the added benefit of acting as deterrent to anyone contemplating swimming across it with robbery on his mind. And there were things worth stealing in there all right.

An inventory from when the castle was taken in 1640 shows just how sumptuous the furnishings and furniture were, best illustrated by five of the beds of which two had silk curtains and three had cloth. All had silk fringes with a silk counterpane, decorated with braid and silk lace with matching stools and chairs. Or, if you were in search of a good book, there also was a library, showing that Robert was not just a rich man, but a man of culture and learning too.

For the visitor today, the best remaining evidence of just how splendid the Lodging must have been can be seen from the ornate carvings over the widows and doorways. They feature heraldic devices and scenes from classical mythology which a noticeboard facing them helps you understand. Some carvings are triangular to echo the castle's shape, whilst above the gatehouse, is the Maxwell coat of arms featuring a deer *couchant*, beneath a holly bush.

Murdoch's Tower, Caerlaverock Castle

● ● ●

Entrance detail, Caerlaverock Castle

The entrance itself is imposing but with this new wing, Robert is saying to his visitors and guests, "See how rich I am – a man of distinction, so refined".

Another noticeboard gives an artist's impression of what the entire castle would have looked like when it was newly built. With its slate roofs, it reminds me very much of a French chateau, while yet another noticeboard shows what the castle was like in 1295, during Sir Herbert's time. What a difference three-and-a-half centuries make! He must have been immensely proud of his *des res*, must Sir Robert, and rightly so. But as so often happens in life, the gods see to it that they're the ones who have the last laugh. Robert had only six short years to enjoy the trappings of his wealth. The siege of 1640 was to be the castle's last. It never recovered.

It wasn't Robert's last throw of the dice, however. In 1644, he was involved in the nine-month-long Siege of Newcastle, taking refuge in the castle when the Covenanters took the town. His life was spared but his lands and titles were forfeited. He fled to the Isle of Man where he died, you imagine, broken-hearted, aged only thirty-three.

There was an earlier siege in July 1300 during the Wars of Scottish Independence. On that occasion, after withstanding two days of attacks by the mighty army of Edward I, which was made up of a force of three thousand foot soldiers, eighty-seven knights and barons, not to mention the weapon of mass destruction of its day – the formidable siege engines which had been requisitioned from castles as far away as Jedburgh and Carlisle. The garrison of only sixty men bowed to Goliath and surrendered. As a contemporary account written by one of the besiegers tells us, some were hanged from the castle walls *pour encourager les autres* while others were allowed to go free and tell the tale.

Shortly after 1312, Sir Eustace Maxwell, who was keeping Caerlaverock as a vassal of Edward II, changed sides and espoused the cause of Robert the Bruce. His is one of the seals that was attached to the Declaration of Arbroath which was sent to the Pope in 1320. Not surprisingly, this brought about the

• • •

wrath of Edward II, and he attacked the castle. But this Edward was not the warrior-king his father was, and this time the castle successfully withstood the siege. That said, the English might just as well have won the day, for in accordance with Bruce's policy of not giving the English a stronghold in the southwest, Sir Eustace dismantled the castle himself. For this act of rendering himself homeless, he was forgiven a debt of £32 (no small sum in those days) by the king.

Bruce died in 1329 and was succeeded by the boy-king, David II, who was only five-years old. He was crowned at Scone in November 1331. Believe it or not, he was a married man! He was four when he married the seven-year old Joan of the Tower, a girl nearly twice his age! She was so-called because she was born in the Tower of London. Her father was Edward II and her mother was Isabella of France. To leap into the future for a moment, they were married for thirty-four years before Joan died aged forty-one, probably a victim of the great killer of the time – the Black Death. They did not have any children. He didn't have any children to his second wife, Margaret Drummond, either, nor, incidentally, with his mistress Agnes Dunbar.

Like a snake shedding its skin, it was time for Sir Eustace to make a third change. Although the boy-king David had Regents, Eustace sensed a wind of change after the death of his father, the great military strategist. It was a wise move. The Balliol faction, with the support of Edward III of England (who had succeeded to the throne in 1327), defeated the Regent, the Earl of Mar, at the battle of Dupplin Moor in Perthshire and Sir Eustace duly attended the coronation of Edward Balliol at Scone in September 1332.

I will spare you the details of Edward Balliol's reign. A game of musical thrones comes to mind. By the end of the year he was forced to flee to England after being defeated by the Scottish nobles at the Battle of Annan, was restored in 1333, deposed in 1334, restored in 1335 and deposed again in 1336. In January 1356, in return for renouncing his claim to the throne of Scotland now and in perpetuity, Balliol took not so much the king's shilling but a king's pension and retired from trying to be a king. He received his pension for ten years before handing in his dinner pail in 1367.

As for Sir Eustace, he continued to cooperate with the English until 1338 when he rebelled again, but was pardoned the following year by Edward III. When David II returned from France in June 1341, he threw his lot in with him. It was his fourth and last change. He died in Caerlaverock in 1342 and was succeeded by his brother, John, who was captured at the Battle of Neville's Cross near Durham in 1346, taken prisoner, and died in the Tower of London the following year.

Two hundred years after the death of Sir Eustace, in November 1542 to be precise, Robert Maxwell, 5th Lord Maxwell (1493-1546), went south with an army to put an end to the burning and pillaging in the Borders which Henry VIII had ordered in response to his nephew, James V of Scotland, who had the nerve to refuse to abjure the Catholic faith. Just because *he* was having a certain little dispute with the Pope over his love life, there was no need to take it out on others...

Like his ancestors, Robert Maxwell was a man of distinction. He was one of the Regents for James V who came to the throne aged only seventeen months after his father, James IV, fell at Flodden Field in 1513. (Incidentally, James has the doubtful distinction of being the last British monarch to die in battle.) Maxwell was also the Regent of the Isle of Arran, his own little kingdom in effect. In 1513, he became Admiral of the Scottish Fleet and in 1515, given the turbulent nature of Anglo-Scottish relations, was handed the poisoned chalice of being made Warden of the West Marches which meant he was responsible for the law and security of the region. In 1537, he had an arguably more agreeable job when he was chosen to be part of the team of ambassadors who went to France to arrange the marriage between the king and Mary of Guise. Reader, he married her, by proxy.

Maxwell was captured at the Battle of Solway Moss but released on James V's death on payment of a ransom. He was later arrested and sent to Edinburgh Castle on the orders of the Abbot of Paisley for permitting the Bible to be read in Scots and English. (Yes, truly a terrible sin.)

He also opposed Cardinal Beaton who objected to the 1543 Treaty of Greenwich, Henry VIII's plan to unite the two warring nations by the betrothal of the 7-month old Mary, Queen of Scots to the five-year old Prince Edward of England. Beaton's objection to the marriage was because Mary was the heir to a Protestant country. You might have thought that this would have endeared Maxwell to Henry forever. Alas not. After his release from Edinburgh, Maxwell was captured again at the Battle of Glasgow on 1st April 1544, though released a month later.

All these releases from chokey aroused the suspicion of Henry, who now doubted his loyalty and sent him to the Tower of London, just in case. To get out of that, Maxwell offered to submit himself to the guardianship of Edward Seymour, Earl of Hertford, who, after the Scots reneged on the Treaty, had been ordered by an irate Henry to burn, sack, and raze Edinburgh to the ground "so there may remain forever a perpetual memory of the vengeance of God lightened upon [the Scots government] for their falsehood and disloyalty".

It didn't wash. Henry was unconvinced, but he did give him a free transfer, so to speak, to Pontefract Castle. He was released from there in October of 1545, provided he handed Caerlaverock over to the English. No greater love hath a man for his freedom than he hand over his family seat to the enemy. But the English were his friends now, were they not?

But that is not the end of Caerlaverock's story, not by any means. In November of 1546, it was captured by the forces of the godly (or the ungodly, depending on your religious persuasion), by Cardinal Beaton's men. Maxwell was captured yet again and imprisoned in Dumfries. He claimed he had only been a supporter of Henry VIII and the Great Marriage Plan under duress and in fear of his life. He convinced his captors, and not only did he regain his freedom and receive a free pardon, but he was made Chief Justice of Annandale to boot. Not bad for an old lag who had more twists in him than a two-foot long snake.

But there's more. In June 1546, he got his old job back. He was reappointed Warden of the West Marches. Who would want it? Maybe it was a job he couldn't refuse anyway. But there was one more twist left in the snake. A month later he wriggled out of that job-from-hell by going to that land "from whose bourne no traveller returns," as Hamlet put it. Hell or heaven? I don't think there's much doubt about it, frankly.

And so, with the castle explored, and accompanied by swallows putting on a dazzling display of aerial acrobatics, we make our way over the green sward to where, attached to the visitor centre, we see a display of another sort – noticeboards and a film documentary of the siege of 1312.

A great deal is known about it thanks to an unfinished poem, *The Roll of Karlaverock,* written by an English herald. We know the names of all 87 English knights but nothing at all of the 60 brave Scottish defenders. You know what they say about history being written by the victors.

On noticeboards in the shape of shields, there is a great deal of information (you might even say, too much) about the background to the conflict, how the siege was undertaken and the art of heraldry. If you can't be bothered to read all the information, help is at hand, at least as far as the siege is concerned, in the form of a film made by Historic Scotland – since 2015, Historic Environment Scotland (HES).

It features Sir Tony Robinson with a fine head of hair (which tells you how long ago it was made), bouncing with energy, as he single-handedly re-enacts the siege. A tour-de-force really, and well done, Tony, but out of this entire exhibition, what catches my eye most is a collection of roughly-shaped sandstone balls. These were the ammunition for the trebuchet, the mighty wooden catapult that, before the invention of the cannon, launched those deadly missiles at the foe. You can see the remains of a trebuchet near the car park but it is lacking what must surely be the most fearsome part, the long arm that flung the boulders hundreds of yards with devastating force against the hapless defenders.

If you prefer your history natural, a path from the castle takes you past the foundations of the old castle, through the castle woods to Caerlaverock National Nature Reserve (NNR) and the nearby Wildfowl and Wetlands Trust (WWT).

Interesting though that may be, we are not going there on this occasion. We are heading instead for the village of Caerlaverock to seek out the grave of *Old Mortality*. If you decide to pay a visit, you will need to be vigilant. The road there is narrow, the sign to the church is hard to spot and it lies down a track even narrower than the road, and that is saying something. There is not a passing place to be had should you meet a vehicle coming in the opposite direction.

It is most likely to be a tractor because at the end of the track, as well as the church and graveyard, there is a farm. Our luck is in: nothing coming or going. There is plenty of room to park, but nothing to indicate where the grave we seek is in a place fairly bristling with red sandstone headstones.

Gravestone of *Old Mortality*

Our luck continues to hold, or was it some sort of instinct that made me turn to the left once through the gate? It took only a matter of moments to home in on it. There is nothing special to distinguish it from the others, except perhaps, its curved top – but a good many others are like that too.

At the top are carved the tools of our man's trade, a crossed chisel and mallet, then the word "ERECTED" engraved upon a ribbon of stone and then this:

TO THE MEMORY
OF
ROBERT PATERSON.
THE

OLD MORTALITY
OF
SIR WALTER SCOTT.
WHO WAS BURIED HERE
FEBRUARY 1801.

There are four lines of verse beneath that which I'll leave to you to read if you decide to come here. If you decide not to bother, it doesn't matter. They're not important.

What *is* important is that *Old Mortality* has joined the immortals now and must surely be in heaven.

● ● ●

Chapter Ten

The Brow Well: The Cure That Killed

WE continue our way along the B725, heading towards Ruthwell, but before we arrive there, there is something else we must stop and visit. You can't miss it. The brown sign with Burns's portrait at the top, the legend "Burns Heritage Trail" beneath, and below that, in even bigger letters, "Brow Well". There is a lay-by nearby, not very big, but we are the only visitors so it is roomy.

It was here Burns came for the good of his health to drink the rust-coloured chalybeate waters and bathe in the chilly waters of the Solway Firth, as prescribed by his friend and doctor, William Maxwell, who had diagnosed "flying gout", what we would call "rheumatic fever". Three days after leaving the Brow Inn, where he had been staying for two weeks whilst taking the treatment, Burns died on 21st July 1796 of endocarditis. He was buried, for the first time, in St Michael's cemetery on 25th July, the same day that his son, Maxwell, was born, named after the doctor aforesaid. What a rollercoaster of a day for poor Mrs Burns! Clearly she bore no ill will to the well-intentioned doctor.

Incidentally, in an interesting footnote, Maxwell was present at the execution of Louis XVI and dipped his handkerchief in the decapitated monarch's blood. It seems a strange and grisly thing to do and betrays the doctor's Republican sympathies – the same sentiments that Burns was accused of having and for which he found himself in hot water, by way of a change.

You may not realise it, but the road that took you here follows the ancient drove road to England where Scottish beef farmers took their cattle south to market. In Burns's day, the village of Brow consisted of only a dozen houses (it's pretty much the same today), but the inn where those stayed whilst they were taking the waters, was demolished in 1863 when the road was widened. No matter, there are plenty of other places in this area which have associations with Burns, as you know.

The Brow Well

The well from which Burns drank the water looks more like a plunge pool than a well, as if what you are meant to do is bathe in it and somehow absorb the nutrients through your pores rather than ingest it.

It was given a facelift in 2016. It is L-shaped, hemmed-in by slabs, with steps that Burns never stepped on, leading down into the rusty water, ankle-deep now, but when full, surely the invalids were expected to immerse their bodies in it rather than drink it. Around the perimeter, appropriately enough, are engraved some lines from Burns's poem of premonition of death: *A Prayer, in the Prospect of Death.*

A notice in big, bold, red letters, draws the visitor's attention to the fact that the water is not fit for human consumption. Whoever wrote and erected that notice was wasting his or her their time, though of course, in these litigious times, one can't be too careful. Even if you didn't know that it didn't do Burns the slightest bit of good, the instant you see the colour of the water, you wouldn't dream of taking as much as a sip from that most disgusting-looking brew.

The colour is due to the concentration of iron, the very thing that is meant to be good for you, to build up your strength, which Scotland's "other national drink", the bright-orange Irn Bru, proudly boasts is "brewed from girders" with a strong emphasis on the rolling of the "r"s. In Scotland it outsells that universal soft drink, Coca-Cola. The only other country in the world that achieves this feat is Peru with its Inca Kola, which is an unappetising shade of sickly yellow. Personally, I prefer to stick to *uisge bheatha.*

The other part of the "cure" that the poor poet (in both senses of the word) was required to do, was to wade out each day into the freezing waters of the Solway Firth, up to his armpits. Never was the saying "you'll catch your death of cold" been more prophetic than in Burns's case. He had also probably been told by his misguided doctor that there was "no gain without pain", and therefore the more unpleasant he found being immersed in that freezing water, the more it was doing him the world of good.

● ● ●

There was one comfort allowed him however, or should I say part of the remedy – the drinking of port, which seems strange when you remember that Dr Maxwell had diagnosed a severe bout of gout. Alas, the Brow Inn did not supply such a medicine but fortunately mine host knew a man who did, and pointed Burns in the direction of his son-in-law who kept the hostelry in Clarencefield only a mile or so away. A mere step for a fit man, which Burns obviously was not, otherwise he would never have been there in the first place. But doctor's orders are orders.

The story goes that Burns, arriving with an empty bottle in order to receive the life-restoring elixir, plonked it down on the bar and confessed he had no money to pay for it. This, of course, was long before the days of the NHS where in Scotland prescription medicines have been free for a good number of years. That said, I doubt if I will ever live to see the day, considering how cash-strapped the NHS is at the moment, when I will ever be prescribed a medicinal malt whisky before bedtime to ensure a good night's sleep.

In lieu of payment, Burns offered his dearly-beloved watch seal until such time as he had the wherewithal, but the landlord's wife, Mrs Burney, persuaded her husband to let Burns have the port for free and without surety. Was it out of common humanity, seeing how ill Burns looked, or was the old charm with the ladies still working?

Burns *was* short of money as a matter of fact, as due to his ill-health, he had been unable to undertake his duties as exciseman for the past three months and was now on a salary of £35 per annum, reduced from £50 and with a heavily-pregnant wife and kids to keep. No wonder he was worried about money. To add to his troubles, he had recently received a solicitor's letter from a haberdasher for non-payment of an account for the making of his Dumfries Volunteers' uniform. He lived in fear of being arrested and dying in a debtor's prison. He wrote to his friend, George Thomson, begging for money to clear the debt.

He wrote several other letters beside, which fortunately survive. He was invited to tea at Ruthwell Manse and when the minister's daughter, Agnes Craig, went to pull down the blind to shield Burns's face from the glare of the sun, he asked her to leave it alone, prophetically remarking, "He has not long to shine upon me." It reminds me very much of Wilfred Owen's *Anthem For Doomed Youth* where the "drawing-down of blinds" is a symbol of all those young lives wasted in WWI.

On 5th July, the day after arrival at Brow, Burns's friend Maria Riddell, who was also in the area for the good of her health, similarly invited him to tea.

She was shocked by his appearance. She thought he had "the stamp of death" on his features and he was "touching the brink of eternity".

Mrs Riddell later related that at their meeting, Burns greeted her with the words, "Well, madam, have you any commands for the other world?" Black humour to be sure, and once again shows that Burns realised he was not long for this world, but neither she nor he probably realised just how close to death he actually was. Whether or not there is another world, we will all find out one day, hopefully later rather than sooner, but I am left pondering what the word "commands" says about the personality of Mrs Riddell and her relationship with Burns. Two years previously, Burns had been banned from her house at Friar's Carse near his farm of Ellisland, because of his drunken behaviour. It is a tale that will be told in greater detail later.

The tides were no longer suitable for bathing in the Solway and Burns decided to return to Dumfries. To do so, although he had his horse with him, he requested the use of the spring cart belonging to his friend, John Clark, because as he put it, "getting wet is perdition" – which tells you all you need to know about what he thought about his daily *dook* in the Solway. It also tells you that while the sun may have shone on his face at Ruthwell, the Scottish summer had reverted to type by the 18th July, the day when Burns left for home.

As soon as he arrived there, he wrote an urgent letter to his father-in-law in Mauchline, begging him to send his wife to help their daughter with her confinement, adding that he thought the "disorder" he was suffering from would be "fatal".

Once again, his intimations of mortality were correct. It was the last letter he ever wrote. Three days later, he was dead.

Chapter Eleven

Ruthwell: The Cross and the Savings Bank

S O it's farewell to the Brow Well, hello to Ruthwell. We've come here for two reasons: to see the Ruthwell Cross and the Savings Bank Museum.

We pick up the key to the church from a box outside the new manse and presently, we find the cross towering over us despite it standing in its own well. It is an elaborately-carved Anglo-Saxon Cross, dating from the 7th century when this part of Scotland was in the kingdom of Northumbria. The runes are a later addition, probably dating from about 900 AD.

It's an elaborate visual aid, depicting episodes from the New Testament, and in the same way that Giotto's frescoes tell the story of St Francis so the illiterate could understand, I can imagine a monk standing in front of it in 900 saying, "Right, listen up you lot. Starting on this side, at the very top, we have John the Baptist and an eagle, then below the arm of the cross, an archer shooting an arrow into the sky (don't ask me what that means as I haven't a clue). After that, we have industrious Mary and contemplative Martha," and at this point the monk would break off and tell the listeners that story before continuing, "and here you can see Mary Magdelene washing Jesus's feet... then Jesus curing the man who was born blind... next is the Annunciation of the Virgin Mary... and the last one, I need scarcely tell you, is the Crucifixion.

"Now if you would just follow me round to the other side...at the top is a bird, which, as you can see, is a dove. (What's that, my son, you think it looks like an eagle? Well it isn't, it's the dove of peace.) Now where was I? Ah, yes, next you see two evangelists, followed by John the Baptist and the *Agnus Dei*... then Christ standing on the heads of two animals. The Latin around it says it's the beasts of the desert recognising Jesus as the Saviour of the world. After that you see St Paul and St Anthony breaking bread... and lastly the flight into Egypt.

"On the sides you can see vines and animals eating grapes. That symbolises the Eucharist. And now that I have explained all that to you, next time you see the cross, when you look at the carvings, you will be reminded of the stories. Now go in peace."

Talk about "sermons in stones"! Actually scholars are still arguing about what the scenes depict – even if it was a cross at all. Some argue that it really was a column, although a fragment of stone, securely anchored down by iron bars in front of the cross is described as being "all that remains of the cross beam". Well maybe it is and maybe it isn't. It's just a small block of stone and in my opinion, could have come from any part of the cross or not actually be part of it at all. The cross beam has never been found. Could that possibly be because it never existed in the first place?

The cross beam that now graces the top, is clearly a later addition. It was designed and commissioned by the Reverend Henry Duncan of whom much more, soon. And another thing that is perfectly obvious is that some of the stones at the top are distinctly redder than the rest. Could it possibly be that they don't belong here at all and there was another cross or column once upon a time?

This is quite a possible scenario for the cross was once a sort of massive stone jigsaw. What happened was that in 1640, in its wisdom and anti-Catholic zeal, the General Assembly of the Church of Scotland decided that "idolatrous

monuments" were an abomination and should be destroyed. The parson at the time, the Rev. Gavin Young, delayed for as long as he could but finally and reluctantly broke the stone into pieces. We know he did so reluctantly because he broke it very carefully. Some found shelter in the church, some were scattered about the manse gardens, while others were buried under the floorboards where they lay undiscovered until the 19th century when the church was being revamped.

In 1771, the bigger pieces were hauled outside to make way for wooden pews. And there they lay, weathering away for thirty years

The Ruthwell Cross

before along came the Rev. Henry Duncan who began reassembling the fragments in the garden of the manse. (You may remember his fossils in the Dumfries Museum.) In 1823, the reconstruction of the cross was complete, except that the stone at the tip of the cross was put the wrong way round, so the experts think. In 1840, J.M. Kemble of the British Museum identified the runes as being Anglo-Saxon, or Old English, and duly translated them in 1842 – *The Dream of the Rood.* I studied it at University and it was good to meet the original in the flesh, so to speak.

In 1887, the cross was taken inside the church where it remains to this day in its own purpose-built apse thanks to the foresight of the Rev. James Macfarlan – only it was too tall and had to be planted in a pit surrounded by a railing to prevent viewers from toppling in. And there's one other thing; why we may not be seeing the stone as it was when it was first carved. It's possible the figures on the stone were brightly painted. We knew the Picts painted their cross-slabs, so my money is on the Ruthwell Cross having been gaudily painted too when it was new.

Facing you as you leave the church and built into the kirkyard wall, is a memorial tablet to the Reverend and his family, amongst others, his first wife, who died in 1832 "in the 61st year of her age". I quite like that way of putting it. She was his predecessor's daughter, Agnes Craig, she who wanted to protect Burns from the sun. Incidentally, when he was eighteen, Henry had met Burns when he was visiting the manse at Lochrutton. His father said to him and his brothers: "Look well, boys, at Mr Burns, for you'll never again see so great a genius."

But to begin at the beginning. Henry was born in Lochfoot near Kirkcudbright in 1774, the son of a minister, and another of Dumfries Academy's distinguished alumni. When he was sixteen, his father had sent him to Liverpool to join two of his brothers, destined for a career in banking. After three years, he decided it was not for him and he came back to Scotland to study for the ministry. He was following in the family footsteps: his father and grandfather were both ministers. In 1799 he was appointed the minster at Ruthwell but it was not until he attended a meeting of Quakers five years later that he got God, so to speak.

In 1839, he served as the Moderator of the General Assembly of the Church of Scotland and after the Disruption of 1843, he became one of the founders of the Free Church.

The Disruption was a seismic event in the Scottish Church where 474 members out of about 1200, broke away over the issue of the right of parishioners to chose their own minister, not have him thrust upon them by the landowner. It was not a decision to be taken lightly. Being a member of the Free Church meant you were ostracised from the parish, losing not only your job, but a roof over your head. The ex-Moderator was reduced to living in a little cottage in nearby Clarencefield.

He was always tireless in the causes he espoused and aged seventy-one, he had travelled to Manchester and Liverpool in order to raise money for the Free Church. On his way home to Edinburgh he stopped off at Ruthwell. He was invited to preach at nearby Cockpool but unfortunately suffered a stroke and died two days later at his sister's house. It looks as if he had been pushing himself too hard.

As you can imagine, his funeral was very well attended. Unfortunately no-one knows where he was laid to rest as no record was kept. Probably one place it is not, is with Agnes, as the second Mrs Duncan, Mary Grey Lundie, might have had something to say about that. She was the widow of one of his good friends, the Rev. Robert Lundie of Kelso. Henry's son, William, was already married to her daughter, also called Mary. They were, you might say, a close-knit family. The older Mary, Henry's junior by fourteen years, survived him by thirty-one years, dying in 1877 in the 89th year of her age.

So much for the Cross. Now for the Savings Bank Museum.

We retrace our steps to the village and park right at the door – a neat, whitewashed building with the window and door facings picked out in black. We are just about to take photos when the door is thrown wide open. Kay (as I later discover her name to be), has heard us and warmly welcomes us inside.

It was here, in this very room that the very first Savings Bank in the world was founded by none other than the Reverend Henry Duncan, aforesaid, in 1810. There is a desk and a chair, the original (how I would have liked to sit in it), and a 1/5th scale model of the Ruthwell Cross made of beeswax. And here's the amazing thing: it was made by Henry himself and later given a good lashing of masonry paint by his family to preserve it. I'm glad they did.

And if that were not already enough, there are the sketches Henry made of the cross and, on the wall, sketches of his landscapes. Fine art it certainly is. His lack of neatness in the keeping of the bank ledgers in Liverpool was allegedly why the Heywoods Bank in Liverpool "had to let him go" as the present-day euphemism has it. Frankly, I don't believe a word of it. Anyone who could draw with this amount of precision could surely manage to put some neat figures within the margins of the red lines if he had wanted to. No, his massive brain could not be constrained within such narrow margins. He saw a way out from this mind-sapping drudgery by crossing the red lines and he was free at last from his father's will, but who surely, must not have been disappointed when Henry chose to follow in the family footsteps.

We know he made it to the top of the tree in the Church, and how proud his old man would have been, one imagines. But that was just one thing. He was so much more besides. For starters, he was a

The Savings Bank Museum, Ruthwell

writer of essays and articles, mere minnows to the four-volume *The Sacred Philosophy of the Seasons* or *Seasons* for short – which they certainly are not, by any stretch of the imagination.

But good old Henry didn't stop there. He was the founder-editor of *The Courier*, Dumfries and Galloway's first newspaper and still in print today. After the Disruption, his voice was officially silenced, so what did the indefatigable Henry do? He simply started up another newspaper – the *Dumfries and Galloway Standard*, also still in print today.

Was there nothing the man couldn't do? It was a bit rude of him, really. While the majority of us found ourselves at the back of the queue when the talents were being handed out, there was Henry at the front of so many. It's just not fair.

To this list and arguably at the top of it, you can certainly add "philanthropist". In fact it has been said it was his desire to serve his fellow man that inspired him to enter the ministry. The times were desperate. Britain was at war with France, bad harvests meant corn was in short supply and the price went through the roof. At his own expense, and with the help of his banker brothers in Liverpool, he arranged for the shipment and distribution of grain to be sent from there. He also provided employment for his women parishioners by supplying flax to spin while the men delved in the church grounds or glebe turning it into a model farm. He also took over the running of the Friendly Society, which in time of severe hardship, such as a death or illness of the breadwinner, saw to it that the family did not starve.

His creation of the Savings Bank in the premises of the Friendly Society was also born out of his philanthropy, the need to help his poorest parishioners who received interest on what savings they could scrape together. Whereas other banks required the unimaginable riches of £10 to open an account, all

Duncan's parishioners required was sixpence. The parishioners received 5% interest as long as they remained members for three years. If they withdrew all of their deposits before that time they only received 4%. In this way Duncan brought a measure of self-respect and pride to his parishioners, helping free them from the shame and ignominy of having to rely on charity. Not only that, but the entrepreneurial minister used the surplus interest to set up a charity fund and build another school. He was tireless in promoting the idea throughout the country, which he did at his own expense, printing leaflets and addressing meetings.

It caught on. At the end of the first year, £151 had been deposited. It may not sound much now but allowing for inflation and considering the poverty of the members, it was an enormous sum. By the time of Duncan's death in 1846, there were 577 Savings Banks in the UK with funds in excess of £30 million.

There are quite a few artefacts to be seen, such as ledgers and records from the original bank, as well as bank notes and coins from all over the world. I was delighted to renew my acquaintance with a half-crown. Now that is what I call a coin! Solid and heavy, it could have come from a bygone age and when I had one, I knew I was rich indeed.

Kay shows us an ancient-looking money-box which required three people to be present when it was opened as it had three different locks. Savers could see that all was above board, that their money was safe from any *pochling* – not that they would ever suspect the good Reverend, to name but one, capable of such a thing. Indeed, it cost him a great deal of money from his stipend to run the bank for such things as postage.

In the little room next door is an amazing collection of piggy banks. (Is it still a piggy bank if it's a cow or a teddy bear or a mouse or a bee or a tortoise or a ladybird, to name but a few?) There are several like a book, a whole library of them in fact. I used to have one like that and one day I broke into it, not being able to wait for whatever it was I was so desperate to buy.

I had never heard of the Rev. Henry Duncan in those days but I can see now that he would have been shaking his head in sorrow in heaven. I have to laugh at the irony of his father's words when he introduced him to Burns. No-one could have foreseen that there were two geniuses in the room that day, but I hope all the same that Burns repaid the compliment and took a good look at Henry.

Chapter Twelve

Annan and Eastriggs: The Rose-Red Town, the Devil's Porridge and the Rail Disaster

I GNORING the bypass, we come to Annan on the B725 and as soon as I see it, John Burgon's immortal lines, *A rose-red city, half as old as time* came unbidden to mind. He was writing about Petra and the two are different in many, many ways, but Annan is most decidedly red, for every building, with a few white-washed exceptions, has been constructed out of dark-red sandstone. Unlike Petra, however, these buildings are only a couple of centuries old.

But then you have to bear in mind that the town is only eight miles from the English border, and given the strained relationships between the two countries of England and Scotland, you will understand at once why no old buildings from the *days of old when knights were bold* have survived – apart from a green mound which is all that remains of the motte-and-bailey castle that Robert the Bruce's family built in the 12th century.

In December 1332, at the Battle of Annan, the newly-crowned king, Edward Balliol, and his forces were taken by surprise, as they lay a-bed, by the Bruce faction under the leadership of Sir Archibald Douglas. I suppose all is fair in love and war. With your life and a cause and a throne at stake, there seems little point in waking up the opposition and telling them to put on their armour and prepare for a battle. Edward was ignominiously chased out of Scotland, in his night-shirt, so it was said, and on the back of a carthorse, to hide under the skirts of his namesake, protector and puppeteer, Edward III.

The town's name probably derives from *Anu*, the Gaelic goddess of prosperity and indeed, it was a well-to-do market town. It was given a royal charter by James V in 1538 and made a Royal Burgh in 1612 by James VI. In that century and the next, it was a busy and prosperous river port.

Annan

Shipbuilding, fishing and quarrying were the major industries, and of course not forgetting farming, perhaps the most traditional of industries.

The Annan river is crossed by a fine three-arched bridge designed by Robert Stevenson (more famous as a builder of lighthouses, and grandfather of the novelist), and built by John Lowry. It was completed in 1827 at a cost of £60,000. It is said that to wet its head so to speak, the workmen drank a gallon of whisky.

A railway bridge crosses the river too, but before the present structure was built, there used to be a viaduct. In our present times of global warming (although some deny it despite what seems to be irrefutable evidence to the contrary), it may give you some pause for thought when I tell you that the viaduct was damaged by ice floes in 1881. It took three years to repair. Alas, for the viaduct, it was only a stay of execution. It was closed in 1921 and demolished in 1934. Now only the embankment remains.

If you were to come to Annan on the first Saturday of July, you would be treated to the spectacle of the Riding of the Marches where a hundred riders or more make a tour of the town's boundary markers to check all is present and correct. The tradition goes back to James V's time when the "marches" or common land, were checked to ensure they had not been encroached upon by rapacious landlords. You can see where the good townsfolk of today are coming from. When they discover that all is present and correct, it's a cause for a great celebration with pipe bands and much, much more.

The Bridge House, at the western end of the High Street, was a fine three-story Georgian mansion built in 1780 and saw service as the town's academy from 1802-20. Thomas Carlyle was here as a pupil and loved it so much that he returned as a teacher. Actually that's not true. He did come back to teach there, but he hated it on both occasions.

Dominating the High Street is the Town Hall of 1876 with its impressive clock tower. The statue of Bruce lower down only dates from 2013. He is shown holding his mighty two-handed sword by the blade in his right hand, while his left clutches the tightly-rolled up Declaration of Arbroath. Victory over English rule and domination accomplished. No prizes for guessing what he is thinking.

On the southern side of the High Street is the Queensberry Arms Hotel, an old coaching inn. In the rear is a *doocot*, or dovecot, from 1690, the oldest building in Annan. Across the street is a close called "Hare's Den" because, according to legend, that was where the infamous grave robber and murderer once stopped after being freed when he turned king's evidence against his former partner in crime, William Burke.

We turn up Bank Street and make for the Museum.

It's housed in two storeys, the lower one being turned over to rotating exhibitions. At the date of our visit, it was dedicated to Lady Florence, Dixie (1855-1905). It's a pity I don't have the space to tell you about her here and the exhibition is long since gone. She was a prolific writer, traveller and campaigner for women's rights. Her father was Archibald William Douglas MP, 8th Marquis of Queensberry. Her brother was the 9th Marquis, after whom the boxing rules are named, but who more famously hounded poor Oscar Wilde to death because of his affair with his son *Bosie*.

Upstairs you can read about the life and times of Annan, from prehistoric times to the nuclear age including the history of the harbour, more about the Marches, and about RAF Annan which operated from 1942-44 as a fighter pilot training school. In 1955 it became the construction site for the Chapelcross Nuclear Power Station. It opened in 1959 and used six million gallons of water every day. Imagine that! The four three-hundred-foot-high cooling towers, once the symbol and icon of the UK's embryo nuclear industry, were a familiar sight to travellers heading south to England or north to Scotland on the A74.

Built in 1959, the reactors were intended to create plutonium for military use as well as supplying electricity for the domestic market. At full capacity, it produced enough electricity to supply not just every home in southwest Scotland but the Borders and Cumbria too. Isn't that an amazing thing! However, as *Ecclesiastes* poetically reminds us, as well as a time to build up there is a time to break down and in 2005 the decision was taken to decommission Chapelcross as well as its sister plant at Calder Hall, now known as Sellafield, in Cumbria. In May 2007, by a controlled explosion, the Chapelcross towers were demolished in just ten seconds to 25,500 tons of rubble and dust.

If you have a penchant for the curious, then this excellent little museum provides some interesting specimens, such as a mummified baby crocodile, a one hundred-and-ten-year-old piece of chocolate, a wispy grey lock of Thomas Carlyle's hair and the blood-stained jacket of Lieutenant-General Colin

Mackenzie (1805-81) who served in the Indian Army in Afghanistan. He was wounded in Hyderabad in 1855 during a mutiny by one of the cavalry regiments, but lived to tell the tale – which is surprising when you see the amount of blood on the uniform.

If you have the time (and your wife permits) you can visit the Annan distillery in Northfield. It opened in 1836 and closed in 1918 and, like Sleeping Beauty, went to sleep for nearly one hundred years until it woke up again in 2014. You can take a tour and have a taste of course. Oh, and if you happen to have a spare £2,300 rattling about in your pocket, you can buy a peated cask from the 2015 production or £2,100 for the unpeated. It's my lucky day: I am not a fan of the peaty.

We are heading east towards Gretna and Gretna Green, the last village in Scotland. It is thanks to the latter's location as also being the first village, and the differences between the marriage laws of England and Scotland, that it found itself at the heart of the marriage industry.

Gretna, on the other hand, has a less romantic past. It was built during the First World War to house the 30,000 workers in the munitions factory at Eastriggs which also grew to accommodate the works. They arose out of the Shell Crisis of 1915 when it became apparent that there was a shortage of high-explosive shells and if the war was to be won, something needed to be done. The following year, David Lloyd George was appointed Minister of Munitions and became Prime Minister in December of the same year after the Asquith government fell.

At the time, HM Factory, Gretna, as it was called, was the biggest munitions factory in Britain, bigger than all the rest put together, and a mind-boggling nine miles long and two miles wide, stretching from Eastriggs to Longtown over the border. The work force was composed mainly of women – 12,000 of them. In 1916, 60% of them were under nineteen, the men being otherwise engaged elsewhere. Their main job was to stand in front of huge earthenware basins mixing nitro-glycerine with guncotton. A single spark such as from static electricity and they would be

Eastriggs

blown to kingdom come. They were making cordite, propellant for the shells and dubbed the "devil's porridge", by Sir Arthur Conan Doyle, who as a war correspondent, visited the factory in 1916. It was an appropriate image; the maw of the guns was insatiable. It goes without saying that without the munition factories, and this one in particular, the war would most certainly have been lost.

The name stuck, like porridge tends to when it goes cold in the bowl. The words, writ large on the side of the building ahead of us, tell us we are approaching our destination. One of the volunteer museum staff, David, gives us some background information.

Gretna, he tells us, was once known as "Timber Town" but the houses were later built of brick due to the scarcity of timber since that slow-to-replenish source was being gobbled up by the trenches. It came to be called a "Garden City" and was emulated elsewhere, both at home and abroad – the cutting edge of modern housing with central heating and indoor toilets. Today it is also known as the "Commonwealth Village" due to the large number of scientists who came here from all over the world to play their part in creating the factory.

It was built by 10,000 Irish navvies, who were well known for their fondness of drinking often followed by a jolly good punch up. After the Germans, alcohol was seen as Public Enemy Number One. George V set an example by becoming teetotal, whilst Lloyd George's budget of 1915 drew the line at Prohibition but hiked the tax on alcohol. As far as Gretna was concerned, the Government took up preventative measures by the compulsory purchase of all the pubs in the district, and even as far as Carlisle. They appointed managers who received commission on the food they sold, as well as watering the beer down to 2% and spirits being *Verboten*. At this time, the legal age for the consumption of alcohol was set at 18, just as it is today.

Before these measures were introduced in 1916, there was the legendary tale of the "Night of a Thousand Whiskies". What happened was the navvies phoned the nearest pub to the station in Carlisle to say they were on their way and bribed the fireman to put on more coal so they would get there before closing time. They made it by five minutes before closing time and, when they got there, there were 1,000 glasses of whisky lined up on the bar.

After the navvies left, the "Gretna Girls" – as they were called – moved in. It was a settlement of 30,000 souls, a good deal bigger than a great many villages, with all the trappings of a town: five churches, two dance halls and two cinemas, not forgetting shops, banks and sporting facilities. There were several football teams, and remember we are talking about ladies here, mostly. What there was not, was a brewery or a pub. The Government wasn't making it easy, even to imbibe the 2% beer. Cheers!

The girls were paid well, earning five times above the average wage. It was dangerous work certainly, but their remuneration was controversial – that they should be earning so much and the men half as much again for the same work, while their compatriots were facing bullets and bayonets amongst the blood and the mud of the trenches. Some men were conscientious objectors but many accused them of being cowards or "yellow". While that may be unkind, there is no denying that the munitionettes were also known as the "Canary Girls" as their skins turned yellow due to the acid that was mixed with the gun cotton to make nitro-cotton. Because it was so unpleasant, it was the best-paid part of the process and five months at a stretch was the most that was allowed.

Anyway, well done to them and it could be argued that as well as the incalculable contribution they made towards the war effort, they did more for the voting rights of women than the Suffragettes. Sir Arthur Conan Doyle took his hat off to them, though he put it somewhat perversely: "Even all the militants shall in future not prevent me from being an advocate of their vote."

We thank David for his extraordinarily-detailed exposition, and thus armed, so to speak, we are set loose to explore the two-storey museum at our leisure.

The first thing we come to is an exhibition of a disaster. It took place on 22nd May 1915, and it had nothing to do with the factory as you might have expected given the volatile nature of the premises. The Devil must surely have had time on his hands when he brewed up the series of incidents that became known as the "Quintinshill Railway Disaster", still to this day Britain's worst. Let's hope that unenviable record is never overtaken.

Quintinshill was a signal box near Gretna and what happened was a troop train taking the 7th Royal Scots on their way to Galllipoli ran into a stationary local train. Bad enough, but the killer blow came when an express train, heading north, ran into the wreckage of both trains which had been strewn across the tracks.

Compressed and twisted metal, then fire. The surviving officers drew lots and two were given the gruesome job of shooting the trapped soldiers to save them from being burned to death. One soldier was freed by amputating both legs; another saved himself by cutting off his own arm. 229 people were killed and 246 were injured, many seriously. Only 64 walked away unhurt. A scene of carnage to be sure, and – you would think – must surely rank amongst one of the world's worst train disasters. You may be amazed to learn, however, that it just manages to creep into the top thirty at number twenty-seven. If you have ever seen photographs of those trains in India with crowds of people squatting on the roof, it might explain why this was such a relatively modest loss of life.

Talking of loss of life, just around the corner is an eye-arresting photograph of a soldier standing up to his knees in a massive mound of spent shells. It stretches behind him as far as the eye can see, but how far in front of him the photograph does not show. Imagine if one shell killed just one person, then this would amount to a massacre, but the truth of course is that there were a good many more deaths than that. The most graphic portrayal of the horror of war I have seen without a body.

Other panels on the ground floor tell the story of the factory in words and pictures. One shows the girls with their fetching overalls and shower caps, posing for the camera and looking for all the world like a chorus line from some musical show.

The upstairs gallery features the district and WWII. *Plus ca change, plus c'est la meme chose.* HM Gretna became the Powmill Munition Factory in January 1941 with its own "Canary Girls" making TNT. They were also known as the "Broom Lassies" after the farmland the factory was built on. At its peak it had a workforce of 4,000. There were several accidents, the worst being in October 1943, when an explosion resulted in the death of five girls. The factory was closed in 1945, but saw service again during the Korean and Falkland wars.

There is also a mock-up of a 1940s kitchen. It looked familiar in so many ways: a cooker just like the one my mother used to have and the same sink, and there's the blue-and-white tin of National Dried Milk with added vitamins that we children used to get. There was also orange juice, which was lovely, and cod liver oil which was ghastly. My mother had to chase me round the kitchen table to get it down my neck.

Time marched on and the weapons got nastier. That's called progress. Chapelcross was built on the site of the former RAF Annan (of which there is also a display) to produce weapons-grade plutonium. In 1980 it was the only nuclear facility in Britain to produce tritium, required for the Polaris and Trident programmes. It continued to do so until the decision to decommission it in 2005, as I said earlier. As well as a lot of information on how the reactors work (or worked, rather), the visitor can don a 3D visor and be virtually inside the reactor if, of course, first of all, you can get your hands on the visor. It's virtually impossible. There is only one.

Back out in the car park, I can't believe my eyes when I see a car whose registration plate has writ large upon it, "TNT" with some digits after it. Clearly a personalised number plate, but how apposite for this place! What a coincidence! I must speak to the driver and find out more.

• • •

It turns out that the driver is Tina and her husband is Tony. Just how romantic is that, like a heart bearing lovers' initials carved on a tree trunk! All the same, I wonder if their relationship doesn't get somewhat explosive sometimes.

Chapter Thirteen

Gretna Green: The Marriage Business

THE marriage industry really took off in Gretna Green in 1754 with Lord Hardwicke's Marriage Act designed to put a peep to the number of irregular marriages which were going on all over England. It did not apply to Scotland where there was no change, but what it did south of the border was to restrict the number of places where marriages could take place, and more significantly, if you were a minor (which at that time was twenty-one), you were required to have parental consent before you could marry. Any clergyman who was found guilty of contravening this law was liable to fourteen years' transportation, which – I imagine – focused their minds admirably.

If that seems rather old to be a minor today, in Scotland, by contrast, it seems inordinately young for boys to be able to marry at fourteen and girls at twelve – and without parental consent to boot. It was Celtic custom, though in practice it hardly ever happened. You can understand, however, why young lovers in England beat a path to the door of Gretna Green. Elopements were facilitated in the 1770s when the toll road arrived. Couples wishing to tie the knot deemed it a small price to pay for this easier access to married bliss.

Another peculiarity of the Scottish system was that almost anybody could conduct a legal marriage service as long as it was conducted in front of two witnesses. Almost by accident, to the blacksmith fell the honour. For one thing, the blacksmith's smiddy was easy to find and for another, he was the one most likely to be at home, chained to his anvil so to speak. And symbolically, the forging together of two pieces of metal could be seen to represent the union of two people who were in haste to marry before those opposed to the match discovered they had fled and set off in hot pursuit. For this reason the blacksmiths became known as "anvil priests".

In 1857, a law was passed in England that required at least one of the pair to have been resident in Scotland for at least three weeks before the marriage could be recognised as legal in England. This obviously put an obstacle in the way of runaway couples who needed to be a bit more devious and cunning, but as everyone knows, the course of true love never did run smooth and true love will find a way. The law did not have any jurisdiction in Scotland and the flow of those fleeing, seeking marital bliss scarcely slowed.

In 1929, in Scotland, the age of marriage was raised to sixteen for both sexes, although parental consent was still not required. That is how the law stands at present. England and Wales have caught up and you can get married at sixteen as long as you have the blessing of your parents. If you don't, you have to wait until you are eighteen before you can tell them to sod off, you're doing it anyway, only to have to confess a couple of years later, "Sorry, mum and dad – you were right all along. I should never have married the idiot."

In 1977 the three-week residency rule was repealed and two weeks' written notice had to be given instead. In 1994, you could be married over the anvil instead of a church as long as the ceremony was conducted by an ordained minister. In 2002, registrars were allowed to conduct a civil wedding in a venue outwith the registry office. Finally, to end this gallop through Scottish wedding law, same-sex marriage was legalised in 2014.

But back to the past. The "World Famous Old Blacksmith's Shop" aka *The Old Smiddy* has expanded unrecognisably from the original to no fewer than three wedding rooms, each with an anvil, not to mention a museum and a shop, as the name implies. The last and best known "anvil blacksmith" was Richard Rennison (1889-1969) who, from 1926 until 1940 was responsible for the happiness (at least on the day) of no fewer than an incredible 5,147 couples.

The previous incumbent and owner was Rennison's boss, Hugh Mackie, who had purchased the property in 1890 but gave up doing any metalwork by the turn of the century. Rennison was a bit of a joker who told his couples that although he was not a member of the clergy, he was well qualified to marry them as he was "no sinner". If the joke does not immediately strike you, notice his surname is a palindrome of those words. (I wonder how long it took him to notice that happy coincidence.)

He charged a suggested donation of £1 per ceremony or whatever people could afford (probably not very much if the couple were a pair of sixteen-year-old runaways). He often did it for free, the old, romantic softie, but on one occasion apparently was given £20, worth about £4,000 today.

The Old Blacksmith's Shop, Gretna Green That's a very expensive bride to be sure, but then he was saving the expense of having to spend all that money on giving the guests a slap-up meal. Nice work if you can get it: a few preliminary words, a blow of the hammer on the anvil followed by, "I now pronounce you man and wife. You may kiss the bride." And that's it!

And if you did not bring your own witnesses with you (and you can imagine many runaway couples did not), if you crossed Mr Rennison's palm with silver in the form of half-a-crown, he could supply them too, Mrs Rennison being happy to oblige. Indeed, she performed some marriages herself on the odd occasion. In 1930, 2/6d was the equivalent of nearly £20 today. That seems a bit pricey for the autograph of a not-very-famous person. Anyway, it seems Mr and Mrs Rennison weren't doing too badly out of the marriage business. You can imagine theirs was a very happy marriage and you can imagine them laughing all the way to the bank.

But poor Mr Rennison probably wasn't laughing, more in danger of having a hernia when, in 1931, when he went to London on holiday, he took the 240-pound anvil with him. He claimed it was because it was he was afraid it might be stolen. He may have a point there – some people will steal anything unless it is nailed down (take the cross arm fragment at Ruthwell, for example), but it seems more likely to have been some sort of publicity stunt or a very heavy business card.

All good things come to an end, and Mr Rennison's days as an anvil priest were drawing to a close. In 1935, a committee was set up to look into "irregular marriages" and he was called to give evidence. In his defence, he said he did not describe himself as a priest, nor did he dress like one – and furthermore, he advised his clients they had to ensure the marriage was recorded with the registrar in Dumfries. His testimony didn't do much good for his livelihood. The Committee's report resulted in the Marriages (Scotland) Act of 1939 which came into force the following year. Under it, the marriages which he had been conducting, became not so much "irregular" but illegal. It was the end of an era that began in 1754.

As well as the wedding rooms aforesaid, there is a museum where pride of place is given to the original anvil. If you are of a superstitious nature, you are free to touch it in order to ensure an ever-lasting marriage. But before you do so, touchers beware! Remember the saying "Be careful for what you pray for." You might like to think twice before you stretch out your hand. There is also a fascinating audio-visual display which brings to life the dramatic stories of some of the people who eloped here.

The Gretna Green Story, Gretna Green

About 5,000 couples a year come to the Gretnas to be joined together in holy matrimony in a variety of venues. That's an incredible one-in-eight of all marriages in Scotland. I wasn't married here, but I did spend my wedding night in one of the hotels and I didn't get a wink of sleep. It's not what you may be thinking. The less interesting truth is I am not an afficiando of dancing and baled out of my own nuptials early, leaving the guests to face the music only to be subjected to the infernal decibels of someone else's wedding band.

Other border towns tried to follow in Gretna Green's example to cash in on the lucrative marriage trade, but the Marriage Act of 1857 sounded their death knell rather than wedding bells. Across the Atlantic, cities such as Las Vegas and Reno have since cashed in on the wedding business.

Whether or not they get married in Gretna Green, an amazing number of people who have no Scots blood in their veins to offer the midges, nevertheless choose Scotland to get married. It does have scenery of course, and kilts and castles, but what it does *not* have is a settled climate. Every bride wants a nice day for her wedding and especially doesn't want to be eclipsed by the men in their full-kilt regalia – yet they still choose to get married in Scotland. Isn't that an incredible thing!

After a time, some people find themselves trapped in a loveless marriage, but everyone who comes here finds themselves in a tourist trap. At the time of our visit, it was inundated with coachloads of Japanese tourists availing themselves of the opportunity to pose in front of a variety of romantic backgrounds which they take inordinately seriously, spending a great deal of time over each photograph. A snapshot it most definitely is not. They also spend a great deal of money on souvenirs.

Once again Gretna Green's location has turned up trumps, but it's a fake Scotland. It wouldn't surprise me if next these tourists are heading north to Loch Ness hoping for a sighting of Nessie – another fake Scotland. They are by no means the only ones to batter on up the A74 heading for the Highlands. They don't know what they are missing by not turning left and heading west instead.

Galloway is Scotland's secret corner.

Chapter Fourteen

Ecclefechan: The Birthplace of a Genius

MANY years ago, when I was a schoolboy just being exposed to the complexities of French grammar, our teacher issued us copies of *Paris Match* to look through, no doubt with the intention of exposing us to some French culture. Funnily enough, the copy I happened to get contained an article on Thomas Carlyle. I remember it like yesterday because I found it deeply shocking. I don't remember anything else in the magazine, but this sentence rocked me back on my heels: Thomas Carlyle, *né á Ecclefechan en Angleterre... Angleterre* for God's sake! Was there ever a town that sounds more Scottish than Ecclefechan! Conflating England with the United Kingdom is a mistake commonly made by many foreigners, but it's also done by some English people – who should know better.

Anyway, we are making for Ecclefechan now on the B7076. As we do so, we are keeping a sharp lookout for the Merkland Cross. It's a sixteen-foot-high medieval monolith and reckoned to be one of the finest in Scotland, if not *the* finest. There is a bit of mystery surrounding it. It is thought to date from about 1400 and dispute rages around what its purpose was.

Some suggestions are it marks the place where a market was held or where people gathered around to hear the word of the Lord. Another theory is that it is a memorial to John, Master of Maxwell (so-called because his father was still alive) and Steward of Annandale. As a Steward, it was his responsibility to administer law and justice in the region.

On 22nd July 1484, the day of Lochmaben Fair, there was trouble. Two proscribed outlaws rode into town, namely Alexander, Duke of Albany, the younger brother of the unpopular James III, and James, 9th Earl of Douglas who was the son of James the Gross. He was the older twin, by a mere matter of minutes, of his brother Alexander. In 1452, the twins' older brother, William, the 8th Earl, had been lured to Stirling Castle by James II under a promise of safe conduct to discuss their relationship. Maybe the king's intentions were good, but you know what the road to hell is paved with and that's very probably where James is now. During the meeting, he stabbed William in the throat and the job was finished by the Captain of the Guard who poleaxed him before throwing his body out a window.

According to another account – if you prefer your tales, like your steaks, bloody – then listen to this. In this version, the king stabbed Douglas twenty-six times and then *he* threw his body out of the window. If this version is the correct one, then James must have been very, very angry. His nickname was *Fiery Face*. The unfortunate fellow had a bright-red birthmark on his face, an outward sign, so contemporaries believed, of a hot temper. Regardless of your choice – the single stab to the throat or the multiple stabs to the body – either would seem to add substance to the theory of the king's hot-blooded temperament.

James had previous. In 1440, when he was only 10-years-old, he invited the 16-year-old 6th Earl, also known as William, and his younger brother, the 12-year-old David, to tea. It all sounds very polite and civilised, but the boy king had murder on his mind. Well, to give him the benefit of the doubt, after the death in 1439, of the 5th Earl who was his Regent, it was his new Regents – Sir Alexander Livingston, Sir William Crichton and Sir James Douglas – who were the ones up to mischief. The Douglases were just too powerful for their own good. They who looked after the crowned head were feeling uneasy.

The event has come down to us in history as the "Black Dinner". During the meal, the head of a black bull was brought in. It would be enough to make me put my knife and fork down as I hypocritically cut my way through my steak. The last thing I would want to see is the head of the donor, appearing like Banquo's ghost at the feast. But for the Douglas brothers it was much worse than that: they knew exactly what it meant. It was a symbol of death. They were given a mock trial, found guilty (there's a surprise), taken outside and beheaded on the spot.

So that explains why there was no love lost between the 9th Earl of Douglas and Albany. The latter hoped his former tenants would join them and rise up against James III, which is why he chose Fair Day at Lochmaben as he knew there would be a good gathering of people there. Unfortunately for him, they didn't love him as much as he thought and didn't rise up.

Reinforcements for the loyal royalists arrived, and the Battle of Lochmaben Fair raged from noon to night. In the end, Douglas was captured and died in 1488, at Lindores Abbey in Fife, the last earl of the Douglases. Albany and his troops were pushed back over the border. Eventually he made his escape to France where he died in a joust when his lance shattered and a piece lodged in his eye. Ouch!

• • •

As for the tale about Master Maxwell, he was foully-murdered when, resting on his sword trying to recover from a wound, a dastardly man called Gask stole up behind him and stabbed him in the back as revenge for Maxwell having sentenced a cousin of his to death. The cross is said to mark the place where the fifty-year-old Maxwell was cut down.

It's free to visit the stone which you will find in a field on Woodhouse Farm, Kirtlebridge. Like the Ruthwell Cross, it is surrounded by an iron railing, only whereas that is in a pit, this stands on a mound like the sort of thing you would build on the beach for the kids with the pillar looking like a flag that you stick in at the top. The top of the cross is unlike anything I have seen on a stone cross before. It's what in heraldry is called a "fleury cross" – four fleur-de-lis pointing to the four points of the compass with a little hole in the centre where the stems meet. The column, by contrast, is octagonal and plain. You would have thought if it really *was* a memorial to Maxwell, they would have said so on it somewhere. After all, there is plenty of room to do so.

If you are short of time, or if mysterious, medieval, monoliths are not really your thing, then if you keep your eyes peeled, you should be able to see as much of the stone as you would want because the A74 (M) unreels its way north and south at the bottom of the field.

And so we come to Ecclefechan where that well-known "Englishman", Thomas Carlyle (1795-1881), philosopher, satirist, historian, mathematician, translator and teacher was born. We shall be visiting his birthplace – for us, not for the first time. The house was built by his father (who was a stonemason as well as farmer), and with the help of his uncle. It is now in the care of the NTS. The birthroom is said to be the one with the two little windows above the arch.

Annan Academy is proud to boast him as their greatest former pupil to date but when he was there for the first time, he was remorselessly bullied. He bailed out aged fourteen and walked the eighty-odd miles to Edinburgh (they don't make them like that any more) to attend university. After four years, he chucked that in too and returned to his alma mater as a teacher of mathematics, where he presumably was not bullied this time. Obviously this was long before the days of having a degree and teacher training was a requirement. And if his subsequent career serves to tell you anything, it tells you that you don't need to have a degree to get on in life. But it does help to be a bit of a brainbox.

In 1817, Carlyle turned his back on the chalk face and decided to go back to university and study theology, as his parents had originally wanted him to. However he began to have doubts about his religious convictions and decided to jack that in after a couple of years, and live by his pen instead.

Birthplace of Thomas Carlyle, Ecclefechan

He wrote articles for Brewster's *Encyclopaedia* and the *Edinburgh Review*. His first most notable work was *Sartor Resartus*, or *The Taylor Retailored*, which first appeared in instalments in *Fraser's Magazine*. In his own words, he describes it as "simultaneously factual and fictional, serious and satirical, speculative and historical". It was partly autobiographical and partly philosophical. In fact no-one had seen anything quite like it before.

He was an admirer of Oliver Cromwell and Frederick the Great. His *On Heroes And Hero Worship And The Heroic In History* (1841) puts forth his ideas on heroic leadership. His ideas resonate very much with Fascism. Arguably, even worse, in 1849 he published an essay in which he states why slavery should not have been abolished. In it he uses the "N" word, though at the time it was not deemed as offensive as it is now. In a collection of essays published under the title *Latter-Day Pamphlets* (1850) he attacked democracy as a nonsensical idea, though admittedly, he denounced aristocratic leadership also – music to the ears of Marx and Engels. So if leaders were not to be elected democratically nor through the hereditary aristocracy, just how were they to be appointed? The answer, according to Carlyle, lies in the Great Man Theory. In his view, the "history of the world is but the biography of great men". These views, in particular his views on slavery, caused a rift between Carlyle and his friends and followers.

In Jamaica in 1865, the peasant Morant Bay Rebellion was savagely put down by the governor, Edward Eyre. Uproar broke out back home, and John Stuart Mill formed the Jamaican Committee which demanded Eyre be prosecuted for murder. Amongst the members were Charles Darwin, Thomas Huxley, aka *Darwin's Bulldog*, and John Bright, the Quaker and Liberal politician. For his part, Carlyle set up a *Defence and Aid Committee* for Eyre which included such people as Tennyson, Dickens, Ruskin and Kingsley. Naturally this led to a cooling off of the relationship with Mill and even to some extent with Ralph Waldo Emerson, who had been one of his earliest and staunchest admirers. Eyre was charged twice for murder but was never tried.

The Carlyles moved from Dumfriesshire to London in 1831 and three years later moved to Cheyne Row, Chelsea, and there they stayed until their deaths, Jane in 1866 and Thomas in 1881. This is where anyone who was anyone in Victorian society came to hear the great man, giving rise to him being given the soubriquet the "Sage of Chelsea". The house has now been turned into a museum. There is not a blue plaque outside, but there is a big white marble bust, so there is no mistaking you have arrived at the right place. And that's all I am going to say about it, as it is not where he died that is of interest to us, but where he was born.

But before we go, an interesting little diversion about arguably Carlyle's best-known work – his three-volume *History of the French Revolution* (1837), which Charles Dickens used as a source in his *A Tale of Two Cities* (1859). That's interesting enough, but there is another story attached to volume one of Carlyle's tome. The story is that he gave it to John Stuart Mill whose maid used it to light the fire. To be fair to her, with its crossings out and re-workings and dreadful handwriting, not so say generally rather messy appearance, it did look like a pile of waste paper. All the same, when Ruskin found out what she had done, and imagining the sound and fury of Carlyle's wrath descending on his head, my bet is rather than forgiving her on the spot, understanding she knew not what she did, he let her have it in the neck.

Alas, the details of the aftermath are sketchy. It would be great to know for sure how Mill broke the news to Carlyle and what his reaction was. All I can say is when I have written a long e-mail and inadvertently pressed something which results in the screen going blank, losing everything I have written, not only do I lose the will to begin all over again but also the will to live. Carlyle's loss was much, much greater and I can only imagine that his despair was of a similar multitude. Worse, Carlyle claimed that he had kept no notes. However, as I explained above, the friendship did not cool until 1865 so presumably Carlyle did not vent his spleen too much and sat down to write the whole thing again from memory. He was said to have a photographic memory, but he was also said to have been of a curmudgeonly disposition as he suffered from a severe case of dyspepsia – probably stomach ulcers – and I can imagine Mill hoping Carlyle's inner man was having a good day when he broke the news. When the first volume was eventually published, Mill rushed to be the first to write a rave review. It was the least he could do.

As for Carlyle, when the news was broken, if he took it on the chin – merely shrugged and said, "Don't worry, John. I'll just write it again" – it would be an admirably calm and sanguine response, and I would take my hat off to him.

• • •

Actually it wouldn't be for the first time. That's exactly what I did when I was here the time before. The great man's hat (the label said so) was lying carelessly on a chair in the birth room. I was alone. I searched the room with my eyes for cameras. I didn't see any. I needed to act quickly. It was the matter of a moment to doff mine and pick up the big, broad-rimmed, black felt affair that was just begging me to try it on. In an instant, all was dark as the hat flopped over my eyes. How conceited Carlyle was I couldn't say, but nothing I have read about him leads me to believe he was. What I can do is testify to the fact that while he may not have been in possession of a large fortune, he certainly was of a big head. But then he needed a large cranium to house that massive brain of his, even if he never got a university degree.

Inside the house you can see many of Carlyle's personal belongings. Is that *the* hat, now hanging on a chair beside the fireplace, and removed here out of temptation from those vandals and ignoramuses who would like to try it on for size? But mainly, what the house does (and it does it supremely well), is let the visitors use their imaginations as they look at the period artefacts and picture young Thomas and his eight siblings (he was the oldest) squashed into this little dwelling. But if the thought of exercising your imagination wearies you too much, you can always refer to the information boards or ask a guide if there is something in particular that attracts your interest.

You can also see, from photographs and paintings, what the Carlyles looked like in the Chelsea days when they were at the height of their powers. I use the word "their" advisedly. Jane, whom Thomas had met when he was at university, was no intellectual lightweight in her own right. Before Currer Bell was revealed to be Charlotte Bronte, Jane was one of the suspects.

Theirs was a stormy relationship by all accounts. I think Samuel Butler summed it up best when he said, "I think it was very good of God to let Carlyle and Mrs Carlyle marry one another, and so make only two people miserable instead of four." Well said, Sam! It is possible that the marriage may never have been consummated, being more a marriage of minds, apparently. Indeed, the love of Jane's life was the feminist writer, Geraldine Jewsbury, not there is any evidence that was consummated either. It was a stormy relationship too, as Jane was jealous of Geraldine's many liaisons.

It's a funny thing that the word "Victorian" conjures up images of prudery and sexual repression, where piano legs, in their nakedness, were covered up as being too rude. That may be a myth, like Marie Antoinette's breasts are supposed to have been the mould for champagne glasses, but in fact, nothing could be further from the truth – the Victorians were at it like rabbits, not least their Queen.

After Jane died, the spirit seems to have gone out of Thomas. You might say that the spark had gone that made him fire. He was a widower for fifteen years and when he died, he was not reunited with her. As he had promised her forty years previously, Thomas took her back to her origins in Haddington, to be buried with her parents. After all, if they didn't sleep together in life, so why should they sleep together throughout eternity? Whether they were reunited in heaven, no-one knows. Perhaps if peace is to reign there, maybe it would be better if they were not.

Thomas was awarded the honour of being buried in Westminster Abbey but put in his will that he wanted to be planted in Scottish soil and be buried in his home ground along with his ma and pa, in the local cemetery and it is there we now direct our steps.

The grave is enclosed by railings and the tombstone bears the family crest of two wyverns (winged dragons with a barbed tail) and the motto *Humilitate* and these words: "Here rests Thomas Carlyle, who was born at Ecclefechan, 4th December 1795, and died at 24, Cheyne Row, Chelsea, London, on Saturday, 5th February, 1881."

It's a humble enough memorial, to be sure, but of course his real memorial is his immortal works.

Chapter Fifteen

Hallmuir and Lockerbie: Prisoners and Disasters

E'RE bowling along the B7076, heading north towards Lockerbie. Note the word "bowling". You never saw such a splendid B road in your life; it's even a dual carriageway in places. The reason for that is just to our right – the M74, which was built in the Nineties. Since its inception, the B7076, once the major artery through the Southern Uplands, is now rather like a dowager duchess – much reduced in status, but secretly delighted with the lighter duties. And, I have to say, it is indeed a pleasure to drive along it.

Before we get to Lockerbie, a brown sign directs us to the Ukranian POW camp at Hallmuir. Most people have heard of the Italian Chapel in Orkney, but I, for one – although I lived in this area for five years – had never heard of the Ukrainian Chapel in the former prisoner-of-war camp.

Dear, oh dear, oh dear! What a sorry sight it is! It's a graveyard for lorries, caravans and cars as well as being a lorry depot. There are a few corrugated huts, one of which is the chapel and, like the huts, in a very bad state of repair. The paint is peeling and the roof has an alarming bow. It is locked and the windows are curtained, but a gap at one in the front offers a slight glimpse of the interior.

Outside, there is a little shrine and a memorial with a marble cross. But what's the story? How did this chapel come to be here? To find that out, as well as see inside the chapel, I had to have recourse to the Internet.

The camp was built in 1942, designed to hold up to 450 German and Italian prisoners-of-war. In 1943, volunteers and conscripts from Nazi-occupied Ukraine had been formed into the 14th "Gallicia" Division of the Waffen SS. Ukrainian nationalists at heart, from the volunteers' perspective, they thought they would be more likely to gain independence from the Nazis than the Soviets.

Chapel of the Ukrainian Prisoner of War Camp, Hallmuir

For two years, the Division fought the Soviets on the Eastern front. Then in 1945, at Graz, Austria, in the face of fierce fighting, the Nazis renamed the Division, the "1st Division of the Ukrainian Army" in a last-ditch attempt to save the day, as if by so doing it would put fresh vim and vigour into the Ukrainians' resistance. It didn't make any difference. On 10th May, the ragged remains of the Division surrendered to the British and the Americans, and the prisoners were interred at Rimini.

Under the terms of the Treaty of Yalta, any person in UK or US hands who could be classed as a Soviet citizen and who had fought against them, was to be handed over to them where they faced the unenviable fate of either being shot by firing squad more or less right away, or facing an extended death by suffering in a Siberian labour camp. After the Ukrainian Greek Catholic Church made representation to the Pope, Pius XII, he in turn appealed to the allies to spare the lives of the 1st Division, describing them as "good Catholics and fervent anti-Communists".

It worked. The status of the 1st Division was changed from "prisoners-of-war" to "surrendered enemy personnel". We all know what Juliet said about a rose, and the Ukrainians must have thought it incredibly sweet news when they were given the choice of either being sent to Canada or the UK. Which would you choose? 7,150 of them chose the UK, and on 15th May 1947, one-and-a-half thousand of them arrived in Glasgow on board the troop ship *India Victory*. Of those, 450 found themselves here in Hallmuir.

Looking at the few huts left standing today, I can imagine what they must have thought when they first clapped eyes on the accommodation, and I wonder if they thought they had made a mistake, should have opted for Canada where they might have been offered a nice log cabin somewhere instead of these corrugated iron huts in the backwoods of Scotland. That said, anything was better than a Soviet labour camp in Siberia, even death.

Most of them found employment on local farms or in forestry. And when they weren't doing that and getting to know the local lassies, they occupied their time by transforming the rude hut into a splendid chapel that we can't see today except on the Internet. It is at least the equal of the Italian Chapel in Orkney which tourists flock to in their droves. By contrast, this chapel has been

• • •

neglected and left to decay. Something needs to be done to preserve this proud legacy – and the sooner the better.

And so we come to Lockerbie, whose name betrays its Viking origins. It means "Lochard's Village" in Old Norse but there are the remains of a Roman camp nearby, which of course means this area was occupied by other invaders long before that. At the entrance to the

Memorial at the Ukrainian Prisoner of War Camp, Hallmuir

cemetery is Dryfsedale Lodge, formerly the caretaker's cottage, which tells Lockerbie's story on a series of panels around the room from prehistoric times to the present. There are a couple devoted to the Air Disaster, as well as a Book of Remembrance called *On Eagles' Wings.*

By the middle of the 18th century, the town had grown to a town of some size; by the end of the century, it was a staging post on the Glasgow-London carriage route. In 1816, Telford's road drove through the town, making it a link in the Glasgow-Carlisle route, then in 1847 along came the railway, putting Lockerbie even more firmly on the map.

In 1883, an accident occurred which eerily foreshadowed the Annan railway disaster. There was a collision involving three trains. A passenger train ran into the rear of a goods train, sending some carriages onto the parallel line and into the path of a speeding express, rushing north. Seven were killed; three hundred were injured. That was Lockerbie's first disaster. You have probably never heard of it until now. The second is world famous.

Thirty-one thousand feet above Lockerbie's skies on Wednesday 21st December 1988, occurred one of the most notorious terrorist attacks known to man. Because I remember the event so vividly, listening to the radio for news updates, it brings me up short to realise it was actually thirty years ago.

On that day, the day that a bomb blew Pan Am 103, *Clipper Maid of the Seas,* out of the skies, all our lives were changed forever. It was, and hopefully will remain, the worst aircraft disaster and terrorist attack in the UK. The death toll was horrendous: 243 passengers, 16 crew and 11 victims in the town, in Sherwood Crescent. That was where the wings fell to earth, creating a crater 155-foot broad and 196-foot long. That, along with the nose cone which landed in a field near Tundergarth Church, are the two enduring images of that dreadful day.

• • •

On board were people from twenty-four different nations. The oldest victim was eighty-two, on the ground; the youngest, two months, on the plane. One had had a full life but was not nearly ready to die yet; the other never really knew his parents, never knew the children and grandchildren he might have had. From whatever end of the telescope you care to view it, it was a wicked waste of life.

I reflect on the vagaries of life, how the seemingly most trivial inconsequential thing, or just one brief moment, the spin of the wheel of fortune, can alter your life forever or even bring it to a sudden end. This truth is borne out by the following stories of those who, by missing the plane, also missed a premature encounter with death.

There was Jaswant Busata, a 47-year-old Sikh car mechanic who arrived at the boarding gate too late. Because his luggage was on board, but he was not, he was considered a suspect. Then there was John Lydon, better known as Johnny Rotten, who missed the flight because his wife took too long to pack. It may just be me, but when Johnny discovered they weren't going to make the flight, I can imagine him cursing his rotten luck but more likely cursing his wife, only when he heard the news, thanking her for being such a fastidious packer. Then there were *The Four Tops* who overslept after a performance the previous night and booked another flight. Finally, the actress Kim Cattrall, who cancelled her reservation to do some last-minute Christmas shopping in London. Who would have thought that such a thing could be a life-saving experience?

On the ground too, there was a narrow escape for Father Keegans who lived at No 1, Sherwood Crescent. His was the only house that was not either totally destroyed by the impact or so badly damaged they had to be demolished. In a further twist of fate, he was preparing to visit his neighbours at No 13, Maurice and Dora Henry, at 7pm. The bomb detonated at 7.03pm. Their bodies were never found.

Remembrance Monument for the Lockerbie Air Disaster

At No 16, fourteen-year-old Steven Flannigan was having his sister's bicycle, intended as a Christmas present, checked over by a neighbour when he saw his house, with his parents and sister inside, engulfed by a fireball. Because of a family argument, his older brother, David, was staying with a friend in Blackpool. He had been planning to return on Boxing Day.

In a coda to this tale of tragedy and near-death experience, death was not that far away for the Flannigan brothers. Five years later, David died of heart failure in a hostel in Thailand. With his share of £2 million compensation, he had lived a George Best lifestyle. Seven years later, Steven was hit by a train. He had been drinking with his friend, mine host at the Royal Oak in Heywood, Wiltshire until one in the morning, but was not drunk. There was a shortcut home over a three-foot high railway embankment composed of gravel. What happened next, no-one knows for sure. Did he trip and knock himself unconscious or did he sit by the tracks contemplating his life (which also included a failed relationship) and when he heard the 3am maintenance train slowly lumbering towards him, did he deliberately put himself in its path? The drivers saw him and even although it was moving very slowly, they were unable to stop the juggernaut. David never regained consciousness and died in hospital two days later.

The road to the Aircraft Memorial is bordered by flowerbeds, through the old cemetery, until eventually you come to a plain triptych of grey granite, where, in sombre black letters, are inscribed the names of the dead. There is a raised platform below, like an altar, where, for remembrance, you can lay some flowers, and where some have done so before us. In front of them is grouped the graves of those who died on the ground.

Having paid our respects we leave in sombre mood.

Chapter Sixteen

Lochmaben Castle: The Struggle for Power

WE'RE on the road again, this time on the A709, heading back towards Dumfries via Lochmaben where we are going to visit the ruins of the castle.

In the 12th century, the Bruces built a castle here but all that remains of that is a hump on the golf course where the motte would have been. The history books tell us that Robert the Bruce was born in Turnberry, Ayrshire. On the other hand, the motto of Lochmaben – *From us is born the Liberator King* – tells us they claim the lad was born somewhere under, or above, that mound of grass. I suppose he might have been.

In 1298, Edward I captured the wooden keep and built a sturdier edifice on a triangular promontory in the loch. He was playing for keeps, but in fact, the castle changed hands more often than people changed their underwear in those days – which comes as no surprise, given the times and its location in the border zone between warring nations.

We've come to see the ruins of the subsequent 14th century castle. It lies at the end of farm track, but there is plenty of parking at the end. The loch is a local nature reserve and I'm drawn initially to a photo of a damselfly on a noticeboard and marvel how exceedingly like a helicopter it is. As for the ruins, they are very aptly named, most of them fenced off to ensure they do not happen to collapse while we are standing beneath them.

In 1299, the Earl of Carrick, better known as the future Robert the Bruce, laid siege to Edward's castle for five days, without success. If at first you don't succeed... He managed to do so in 1306. It was retaken, and taken again by Robert the Bruce in 1314. The English took it again in 1333 but in 1385, Archibald, 3rd Earl of Douglas, Lord of Galloway and the illegitimate son of Sir James Douglas, aka *Archibald the Grim* (1328-1400) captured it again for the Scots. It was at that time he was given his unflattering nickname (or maybe he was rather chuffed by it) by the English defenders, on account of his "terrible countenance in wierfare", as a contemporary writer put it.

After that, the Grim One's power and influence grew and grew during the reigns of, as Sellar and Yeatman might have put it in *1066 and All That* – the "not-very-good king" Robert II – the first king of the Stewarts. It was a dynasty that was to last for 230 years. That's some legacy!

In 1384, his brother, John, Earl of Carrick, more or less deposed him to become the *de facto* ruler of Scotland. When Robert died in 1390, John became the legitimate king in name too, styling himself Robert III, since "John" was a hated name for a Scottish king after the Bad King John Balliol experience.

He did not enjoy robust health. In 1388, he had been kicked by a horse – I imagine in a very sore place – and had never fully recovered. In 1399, the General Council appointed his son, the 21-year-old David, Duke of Rothesay, as Lieutenant of the Kingdom. He was to be advised by a committee headed by his uncle, Robert – the *real* Robert, his father's younger brother – whom they made the 1st Duke of Albany at the same time.

It wasn't long before David fell foul of George Dunbar, the Earl of March, by reneging on a deal to remarry his wife. Yes, you *did* read that correctly. In 1395, David had married Dunbar's daughter, Elizabeth, but the Papal disposition required because they were blood relatives, never came. They separated, and in 1397, probably bigamously, David married Mary or Marjory, the daughter of Archibald the Grim.

Archibald was the architect behind this union. He saw himself as a peacemaker and the grandfather of kings, as did Dunbar. By uniting the mighty Douglas family with the royal house of Stewart, Archibald sought to remove the Stewarts' fear of being usurped by them – make the head that bore the crown lie less "uneasy" on the shoulders.

Lochmaben Castle

Dunbar, however, was more than a bit miffed, and he dashed off a letter of complaint to Henry IV (1367-1413). In August 1400, Henry's army marched on Edinburgh and laid siege to the castle. It must be great to have friends in high places who are prepared to go to war just because of someone else's domestic disputes. The castle was not taken, but the

Scots nobles were far from amused at this unwelcome invasion that David had provoked.

He further alienated the nobles by making decisions they thought fell far short of the sort Solomon would have made. But what was really rattled their cages, especially Albany's, was he making them without consulting the Council, as he should have done. He was acting more like a king than the Lieutenant of the Kingdom.

Albany arrested his nephew and initially imprisoned him in the Bishop's Palace at St Andrews before transferring him to Falkland Palace where he died, aged 24, in 1402. Before his arrest he had been a fit and healthy young man. Death was said to be by "divine providence". Oh, yes? Most likely Albany starved him to death in a bottle dungeon. The troubles within families. You should choose your uncles carefully.

The rest of the history of the castle is briefly told. In 1455, James, the 9th Earl of Douglas, and his brothers rebelled against James II after their brother, the 8th Earl, had personally been stabbed to death by the king. It was to prove decisive. The 9th Earl lost his castle at Abercorn, and at the Battle of Arkinholm, near Langholm, he lost again. He wasn't there, having gone to England to get help from Henry VI. His three brothers *were* present, however: Archibald, Hugh and John. Archibald was killed and his head presented to the king, Hugh was captured and executed. John escaped to England and was never heard of again.

As I mentioned earlier, in connection with the Battle of Lochmaben Fair, where the 9th Earl was captured, the new king, James III, in a surprising show of clemency, sentenced him, not to death, but to the monkhood at Lindores in Fife. I suppose there are worse fates, depending on how secular you are and how high your sex drive is. He died there in 1488 aged sixty-two.

And that spelled the end of the power and threat of the Black Douglases. In the eyes of the Stewarts, the Douglases had committed treason, thus they forfeited not only their lives, but their hereditary titles too. Lochmaben Castle was "attainted", that is to say "stained" or "corrupted", and therefore forfeit to the crown. It now became a royal residence. James II set about improving the grand hall, making it a residence fit for a king.

Fast forward in the castle's history until we come to James V and his army which mustered here in 1542, on their march south to their humiliating defeat at Solway Moss. In 1544, the castle was captured by the English during the *Rough Wooing* (Henry VIII's plan to forge an alliance between England and Scotland by the marriage of his son, Edward, to the infant Queen Mary), but reverted to the Scots the following year.

Cruck Cottage, Torthorwald

In 1565, it had a famous visitor when Mary, Queen of Scots slept here. Perhaps I shouldn't bother to mention it as she did sleep around a bit, so it's not really a very remarkable event. An event that *was* remarkable, however, was in 1588, when James VI besieged the castle and took it from John, the 8th Lord Maxwell, for his part in planning the Spanish Armada.

After the Union of the Crowns in 1603, peace broke out between England and Scotland and there was no longer any need for the castle as a fortress against the former enemy. It began to fall into ruin, a process that was accelerated when it served as a convenient quarry for the building of houses in Lochmaben. Most of the facing stones were removed, but one unintended consequence of the quarrying is it gives you an insight into the construction of a medieval castle wall. As the old song has it about there being *an awful lot of coffee in Brazil,* there's an awful lot of stones needed to fill the core of a castle wall, they being so high and thick.

Some of the walls have toppled over, but you still get an idea of how tall they once were and how imposing the castle would have appeared in its heyday. The best view is seen along the emerald-green of the moat where an arch props up an ivy-clad wall. In fact there is a great deal of ivy hereabouts – the last invaders.

We leave it to get on with its insidious takeover along with the nettles that grow as *high as an elephant's eye*, and continue on the A709 until we come to the very Viking-sounding name of Torthorwald. Its castle is in such a ruinous state that it is hardly worth mentioning, so I won't.

We do stop, however, to see from the outside, the charming 19th century thatched cruck cottage which has been lovingly restored and maintained by volunteers. If you would like to see inside, a notice in one of the curtained windows provides a number to phone.

Like Lochmaben Castle, time is against us. We have to move on.

Chapter Seventeen

Lincluden Abbey and the Twelve Apostles: The Naughty Nuns, the Pious Earl and the Vandals

THE brown sign on the A76 directs us round the outskirts of an enormous housing scheme, to Lincluden Abbey or Lincluden Collegiate Church as it is also known. It's one of Historic Environment Scotland's unmanned sites, open all year in all weathers, any time of the day. There is not a lot of space to park and what little there is, is occupied by some Historic Environment Scotland vehicles. Down by the ruins of the Church there appears to be a conference going on.

About 1160, in a piece of land between the River Nith and Cluden Water, a Benedictine nunnery was founded by Uchtred, son of Fergus of Galloway. It was manned (if that's the right word) by ten nuns, but by 1389, there were only four. But what nuns! None like them throughout the length and breadth of the land. In fact, the fabric of the building, to say nothing of the moral fibre of the resident ladies, had fallen into such a state of decadence by that time, that our old friend Archibald the Grim, 3rd Earl of Douglas, thought something needed to be done. Accordingly, he picked up his pen and wrote a stiff letter to the Pope.

Lincluden Abbey

In it, he claimed that the nuns lived "disgracefully", that "the beautiful buildings are disfigured and ruinous through their sloth and neglect, but deck with foul clothing and ornaments their daughters born on their immoralities whom they rear in common with them in the same monastery." You can imagine the poor Pope's hair standing on end. He gave Archibald the go-ahead to deal with the problem. He duly drove out the nuns and set about building the collegiate church, the remains of which we see today. The nuns were replaced with a provost, eight priests and twenty-four bedesmen, or professional prayer-sayers. In return for the vast amount of money Archibald sank into this project, they prayed for his soul as well as those of his wife and their descendants.

That's all very well for those than can afford it, but what if you can't? It must have been a scary thing to have lived in medieval times, terrified to put a foot wrong lest you paid for it after death – forever and forever. What if you had killed people, albeit in the defence of your house and home, or your castle? You know what the sixth commandment says.

Soon after this, in 1369, David II awarded Archibald the title of Lord of Galloway *becaus he tuke git trawell to rid the cuntrey of Englis blude*. But Archibald wasn't finished yet, not by a long chalk. He granted the lands of Crossmichael and Troqueer to the adjacent Monastery of Holywood for the support of their charitable hospital for the poor and infirm. Mind you, he wasn't acting entirely out of altruism. For this good deed, the monks were charged with praying for the souls of Robert the Bruce and Edward his brother, King David II and his own father, Sir James, Lord of Douglas, aka *James the Good*. The soubriquet is something of a misnomer. He was utterly ruthless.

It was James who had been entrusted with taking the heart of Robert the Bruce to Jerusalem, but he was killed whilst fighting the Moors at the Battle of Teba in Spain in 1330 and the heart never made it to the Holy Land. It was taken back to Scotland and buried in Melrose Abbey.

Archibald must have violated the sixth commandment many, many times and enthusiastically too, if his nickname was anything to go by. Not only that, but he had broken the seventh commandment too: *Thou shall not commit adultery*. About seven years into his marriage (you know what they say about the seven-year itch), he had an illegitimate son who grew up to become William Douglas of Nithsdale and who went on to marry Robert II's daughter, Egidia, before ending up being murdered by friends of his enemy, Sir Thomas de Clifford.

Archibald the Grim was taking no chances. Three years before his death, in a sort of belt-and-braces arrangement, he made a grant to Sweetheart Abbey in return for prayers for own soul, Joanna his wife, their sons Archibald and James, and his own father and mother. The Abbey, founded in 1273 by Devorgilla, the mother of John Balliol, as I'm sure you will remember, had suffered very badly from fire and pillage over the years.

Lincluden Abbey (Detail)

And that's still not all. In 1398, work began on the founding and building of another collegiate church in Bothwell, near Glasgow and which eventually became the resting place for his body when he died in 1400. Alas it was not completed by then, but you can bet your bottom dollar that the prayers for his soul would have been winging their way heavenward from there along with all the others.

About the time that Archibald died, the church at Lincluden was completed – and let's hope he lived to see it in all its glory. The architect was a Frenchman, John Morrow, considered to be one of the finest stonemasons of his day. All that remains now are the choir and the nave and if the choir is anything to go by, it must have been the wonder of its day. Those who know, tell us that the choir is considered to be one of the finest examples of Gothic architecture in Scotland. When you look at the carvings around the doors and what's left of the tracery of the windows, you can well believe it.

Another point of interest, even if you are not a taphophile, is the elaborate canopied tomb and effigy of Margaret, the wife of Archibald, the 4th Earl, who died in 1451. She was also the Countess of Douglas and the Duchess of Touraine, but most important of all, she was also the eldest daughter of Robert III. In other words, Archibald was doing his bit to cement a union between the two families, which as you know, was dear to his father's heart. He must have been very proud of him.

The 4th Earl continued to embellish the Church, whilst the domestic range, known as the "Provost's Lodgings", was extended onwards and upwards into a four-storey tower house by William Stewart during his tenure as provost of the Church between 1529-36.

I agree that the Princess Margaret's tomb is the most impressive feature in the entire complex but I'm much less impressed with the enormous amount of graffiti on the walls, and not all of it by modern vandals either. Take this by J.

Johnstone for example, whom I suspect must have been a stonemason. The letters been been carved to a good depth with a chisel and he also took the trouble to immortalise the date of his vandalism by framing it in a scroll. Unfortunately for him, some later vandal has made the date illegible but it appears to be in the 19th century. The vandal vandalised. There is a certain rough justice in that.

But the biggest period of vandalism in the Church's history was yet to come. In 1560, along came the Reformation. After this catastrophe, William Douglas paid the enormous sum of £3,000 to have it repaired. He was the younger brother of he who turned out to be the last provost, giving up his post in 1590. The domestic buildings became the property of the Maxwells, who set about doing some house improvements to create a state-of-the-art mansion house.

Although there is nothing of the interior still to be seen, you can imagine how sumptuous it must have been by looking at what they did to the garden. In the smooth, green, billiard-table sward that surrounds the Church, you make out a raised pattern on a grassy mound. This is the knot garden, modelled on the King's Knot at Stirling Castle and – like that – best seen from above, which would have been possible from the fourth storey of the tower. It still remains to a good height, with one wall pointing to the sky like a stern finger issuing a warning.

As we come round the corner to the domestic range, our nostrils are pricked with the acrid smell of smoke. We soon find out the reason. The range, with its vaulted ceilings and gun-ports is very much reduced to a shadow of its former self, and in a corner of one of them, probably a cellar of some sort, there is a massive sooty stain rising up the walls and along part of the ceiling.

"It happened yesterday evening," explains the leader of the group of HES employees into whose hearing range we have just arrived.

Only yesterday evening, eh? No wonder we can still smell the smoke. So that explains the group of people we saw on our arrival. The purpose of their meeting is to discuss what can be done about the vandals, the problem being the open nature of the site and the vast housing estate behind it. We are invited to give our suggestions if we have any. We are afraid we haven't. You can't reason with morons.

Vandalism has a long pedigree here, and the worst took place after the Maxwells abandoned their mansion about 1700. After that it became a quarry, like Lochmaben Castle before it, for the building of local housing. I suppose that's a sort of rebirth for those blocks and stones which, in their new location, might well last for centuries more. Not like us who must come to dust.

* * *

The Twelve Apostles Stone Circle

And so we take our leave of what remains of the Collegiate Church and the mansion. I hope someone comes up soon with a solution to the problem of the present-day vandals while there is still something left to see.

We head back up the A76 and a short way off the B729 we arrive at the Twelve Apostles, a stone circle, the largest in mainland Scotland and the seventh largest in the UK. It's thought to date from the Bronze Age – about 3000 BC.

At first sight, it's rather underwhelming. It's hard to take in because, for one thing, the diameter is so big – 290 feet – and secondly, because, of the twelve stones, only five remain standing. The tallest stands at just over ten feet tall – or it would be if it weren't lying flat. Actually, it's more egg-shaped than a perfect circle, possibly because it's actually two conjoined circles, one joining the circumference of the other.

Legend has it that the stones were erected by the apostles and there were only eleven because Judas Iscariot didn't turn up, or wasn't invited. I am sorry to spoil a good story, but it's just not true – and here is the proof. Back in 1789, a drawing by the draughtsman, antiquarian and lexicographer Francis Grose (1731-1791), clearly shows twelve stones. Judas definitely *was* there.

So what happened to the missing stone? Something as big and heavy as it must have been, just can't vanish into thin air. Apparently sometime before 1837, it was removed by a farmer. So what if it were an ancient monument? As far as he was concerned, it was a convenient source of stone for whatever purpose he had in mind. And he wasn't the only one to commit this sort of outrage. In 1837, at Holm, a mile to the east, another stone circle was discovered. It originally was made up of nine monoliths which were "broken and applied to the purposes of building".

The stones here are a mixture of sizes and shapes. (Look for the one that looks like a couched lion.) Geologists tell us that all of them, bar one, are

Silurian, a mind-boggling 440 million years old, and the other is porphyry. They also tell us that four of them, including the latter, are natural boulders while the rest have been quarried. The nearest source is two miles away. I believe what they say, but I find it incredible. It's one amazing feat to transport them to this location, another to get them standing upright, but quite another to carve them out of the living rock first.

Some of them bear "cup marks" like those found on Pictish stones, and there is one in particular that is intriguing. If you follow the line of the marks, it looks remarkably like an arrow with a long shaft and two lines on either side which form the point. It looks too perfectly formed to be the work of nature – but is it? And if not, to what is it pointing? It has to be admitted there are some other pits in the stone too, and if you look at the arrow the other way, though not so well formed, there appears to be what appears to be another arrow pointing in the opposite direction. What can it mean?

We are told that these "cup marks" are due to weathering. Oh, really? In a straight line like that? Pull the other one. In the absence of any other explanation, my theory is some joker, on seeing a pattern in the holes, improved on nature. Of course he can't actually see people scratching their heads over these mysterious marks, but I'm sure he can imagine it and is having a good chuckle whoever he is, or was.

In 1882, during an excavation here, a four-inch bronze figure dating from the 1100s was dug up and is now in the care of the Dumfries Museum. It is conjectured that it might be St Norbert (c 1080-1134) and it was placed there at the orders of the Pope who was trying to clean up pagan sites by sanctifying them. He's a new saint on me and we need not worry our heads about him except to say that he was the founder of the Premonstratensian order, so severely ascetic that it was responsible for the deaths of his first three disciples.

No wonder it didn't catch on and he's not better known.

Chapter Eighteen

Ellisland: The Failed Farmer

WE are back on the A76 now and back on the Burns trail once again. This time we are going to Ellisland, which as you already know, was where he lived from 1788-91, before he moved to Dumfries.

Patrick Miller, a director of the Bank of Scotland and chairman of the Carron Ironworks in Falkirk, was an admirer of Burns. He was a forward-looking man who had an interest in agriculture. He invented a drilling plough and a new type of threshing machine, and had recently bought the estate of Dalswinton three years before Burns took up the tenancy.

For a man of vision, unbelievably, he bought the estate sight unseen. And when he *did* see it, it he found it in the "most miserable state of exhaustion and the tenants in poverty". Burns was given first choice of three farms, two on the east side of the Nith and one on the west. According to sod's law, he picked the worst one, based on the advice of a friend, James Tennant. Tennant by name, he should have tried being a tenant here himself.

Ellisland did have some fertile land near the river but unfortunately the bulk of the 170 acres was stony ground. If only Tennant's advice had fallen on *that*, Burns would have had an easier time of it. Garden of Eden it most certainly was not, although there was an orchard. What there also was *not* – the most basic thing, you would think – was a farmhouse, nor anywhere to shelter the cattle or house the farm implements. This was farming from scratch. Despite all this, Burns thought he had landed on his feet. He knew his friend was no rapacious landlord and he thought the banks of the Nith as "sweet poetic ground as ever I saw".

It may not have been good agricultural land, but the years he spent here were very productive from a writing point of view. He produced more than 130 poems and songs, including what is undoubtedly his masterpiece, *Tam o' Shanter* as well as *Auld Lang Syne*. He also wrote 230 letters out of his life's output of 700.

It sounded like a bargain – £70 a year, restricted to £50 for the first three. But first of all, things needed to be done. With the £300 Miller gave him, Burns constructed a farmhouse, a byre and other farm buildings, fenced fields and bought stock. Obviously a pound went a lot further then than it does today.

The cottage consisted of four rooms, including the kitchen. It was spacious for its day with, at its centre, the master bedroom. The family eventually moved in, in June 1789, a year after the lease had been signed. To ensure good luck, they wore their best clothes, preceded by a servant girl carrying the family Bible on which sat a bowl of salt. Every house had a Bible, even if, like most houses today, it is never opened from one year to next. Then an oatcake was broken over Jean's head. How they laughed to see such fun, then they drank a toast to their happy life in the new house. They were full of optimism, looking forward to a bright new future. But in heaven the gods had other plans.

At this time, the family consisted of two-year-old Robert as well as Francis and William who were born here. In addition, until he found a job as an apprentice saddler, Burns's younger brother, William, lived here too. You can understand brotherly love and all that, but what is harder to understand is that the household also included Betty, Burns's daughter by Anna Park, former barmaid at *The Globe* in Dumfries.

You may remember from Chapter Two that Betty was born just nine days before William, and Jean brought her up as if she had again given birth to twins. She had a natural tendency towards bringing twins into the world. You really have to take your hat off to her for being such an understanding and forgiving wife.

Right from the start, Burns did not put his eggs into the Ellisland basket alone – wisely as it turned out. He had applied to become a gauger, the equivalent of today's customs and excise officer, which in most people's opinion, must rank third after the taxman and politicians in the list of most reviled occupations. His job was to go around measuring the productivity of goods on which tax was payable, which in Burns's day was nearly everything, including household essentials such as salt and candles, not to mention the one we are most familiar with today – alcohol.

Despite this, Burns was so keen to become one of that unloved bunch of men that in January 1788, and anticipating that he would need a "patronising friend" to secure the position, he wrote to his new friend, a certain Richard Graham of Fintry, telling him that he had requested an "Order of Instruction" from the Scottish Board of Excise. He had met Graham in August of the

● ● ●

previous year when they had been staying in Blair Atholl as the guests of the Duke and Duchess of Atholl. It just so happened that Graham happened to be the Chief Commissioner of Excise for Scotland. It seems to me entirely possible that it was *because* of that meeting that Burns thought of this career move, having such an influential friend on the Board, as he did. As the old adage has it, it's not what you know, but who [sic] you know.

Ellisland

In September, still not having heard from the Board, but having discovered that after he had paid his rent, Ellisland was not providing the living he had hoped for, he wrote to Graham again. It's not to Burns's credit that not only did he ask Graham to use his influence to have him appointed as exciseman in his local area, but also went so far as to suggest that the present incumbent, having recently inherited some money, was not short of a bob or two and could afford to retire. But what really takes the biscuit is the way Burns assumes it was a formality, intimating that he could start at the beginning of the following summer.

Of course, being a famous poet in your own right does help a bit. The request in the letter was repeated in verse form bearing the title *First Epistle to Robert Graham of Fintry Esq.* It's clear from the title that more would be coming and indeed, there were two more.

Burns did not rely on those letters alone. He also had written a cringe-making crawling letter to his old patron, the Earl of Glencairn, asking *him* to use his influence. How much effect that had it's hard to say, but it was not until September of 1789 that Burns landed his dream job. The remuneration was £50 a year – the same as the rent.

From Mossgiel, Burns had brought three Ayrshire cows. When the locals saw the yield they produced, they were mightily impressed. He had some other cattle besides, four horses and a number of sheep. As for his other job, his was a large area consisting of ten parishes, sometimes involving a ride of two hundred miles a week, in all weathers, five days a week. And when he got back home there was the paperwork – four different kinds of records to be kept. Something had to give. Burns turned the unfruitful arable farm over to being mainly dairy

• • •

and it fell to Jean and the servants to milk the cows and make the butter and cheese from both cows' and ewes' milk.

His time at Ellisland was not a happy one. As I mentioned earlier, Burns was not averse to scribbling some lines of verse on a windowpane, the vandal that he was, and it is a measure of how much he hated Ellisland, which he described as that "accursed land", that he requested his brother-in-law to smash the windows on which he had scratched some lines. It's as if he wanted to expunge all memory of his ever having been there.

The cottage has seen many changes since Burns's day but in other respects it's easy to imagine the family living here, and in fact, it has been continuously inhabited for two hundred years, the present householder being the curator of the museum. The kitchen looks as if Jean has just popped out to do a spot of milking and the kids have been sent to the orchard to pick up the windfalls. The restored *cludgie*, or toilet, stands in a corner.

There are so many personal effects belonging to the poet you can almost see his ghost sitting in that chair in front of the desk, and once the light has failed, by the light of a guttering candle, dashing off all those verses and letters. Information panels on the walls celebrate his life, making much of the fact that it was here he wrote his most famous poem, *Tam o' Shanter* – not in this room exactly, although it was probably where he committed to paper the words he had composed in his head as he paced up and down the riverbank. It was also on that stretch of river that one day he saw a wounded hare limp past him and wrote *To a Wounded Hare.* I come from farming stock and in my experience, farmers are not much given to sentimentality as far as animals are concerned.

One other thing that was confirmed for me here by reading the information boards was just how musical Burns was. I always assumed he must have been, composing so many lyrics to so many songs, many of them on the

Ellisland (Alternate Angle)

hoof in the course of his exciseman duties, but here I learned that he could play the fiddle and the stock 'n' horn, a traditional wind instrument played by the Scots peasantry, consisting of a reed and a chanter with a bell made of horn. I also learned that Beethoven, Haydn, Weber and Hummel, to name but four, turned the tables on Burns, so to speak, when they composed music to his words.

The visitor can also learn what happened to Ellisland after Burns left and how the last owner, George Williamson, bequeathed it to the Ellisland Trust in 1922. It looks after the property to this very day.

Burns is often referred to as the *Ploughman Poet*, conjuring up an image of a haggis-fed rustic who had no time for books. In fact nothing could be further from the truth. He was extremely well read. At school, he was taught grammar, syntax and theology. Enthralling subjects I don't think, but they did nothing to diminish Burns's thirst for knowledge. In 1773, he was sent to board with his tutor, John Murdoch, who taught him French. In Tarbolton, aged only 18, he founded the Bachelor's Club, a debating society which met monthly. Here, at Ellisland, he founded a Library. It was five shillings to join and there was sixpence a month subscription charge, all of which went towards buying stock.

In the granary, amongst items such as Jean's mutch and a pillowslip she made, you can see an audio-visual display of Burn's time here but what intrigues me most of all is a framed photograph of a slave with an iron collar, linked by a chain to manacles on his wrists. What on earth could that have to do with Burns?

The answer is the poem *On Glenriddell's Fox Breaking His Chain*, more commonly known as *Liberty Regained*, which accompanies the photograph. Robert Riddell was Burns's neighbour and friend at Friar's Carse. Somehow, he had captured a fox and kept it chained up outside the house. On visiting him one day, Burns was delighted to see that the fox had somehow managed to escape. Whilst it is another example of Burns's compassion for animals, it is also of course, in the wider sense, an attack on slavery upon which many of the rich and powerful built their fortunes and big houses.

Another poem featured in the granary is *Elegy on Willie Nicol's Mare*. The servants dubbed her "Peg Nicholson" after a Margaret Nicholson who had tried to assassinate George III in 1776. Burns's good friend (no greater love for a man than he name one of his sons after him), William Nicol, being unable to get an acceptable price for the poor clapped-out creature, gave her to Burns to keep until such time he could get a better price for her at some fair or other, or so he hoped. Unfortunately she did not survive the winter, and her body was thrown into the Nith according to the accustomed method of what to do with a dead horse. It certainly makes you see the Nith in a different way, the sight of all those bloated horses' corpses being swept down river to provide food for the fishes.

The other farm buildings have an exhibition of farming life, which may or may not interest you, but if you *really* want to follow in Burns's footsteps, you can do so literally, by taking the riverside walk to Friars' Carse, or conversely, if you are staying there, walk to Ellisland. That's what we did on our first visit.

The bluebells were in full bloom and they were beautiful.

Chapter Nineteen

Friars' Carse: The Shocking Scandal

IT was a walk Burns did many, many times, from Ellisland to Friars' Carse, the home of his friend, Captain Robert Riddell, whom we met in the previous chapter. If you are taking the same walk, on the way there, you will come to the Hermitage – a "summerhouse" so-called; a stone building with crow-stepped gables. It is surrounded by trees and looks about as summery as a Siberian winter. All right, I exaggerate, but this is a place where the sun does not penetrate. So what is it doing here?

It is a man-cave if ever I saw one, where the Captain could seek shelter from the vicissitudes of married life and indulge in such manly pursuits as having a wee dram from this secret store in the woods away from the watchful eye of the Drinks Police, aka Mrs Riddell. The good Captain gave Burns a key and if you can't imagine those "drouthy neebors" sharing a bottle of claret, whether or not the sun was over the yardarm, then you know nothing at all about Burns.

It was here he composed some of those 130 verses attributed to his period at Ellisland, and not just on paper either. Once again, he indulged his penchant for laboriously scratching a verse on a pane of glass. Being a friend of the owner, he probably was forgiven for defacing the property. The building itself is not the original, but a copy, erected in the 19th century and restored in 2009.

The house itself is only a mile south from Auldgirth. Before I get on to the story of the scandal, I must tell you an interesting one about the village. One day the Devil came to claim the wife of a farmer. "Take her," said the farmer, "but you'll soon bring her back." If he'd stopped to think about it for a minute, the Devil should have been warned by the husband's cavalier attitude to losing his lovely wife, but he didn't. He carried her off to hell on his back, and sure enough, back he came with her a couple of days later. He said her cursing had upset the demons so much they demanded he got rid of her. As for the farmer, we don't know if he rejoiced at seeing her back again but he refrained from saying, "I told you so." It's best not to annoy the Prince of Darkness.

Friar's Carse

Friar's Carse is a hotel now in the Scots Baronial style and bears no resemblance in any shape or form to the house that Burns knew, so there is no use in narrowing your eyes and imagining him seeing what you see when you emerge from the woods. The building Burns knew had only been built in 1771. A century later, it was totally remodelled, and extended in 1909. It was built on lands which in the 13th century were granted to Melrose Abbey, and a nice little earner it was for them too since they feued it out.

Anyway, it was at here that Burns met the antiquarian Francis Grose whom we met briefly in Chapter Fifteen. Grose by name and gross by nature – he was a very large man whom Burns described as "fine, fat, fodgel, Grose" – and don't tell me he was not an imbiber too with a figure like that. It is a little-known fact that it is he whom we have to thank for *Tam o' Shanter: A Tale.* Here's that story – not the scandalous one I refer to in the chapter heading.

Grose was writing a new book on Scottish antiquities and agreed to include a sketch of Kirk Alloway, provided that Burns gave him something to accompany it. I doubt if he expected something as long as he got. Along with the poem itself, Burns told him there were three "authentic" stories about witches and the church and gave him a synopsis of the poem which he reputedly wrote in a day. He sent it to Grose in December 1790. It appeared in print for the first time in the *Edinburgh Magazine* in March 1791 and in Grose's second book of *Antiquities of Scotland* the following month. The rest, as they say, is history. (And where would Burns Suppers be without it?)

And so to the scandalous tale. On 16th October 1789, a notorious drinking contest took place at Friars' Carse which Burns commemorated in his poem *The Whistle.* The contestants were Sir Robert Laurie, Captain Riddell, and Alexander Fergusson of Craigdarroch near Moniaive. The winner was not so much to be the last man left standing but the one who could get a note out of the whistle, which was apparently made of ivory. Fergusson emerged the victor after consuming eight bottles of claret, though that may be an exaggeration – he may only have drank five or six. (Incidentally, his grandmother was Annie

Laurie, immortalised in the song, and who happened to die at Friars' Carse on 5th April 1764, aged 81.)

The whistle had an interesting genesis. According to Burns's own account, it once belonged to a Danish gentleman at the court of Anne of Denmark, the wife of James VI. The Dane was of "gigantic stature and great prowess, and a matchless champion of Bacchus". He literally drank for Denmark. Throughout the courts of Europe, his party trick was to lay the whistle on a table and issue a challenge to drink him under the table. In contest after contest, he emerged victorious and he had the credentials to prove it. He had won victories in Copenhagen, Stockholm, Moscow, Warsaw and several minor courts in Germany.

After several more victories in Scotland, he finally met his nemesis in the shape of Sir Robert Laurie of Maxwelltown. When it comes to the drinking stakes, it takes a Scot to show these Danes how to drink. As the popular toast has it, at least in Scotland: *Here's tae us. Wha's like us? Damn few an' they're a' deid [[o' liver failure]]*. His son, Sir Walter, in his turn, lost the whistle to his brother-in-law, Walter Riddell, and that is how it came into the Riddell family. At least the whistle and the title remained in Scotland and the pride of the nation remained intact.

Alas, the friendship between Burns and the Riddells came to a sudden end in December 1793 in an incident known as the *Rape of the Sabines*. You can imagine a great deal of drinking had been going on during the evening and as to who proposed the notion that they should re-enact the Roman original, I can only hazard a guess, but it was so realistic that it terrified the ladies out of their wits and Mrs Robert Riddell ordered Burns out of the house and to never set foot in it again.

Returning to Ellisland, in what must have been a wavy sort of way, you would think, Burns did not lie him down to sleep, but instead wrote a grovelling letter of apology to his hostess. After all, he had much to lose: a merry social life at the mansion (whilst Jean looked after the kids) and his trysts with the lady's husband in the shed at the bottom of the garden, so to speak.

From the benefit of personal experience, I have to confess, had I been sitting on Burns's shoulder on that early morning when he returned to Ellisland, I would have advised him to get some kip before he began writing. Anyway, the shameful letter was sent and still exists. In another of his inglorious moments, Burns puts the blame on her husband for leading him astray and claims he only acted under the influence of alcohol. It smacks very much of Holy Willie's excuse:

But Lord, that Friday I was fou,
When I cam near her;
Or else, Thou kens, Thy servant true
Wad never steer her.

Apart from begging her forgiveness for the "impropriety of his conduct", he asked if she would be so kind as to pass on his apologies to the other ladies, in particular Miss I and Mrs G whom he has some hope to believe he has "not outraged beyond all forgiveness". I would have loved to have been there to see what actually took place, as the exact details are somewhat shrouded in mystery.

The letter is embarrassing to read, it really is – very much overwritten. Burns pretends to be in hell and suffering torment for his conduct. Just too, too contrite, but I'm sure he must have had faith in the power of his pen. Having written it, he should have re-read it in the morning, put it in the fire and begun all over again. That said, I can see he must have been desperate to send it off and make amends as soon as possible as the consequences of a severance with the Riddells must have been too dreadful to contemplate, from Maria especially, with whom he was becoming increasingly more involved, her husband attending to business in the West Indies.

Do not be misled. Despite the events at Friar's Carse, it was more a meeting of minds, Maria being a bit of a poetess, like *Clarinda*. Actually, it was a bit of a fashion for ladies of a certain standing in those days to try their hand at writing some poetry. Once he was officially married to Jean, Burns never was unfaithful to her.

Alas, he *was* wasting his time. Mrs Riddell never forgave him and never spoke to him again. Unfortunately, neither did her husband. You can imagine he was under orders not to do so from her, or else face the consequences. She may, or may not have been a bit of a prude, but whatever she was, she certainly was unforgiving. Maria, the wife of Riddell's brother, Walter, was made of more bendy stuff and she did forgive him later. You may recall their encounter at the Brow Well when Burns told her of his intimations of mortality and which she could plainly see for herself.

Unfortunately, the rift between the two Roberts became even wider and impossible to mend when the friends were separated by death. Just a few months after this sorry scandal, on 21st April 1794, to be precise, Riddell was dead, aged only thirty-nine. Burns was devastated. It is a terrible thing to lose one of your best friends; it's a far, far worse thing to be parted by death under the shadow of a quarrel.

• • •

Two years and two months later, Burns was also dead. He was two years younger than Riddell. It's a terribly young age to die. Let us hope there was a reconciliation in heaven and there was a bar where they could have a *richt guide willy waught for auld lang syne.*

Chapter Twenty

New Abbey: The Heart, the Banker and the Monks' Mill

I T'S a new road, the A710, and a new direction – south towards the coast and back on the official SWC300.

The first stop is to renew our acquaintance with a lady we met in Chapter One. We have come to the village of New Abbey which nestles at the bottom of green-clad, double-humped Criffel, which at 1,871 feet, is Galloway's highest peak. That makes it a Marilyn, by some distance. As I know you know, any mountain over 3,000 feet in Scotland is called a *Munro*. Some bright spark thought of calling any hill over 150 meters (492 feet, for the unconverted, like me), a *Marilyn*. There are a good number of them in Scotland.

But that is not the name of the lady we seek. Her name is Devorgilla and the Cistercian Abbey, which was new in 1273, was founded by her here in memory of her husband, who, as you know, was the father of the late and much-unlamented John Balliol, the once and former king of Scotland.

She married when she was only thirteen and she loved her husband to bits. In fact, so much in love was she that when he died in 1268, she carried a bit of him, his embalmed heart, about with her in an ivory-and-silver box until her own death in 1289. It's a grisly object to be sure. Did she open it and gaze at it fondly every day I wonder?

She was buried clutching the box to her bosom in front of the altar in the Abbey. After that, the monks referred to it as *Dulce Cor*, or Sweetheart, and that is what the abbey is known as today. Its former name, "New Abbey" was because it was built as a "daughter" abbey to nearby Dundrennan Abbey. It turned out to be the last Cistercian monastery built in Scotland. Part of their creed is manual labour and self-sufficiency. When they were not engaged in holy pursuits, they tilled the soil and brewed the beer – which just goes to show, they weren't all bad.

Alas, after the Reformation, the altar was destroyed, and with it, Devorgilla's tomb, itself a 16th century copy of the original. Clearly, it had suffered some severe damage in the past. In 1932, surviving pieces of the 16th century tomb, including part of an effigy of Devorgilla, were erected in a new position in the south transept.

One of the monastery's most famous guests was Edward I, who came here in 1300. For some reason he spared it, which is more than can be said for the fate of other abbeys as the Wars of Independence raged around them. Perhaps the *Hammer of the Scots* liked the story of the heart, the old softie. However, only thirty years later, the Bishop of Galloway was lamenting its "outstanding and notorious poverty".

Towards the end of the century, the abbey came under the protection of our old friend Archibald the Grim who by then had moved to his new castle at Threave in Castle Douglas, where we shall meet him again in due course. As I mentioned earlier, he put his hand in his pocket and financed extensive rebuilding and repairs.

Despite what they did to the altar and Devorgilla's tomb, Sweetheart continued to practice "papistrie" under the protection of Lord Maxwell, a devout Catholic and who ignored orders to arrest the abbot, Gilbert Broun. As a matter of fact, he turned out to be the last abbot. Volume 7 of the *Dictionary of National Biography* describes him as a *perverting papist, quho evir since the reformatioun of religioune had conteintit in ignorance and idolatrie almost the haill south west partis of Scotland and had been continowallie occupyit in practiseing of heresy.*

I love the spelling, in particular, "*continowallie*". You can just see the writer spelling out the syllables as he bent over his quill. For these misdeeds, despite the best efforts of his flock who rose up in arms to prevent it, Broun was imprisoned at Blackness Castle in 1605. All his wordly goods were publicly burned in Dumfries and he was packed off to Edinburgh. Thanks to the mercy of James VI, he was merely banished to France where he became a rector of the Scots College in Paris. He did not learn his lesson, however, because he boldly returned to the Abbey in 1608. After a cache of "Popist trash" was found in his rooms,

Sweetheart Abbey

he fled to France and never returned. He died in Paris four years later.

Even so, the abbey continued to limp along until the last monk died in 1624. It's an amazing achievement to have lasted so long after the Reformation of 1560. The abbey and its lands passed into the hands of Sir Robert Spottiswoode, son of the Archbishop of St Andrews, who assumed the title of *Lord of the New Abbey*. In 1633, Charles I created the Diocese of Edinburgh and it was his dearest wish to grant the lands of the abbey to the new diocese. Spottiswoode wasn't very happy to sell the lands, but when a king commands... You can imagine he was even less happy when the king's payment never came. The lands were briefly restored to him in 1641, however. But shortly after that, he was forced into exile, like the last abbot.

That also marked the death of the monastery buildings. It's the same old story: it was used as a quarry to build the new town of Dumfries. Then, in 1779, a public subscription was raised to preserve the shell of the abbey, and thank God they did. To stand in the nave and look along it through the central bell tower to the delicate tracery of the window at the west end is an impressive sight. That's what catches the eye, but there are also the remains of some of the domestic buildings, among them the warming room or calefactory, where monks could warm themselves around the communal fire. You can imagine just how bitterly cold those stone buildings would have been with their bare walls and high ceilings.

The remains of Sir William Paterson (1658-1719) who was born in Tinwald, just outside Dumfries, lie in the cemetery. He is most famous as being the founder of the Bank of England (note it took a Scotsman to do it). He is also known as the architect of the ill-fated Darien Scheme – but that's more a case of being infamous. The scheme was to make poor Scotland a major trading nation like its much richer nation to the south by creating a colony on the narrow Isthmus of Panama.

It was where the Panama Canal is now, so on the face of it, it looked like a good plan – to create a route overland which would link the Pacific and Atlantic oceans. Sadly, we all know what Burns said about *best-laid plans*. For several reasons the scheme failed, of which I will only mention dirty deeds by the English and the East India Company who had a vested interest in seeing the Scots' project fail.

In fact, it not only failed, but failed spectacularly. Had it worked, Paterson would have been a national hero. But it was not to be. After only eight months of hardship and suffering, the new colony of *Caledonia* was abandoned in July 1699. Of the 1,200 would-be settlers, only 300 survived, dead of disease or famine or malaria – including Paterson's wife and child. He only barely survived himself.

Far from making Scotland a wealthy trading nation, the scheme not so much impoverished Scotland, but brought it to its knees. The Scottish nobility, who had invested heavily in the venture, was almost bankrupted. The economy was in such a bad state that it is cited as one of the reasons, if not *the* principal reason, which brought about the Act of Union in 1707. If you can't beat them, join them.

And guess who was a key player in bringing about that union? The former founder and director of the Bank of England, William Paterson, that's who! After the doomed Darien venture, he came back to Scotland but spent the last few years of his life in London where he died. Now he's spending eternity in an obscure plot in the little village of New Abbey. Had the Darien Scheme been a success, they would have dug him up and built a mausoleum over him.

The abbey may be the jewel in the crown of this charming little village, but it has another attraction – an 18th century corn mill. It was built by the Stewarts of Shambellie House and is still known today by the locals as *Monks' Mill* which tells you that it was monks from the monastery who first operated a mill on this site.

The present mill was originally two storeys high, and it is a sign of the efficacy of the new agricultural methods introduced in the 1800s that a third storey had to be added to cope with the increase in grain production. It was used for storage, but first the grain had to be hauled up there in sacks weighing 22 stones on the back of the miller. Can you imagine that! At some stage, a sack hoist was introduced – and not before time too. Just ask the miller, the appropriately-named Thomas Millar, the first on record, and whose millstones first began to grind in 1825. The last miller was John Clingan, who ceased operations in 1948.

The miller's house now serves as the visitors' centre, where you can see and try your hand at grinding corn as it was done before the invention of water mills. And what a laborious process it is – and women's work too, while the men out a-hunting they did go. Believe it or not, the water wheel was invented by the ancient Greeks. Well done them! Pity their labour-saving device didn't make it to Scotia's shores until much, much later.

Now the millstones are turning again thanks to Historic Environment Scotland, as long as there are visitors to make it worthwhile – and water. There were only the two of us, so there was *nae chance*. It didn't matter. We could have been an army and still the stones would not have turned. There simply was not enough water in the mill pond due to the long, hot summer we had enjoyed. There is always a price to pay.

Our visit began upstairs in the visitor centre with a video called *The Miller's Tale* which, of course, has absolutely nothing to do with Chaucer's bawdy tale. But it does let you see the mill in action – the next best thing to seeing it in real life.

Outside is the restored waterwheel which is of the "pitchback" variety, where the wheel rotates in the opposite direction to the flow of the water. From there we take a stroll to the mill pond and sure enough, the water is so low it looks more like a muddy field than a pond.

We are taken inside the mill itself, where our guide explains how it works. I nod like one of those indefatigable donkeys you see at oil wells to show I am following the exposition and understanding everything he says. I *do* understand the principle that the waterwheel, turning vertically, is connected to a cogwheel which drives another wheel, which revolving horizontally, is connected to a shaft that in its turn, drives the massively-heavy top stone. What beats me is how those ancient Greeks dreamed up such a complicated system in the first place.

The oats are fed into a hole between the stones by a three-cornered cam on the drive shaft and which hits the feeding trough at regular intervals, resulting in a clacking sound. The millers wittily nicknamed it a *damsel*. To their ears, it reminded them of the sound of young ladies gossiping.

The highlight for me is the cunning way that the miller began his day by lifting a counterweight (a curling stone) connected by a rope to a trapdoor above which then opened to allow the stream of water to escape from the *launder*, the wooden trough that carries the water from the mill pond. It's as easy as, and the equivalent of, turning on a switch. That done, the mill is ready for the daily grind. The water in the millpond (when there is some) comes from Keldar Loch, a mile a way.

In June 2017, the corn mill had the distinction of being chosen as one in a set of six stamps featuring UK watermills and windmills. Not only that, but it was given pride of place as the first-class specimen.

There's a third thing you can do here, should you have the energy and time enough. You can climb the hill behind the abbey and see, at closer range, the Waterloo monument that stands on the summit. It should only take you about twenty minutes to get there.

However, if you don't have the puff, or the minutes to spare, I can save you the hike and tell you it's a four-story circular tower on which a plaque reads: *Erected 1816/To record the Valour/of those British, Belgian,/and*

Prussian soldiers/Who under/WELLINGTON and BLUCHER/on the 18th of June, 1815/gained the Victory/Of/WATERLOO/By which French Tyranny/ was overthrown/and Peace restored/To the World.

So now you know.

Chapter Twenty-One

Kirkbean: The Father of the American Navy

I N the last chapter we met the Founder of the Bank of England; in this we are going to visit the birthplace of the Father of the American Navy. (Those Scots, they get everywhere!) And if that weren't quite enough, later in life, he became a Rear Admiral in the Imperial Russian Navy. That's quite a career, if I may indulge in a little litotes. I probably don't have to tell you his name but I will anyway. John Paul Jones, though he was just plain John Paul then. The reason for the "Jones" you will find out later.

We've only come half-a-dozen miles from New Abbey to Kirkbean. It's a charming little village with whitewashed cottages that were built in the late 18th and early 19th centuries to house the workers on the Arbigland Estate. The "big house" was built in 1755 by the agricultural reforming landlord, William Craik (1703-98). His daughter, Helen, poet, novelist and friend of Burns, lived there until she left abruptly in 1792. There was a bit of a scandal attached to her departure. She was supposedly engaged to a groom, who after he was given his marching orders by her father, committed suicide. Or did he? An alternative version is he was murdered by a member of the family who thought she was letting the side down by marrying beneath her. Whatever the truth may be, she never came home again and died at the home of relations in Cumbria in 1825, aged 74.

Her half-brother, James Craik (1727-1814), became the Physician General or top doctor in the United States Army – the personal physician to George Washington, no less. He was also one of the three who attended the first President on his deathbed. I will not weary you with telling you how he got from Arbigland to Virginia, a mighty big step to be sure, except to say it wasn't all done at once.

That they were a distinguished couple of half-siblings is beyond doubt, but hang on to your hat. According to another story, or rumour, if you want to put it no more strongly than that, John Paul might more appropriately, have called himself "Craik" – since he was William's son. Who knows for sure? Only the dead and they're not telling. I know no more than the next man, but I do know things tend to happen in threes and it wouldn't surprise me if he were the third talented child to be fathered by William Craik.

Who would have thought that this unremarkable place in rural Scotland that few have heard of, even today, should produce two boys who would grow up to play such a big part in American history? And if your credulity is not already stretched beyond the sticking place, there was another famous seaman born here, although you have probably never heard of him. John Campbell (1720-90) by name, he was the son of the minister, and went on to become a Vice Admiral in the Royal Navy and Governor and Commander-in-Chief of Newfoundland. Incredible!

It's worth having a little poke about the cemetery while you are in the village. There you will find the table tomb of John Paul, the acknowledged father of the Father of the American Navy. He was a gardener on the estate. That may not be of special interest to you but there are also some interesting carvings of women wearing pleated skirts and lacy collars. I'm not unfamiliar with cemeteries as you may have gathered by now but I've never seen the like of that before.

Taking the road towards Southerness, we branch off to see the place where John Paul was born on 6th July 1747. When you go round to the side of the cottage that faces the sea, you might be amazed to see a couple of clumps of palm trees. Strictly speaking, they are *Cordyline australis*, commonly known as the "cabbage tree" and native to New Zealand. You might well wonder what they are doing in these northern climes. The answer is the Gulf Stream swings in pretty close to the shore here, bringing with it a milder climate.

The cottage is a small, whitewashed building, a humble affair, as you would expect, being the home of a gardener. It's a bit of a miracle that it still survives. Had it not been for a certain Lieutenant Pinckam of the US Navy who came here in 1832 looking for the place where its founder was born, it probably wouldn't have been. He found it in a shocking state – a roofless ruin. With twenty-five guineas of his own money, he paid for repairs to be made by the workers on the estate.

But that was only the beginning of the story. In 1947, it occurred to retired Admiral Jerauld Wright of the US Navy that something should be done to restore the building to the way it would have looked at the time John Paul lived there. Had it not been for Lieutenant Pinckam's timely intervention, it would probably have been beyond redemption. Wright was supported in his plan by Admiral Sir Nigel Henderson of the Royal Navy. No hard feelings then.

The third part of the story took place in 1990 when a charitable trust was set up and, in 1993, the museum was finally opened by Vice Admiral Edward Clexton of the US Navy. The visitors' centre was opened in 2003. The main exhibit, which you can't help but notice as you

John Paul Jones Museum, Kirkbean

enter, in the centre of the floor is a 3/16 inch: 12 inch scale-model of the fully-rigged *Bonhomme Richard,* the significance of which you will soon find out.

Here too, you can see the gold medal Jones was awarded by a grateful Congress, as well as a bronze bust of him, by Jean Antoine Houdon, when he was the toast of Paris in 1780. Jones liked it so much he had twenty copies made to give to his friends. Why not? We used to hand out flattering photos of ourselves before the digital age made the printing of photographs redundant. Actually, the bust had another bizarre role to play after Jones' death, but that comes later in the story, naturally.

The cottage consists of three rooms, a living room and a bedroom which have been made to give an impression of what they would have been like in John Paul's day. In the living room, through earphones, you can hear Mrs Paul tell you what everyday life was like in the cottage. Unfortunately you can't ask her if her husband really was the father of her famous son. Even if you could, she'd probably be mortally offended by your impertinence and order you out.

A third room has been designed to look like his cabin in the *Bonhomme Richard* (named after a French translation of Benjamin Franklin's book *Poor Richard's Almanac*) and where you can see and hear an audio-visual account of Jones' most famous battle out of so many. It was the command ship of a fleet of seven US ships whose mission was to harry British merchant shipping in the Atlantic. In a bloody, three-and-a-half hour battle off Flamborough Head in Yorkshire on the 23rd September 1779, the *Bonhomme Richard,* outgunned by the *Serapis*, with its masts shot down and beginning to sink, Jones was asked by the captain of the *Serapis* if he wanted to surrender. Jones' reply has passed into legend. "I have not yet begun to fight."

He rammed the *Serapis*, boarded it and captured it. He also captured the *Countess of Scarborough*. More than half the sailors on both sides were either killed or wounded. With these prizes, he made for Texel in Holland (which was neutral), and when the French got to hear of these deeds of derring-do, Louis XVI made him *Chevalier John Paul Jones* and presented him with a gold sword and a certificate of merit from *L'Instute de Militaire*.

Arguably, that was his finest hour in a glittering career but his beginning as a British seaman was far from glorious. Aged seventeen, his first job at sea was as third mate on the *King George*, a slave trader. Two years later, he was first mate on the brigantine, *Two Friends of Jamaica*, with a crew of six and a cargo of seventy-seven slaves. The stench was so appalling that Jones called it an "abominable trade" and turned his back on it forever.

At twenty-one, he unexpectedly found himself captain of the brig *John* when both the captain and the first mate were struck down with yellow fever. He was confirmed as captain but on his second voyage he faced a charge of murder when a man died after being flogged. He got off with that and went to the West Indies, where he did very well for himself until an event in 1773. In a dispute over wages, he killed, with his sword, the ringleader of a bunch of mutineers – in Jones' own words "a prodigious brute of thrice my strength". He fled to Virginia, where he adopted the name of plain John Jones but which he later changed to the one by which he became famous. You've got to admit it has a better ring to it. John Craik Jones wouldn't have sounded half so good either.

When he arrived in Virginia, the American Revolution was just getting underway. Jones sympathised with the colonists and when Congress formed a "Continental Navy" he volunteered. The navy at that time consisted of a grand total of five vessels. Jones was appointed lieutenant of the *Alfred* on 7th December 1775. Thirteen frigates were commissioned to be built. He was soon promoted to captain of the *Providence*. And providence shone upon him. Harrying merchant vessels off the coast of Nova Scotia and in the Great Lakes, he soon attracted the attention of the powers-that-be and he advised Congress on the drawing-up of Navy regulations.

France joined the war on the side of the Revolutionaries on 6th February 1778. Operating from Brest, in command of the USS *Ranger*, Jones revisited his home waters and attacked the port of Whitehaven across the Solway in Cumbria. He personally accompanied two raiding parties ashore and spiked the cannons of the two batteries that were defending the harbour, as well as setting fire to the collier brig *Thomson* while he was at it.

Then, in a tactic more like an act of piracy than an act of war, he set sail for St Mary's Isle in Kirkcudbright Bay in an attempt to kidnap the Earl of

Selkirk. Fortunately for the Earl, he was away from home so Jones made off with the family silver instead. No wonder the British regarded him as a pirate. Rightly so, but he was a pirate with honour...

On his return to Brest on 8th May, Jones wrote a letter of apology to the Countess explaining he had only taken the silver to pacify his men who were disgruntled at having come away from Whitehaven empty-handed, while by contrast, in America, the British went about burning and looting, not just the rich, but the poor too. He had ordered that officers only were to enter the house, that only the silver plate was to be taken, that no damage was to be done and no-one was to be harmed. Furthermore, he promised that when the silver came to be sold, he would buy it himself and return it by "any conveyance as you shall be pleased to direct".

He was as good as his word. As he wrote in an accompanying letter to Selkirk, in February 1784, he said there was nothing personal in his plan to kidnap him, his motive was merely to hold him hostage in exchange for several prisoners being held by the British as "traitors, pirates and felons".

But that was in the future. After the events of St Mary's Isle, the *Ranger* came under attack from the HMS *Drake* out of Carrickfergus in Northern Ireland. Despite the latter's superior gun and manpower, after an hour-long battle in which both its captain and lieutenant were killed, the *Drake* was captured and Jones returned to France in triumph. Earlier, the American flag on the *Ranger* had been saluted by the French – a first for the new nation's navy. Not a bad little excursion for the Revolutionaries indeed. In fact it was the first major victory for the colonists in their struggle for independence.

1781 found Jones back in Virginia, where Congress passed him a vote of thanks for the way he had "sustained the honour of the American fleet". In 1787, he was awarded a gold medal for "valour and brilliant services". He was to be awarded the command of the *America*, at present under construction, but in fact he got a desk job instead and spent the rest of the war advising Congress on the establishment of the Navy and the training of naval officers. And if all that doesn't entitle him to be called the "Father of the American Navy" then I don't know what does.

What does a man who is skilled in the art of naval warfare do when the war comes to an end as it did in 1785? Fortunately Jones knew a man who knew the answer. That man was Benjamin Franklin, who advised him to offer his services to Russia. In 1788, Catherine II created him *Kontradmiral Pavel Ivanovich Jones* where he served in the Black Sea Fleet under Prince Potemkin. (Bizarrely, Jones only ever reached the rank of captain in the navy he founded.)

At the two battles of Liman in the Dneiper-Bug estuary of the Black Sea, and although the Russians defeated the Turks, Jones fell foul of the Commander of the Dnieper flotilla, Karl Heinrich von Nassau-Siegen. Jones regarded him as incompetent – probably with some justification. Alas the Commander had the ear of Potemkin, and Jones, who knew nothing of Russian Imperial politics, was recalled to St Petersburg where once again, scandal dogged him. In 1789, he was arrested and falsely accused by Nassau-Siegen of raping a twelve-year-old girl. He was defended by the French Count de Segur who managed to convince Potemkin that Nassau-Siegen had an axe to grind and was acting in his own interests. All the same, Jones left Russia, never to return.

In May 1790, he returned to Paris where George Washington made him an American citizen and appointed him ambassador to Algiers in 1792. He wanted him to sort out a problem with pirates along the Barbary Coast who were holding American ships to hostage. It would have been intriguing to see how Jones would have dealt with them, but he died before he could take up the post. He was only forty-five, but no-one could say he had not lived a full life. He was suffering from nephritis, jaundice, and pneumonia. (I told you things tend to come in threes.)

He was buried in the Saint Louis Cemetery in Paris, a plot in a foreign field reserved for alien Protestants. In a far-sighted move, Pierrot Francois Simmoneau stumped up 462 francs to preserve the body in a lead coffin filled to the brim with alcohol in anticipation of the day the Americans would claim their boy. An alcoholic's dream.

The cemetery happened to belong to the royal family and after the French staged their own revolution, the land was sold off and over the next century, variously used as a garden (which you can imagine was very fertile) and as a depository for dead animals. After that it was built upon.

Anyway, during all this activity, Jones slept on, preserved in alcohol, to all purposes forgotten, until along came the Ambassador to France, General Horace Porter, who in 1899, began his search in the former cemetery for the coffin. The only clue Porter had was that he was looking for a lead coffin. The workers dug shafts supported by timbers, like miners, only theirs was much more grisly work encountering skeletons along the way whose wooden coffins had long since rotted away.

Eventually they found five lead coffins. It turned out that the third was the one they were looking for. It did not have anything on the outside to identify who lay inside, but Professor J. Capitan of the School of Anthropology in Paris, and his two fellow doctors, reached the "clear and well-founded conclusion" that the corpse in the coffin was none other than the dead American hero. The search had taken six years.

In case you are having your tea as you read this, I won't go into details about the condition of the various organs that the professor examined, or the incredible stench when the coffin was first opened, except to say that it was confirmed that it was indeed nephritis that carried Jones off – in fact another piece of proof that they had got the right man. And this is where the bronze bust by Jean Antoine Houdon comes into play. Believe it or not, it was another determiner in establishing the identity of the body in the lead coffin, despite him having been laid in earth for more than a century. It says much for the pickling properties of alcohol. I wonder why doctors don't recommend it for a long life instead of telling us that it is bad for us.

Jones made his last voyage aboard the USS *Brooklyn* to Chesapeake Bay where he was met with a great deal of pomp and circumstance. I'm sure, looking down from heaven, he would have been touched and proud to see the welcome they gave him – enough to forgive them for disturbing his Big Sleep by digging him up, not to mention the humiliation of being *unseamed from the nave to th' chaps* like Macbeth did to the *merciless Macdonwald* and having his innards cut out and dissected.

Having taken him back to his adopted country, it took seven years before they decided what to do with him. It was not until 1913 that his well-preserved remains were laid to rest in the chapel crypt of the Naval Academy in Annapolis, Maryland.

They put him in an absolutely hideous marble sarcophagus, modelled after Napoleon's. The marble is black with so many white splats and streaks, it looks like it has been the lavatory for all the seagulls in Annapolis. It rests upon some brown sea creatures of indeterminate species but which look suspiciously like slithery sea slugs. The laurel wreaths on the top, because they are made of bronze, look withered and decayed as if no-one could be bothered to lay down fresh ones. Poor John Paul. I can just imagine him birling around in there at a hundred miles an hour.

There is a photograph of it in the museum. Despite its appalling awfulness, I sincerely hope you are able to see it, as well as all the other artefacts. The museum was saved from closure for a year, at least, thanks to the generosity of Jim Poole, a retired US Navy commander from San Diego. He had previously donated $5,000 in March 2017. The museum and the cottage especially, have a special place in Jim's heart. It's where he proposed and where he got married in September 2017.

Chapter Twenty-Two

Carsethorn and Southerness: Beginnings and Endings

KNOWING all you do now about John Paul Jones, you might like to go to Carsethorn where it all began for the thirteen-year-old boy, though it does mean a bit of a back-track. As for John Paul, he seemed to be drawn there, as if saltwater was flowing through his veins, to absorb the activity of the port, to watch the ships come and go.

It was but a step from his home to here but a giant stride across the seas to fame and fortune although that deserted him at the end of his life, dying practically penniless and friendless. A sad end for a man who had once rubbed shoulders with the great and the good, crowned heads, empresses and presidents. It's worth coming here to reflect that it was from this very spot that the beginning of that inglorious end began.

It was from here he took ship to Whitehaven across the Solway. It's a romantic notion, running away from home to sea, but one wonders what his parents made of it. They had already lost one son to the lure of making a fortune in the colonies, to Fredericksburg in Virginia to be precise, and who was doing very nicely as a tailor, thank you very much. Now they had lost another to the sea. They could never have imagined the heights that his small frame of five feet, five inches would reach, which might have put at ease the maternal breast, not to mention make it swell with pride.

He signed on for seven years as an apprentice, went first to Barbados, then spent some months in Fredericksburg with his brother whilst his ship, the *Friendship*, lay idle. When he did eventually return to Whitehaven, it was to find the ship's owner in straightened circumstances and he duly released him from his contract. It was at that point John Paul entered the shameful slave trade, as mentioned in the previous chapter.

Carsethorne began as a trading port set up by Danish Vikings. There's not a lot to see nowadays, only the enormous sea and the sky (which is reason enough) and a single street of neat whitewashed cottages with the Steamboat Inn at its hub, but when John Paul was in short trousers, it was very different indeed, a bustling place, although the Inn wasn't there yet. It dates from 1813.

By the sixteenth century, the port was thriving. Boats would anchor or beach on the sands where they would be unloaded at low tide, the cargo being taken by cart across the sands. There was also a thriving illicit trade in smuggling, hence the need for someone like Robert Burns, exciseman, but better known as the scribbler of some lines of verse.

There was another exciseman named Blackett of Arbigland who supplemented his income by being a smuggler himself. If he thought to impress his bosses by informing on his fellow smugglers, it badly backfired when they ratted on *him* and he lost his job. I imagine he lost a lot of friends too.

Over the years, the channel of the Nith moved closer to the shore and in 1831, a jetty was built by the Nith Navigation Commission for the Liverpool Steam Packet Company. During the 19th century, this was the departure point for destitute people seeking a better life abroad. They came with all their worldly goods by horse and cart, and which they sold for whatever they could get before setting off into the unknown with sacks of oatmeal which was to be their sustenance on the voyage. Whatever the perils of that held in store for them, not to mention the uncertainties in the New World and elsewhere, it had to be a better life than that which they were leaving behind.

In 1850 alone, it is estimated 10,000 people left for Canada and the United States, 7,000 to Australia and 4,000 to New Zealand, all from here. All that remains of the jetty are some skeletal posts sticking out of the beach. You have to imagine the thousands of people who once walked over it and hope all went well with them in their new lives.

When it wasn't being used for the emigration of people, it was used by the aforementioned Liverpool Steam Packet Company, which, as its name suggests, shuttled between here and Liverpool, carrying a cargo of cockles, mussels and people. In the hardship years, the export of those crustaceans across the Solway to the big city was a life-saver for the starving people of the "Carse", as it was popularly known. With the proceeds, these hostages to hunger tramped the thirteen miles to Dumfries to sell them and supplement their diet with food of a different sort.

Since 2006, there has been a revival of the cockles and mussels industry, but it's not something you should try for yourself. Remember, remember, the fifth of February 2004, when twenty-one Chinese cockle pickers were tragically drowned in Morecambe Bay. The Solway has patches of quicksand. Best leave the cockle-gathering to the professionals.

• • •

Another relic of the grim days in the 18th and 19th centuries is the whitewashed warehouse you can see near the shore. It used to be a barracks where convicts were incarcerated before they were transported to Australia, often for the most trivial of crimes, such as stealing a loaf of bread because they were starving. They were marched here under armed escort from the Tolbooth Jail in Dumfries.

Despite the vast number of emigrants in 1850, it also marked the year of decline for the Carse as a port. This was due to the arrival of better roads, but more significantly, the railway. Another reason was the cost of maintaining the channel to keep it navigable. Nevertheless, the Carse continued to be a port of sorts until the 1920s.

On the shore, a colourful finger-sign points the way to Liverpool, 320 miles, and Svalbard in Norway, 2,000 miles exactly, which, no doubt, is why it was chosen to feature on the post. Not a town, but an archipelago in the Arctic Ocean between Norway and the North Pole. It's hard to see why anyone would want to set sail from here to there unless they wanted to feed the polar bears, by which I mean become fodder for them. It is better known as "Spitzbergen", which, translated into English, means *Jagged Mountains.* Outstandingly beautiful, and a damned sight colder than the mild climate of the Carse.

So much for Svalbard. We're going somewhere much, much nearer on a minor road which takes us, straight as an arrow, to the broad horizon where the road ends in Southerness. It's another whitewashed-cottage village, the cottages being a legacy from an insane venture by Richard Oswald towards the end of the 18th century. Somehow he had got it into his head that there was coal in them there flat lands, and the houses were built to house the miners. They never found any coal.

Southerness is as different from Carsethorn as chalk is from cheese, and not a cheese to my liking either. But plenty of people come here and must like it very much. It is a holiday destination with a golf course which was established in 1947. The 1970s saw the arrival of the first holiday park and

Southerness Lighthouse

the caravan park followed shortly thereafter, and that's what you first notice when you arrive – not the sea and the sky, but the wall-to-wall caravans. There are hundreds of them of the residential sort, some of which are owner-occupied and some that are available to rent. To accompany them are some activities for the kids, while the Paul Jones Hotel, as if was Paul was his first name, was built in 1954.

Its most striking landmark, the lighthouse, was built in 1749 and has the distinction of being the second-oldest in Scotland, built to guide vessels into the Nith estuary. It grew taller in 1785 and once again in the 1840s. The light went out in 1931.

It's the most unusual lighthouse I have ever seen, the body being square or rather wedge-shaped, and tapering at the top. A railed gallery runs round the top, apart from a small gap on the landward side. On the seaward side, the curve of its glass frontage stares out to sea like a blind Cyclops to where a blur of windmills in the Firth are semaphoring that it's pretty windy out there.

Here on land, it's pretty windy too, the flags of the caravan park standing stiffly at right angles to the flagpoles. I wonder if the golfers relish the challenge or curse it as an ill wind that drives up their handicap.

As for us, we are relishing the next part of the journey. This is where the coastal part of the SWC300 really begins. It's an exciting prospect.

Chapter Twenty-Three

Dalbeattie: The Granite Town and the Titanic

FROM Southerness we continue along the A710 to Sandyhills. Never was there a place so well named. From here, all the way east to Southerness and beyond, round the bend at Gill Foot Bay and onwards as far as Carsethorn – sand, sand and more sand. Admittedly, the beach does narrow considerably at Carsethorn but there is still no shortage of sand to get in your sandwiches should you decide to picnic on the beach. Turning to the west, the sand extends all the way to Auchencairn Bay.

When the tide is in, because of its shallow waters, it is perfect for swimming or paddling, and when it is out, for letting your pooch off the leash. Acres and acres of space to have fun in – and let's not forget the Gulf Stream which warms the waters. Meanwhile, narrow streams meander and twist their way across the broad expanse as if lost, looking for the sea.

The errant sun is harder to arrange and cannot be guaranteed, but remember you are at latitude 54 degrees north which is a lot further south than Svalbard and a hell of a lot warmer too, so I don't want to hear any moans, if on your visit, it doesn't come out to play.

Soon we come to Rockliffe along what is known as the "Colvend Coast". It's yet another of those pretty little villages that you should not miss. But what Rockliffe has to offer, which others don't, is a view across to Hestan Island and Rough Island. Hestan has a lighthouse and cottages; Rough, which is a lot nearer, you can walk to across the sand, but check the tide times before you go. They come in quickly, and the last thing you would want to do is to embarrass yourself by appearing on the front page of the *Galloway News* as having to be rescued by the RNLI from a rough night on the island. One further word of caution: you wouldn't want to be a voyeur would you? Please don't go during May and June. There are hundreds of couples having sex on the beach. By that,

I'm referring to the breeding birds, naturally; oystercatchers and ringed plovers. It happens to be a bird sanctuary.

From here, you can take the coastal path to Kippford of Scaur (Kippford for short) where you will pass the Mote of Mark. It was a hill fort during the Dark Ages, that period during the 5th and 6th centuries after the Romans left, and before the Viking invasion began. It was occupied during the 5th and 6th centuries until it was destroyed in the 7th century, probably by the Northumbrian Angles. According to legend, Mark was King of Dumnonia, the third person involved in the Tristan and Isolde love-triangle, and indeed, excavations have uncovered high-class jewellery and decorated horse-gear from the time of the historical characters.

Far be it from me to spoil a good story, which of course Wagner fans will know well, and which I won't repeat here, but actually, since Dumnonia was in the area covered by present-day Cornwall, Devon, Somerset and Dorset, it is much more likely that the Mark of the Mote had nothing to do with that region or legend but he was a Reghed chieftain. Rheged was the ancient Briton kingdom that existed in the north of England and southern Scotland from the post-Roman era until the early Middle Ages.

It's just a grassy hump now, but when it was inhabited it would have had a large circular wooden hut protected by a wall of timber and stone with a wooden gate to the south. Part of the wall was vitrified and there's not much mystery about whodunit. A smoking gun, so to speak, remained in the form of runic inscriptions left behind by the Angles.

And just because they lived in the Dark Ages, don't go thinking the people who lived here were uncultured and uncivilised. They were metalworkers, importing iron from the Lake District and jet from York to make jewellery. And that's not all: they were traders – pottery from Bordeaux and glass from the Rhineland were amongst the archaeological finds.

That was a slight detour. The road snakes away from the coast through lush green countryside and woodland. We're making our way to Dalbeattie. The name derives from the Gaelic "valley of the birch", the first syllable of which has resonances with the Germanic languages and means "valley". There are no birches to be seen now, only armies of soldier pines marching through the Urr valley in which the town nestles.

I have to declare a special interest here. This was where, when we were newly married, we had our first home, initially in a caravan on the municipal site. We had been enticed to Galloway on the promise of a house. On the day of the wedding, I received a letter from the County Council bearing the glad tidings that we had been granted a house "at present under construction". I'm not going to give the date away as it will betray my age, but there had been a building strike that year and the promised house was well behind schedule.

For auld lang syne, we checked it out. No sign of a blue plaque yet. Of course these things are normally erected after the death of the one so-honoured. There's plenty of time left, I hope – but do not expect. Not the plaque, the time.

It's not a blue plaque, but there *is* a memorial, probably more permanent, since it is made out of Dalbeattie granite, on the wall of the Town Hall, at the top of the High Street. The one honoured on it has been portrayed on the silver screen, in TV films and documentaries many, many times, but most famously by James Cameron in 1997 in the *Titanic.* His name is William McMaster Murdoch (1873-1912).

He first became a hero in 1903 when, as second officer of the *Arabic,* he avoided a collision with a ship that was bearing down on them by countermanding the order of a superior officer to steer "hard-a-port" and by seizing the helm himself, he kept the ship steady on its present course. After that you can imagine him closing his eyes, bracing himself and praying very, very hard. Imagine the repercussions if there had been a collision, but fortunately, the ships missed by inches. If he *had* swung to port, almost certainly, the *Arabic* would have been hit by the other vessel.

In 1911, he joined the crew of the *Olympic* as First Officer with Edward J. Smith as master. She made her maiden voyage in June to New York. In September, she was involved in a collision with HMS *Hawke* and had to go to Belfast for repairs. After that she was involved in another collision with a sunken wreck and on another occasion, nearly ran aground in Belfast. Some might say she was an unlucky ship.

Sailors are a superstitious lot and when Murdoch arrived in Southampton he must have thought that it was his lucky day when he heard that along with Smith, he was being transferred to the sister ship, the *Titanic.* Oh, the irony!

He was on the bridge on the night of the disaster when, at about 11.40 pm, an iceberg was spotted in the *Titanic's* path. In the light of Murdoch's split-second thinking on the *Arabic,* I would have thought there's no-one you would want more to be at the helm in that situation than Murdoch. He gave the order "Hard-a-starboard!" What happened next is a matter of debate and disagreement: was the order misunderstood, was it misheard, did the quartermaster turn the helm the wrong way, or was there simply just no time at all to take evasive action?

After the collision, Murdoch was put in charge of evacuating the starboard side, the side that had come into contact with the iceberg. It was buckled and breached, causing the first five forward compartments to be flooded, including a boiler room. He successfully launched ten lifeboats and was last seen trying to launch collapsible lifeboat "A" when he was swept overboard. His body was never found.

A myriad of myths have arisen about his death, which I won't repeat here and which you probably know anyway. What I *will* tell you is that in 1998, the vice-president of 20th Century Fox, Scott Neeson, paid a visit to Dalbeattie and also paid £5,000 into the Murdoch Memorial Prize at the High School. These gestures were met with a lukewarm reception from the people of Dalbeattie and by Murdoch's nephew, who was 80 at the time. As he rightly pointed out, the vice-president's visit, apology and donation, would soon be forgotten, whilst the film goes on and on, perpetuating the myth.

Sportin' Life in *Porgy and Bess* memorably sang, *The things that you're liable to read in the Bible, they're not necessarily so* and that goes for the movies too. Having said that, the myth was not spun out of fresh air – two independent witnesses claim to have seen an officer (they did not know who he was) do what Murdoch was seen doing in the film. Such dramatic stuff is meat and drink to the moviemakers, as if the sinking of the *Titanic* and the loss of 1,503 souls were not dramatic enough.

Considering the amount of money Mr Cameron's film made, namely $2.19 billion, £5,000 seems an insulting amount of compensation – you might call it a spit in the ocean, if that doesn't sound too disrespectful. 20th Century Fox, on the other hand, may well consider it generous, as according to Mr Neeson, from the outset, the director held Murdoch in the "highest esteem" and indeed portrayed Dalbeattie's most famous son as the hero he was – "one of the film's most humane, selfless and sensitively-drawn characters". You can see the letter, quaintly written in block capitals, as well as some memorabilia from the *Titanic*, such as china, in the Dalbeattie museum.

When you step in the door it is like stepping through a portal into the past, as you seem to have entered an old-fashioned shop, even older than when I was in short trousers, and that is saying something.

The museum, or should I say, repository of artefacts from the past, was the brainchild of Tommy Henderson, and after a lot of hard work by him and his team of volunteers in preparing the premises, it opened in April 1993. Since then, like Topsy, it has grown and has expanded to accommodate the ever-growing number of exhibits as more and more people donate items.

It is so *clamjamfried* with objects you could easily spend hours here wallowing in nostalgia, or see the sort of things that were familiar to grandma and great-grandma when they were girls. It's great fun pointing out various items to each other and saying in a tone of excitement mixed with awe, wondering where all the years have gone: "I remember that... and that... and that!" You know you are getting old when you recognise in a museum so many items from your childhood.

Dalbeattie Museum

One thing I don't remember is a hundred-year-old washing machine – and get this, it is still in working order, but happily forced into retirement now. And another thing before my time: a barrel organ, and yes, it works too. And a commode, as fine a piece of furniture as ever I did see, with drawers. It has been opened up so we can see what it really is. But for that, we would never have guessed its hidden purpose. Posh people don't do that sort of thing, you know!

Amongst the displays, as you might expect, there's an exhibit on what was one of the town's major industries. The Dalbeattie Granite Works was established in 1820, the main source of the material coming from Craignair Quarry. As Dick Whittington found out, the streets of London were not paved with gold, but, a long time afterwards, the Thames Embankment *was* made of Dalbeattie granite. Other notable structures that owe their foundations to Dalbeattie, are the Merseyside Docks in Liverpool and several lighthouses of which the Eddystone is the most famous – even a lighthouse at the tip of Sri Lanka.

There's a War Bunker and a bowed window like the *Old Curiosity Shop*, which must make the children's eyes pop to see the number and variety of toys on display. Actually, it's quite impossible to convey the variety and number of curiosities this Aladdin's Cave contains. I sincerely doubt if the volunteers themselves could tell you even half of the items so I won't even try to tell you more, except to mention a couple of things that filled me with a grisly sort of fascination.

• • •

In a glass cabinet, a mannequin is holding a primitive dentist's drill. It looks more like an instrument of torture than a cure for the toothache. (Burns might have preferred to suffer it.) In the same cabinet, what really took my eye, if you pardon the expression, is a collection of pop-eyed glass eyes which unnervingly seem to stare back at me, laid out like cockleshells all in a row, like trophies from some sad, mad and dangerous serial killer.

You would be mad not to spend a lot of time here. Hey big-spender, spend more than a little time here – it's completely free.

Chapter Twenty-Four

Castle Douglas: Threave Gardens –
Nature, Not Always Naturally

WE'RE on a slight deviation from the SWC300, but only for a mere matter of six miles or so, to Castle Douglas, abbreviated to CD by the locals. This was long before that thin disc with more tracks than Glasgow Central came along.

CD proudly boasts it is to food, as granite was to Dalbeattie. It's astonishing that the granite that found itself so far from home has, as far as I can see, not made the short journey here, yet there are half-a-hundred businesses in and around the town involved in the food industry. You certainly won't go hungry when you come here.

It wasn't always a food town: it used to be a cotton town, as one of the three main parallel streets in the town attests. It was doomed to failure. This homespun cottage industry could never compete with David Dale's water-powered looms in New Lanark. They had already been up and running for seven years before Sir William Douglas and his brother Samuel laid out the new town of Carlingwark in a grid pattern in 1785.

Despite this setback, the new settlement was named after William in 1792. He also set up a woollen mill, a brewery, soap works, and a tannery. With Samuel who, incidentally, was a friend of Jean Armour, he also set up a cotton mill in Newton Stewart. It was renamed Newton Douglas before reverting to the original name in 1826 after the mills were sold.

William started out in life as a poor pedlar who made his fortune in the "American Trade". That seems rather vague, but it probably involved trading with the indigenous tribes. He came back in the late 18th century to the original Carlingwark, a settlement around the loch at the bottom of the town. In 1796, he became a baronet. He never married and died in 1809, whereupon the baronetcy died with him and his estate was divided amongst his nephews and nieces. Incidentally, it's worth mentioning in the passing that his niece,

Elizabeth, known as "Betsy", the daughter of his brother George, was married to Colonel James Monroe, nephew of the US President.

William was buried in a mausoleum on the outskirts of the town and has since been joined by his family. He must be glad to have some company and not rattle about in that enormous house of the dead by himself.

We leave the town by the B736 with the loch on our left. It's a Site of Special Scientific Interest (SSSI) because of the birds and grasses. If you are a fisherman you might well be interested in it too, but we're interested in it because of its links with history.

The name comes from the Scots Gaelic *caer*, meaning a fort, while *wark* comes from the Old Scots word meaning "work" in the sense of a building. There are four tiny artificial islands in the loch, settlements in the much more distant past, long before the one which William Douglas knew. In a survey conducted in 1847, on the most southerly island known as "Fir Island", they found a forge which they reckon was used for the shoeing of Edward I's horses in 1300.

But that is only yesterday, comparatively speaking. Two of the islands are built on piles: crannogs, in other words. When the loch was drained in 1765, as well as finding the islets, two dugout canoes were also discovered. Then, in 1866, fishermen dredged up a bronze cauldron filled with smith's tools dating from the late 1st or early 2nd century AD. Archaeologists think they may have been a votive offering. You've got to keep the gods sweet if you know what is good for you.

Next time you are in Edinburgh, you can seek out the items above in the National Museum of Scotland – apart from the canoes, which have disappeared off the face of the earth.

It's only a short distance before we take the road off to the left to Threave Gardens. It's a National Trust Property, and is included in the *Inventory of Gardens and Designed Landscapes in Scotland* – a compilation of those of artistic and/or historical significance. And if that is not enough to tempt you, then let me tell you in 2013 it was placed 2nd in *The Independent's* "10 Best Gardens to Visit" in the UK.

If you have ever wondered where all the gardeners come from that do such a great job maintaining the gardens of the NTS properties and gardens of Stately Homes across the land, and yea, also in gardens in lands across the seas, then wonder no more – this is the place. This is the Oxbridge of the horticultural world. Well, all right, not exactly *all* the gardens; that's a bit of an exaggeration, I must confess. Actually, only eight lucky students are selected each year for a two-year residential course. The accommodation and classrooms were originally situated in the house, to which you can add 64 acres of living classrooms outside. That's some size of a classroom.

There are more types of garden here that you can shake a rake at. There's a walled garden, a rock garden, a conifer garden, a heather garden, a woodland garden, a water sculpture garden and a walled garden – to name but a few. There's also a secret garden but I'm not going to tell you where it is. In addition, there's an arboretum and two woodland areas, as well as a wildlife meadow and children's play area, not to mention ponds and waterfalls and shrubs and bushes and herbaceous borders and lawns.

We tend to take for granted today being able to pop down to the supermarket for, say, a pineapple from Hawaii, a lemon from Sicily, or grapes from Chile (though I prefer to take mine in liquid form). And not just for fruit, but vegetables too. *Ecclesiastes* tells us "there is a season for every activity under the heavens" and since the invention of the jet engine, this was never truer. Somewhere, someone on the planet is growing something that is either out of season here or not grown at all, packing it and possibly freezing it, to appear on a supermarket shelf somewhere near us the day after tomorrow.

Back in the eighteenth and nineteenth centuries of course, this was not possible and the walled kitchen garden and its greenhouses kept the privileged few in fresh fruit and vegetables throughout the year and without the benefit of chemical fertilizers and electric heaters either.

The original glasshouse had hollow walls in which coal fires were lit to prolong the growing season of flowers as well as fruit and vegetables. Cunning, eh? Alas, it's no longer here. The present glasshouse is a mere youngster, having been built in 1997, and here is *its* cunning thing – it includes three temperature zones. The cool house has rhododendrons from Asia, while the tropical house, as well as having a wonderful display of orchids and bird-of-paradise plants, also produces bananas. Bananas home-grown in Scotland! How mad is that!

It all began with William Gordon, a rich businessman from Liverpool who bought the estate in 1867. His "little" house for the summer in southern Scotland was completed in 1872 in the Scots Baronial style in order to entertain his shootin'-'n'-fishin' set of friends. It's built of red sandstone, like many of the much more humble buildings in the town, though many of them have been whitewashed over. It is called "Threave House", but "Hall" or even "Castle" would be more fitting since it is so grand and impressive. But what's in a name? That said, in my view, Dalbeattie granite would have been even more imposing and it's not as if he couldn't have afforded it had he wanted to.

Gordon's bachelor grandson, Major Alan Gordon, generously bequeathed the entire estate of 1,500 acres to the National Trust for Scotland in

Threave House and Gardens

1958. The School of Gardening was set up in 1960 with Mr W. Hean as the first principal.

The Gardens are open all year, for all seasons. In the Spring, the Woodland Garden is a carpet of blue, while as you approach the house, you might well be forgiven for thinking that King Midas had preceded you, for the green of the grass is transformed into a sea of golden daffodils. There are nearly two hundred varieties running riot throughout the grounds. Who would have thought there could be so many different types? And in the winter, there are snowdrops in their shoals and drifts.

You don't have to visit the house, but it's included in the price (which is nothing to us as NTS members), so why not take this portal back to the past too? There is time to spend before our tour begins and we wander towards a huddle of red sandstone buildings, formerly the stable block.

It's near there that we get our first sighting of the indigenous cattle, the Belted Galloways – a family of four consisting of Mum and Dad with a couple of kids. No-one knows for sure how they got the white belt around the middle, but it is supposed they originated from a cross between the black Galloways and the Dutch Lakenvelder belted cattle. Whatever the reason, it gives them a very distinctive appearance and also why they are nicknamed the "panda cow", which most of them are not since they are primarily bred for beef. But what really takes the biscuit is that it's also known as the "Oreo cow".

Their shaggy long hair is well suited to shedding rain, so they can be left outside in the comparatively mild (for Scotland) but wet Galloway winter. Not only that, but they can graze on rough pasture that other cattle turn up their muzzles at. Their flesh is marbled, and as any chef worth his salt will tell you, a little bit of fat is what gives the meat its flavour.

As we get nearer, we note they are curiously motionless, like painted cattle upon a painted field. Not painted actually. Plastic. These have no need to fear ending up on a plate one day.

Carrying on, we come to a waterfall. On some rocks at the bottom, Chiroptera have been carved in flight: *Fledermaus, bawkie bird, chauve-souris* and whatever the Japanese for "bat" is. You won't see them for real, especially if you are here in the daytime, but the wider estate has a Special Protection Area for bats – the only one in Scotland, so no doubt that is why they have been carved in stone for us to see here. To tell you the truth, that's how I prefer them. I hate their horrible membranous wings. Can't understand those people who are batty about them.

Howard and Martin, our guides, escort us on a tour of the house, taking it in well-choreographed turns to provide the exposition, supporting each other, like a good double act does. But before the show starts, Howard has a question for us: what is unusual about the front door? The answer is not that it is curved, being set into a turret, but that it has no handle or keyhole. If you read this before your visit, please do not spoil his day or at least discombobulate him by piping up with the correct answer.

The other questions, the other curiosities, as well as the other interesting details of the house I will leave you to discover for yourself.

Chapter Twenty-Five

Castle Douglas: Threave Castle – Murder, Treason and Plot

W E'RE making for Threave Castle now and back on the trail of our old friend, Archibald the Grim. From the car park it's seven gates and twice as many minutes to the landing stage where we climb aboard the little boat that takes us on the very short journey across the river Dee. Visitors today land on a wooden jetty, but once on the island, you can see the original stone harbour on the far side of the keep.

Names can tell you a lot about a place's origins. *Threave* comes from the Welsh word *tref* meaning a "settlement", which tells you that long before Archibald the Grim came here it had been occupied by Welsh speakers. Those who know about such things, think they were here in the 6th century until they were chased out by the Gaels from Ireland. If it's not one bloody lot of invaders, it's another.

It is supposed that this was the site of a castle built by Fergus, Lord of Galloway, in the early 1000s. His heartland was in the Dee valley, but he also had a stronghold at Whithorn. The site, standing as it does within a loop of the Dee, does seem a natural sort of place to build a castle for defence.

It is thought the original castle was destroyed in 1308 by Robert the Bruce's brother, Edward, after his victory over the Gallovidians, or Men of Galloway. They were supporters of John Balliol who fought on the English side at the Battle of the Dee that year. Then in 1361, David II appointed Archibald the Grim as Warden of the West March and in 1369, Lord of Galloway also. His brief was to subdue the Gallovidians, preferably get rid of them for good. For that, Archibald needed a secure base and he must have looked at this place and saw that it was good. He began building the new castle in the 1370s.

In 1372 he bought the lands of Thomas Fleming, the Earl of Wigton, that fellow being a bit strapped for cash after having had to pay a ransom to the English for his release. This made Archibald by far the most powerful landowner in all of Galloway. But he wasn't finished yet. In 1388, he inherited the title of 3rd Earl after his cousin, the childless 2nd Earl, James Douglas, was killed at the Battle of Otterburn. Talk about the irresistible rise of Archibald Douglas!

Archibald not only managed to subdue the Gallovidians but gave the English a bloody nose too. In 1384, he successfully captured Lochmaben Castle after a siege of nine days. It was there, as I said, that he gained his nickname and it is here that our trail of Archibald comes to an end because this is where, after a life of fitful fighting, he hung up his sword and died peacefully in his bed on Christmas Eve. It's not an anniversary you forget very readily, thus he ensured that Christmases to come for the family were not very merry.

I will not weary you with too much detail about the three-hundred-year story of the five-storey (the equivalent of a ten storey block today) castle, after Archibald died – but now's the time to tell you a little about his daughter-in-law, Margaret, daughter of Robert III, whose tomb we saw in Lincluden Abbey. And, as you will see, in so doing, we will come across other characters who have made an appearance earlier in this story. No surprise in that. This was the Black Douglas HQ after all.

In 1390, Margaret married Archibald's son and heir, also named Archibald. He led a Scots force to France against the English, where he was killed at the Battle of Verneuil in 1424. Also killed was his son-in-law John Stewart, Earl of Buchan. It was a particularly bloody battle. 4,000 Scots were killed, as well as 3,000 French, while the English lost "only" 1,600, despite being heavily outnumbered.

A sad day for Margaret it must have been when she heard the news, but she hitched up her gown and got on with ruling Threave as the Lord of Galloway (should that not be Lady?) for the next twenty-three years. She outlived her surviving son, William, the 5th Earl and Regent of James II. He died of a fever in 1439 at Restalrig in Midlothian. He was succeed by a son, also named William, who was murdered, along with his younger brother, David, at the infamous event known as the "Black Dinner" the following year (as recounted in an earlier

Threave Castle

chapter). William was succeeded by his great-uncle, James Douglas, aka James the Gross, younger son of Archibald the Grim and yes, one of the conspirators at the Black Dinner.

William, the 8th Earl, the son of James the Gross, forced Margaret to cede to him the Lordship of Galloway in 1447. We don't know the exact date of her birth, only that it was sometime between 1367 and 1385. Nor do we know the precise date of her death, but we do know it was at Threave sometime between 1450 and 1456. Even if we take the later year as her birth date, by the time of her deposition, she would have been considered an old woman for those days, no doubt considered, like Elizabeth I later said about herself, as having "the weak and fragile body of a woman".

The times they were a-changing, and William perceived a new threat on the horizon and which he undoubtedly thought only a man had the stomach for. The art of warfare had taken its first steps towards a more efficient method of capturing castles – the cannon. He set about tightening the defences at Threave. His plans involved destroying most of the outbuildings and using the stone to build an "artillery house", a wall with three drum towers along two sides of the tower house, the other two being protected by boggy ground and the river.

Much of the artillery wall has gone now with only one tower still standing, but to a goodly height, so it's easy to imagine the other two. Note the "dumb-bell" apertures – the top one to see through, the lower one to poke your firearm through. These improvements were considered to make Threave the last word in defence, and you can imagine what James II thought of *that* before a cannon blew up in his face in 1460 when he was besieging Roxburgh Castle.

An uneasy truce persisted, but not without incident such as when William executed Patrick MacLellan, the Sheriff of Galloway, here at Threave, because he refused to join him in a coalition with some other nobles against the king. For his part, when William was on pilgrimage in Rome and his back was turned so to speak, James attacked his lands, alleging the Douglases had been harassing nobles loyal to him.

The truce really fell apart in 1452, when James II asked William to tea at Stirling Castle. It was an invitation he could scarcely refuse, and the Black Dinner of 1440 must have been very much in his mind when he rolled up. He was right to be worried. If you recall from the Lochmaben chapter, he *was* most foully murdered, according to one story, stabbed twenty-six times by the king himself.

His brother James, the 9th Earl, rose up, proclaiming the king a murderer and an outlaw. Parliament responded: "The Earl was guilty for his own death by failing to respond to the king's gentle persuasion." "Gentle"! I like that!

James conspired with the English against the royal murderer and hastily began strengthening the defences of Threave even more. This he did by completing the artillery house and creating a grassy ditch to the north of the keep, all generously funded by Henry VI of England – which I imagine, when his Scottish counterpart got to hear of it, was enough to make him choke on his porridge.

The rest you already know, but just to remind you, briefly, the 9th Earl hied him to England to gather support. While he was absent, James II set about systematically destroying the Douglases, defeating them at the Battle of Arkinholm near Langholm on 1st May 1455. Predictably, Threave was the last stronghold to fall, the king personally laying siege to it, having a field-tent erected at nearby Tongland Abbey.

The castle was bombarded by siege engines, and – at enormous cost – a massive one was brought in specially all the way from Linlithgow. So big and heavy it was, on the way there it got bogged down. Of course there were no roads as such in those days. Despite this massive firepower, Threave, with a garrison of only 100 men, gamely held out for thirteen weeks.

Even then, the surrender was not so much due to the might of the king's artillery, but by the revengeful monarch bribing the garrison's commanders and promising them safe conduct. Whether they really were given it or not, I really can't say, but I wouldn't put any money on it as it wouldn't be the first time he had promised such a thing and gone back on his word.

The castle passed into the hands of the Maxwells. From the end of one powerful family threat, to the beginning of another. As you will remember from Caerlaverock, the Maxwells were committed Catholics which did not go down at all well with the Scots Parliament. In 1542, and again in 1568, John, the 8th Lord Maxwell, was ordered to surrender not only Threave but his other castles as well. After Mary, Queen of Scots' execution in 1587, he had travelled to Spain where he helped in the planning of the Armada. He was arrested on his return but freed in 1589 on the payment of a £100,000 bond. He still continued to correspond with Phillip II of Spain, nevertheless.

He got his comeuppance when he was killed at Dryfe Sands near Lockerbie in 1593 in a battle against the Johnstones, who, despite being heavily outnumbered, carried the day. In 1613, his son, John, the 9th Earl, was executed for the revenge killing of Sir James Johnstone.

The end of the castle as a stronghold came about in the summer of 1640, when it was besieged in during the Second Bishops' War. Once again, it held out for thirteen weeks until September, and even then only surrendered on the orders of Charles I himself. After that it was "slighted" – that is to say, made uninhabitable – by removing the roof. Maxwell's lands and titles were forfeited and he fled to the Isle of Man where he died in 1645.

Following that, the castle lay dormant, apart for a brief time during the Napoleonic War, when it was requisitioned as a prisoner-of-war camp, though there is no evidence it was actually put to that use. In 1913, the last owner, Edward Gordon, handed it over to the care of the state.

And that's where we are today. The rectangular tower is 100 feet high with walls up to 10 feet thick. At the top were the battlements, one side with stone machicolations from which they could chuck nasty things down on the heads of the attackers – if ever they got that near. On the other sides, overhanging timber hoardings known as *brèteches* served the same purpose. The entrance was on the east side, protected by a gatehouse and drawbridge.

It's striking just how few windows there are. It must have been as dark as Hades in there during its heyday. It's a lot lighter now thanks to the much larger holes which pepper the walls – the scars of battle – not to mention the top of the castle which is open to the skies.

It was built in the traditional style with the well, the cellar and dungeon at the bottom. Entry was on the first floor, through the kitchen. A spiral staircase gave access to the other floors, the first being the grand hall. The private quarters were above that and on the top floor, beneath the battlements, were the servants' quarters. You can tell they were for people of the lesser sort, because you will search in vain for any fireplaces up there.

Well, you can't have them getting above their station, can you?

Chapter Twenty-Six

Palnackie and Orchardton: Flounders and a Tower

FROM Threave, the SWC300 traveller can take the A75 and then the A762 to Kirkcudbright. We, however, are retracing our steps to Dalbeattie where we will take the A711 towards Kirkcudbright. If you decide to take the short cut, we'll meet you there, but we have a couple of places to see on the way, so find a café or somewhere and have a cup of coffee or something, as we may be some time.

First stop is Palnackie. It's a blink-and-you'll-miss-it sort of place, with the tiniest harbour you ever did see, on the River Urr, but believe it or not, Palnackie has its day in the sun (whether it's shining or not) on the first Saturday of August each year when hundreds of people come to compete in the World Flounder-Tramping Championships. It's a bit of fun nowadays (unless you are a flounder), with the proceeds going to the Royal National Lifeboat Institution, but traditionally this was a method of catching flounders and other flat fish by wading out into the mud flats when the tide is out and waiting for your feet to be tickled.

The port began in the 1660s when millstones were brought here by raft for export to Glasgow. A noticeboard tells us that in 1851 Palnackie had a population of about 200 and it had a customs house, a post office, some grocer's shops and "two or three inns or public houses". (Couldn't they tell for sure?) It served as the port for Castle Douglas, the goods being hauled

Boats at Palnackie

there by horse and cart. Schooners of the smaller sort were towed by horse upstream to Dalbeattie, three miles away. Eventuallly the harbour there silted up. There is no trace of it today, but its memory lingers on in the name "Port Street".

We find Palnackie's harbour surprisingly well patronised with half-a-dozen boats tied up, parked nose to tail, on both sides, though one I have to say, is a bit of a rusting hulk. In proportion to its size, Portsmouth could be no busier. The tide is out, exposing banks that are the last word in mud. It would be a glorious place to be if you were a hippopotamus, but a vessel heading down river would need to be very careful to steer down the middle of the channel.

Next stop, a little later, off the A711, is Orchardton Tower, built in 1455 by John Cairns. Note the date – the same as the demise of the Douglases. Earlier in the 1450s, perhaps because he saw the way the wind was blowing, he espoused the cause of James II. He even got the lands at a reduced rent. Smart move.

This is a very special historic site and the moment you set eyes on it you will see why. It is incredibly well preserved, but that's not the astonishing thing – it's the only freestanding medieval circular tower house or *donjon* in Scotland. Isn't that an incredible thing!

Actually it wasn't always as freestanding as it is now. That's because it once formed a corner of a fortified yard, or to use the Old Scots word *barmkin*. This is where the cattle were herded to protect them from the Reivers if they somehow got wind that a robbing was in the offing. Of course, the walls also sheltered the poor beasts from the biting wind, though their thick, hairy hides could shed water like a duck's back.

Whatever comfort the cattle got from the *barmkin*, there was a lot more on offer for the people. There would have been a bakehouse, a brewery and a kitchen block. The tower provided the living quarters, accessed by stairs to the first floor – not the stairs you see now. They were built in the 17th or 18th century by the simple expedient of converting a window into a doorway. What did they care then about preserving ancient monuments? This was all about making the place more comfortable. And who can blame them? The original stairs would have been wooden and possibly moveable.

Also in the *barmkin* was a two-storey building with a hall on the upper floor, making this a two-hall property since there was another one in the tower. Talk about posh! This is where the laird would have met his tenants and where he hosted banquets and other jolly occasions for their benefit to show what a good laird was he.

The tower is thirty-six feet high and thirty in diameter, tapering to less than twenty-eight feet at the top. The walls are between nine and six feet thick in the cellar, narrowing to five at the top where there is a corbelled parapet which, from below, resembles machicolations.

Orchardton Tower

And to top it all off, there is a gabled caphouse which does precisely what it says, namely caps the exit from the spiral stairs which winds its way up inside the walls.

From the parapet there is a dizzying view down the centre of the tower, but it's also a good vantage point, turning the other way, to peer over the battlements and admire the lush, green countryside all around. The walls are not very high and you can't get all the way round, but the thing that is striking is it's not so much a case of putting your head above the parapet but your head and shoulders too. A place from where to do battle, they most certainly are not – they were never meant for that. Add to that the faux machicolations, and what have you got?

A nod to the architectural past, that's what. Cairns seriously believed he would not be attacked in anger now that the Douglases were subdued, the king now reigning supreme and unchallenged. The future looked rosy. No need therefore to build a home to withstand a siege, more a sort of stately home before the term was ever coined, like a skyscraper, long before *that* word was ever coined. It was not about defence but about showing the neighbours and anyone else just how rich you were. The worst to fear was some Reiver relieving you of your cattle.

And here's an astonishing thing – at the time the tower was built, it was already out of date, *passé*, old-fashioned, harking back to the keeps of two centuries before. You have to go to southwest Ireland before you will see a similar sort of thing. Indeed, it's possible that that is where Cairns got his inspiration from, and it's entirely likely that the Irish got *their* inspiration from the brochs, of which those of Mousa in Shetland and Gurness in Orkney are the best-known in Scotland. They are two thousand years old. Round towers were all the rage then but when the 1400s were ushered in, square keeps became the latest thing.

Outward appearances apart, the recipe is as before as far as the inside is concerned. Cellar on the bottom, great hall on the first floor, private apartments above that, and the servants' quarters on the top.

It's quite amusing really, but at the threshold to the cellar is a slab like a doormat on which is inscribed in block capitals: CAUTION LOW HEADROOM.

The main feature inside the hall is a *piscina* (a stone basin) to the right of the fireplace with a trefoil-headed design (think of a clover leaf or the club on a pack of cards). Such a thing would normally be found near the altar in a chapel, as its purpose was to rinse the communion vessels after mass. This looks as if it has been nicked from some decaying chapel or other – very much at odds with the adjacent plain fireplace. Perhaps the hall doubled as a chapel, or perhaps they used it to wash their hands before a meal, if that wasn't considered too disrespectful, or after paying a visit to the smallest room in the house – if such a hygienic thing ever occurred to them in those days.

Once upon a time, there were two windows here with deep recesses where the ladies could sit and sew because the light was so much better and from where they could glance up from time to time to admire the scenery, although they had seen it so many times before and it was just the same as the last time they looked. There is only one of those windows now. One was sacrificed to make the entrance I mentioned earlier. The other was also used as a doorway in former times, and is now barred with an iron grille lest you accidentally topple over and crack your nut on the boulders below.

John Cairns seems to have been correct in his decision to build a tower house rather a keep with all the defensive trimmings, as nothing out of the ordinary seems to have happened until 1527 when his grandson, William, along with thirty-seven others, were present at the murder in Edinburgh's High Street, of Thomas MacLellan of Bombie, to the east of Kirkcudbright. It seems to have revolved around his mother's remarriage to Robert Scott of Tushielaw and which MacLellan opposed. Eleven years later, the murder was remitted. Murder? What murder?

On the death of William, the estate was divided, like Gaul, into three parts, each of his daughters receiving a slice of the cake. Had he had a son, naturally the estate would have gone to him, but he didn't. Then Sir Robert Maxwell began buying up the slices piecemeal until, at last, the estate was united again in 1615 when he bought the last piece, the one that contained the tower. In 1663, he became the 1st Baronet of Orchardton.

It is a truth universally acknowledged that any country, or indeed any individual in want of a reason to start a fight, need look no further than religion.

Families don't even need that as an excuse, but it was the Reformation that divided the Maxwells. Mungo of that ilk was illegally disinherited by his half-brothers. Whilst he remained true to the Old Religion, his half-siblings turned to the new.

Mungo's son, Robert, grew up in France and obtained a commission in the *Royal Écossais,* a Scottish unit in the French Army. In 1745, he turned out for Bonnie Prince Charlie at Culloden. He was wounded and captured and was on his way to Carlisle for execution when they found his commission amongst his papers. It saved his life – transformed him from traitor to prisoner-of-war. On his release, he returned to France for a while. In 1753, he resigned from the army and then *did* turn traitor, if you want to put it that way – he turned his back on the Catholic Church and embraced Protestantism. It was no crisis of conscience: he did so in order to claim his rightful inheritance.

But it was not as simple as that. A long lawsuit followed before he eventually won his case in 1771 and became the 7th Baronet. If you want to know more details, read Sir Walter Scott's *Guy Mannering.* His adventures and misadventures were the inspiration for the tale.

Should you read it, you will find it doesn't end happily for everyone, and indeed it was not a happy ending for Sir Robert. Six years earlier, he had begun a grand building project – the construction of a modern mansion. His eyes, however, were too big for his belly – or whatever the equivalent is in domestic architecture – because by 1785, the cost of the construction had bankrupted him. He sold his estate, lock stock and barrel to James Douglas, who, as it happens, was the younger brother of William Douglas who built the new town of Castle Douglas and the tower was abandoned.

And there endeth the story of the tower, an architectural anachronism.

Chapter Twenty-Seven

Auchencairn: A Tale of the Supernatural

WE'RE on our way now to Dundrennan Abbey, passing through the sleepy little village of Auchencairn, so-named from the Scottish Gaelic *Achadh nan carn* – the field of the cairn. It's a village with a rather interesting tale attached to it.

It's no longer there now, but at the top of the village, in 1695, there used to be a farm called "Ringcroft of Stocking", owned by a certain Andrew Mackie and family. It is an odd name for a farm, that is certainly true, but odder things went on there. Be prepared to suspend your disbelief.

The local minister, Alexander Telfair, wrote a pamphlet, price twopence, about these odd goings-on. I make no apologies for quoting the title in full: "*A TRUE RELATION OF AN Apparition, Expressions and Actings, OF A SPIRIT, Which Infested the House of Andrew Mackie in Ring-Croft of Stocking, in the Paroch [sic] of Rerrick, in the Stewartry of Kirkcudbright, in Scotland. By Mr. Alexander Telfair, Minister of that Paroch: and Attested by many other Persons, who were also Eye and Ear-Witnesses.*" After a title like that, no-one could complain they didn't know exactly what they were going to get for their tuppenceworth.

Telfair describes cattle in their pens being set free or moved to somewhere else; the fuel for the fire, namely peat, mysteriously catching fire; notes being written in blood; strange voices being heard, and perhaps, most weirdly of all, the family began to be pelted with stones. All that you might understand, if they had somehow offended the neighbours and who were out for revenge. But here's the really weird thing – they were being attacked from *inside* the house by a person or persons, unseen.

And it wasn't just the family. The neighbours themselves, Telfair reports, were stoned and beaten by sticks, whilst he, himself, saw and felt, a

Auchencairn

ghostly arm which then mysteriously disappeared into thin air. Telfair had an explanation and very probably, an ulterior motive – as you shall see.

According to him, it could be traced back to the "Trouble" which included Mackie allegedly having taken an oath to dedicate his first child to the Devil; clothes being found in the house belonging to a "woman of ill-repute"; and a refusal to burn a tooth found buried under the threshold by a previous tenant who regularly consulted a *speywife*, what we call a "fortune-teller".

The affair became known as the *Mackie Poltergeist* and various attempts to exorcise the ghost or spirit, call it what you will, were met by more flying stones and clods of earth. On 30th April, the day the sheep pen mysteriously burned down, the poltergeist spoke, saying it would depart on 1st May. And indeed, that was its final act. Whoever, whatever it was, it never returned. And good riddance!

However, Telfair's pamphlet has another version and an explanation. He and four other ministers, so he claims, said prayers at the farm, after which the troubles ceased. Well done, the power of prayer, Rev. Telfair et al! Give yourselves a good pat on the back.

But that's not the end of the story, not by a long chalk. Two centuries later, the 4th October 1890 edition of the *Saturday Review* denounced Telflair's pamphlet as being "a curious mixture of obvious naked imposture and folklore". The writer was surprised it did not occur to anyone that it was "merely a practical joke". Some joke!

The reviewer concludes that what Telfair's pamphlet really was about was an "argument against atheism". I think there may well be some truth in his theory that Telfair was making the most of the moment to do a bit of proselytising, but on just how this elaborate practical joke was carried out, he is mute.

In our time, historians such as Lizanne Henderson and Ole Grell agree that Telfair did have an agenda, that his little book was designed to be a trumpet-blast against what he and his fellow padres saw, in his own words, as "the prevailing Spirit of Atheism and Infidelity in our time, denying both in

Opinion and Practice the Existence of Spirits, either of God or Devils; and consequently a Heaven and Hell."

As for the mysterious goings-on, Sacheverell Sitwell (just where do some parents get the names to inflict upon their offspring?), claimed in his 1940 book, *Poltergeists*, that the guilty party was one of Mackie's kids who had learned the art of ventriloquism. Now listen to this, and be prepared to be amazed. The voice told Mackie he would be "troubled till Tuesday" and if "Scotland did not repent, it would trouble every family in the land." That's some claim.

Sitwell concluded there can be "no doubt" that one of the children had learned to ventriloquize, but just how this prodigy of a child managed to chuck rocks about by voice control I haven't the foggiest idea. I suppose he (or she) could have been a pyromaniac, and let the cattle loose, for a laugh. You know what a handful teenagers can be what with their hormones and everything.

Everybody likes a mystery, do they not? And I think it's better that way. A conjurer's trick, which filled you with awe and wonder, once it is explained, leaves you feeling disappointed and not a little foolish that you should have been so gullible as not to have seen it though it from the start.

I think it is a far, far better thing that we don't know the explanation for what was going on at "Ringcroft of Stocking". It would bound to turn out to be more than a little disappointing.

Chapter Twenty-Eight

Dundrennan Abbey: A Monk's Life and a Fugitive Queen's Night

RIEVAULX. It sounds as French as frogs' legs, but it's in Yorkshire and it's where the first monks who staffed Dundrennan Abbey came from. They were Cistercians, an austere order who wore white robes in contrast to the Franciscans, who wore black, and who kept themselves to themselves, living apart from the local community.

The order had its roots in Cîteaux, Burgundy, in 1098. St Bernard, the Abbot of Clairvaux exported it to England in 1128 and by 1136 it had reached Scotland. The abbey at Dundrennan was founded in 1142 by Fergus, Lord of Galloway. Or it might have been David I and was patronised by Fergus to show how wealthy he was, and no doubt, devout. The first abbot was Sylvanus who came from Rievaulx – in with the bricks, so to speak. Architecturally speaking, it marks the period of transition from Romanesque to Gothic.

Dundrennan was just the start: its daughter, Sweetheart, was founded in 1273 as I already mentioned, while Glenluce, its grandma in Galloway, was founded in 1191. Once the buildings were erected, all it took was thirteen monks and ten lay brothers, and Dundrennan was in business.

I'm too fond of my bed to have made a good monk. The day began at 1.30 in the morning, arising from a bed in the dormitory that probably was not very cosy, then down the night stairs to the nave of the church for the first prayers of the day and Nocturns. Even in summer, the place must have been freezing. Then it was back to bed until Matins at 3.30 followed by Prime, the first Mass of the day, at 6am, followed by a meeting in the chapter house. There was enough light by then to do a bit of work. Great! Fortunately most of the hard manual work was done by lay brethren, illiterate fellows of lower social standing, most of whom went on to acquire the habit too, in both senses of the word.

At 8am, it was Terce and sung Mass, then more work until Sext at 11.30. At noon, there was the main meal of the day, after which you could have a bit of a lie-down (that would have been me) or have a bit of private pray. At 2.30, it was None (not nothing, but the Latin for "nine", the ninth hour after dawn), followed by more work. That was the longest stretch of secular stuff before Vespers at 6pm, preceded by half-an-hour for supper. At 7.30, there was another supper, but lighter, then Compline and so to bed at 8.15 so you would be bright-eyed and bushy-tailed and ready to go through the same thing the next day and the next and the next...

If you found reading that account of a day in the life of a Cistercian monk a trifle boring, then just try doing it for real. Life expectancy was short and pleasures were few, if any. That said, it wasn't all bad. In winter you could thaw out your chilled-to-the-marrow bones in the communal calefactory or warming room, though it was lacking in the warmth of human fellowship. Conversation was not encouraged, apart from when it was absolutely necessary, not even when you were partaking of your vegetarian meal twice a day in the refectory – but cheer up, you could listen to someone reading a verse or two from the Bible or some other good and improving book.

You also had to attend readings in the chapter house where someone would read a chapter from the Rule Book. It was also where the business of the abbey was carried out – and punishments. Tut! Tut! And if you *still* hadn't had heard enough good words, or were a bit worried that you might have done, or might do something bad like having an impure thought, then you were free to do a bit of contemplation in the cloisters – along with some of your like-minded fellow bretheren.

So much for the proverb *Early to bed and early to rise, makes a man healthy, wealthy and wise.* A monk's life sounds more like a dog's life to me, though probably nearer the mark is Thomas Hobbes' description in *Leviathan* – 'Solitary, poor, nasty, brutish and short" although, to be fair, he was referring to the life of man in general. That said, a silver spoon was found during excavations in the south range where the refectory would have been. Perhaps it came from a monk who was born with it in his mouth.

And yet people were dying to get into the abbey because they knew that when they did, their place in heaven was assured. I don't know what sort of life they expected to find when they got to the afterlife, but I can imagine they wouldn't have been too chuffed if they found it turned out to be just more of the same – forever.

During the Wars of Independence, the abbey suffered at the hands of Edward I's troops and in 1299, the abbot claimed £8000 compensation. A lot of money now; in those days, astronomical. Then in 1328, another claim for compensation was made to his grandson, Edward III, for the restoration of the abbey's estates in Ireland. Two centuries after that, the abbot was replaced by a "commendator" or lay administrator, and by 1529, the abbey buildings were falling into ruin.

Dundrennan Abbey

Another significant date in the abbey's history took place on 15th May 1568. Mary, Queen of Scots is famous for having slept just about everywhere in Scotland and this is no exception, but what is special about here is it was the last place she ever slept in Scotland. How she ended up here is a tale in some ways almost as incredible as the Mackie poltergeist or something out of the *Boy's Own Paper* but there is not enough room to go into that here, unfortunately.

In actual fact, she wasn't a queen any more, just a woman on the run, fleeing the country, accompanied by a dozen-and-a-half nobles and retainers. And whether she actually got any sleep that night is debatable. It wouldn't surprise me in the slightest if she didn't get a wink. The next morning she embarked on a fishing boat from nearby Mary Port from whence the monks used to export their main commodity to Europe – wool.

Legend has it that during the crossing of the Solway, Mary had a premonition and ordered they should turn around and set sail for France instead. Alas for her, the wind she felt on her face was the wind of destiny and the boat's course could not be altered.

She threw herself upon the mercy of her first cousin once removed, Elizabeth I of England – the one who, in the end, was responsible for removing her head.

The abbey's days were numbered too. The wind of change that had been brewed up in Germany by Martin Luther had already reached Scotland's shores. We call it the "Scottish Reformation". After being afforded some protection from the Maxwells for a little while, the abbey passed into the hands of the Crown in 1621. The building fell into decay and then the ultimate disgrace – was used to shelter livestock. Some of the stone went into the making

● ● ●

of the courthouse in Kirkcudbright in 1642 and later on it was a convenient source for the building of the village.

"A glory had passed away from the earth", as Wordsworth said, more or less, but what remains is still pretty impressive: the central west door, part of the west wall, the transepts and part of the presbytery. The glorious nave was 130 feet long with a choir of 45 feet. It was two storeys high with a gallery running round it with a central tower 200 hundred feet in height. Each transept had three chapels. Yes, it must have been quite magnificent, the equal of any of the cathedrals that have survived to our times, and – it is a personal view admittedly – but I much prefer the grey sandstone to the red of Sweetheart Abbey.

The chapter house is especially fine with a 13th century arched frontage and a magnificent four-pointed arched door flanked by matching windows. The interior had an aisle with a vaulted roof, off which there were twelve little rooms, also with vaulted ceilings. They were supported by octagonal pillars, now reduced to stumps, like ground-down molars. You need to use your imagination a bit, but if you let it soar, you will see how splendid the whole thing would have been. Coming down to earth, embedded in the floor, you will see the graves of four abbots.

The oldest belongs to Abbot William, who became second abbot in 1184. That's all we know about him and not a lot more can be said about the next either. At some time in the past, his gravestone had been shattered and reassembled. It belongs to Abbot Egidus, or Giles, and is thought to date from the thirteenth century. The third belongs to Abbot Brian, in office from 1250 until his death in 1273. The last looks particularly well preserved. It belongs to another Abbot Giles, lord Egidus, the 22nd abbot, credited with the reconstruction work after the Wars of Scottish Independence.

Meanwhile, over the stumps of all that remains of the walls of the chapter house, you can see a petrified forest of more recent tombstones. There is also the Maitland Mausoleum, for the land-owning gentry of these parts, which is worth a poke into if you are interested. The enclosure is dominated by the family crest and motto *Esse Quam Videri* – better to be than seem to be. I couldn't disagree with that.

In a niche inside the north transept of the abbey church is the very much-damaged effigy of Alan Fitz Roland, aka Alan of Galloway (c.1175-1234), the father of Devorgilla. He was so powerful he was practically monarch of all he surveyed, but he had to walk a tightrope between offending the kings of both Scotland and England. That was why, in 1212, he led 1,000 troops to assist Bad King John of England in his war against the Welsh. The same year, he sent one of his daughters to England as a hostage to be looked after by one of her uncles. She died the following year. He was chosen by John to be one of his sixteen advisors during the Magna Carta crisis – which shows just how much he must have been respected by the king.

There was precious little of that shown when they moved his effigy from wherever it was originally and cut off his legs and his arms to make him fit in a niche in the north transept. Of course he was well past caring by then.

Grouped together on the west wall of the nave are some interesting gravemarkers. They were originally found in the chapter house in 1838 and moved to the present location fifty years later. One of an abbot is especially interesting. You can tell he was an abbot by the haircut, the robes and crosier. But look closely – there is something incongruous about it. There is a dagger (which you might at first glance, mistake for a cross) sticking out of his chest where his heart would be. And that's not all – he is standing on a smaller figure with a gaping hole in his chest. Could he be the assassin who committed the deed and got his just rewards? But who killed *him*?

Unfortunately, we will never know, as no records have survived. All we know about the abbots is what we see here, carved in stone. To the right of the unfortunate abbot is the gravestone of Patrick Douglas, the cellarer (a very important job), and who died in 1480. He is depicted wearing a pleated, cowled robe with wide sleeves, and his hands crossed above his chest – a sure sign he is dead. To the left of his head is a chalice and to the right, a book which, it is pretty safe to assume, is a Bible or prayer-book. There is some sort of vegetation beneath them and forming a frame around the whole scene, a Latin inscription with a very handy finger in the top left-hand corner indicating where the reader should start.

Facing the cellarer in the same alcove, is a slab with a great deal of Latin writing and a coat of arms. It had been a bit of a jigsaw puzzle for someone at some time and there are a number of pieces missing. It is the grave of Sir William Livingstone of Culter, who the stone says, died in 1607. But did he? According to the Register of the Privy Council, in 1610 and 1611, he was pursing certain people for debt during those years. His first wife was the widow of Edward Maxwell, one of the commendators here. His father was one those who brought Mary here after the Battle of Langside and who accompanied her to England.

Finally, on the adjacent wall, is the tombstone of a nun complete with wimpole and long-pleated robe, her hands in front of her as if in prayer. It is thought she might be Blanche, one of the last nuns at Lincluden Abbey before it was suppressed in 1389 by Archibald the Grim. She died in 1440 and if the accounts of what those nuns got up to have any truth in them, then she wouldn't have been nearly as white as her name suggests.

There is very little left of the outbuildings, but on the west range are the remnants of the lay brothers' residence. This was later converted into the abbots' and commendators' residences with storage cellars beneath. And it was here, a storey or two above them that the doomed Mary, Queen of Scots spent her last night in Scotland.

Chapter Twenty-Nine

Kirkcudbright: Lairds and Artists

AFTER Drundrennan, we come, unexpectedly, upon a strange sight standing in a field off to our right. It must be thirty foot high at least – a wicker man.

Famously, nearby Kirkcudbright (pronounced *cur-KOO-bree*) was the main setting for the 1973 cult horror classic of that name starring Edward Woodward. In the fullness of time, it spawned the Wickerman Festival which ran from 2001 to 2015. It was held at the farm of East Kirkcarsewell, culminating in the torching of the effigy after all the singing and dancing was over.

The origins of burning a wicker man go back as far as the Celtic pagan priests, known as Druids. In his *The Gallic War*, Julius Caesar mentions the Celts' practice of weaving "huge figures of wicker and fill their limbs with humans, who are then burned to death when the figures are set afire". He goes on to say that the preferred victims are "thieves, robbers and other malefactors" but in the absence of such, innocent folks had to do. Fortunately (for them, at least), there was always a ready supply of slaves. It was performed at Beltane or Mayday, the day that the cattle were traditionally driven out to pasture.

The thinking behind the practice of the burning of the effigy is that it represented the Sun God or Oak God who needed to be kept sweet in order to produce next year's crops, especially after a bad harvest. Apart from Caesar's account, there seems to be no evidence that human sacrifice was involved in the burning of the wicker man, but we do know from the Irish bog bodies for

Wicker Man near Dundrennan

instance, that human sacrifices *were* made. It's a matter of speculation, but these victims may, in fact, have been martyrs, sacrificing themselves to save the tribe from starvation.

And so we come to Kirkcudbright, a spacious town with streets so wide and broad that cars can park with their noses facing the pavement, like horses in the Wild West movies. Daniel Defoe (1660-1731), founder of the English novel, journalist, pamphleteer and not least, English spy, was here in 1726 and thought there was not much to write home about. He reported: *A pleasant situation, and yet nothing pleasant to be seen. Here is a harbour without ships, a port without trade, a fishery without nets, a people without business.*

It says more about his prose style than his powers of observation, though to be fair to him, his visit did happen to coincide with a downturn in the town's fortunes. Had he been here in the 15th century, he would have found a harbour bustling with activity. You will scarcely credit it, but over a quarter of all Scotland's textile exports left from this little port. Isn't that an incredible thing!

The town's name comes from the Gaelic *Cille Chuithbeirt* meaning "Chapel of Cuthbert". It *was* a bit of a holy place actually: a monastery had been founded here before 1000AD; in the twelfth century there was a Cistercian nunnery and an Augustan priory nearby; and a century later, there was a Franciscan friary.

At its centre is the ruined MacLellan's Castle built by Sir Thomas MacLellan. It is very much hemmed in by later buildings. We are usually accustomed to seeing castles surrounded by acres of grounds, and indeed this would have been the case, once. On this ground, the Convent of Greyfriars used to stand. It had been there since 1449 and then, in 1560, along came the Reformation – not the first time I've mentioned it in this tale.

In 1569, James II granted the land and buildings of Greyfriars to Sir Thomas. He set about demolishing the convent and built his state-of-the art castle, though town house might be a more appropriate descriptor. Building began in 1570 and was completed in 1582, using stone from the convent of course, a very convenient quarry, as well as stone from the former royal castle at Castledykes.

He didn't demolish the entire convent, however. With an eye to the future, he left the chancel of the convent church standing to serve as a mausoleum for him and his descendents. The windows of the castle stare blankly across the street at the restored Greyfriars Church where inside there is a very impressive memorial erected by their son, Robert, to Thomas and his second wife, Grissel (what a name!) Maxwell. When they married in 1584, she was sixteen – he was about forty. No comment.

Before we move on to the devoted son, Robert, it's worth mentioning in the passing, Thomas's ancestors. His father was killed at the Battle of Pinkie in 1547 when Thomas was a boy in short trousers. He was brought up by his uncle, Thomas MacLellan, known to history as the *Tutor of Bombie*. His grandfather we have already

Kirkcudbright

met – stabbed to death in the High Street of Edinburgh in 1526. His great-grandfather, Sir William, was one of the many *flowers of the forest* who fell at Flodden in 1513, along with the king, James IV – who incidentally, has the dubious honour of being the last monarch of these isles to be killed on the battlefield.

Imagine that, three generations and not one of them died peacefully in their beds! The cycle was broken by Sir Thomas, who turned up his toes in 1597. As I said above, his son and heir was Robert who became provost of Kirkcudbright when he was only fifteen! He rose and rose, serving as a gentleman of the bedchamber to both James VI and Charles I, culminating in his being given a knighthood in 1633 and being created 1st Lord Kirkcudbright.

You could say he made good in the end, but he was a bit of a lad when he was younger. He did time in Blackness Castle for affray in Kirkcudbright High Street and was fined 3,000 merks. Then, in the year he was made provost, he beat up the minister, Robert Glendinning at a kirk session. In the victim's own words: "[he] straick me upoun the head, face and utheris partis of my body, to the effusion on my blood at my neise in great quantitie." Sorry, your Reverend, I know it's not funny at all, but I can't help laughing at your quaint mode of expression and your spelling, especially.

The tearaway's dispute with the Glendinnings wasn't finished, however. In New Abbey, he shot George Glendinning and was detained in Edinburgh Castle and ordered to pay 1,000 merks. 3,000 for fighting in the streets but only 1,000 for trying to murder someone! Doesn't seem right somehow.

Everyone has heard of the colonisation of the New World in the early 17th century but I bet, and although it is much nearer to home, not so many people are familiar with the colonisation, or *Plantation of Ulster*, which was taking place at the same time.

After they lost the Nine Years' War against English rule in Ireland, the lands of the Gaelic chiefs were forfeit. The new landowners were required to be English-speaking, Protestant, and loyal to the king – from which it is easy to make the not-so-giant intellectual leap that the whole thing was conceived as a plan to control and anglicise Ulster, as well as sever the links between the Gaels there and the Gaels of the Scottish Highlands.

Our Robert was one of those landlords but it turned out to be a while elephant, as the cost of protecting his estates was prohibitive. He died in 1639 without a legitimate heir. During the tenure of his nephew and heir, Thomas, the 2nd Lord Kirkcudbright, the estates continued to haemorrhage money. It didn't help that he also sank a lot of money into supporting the Covenanters by forming a regiment in 1640 which left him a bit strapped for cash. He died in 1647.

John, the 3rd Lord Kirkcudbright, the cousin of the above and also a fervent Covenanter, raised a regiment against Cromwell's Parliamentarian army. He lost more than the battle of Lisnagarvey in 1649, when he lost the family fortunes too – at least as much as was left of them.

To cut a long story short, in 1741, the 7th Lord was working his fingers to the bone as a glover in Edinburgh, the castle having been previously taken over by the Maxwells. The following year, the contents were removed and the roof taken off. It's still roofless to this day but it's now in the care of Historic Environment Scotland, who are certainly doing just that if the vast amount of scaffolding is anything to go by.

You know well by now the structure of a tower house, but this shell has some interesting features. At the junction of a passage leading into the kitchen, you will see a curious stone pillar with a recess behind it. What was it for? Your guess is as good as mine. Meanwhile, in the kitchen, there's a cauldron and a noticeboard showing how to cook medieval style which is worth repeating in full: *First, place ye cuts of bacon in a bag, then over them place ye a wooden platform then add ye two clay pots: in one, put ye beef on birch twigs to make soup and in the other place ye a fowl, eggs and onion. Pack around them ye bags of cereals and beans. Now add ye water, cover and leave to simmer.*

Here's another interesting feature – the "laird's lug". Concealed in the fireplace in the great hall was a hole and at the other side was a chamber from where the laird could spy on and listen to what his guests were saying. Paranoid, or just being careful? I suppose there was no such thing as being too careful in those days.

Actually, Sir Thomas was a well-respected man and citizen who entertained no less a personage than the king himself when he came here in

1587. He also served as provost for more than twenty years until death removed him from office, though he did fall foul of the law on a couple of occasions when he wrongfully detained a ship and its cargo in the harbour, and on another occasion, when he bought some illicit wine. Who amongst us has never been subjected to temptation?

As for the castle's defences, the ground-level gun holes and the pistol holes higher up would not have repelled a serious attempt to take it. They were intended more as a deterrent to a would-be bunch of attackers – like a burglar alarm today is meant to make thieves think twice before breaking into your property.

After the MacLellans departed, the next significant event in Kirkcudbright's story was the coming of the railway in 1864 which brought flocks of visitors. Artists, in particular, were drawn to the attractive little town and its picturesque surroundings. The most celebrated of these was Edward Atkinson Hornel (1864-1933), who in his turn, brought in a whole lot more – a regular colony of them in fact. He, however, was not one of those whom the train brought, for the very good reason that he was already here. His boyhood home was No. 18, High Street.

His ancestors had been living in this area since the 1500s, but in 1856 his parents emigrated to Australia. After ten years in the Antipodes, they came back to Kirkcudbright when Edward was two. He attended Edinburgh College of Art before going on to study at the Antwerp Royal Academy of Fine Arts. Two years later, he came back to the family home, where, alas, due to the death of his father, he became head of a household which consisted of four unmarried sisters. Ye gods!

We're on the way now to see the house he bought, Broughton House; numbers 10 and 12 in the High Street, as a matter of fact. You can't say Kirkcudbright isn't compact and doesn't do its best to make it easy for visitors to take in the major attractions. If you are a film buff, you might care to look carefully at the alleyways at numbers 66, 82 and 96 – they all appeared in *The Wicker Man*.

Also on the High Street, at number 46, is the former home of Jessie M. King, one of the distaff side of the *Glasgow Boys*, aka the *Glasgow Girls*. She was born in Bearsden, near Glasgow, and was a protégée of the Glasgow School of Art. She married E.A. Taylor in 1908 and remarkably for her time, she kept her maiden name after marriage. She was inspired by *Art Nouveau* but did not follow it slavishly. She is mostly famous for her children's book illustrations, but she also designed fabric and jewellery.

House of E.A. Taylor and Jessie M. King, Kirkcudbright

Their former house is pretty, with the windowsills and doors picked out in a pastel shade of green. To the right is an *Art Noveau* door with a mosaic above it, informing the reader that she and her husband lived and worked there. And so they did from 1915 until her death in 1949 aged 74.

Through the alleyway beneath the plaque are some artists' cottages. This is the Greengate Close and it was while he was living in the thinly-disguised Bluegate Close that the fictional character, Lord Peter Wimsey, first heard of the death of an artist whose murder he goes on to investigate. The six most likely suspects were artists living in Kirkcudbright or nearby Gatehouse of Fleet. As the author, Dorothy M. Sayers, said in the preface of *Five Red Herrings*: "All the places are real places... all the landscapes are correct, except that I have run up a few new houses here and there."

Out of curiosity, we take a stroll down it, past picturesque cottages, and find ourselves in the strangest garden we've ever seen. There are a couple of skeletons made out of scrap iron with the teeth ingeniously made out of a motorbike chain; a tumbledown shed with an armchair, and vegetation creeping its way in through the walls and ceiling; while on the grass, empty picture frames set on easels have been randomly scattered about.

Dorothy and her husband stayed at the Anwoth Hotel in Gatehouse of Fleet in 1928 before renting a studio in the High Street here next door to the artist Charles Oppenheimer (1875-1961) who lived at number 14. He was born in Manchester but came to Kirkcudbright at the turn of the century, fell in love with the place and stayed and painted it, many, many times. I like his painting a lot, but what I like best of all are his illustrations of Keats' *St Agnes Eve* which transform it into a medieval illuminated manuscript.

You can't miss Hornel's Broughton House, set back from the street and most decidedly pink. If it were not for that striking colour, you wouldn't connect the Georgian frontage of No.10 with the cube of No.12. The house is much more attractive from the rear, and not just because of the garden with its luxuriant foliage, but because of the four-storey round tower at the right-hand side. It's not often that the backside of any building, person, animal, vegetable or object can be said to be its best feature, but in this case it is.

Hornel bought the house in 1901 for £400 which he raised from the sale of a painting (nice work if you can get it), and here he stayed with his sister Elizabeth, known as "Tizzie", until his death in 1933. It was a house of many parts. As well as being his home, it was his studio, gallery and library. At the time of his death, it consisted of 15,000 volumes. It was intended as a service to the community: a library for the locals about the area, and Burns, who was, after all, an adopted Gallovidian. A goodly number of them are displayed in the room to the left of the entrance.

The house was built in 1734 by Thomas Mirrie, a local mason, on the site of an earlier tenement building. It was Alexander Murray, provost, laird and MP, who expanded it in 1740, by buying number 12. After that, it became the *des res* for the great and the good of Kirkcudbright, including ministers, lairds and the 5th Earl of Selkirk, no less. (It was his father who was inconsiderately absent from home when John Paul Jones' men came to take him hostage.)

Hornel made several alterations to the house, notably the studio designed by the Glasgow architect John Keppie in 1901 and the gallery, in 1910, by the same man. It's very impressive because of its great length, gleaming mahogany, reproduction Parthenon frieze and elaborate stone fireplace. What you can't see, because it's covered by a carpet, is the trapdoor through which paintings were brought up from the studio and lowered again to be taken out of the house after they were sold. What you *can* see are a good number of Hornel's paintings which were unsold at the time of his death, while in the studio below, are several which are unfinished.

Styles come and go but Hornel's art remained eminently appealing to the general public, although his style did change and evolve. None of this new-fangled modernist nonsense for him. In the 1880s, along with his friend, George Henry, they became members of an artistic fraternity dubbed the *Glasgow Boys.* Sometimes referred to as the *Scottish Impressionists,* they were interested in the interplay between light and shade. Their subjects were realistic and painted in the great outdoors in order to portray nature as realistically as possible, using free and wide brush strokes.

In 1893/4, Hornel, along with Henry, spent a year-and-a-half in Japan, which greatly influenced his art. (A kimono is displayed in the house.) He also travelled to exotic places such as Ceylon, Burma, Singapore and Hong Kong, as well as back to the land of his birth – Australia – all of which is reflected in his art.

Eventually, he moved away from rustic naturalism to a more decorative style using local young girls as models. He painted them in flower gardens, in woods or on the beach, using photography to help him.

It's unusual for an artist to be appreciated in his lifetime – think Vincent van Gogh for a start – but Hornel was doing very nicely thank you very much, with exhibitions in the United States, Venice, Vienna and St Petersburg, as well as Scotland, naturally. In 1920, he drew up a trust deed by which, after his and Tizzie's deaths, the house was to become an art gallery as well as a library for the town.

Tizzie died in 1950 and the trustees maintained the house until 1997, when they handed it over to the National Trust who spent eight years (and a lot of money, you imagine) on restoring and refurbishing it. And a fine job they have made of it too. As well as the studio and the gallery, you can visit the hall, dining room and library, as well as the cellars, not forgetting the garden which Hornel designed himself, dividing it into various "rooms" and where the Japanese influence can be seen again.

And so we take our leave of Kirkcudbright's most famous artist of which he was just one of many. And still they come to this very day.

Is there another Hornel amongst them? Who can say? Only time can tell.

Chapter Thirty

Kirkcudbright: The Murderer and the Gypsy King

I T'S not far from here to the harbour so we wander down to see what Daniel Defoe was banging on about. He has a point, at least at the time of our visit. It looks a more suitable subject for a painting than a place for fishing boats to tie up at the moment, but that's probably because they are out at sea still. Believe it or not, but the harbour is the fifth busiest fishing port in Scotland!

We are heading now to the Stewartry Museum in St Mary's Street. For once, we have a little bit of a walk to this attraction. It's easy to recognise with its fairy-tale turrets at each corner and portico with battlements. The museum began in 1829 as the brainchild of a few local enthusiasts and was situated on the top floor of the town hall. When the collection outgrew its premises, it moved to its present location in 1893.

Two storeys, with a gallery running round the top floor, reflect the natural and human history of the area. There are more stuffed birds than you can shake a shooting stick at, as well as the six-inch "siller gun" which James IV presented to Thomas MacLellan in 1587 to award as the prize in an annual shooting competition. It is said to be the oldest surviving sporting trophy in the UK.

Like the Dalbeattie Museum, it is chock-full of exhibits from cup-and-ring slabs from a local farm, to works of art by local artists including Jessie M. King, and everything else imaginable in between. I can't say I care for the stuffed birds too much – too much death, some of them posed in grisly depictions of a kill – nature red in beak and claw. For me, the star of the show, the jewel in the crown, and that's just what it looks like – a giant multi-faceted diamond – is the lens from Little Ross Lighthouse.

It was built by a French company, Barbier, Benard et Turenne in 1896, while the lighthouse, you will not be surprised to hear, was built by one of the

Stewartry Museum, Kirkcudbright

Stevensons – Alan, actually – in 1843. It stands at the mouth of Kirkcudbright Bay and is 72 feet high. In the 1900s, it was home to the head keeper, his underling, and their families – a total of sixteen souls. They had their own dairy and piggery, so they had to be farmers and butchers as well. It was a lonely life and would not have suited everyone.

In August 1960, David Collin and his father visited the island intending to have a picnic, when they made a terrible discovery. It's a tale which has much of W.W. Gibson's narrative poem *Flannan Isle* about it. When they arrived, they were surprised to find there was no sign of the keepers. Although it didn't seem likely, they assumed they must still be asleep after their night shift. Then they heard a phone ring but no-one answered. Even more curious. They cautiously entered the first cottage – the head keeper's – and found everything shipshape and in apple-pie order. A budgie was chirping happily in its cage. There was no other sign of life.

Then Mr Collin went into the other cottage and found, what at first sight, he thought was a man lying ill in bed. He was wearing his pyjamas and a towel was partly covering his face. His name was Hugh Clark and it didn't take Mr Collin long to discover he was most definitely sleeping the longest sleep of all. He had been shot in the head at close range by a .22 rifle. Of his fellow keeper, Robert Dickson, there was no sign. They were relief keepers for the head keeper who was on holiday, getting back to civilisation for a while.

It was not the sort of crime that the police needed the help of Poirot to crack. Dickson was swiftly apprehended in Yorkshire, and later faced trial at Dumfries High Court. He offered a plea of insanity but nevertheless was condemned to death. It was later commuted to life imprisonment but Dickson took his own life in jail, so it was the same in the end.

As for the lighthouse, it was automated in 1961, and the 29-acre island put up for sale in July 2017. The properties included a six-bedroomed B-listed cottage, three B-listed ruinous barns (with potential) and a courtyard. To get to it, you would need your own boat or helicopter. Unfortunately, if you like the sound of owning your own little Scottish island, it has been sold – so I'm told.

• • •

It's a lot easier to get to our next destination, by car, up the hill to the cemetery of St Cuthbert's. My heart sank at the sight of the hillside bristling with all those tombstones like a beard of red stubble. How on earth was I going to find the one I sought out of all that – and where to start?

In the event, it turned out to be surprisingly easy. I came across a noticeboard featuring the graves of residents well known in their day. The one I wanted lay directly facing it just a few yards away.

The headstone is not very tall, but is easily identified because it looks so fresh and pink and new. The lettering has been picked out with black paint so it is eminently easy to read, despite the date of when the one lying beneath shuffled off the mortal coil. This is what it says:

The Remains of
WILLIAM MARSHALL,
Tinker, who died,
28th Novr 1792,
at the advanced age of
120 Years.

And if you think that age is remarkable, "you ain't heard nothin' yet," as Al Jolson so memorably predicted in *The Jazz Singer*. You may well suspend your disbelief when you hear the details of his colourful life and might conclude fact has been replaced with myth and legend. I couldn't disagree.

In his extremely long introduction to *Guy Mannering*, Sir Walter Scott tells us that Billy, as he was more commonly called, was born in Kirkmichael (others say he was born in Ayrshire) "about the year 1671". He was variously styled "The King of the Gypsies", the "Caird of Barullion" and "King of the Randies". It may be a bit *passé* these days, but "randy" in the days of my youth, was the term given to young men who always had sex on their minds. Of course I was never called that as it never applied to me, but it certainly seems to have fitted Billy to perfection. He claimed to have been married seventeen times and sired countless children. Well, if you keep on living to that sort of age and don't keep it in your trousers, that sort of thing can happen.

He must have felt a bit like the *Old Woman who Lived in a Shoe* when it came to finding names for all his progeny. He even claimed to have fathered four illegitimate children after he turned one hundred. There is hope for sprightly septuagenarians yet. One of his wives, Flora, is said to have been the inspiration for Meg Merilees in *Guy Mannering*, though in his introduction,

Scott attributes it to another lady before going on to admit the lady in his book may not have actually existed. More a myth than a Mrs Marshall, then.

As for Billy's second title, "Caird of Barullion", Barullion is a range of hills in Wigtownshire, apparently. Really? Is that another myth? I can't find them thar hills on Google, or in an atlas either. *Caird* comes from the Scots Gaelic meaning a "craftsman". That is a fact. In popular Scots usage, the word has suffered some devaluation and come to mean an itinerant tinker (a mender of pots and pans), or gypsy.

That word is actually an exonym – a name given by foreigners to a place or people, different to what they, themselves call it. "Gypsy" was the name given to the Romani or Roma people who, in medieval times, were believed to be itinerant Egyptians, hence the abbreviation to "gypsy". Today it is a word loaded with prejudice, distrust and suspicion – but it was not always so.

The first recorded instance of "Egyptians" in Scotland was in 1492 during the reign of James IV where they enjoyed his favour and protection. And so they did under successive monarchs until 1571, when under a law of stringency, anyone found guilty of being a gypsy was hanged, drowned or deported. Usually it was the fate of women to be dispatched by the watery method, just like the way they disposed of witches. In 1579, a refinement to the punishment decreed that the "idle peopil calling themselves Egyptians" should be nailed to a tree by the ears. Charming!

When he was not making babies, Marshall was many things: soldier, smuggler, robber and murderer. He was also a boxer. If you are one of those who think boxing is some sort form of barbaric sport that should be banned, then think again. It is a pretty tame thing nowadays compared to the sort of sport Marshall indulged in long before the days of the Marquess of Queensberry's rules which did not come into being until 1867, three-quarters of a century after Marshall's death. In his day, it was a bare-fisted affair and anything, and everything, was allowed. You could pull your opponent's hair, gouge his eyes, head-butt him, kick him and grapple with him.

As a soldier, he fought for the Duke of Malborough and William of Orange. But a soldier's life was not for him, nor was a sailor's. He was a serial army-deserter and ran away from the navy three times too. He was his own man.

It's not a title that has been accredited to him, but I would describe Marshall as a sort of latter-day Robin Hood, a champion of the poor against the landed gentry. In an event that foreshadowed the worst excesses of the Highland Clearances a century later, the Gallovidian tenants lost their livelihoods and their homes as the landlords enclosed massive tracts of land to fatten-up cattle for the English market. While the lairds got richer and richer, the peasants got poorer and poorer.

One obvious solution to this unacceptable state of affairs from the peasants' point of view was to knock down the dykes. These peasant militants came to be known as the *Levellers*. They gained a lot of support from the general public, even from the king himself, George I. Billy Marshall also espoused their cause. In the summer of 1723, and putting his army training to use, he organised the peasants, who, armed with scythes and pitchforks, set about tearing down, or levelling the dykes.

The largest action against the dykes took place in four days in May when a thousand Levellers destroyed two miles of dykes built by Sir Basil Hamilton of Baldoon and St Mary's Isle. Two hundred Levellers were arrested but only a handful ended up in Kirkcudbright for trial. The rest escaped, or were allowed to escape.

In the end, no criminal charges were made. The twenty-three captives faced civil action raised by Hamilton. He won his case but since only two were property owners, there was precious little in the way of compensation. And that is how the short-lived and bloodless Galloway Levellers' Revolt came to an end.

On the other hand, Marshall's men, with his infantry and cavalry, were a force to be reckoned with. But they were no match for the tinkers of Argyll. Seeking to extend his "kingdom" from Dumfries to the other side of the River Doon, Marshall was defeated by them at Newtown-of-Ayr in 1712. Never again, in his long life, did he entertain such expansionist plans.

The back of the headstone is very curious. I suppose you could call it Billy's coat of arms. A pair of long-handled spoons crossed, probably represent horn spoons, a traditional gypsy occupation, the making thereof. Superstitiously, we cross our fingers for good luck and it's possible that the idea behind the crossed spoons is King Billy's wish that his subjects would never go hungry. Coins on the top of the stone were probably placed there by visitors for good luck too, or possibly a donation for anyone down on his luck and hungry.

Above the crossed spoons is a very fine pair of ram's horns. They might represent Aries, the ram, which symbolises leadership and strength, the very sort of thing that Billy represented. On the other hand, it might be, as Scott said in his introduction to *Guy Mannering*, the horns of a *tup* – an uncastrated ram. Born to breed.

Seems to me either interpretation would be appropriate.

Chapter Thirty-One

Twynholm and Tongland: A Tale of Two Motorists

IF you are interested in prehistory, you might consider a little detour on the B727 along the shores of Kirkcudbright Bay to Borgue. Near there you will find Castle Haven, an Iron Age hill fort, or dun, from the 8th and 9th centuries. During reconstruction in 1905, as well as uncovering some human bones, worked stone and pottery from the early Iron Age, archaeologists found a blue-and-white glass bead, some bronze spiral rings and the remains of a medieval brooch – evidence that this place had been occupied for centuries.

Iron Age hill forts are pretty thick on the ground in this part of the world but this is unusual in being D-shaped, where the straight line runs parallel with the cliff. The courtyard measured sixty feet by forty. It was protected by inner and outer walls, the inner being up to fifteen feet thick while those on the outside were thinner. There were two entrances, one at the NE and one at the SW, the latter leading down to a small bay where the inhabitants would have harboured their boats.

As for the village, Borgue first appears in the records in 1469. The name comes from the Old Norse *borg* meaning "stronghold". No doubt they had the ancient fort in mind.

According to legend, a boy who used to live here consorted with the fairies. He would disappear for days but would not say where he had been, or perhaps he couldn't remember. The boy's grandfather consulted the local priest, who gave him a cross to tie round the boy's neck. That did it: the boy was never away with the fairies again. But there was a price to pay. The grandfather was hauled before the church elders, who banished him from the kirk for resorting to such a "papist trick".

We're heading west to Gatehouse of Fleet, but before that, we take another little detour. We're following the Dee on the A762 to Tywnholm only a couple of miles out of town to the north. It's another whitewashed little village that has been able to get back to sleep after it was bypassed by the A75 in 1973. The name might come from the Celtic *tywn* meaning a bank or hillock and *hame* Saxon for "dwelling", or it might be from the Scots meaning "between the river banks". Whatever the case may be, there were two mills here on the banks of the Dee in the sixteenth century.

Edward I and his army camped here waiting for provisions. In December 2013, two metal-detector enthusiasts uncovered a hoard of 300 silver coins dating from 1249 to 1325, covering the reigns of the Scottish kings Alexander III and John Balliol and the English Edwards, One, Two and Three. That tells you that it was not Edward I who stashed the loot.

Small though it is, Twynholm has produced a famous son – David Coulthard, the F1 racing driver, born in 1971. Between 1994 and 2008, he won thirteen Grand Prix. In 2008, he finished runner-up in the Race of Champions and went one better in 2014 when he won the Drivers' Cup. Since he hung up his crash helmet, he has become a motor-racing pundit.

The road forks at Twynford and after a short distance, the A711 takes us to Tongland. The name might send a shiver down the spine of readers of a certain vintage. In the 1960s, it was the name given to the Calton area of Glasgow which was ruled by a notorious gang of teenage thugs who called themselves the "Tongs". You knew you were entering their territory when you saw "Tongs Ya Bass" daubed on walls and other handy surfaces. The last two words are short for "you bastard" while the first is said to derive from the film *The Terror of the Tongs*, a low-budget Hammer horror film. Some have argued that "Ya Bass" is a corruption of the Gaelic war cry *aigh bas* – battle or die. Believe that if you like, but to my certain knowledge the Gaelic is not widely spoken in the housing estates of Glasgow.

It should really be "Tungland" from the Norse *tunga*, meaning "a strip of land", the Vikings having come here for a bit of robbing, raping and pillaging before they began to settle down and became domesticated. It stands on the bank of the Dee which was crossed by Telford's single-span bridge in 1806.

The Doon and Old Fort, West of Twynholm

In the 1930s, the river was dammed as part of a hydro-electric scheme, the first large-scale integrated complex to be built in Britain for the purposes of generating electricity. It was completed in 1936 at the cost of £3 million. I have to say, with its numerous rivers and lochs and average rainfall of 40-60 inches a year, this part of Scotland was supremely equipped for this engineering marvel.

It consists of six power stations and eight dams, as well as a network of tunnels, aqueducts and pipelines. The nerve centre is Glenlee near St John's Town of Dalry, from which the other stations can be operated remotely. Isn't that an amazing thing!

You can visit the power station and see the control room just as it was in the 1930s, as well as the turbine room. It's especially geared towards kids, with video presentations on how this cleaner form of energy is produced. You can also walk across the breadth of the 950-foot dam.

If you are lucky, you might see the salmon leap up the ladder that was built to let them get back to the ancestral breeding grounds, and where instinct dictates they should return to spawn and to die. It's not hard to imagine what the fishy brain thinks of this new scheme. As if swimming halfway across the Atlantic were not enough, to be faced with a mighty obstacle like this at the end of your life is, frankly, a step-ladder too far.

Of the Abbey where James IV stayed in 1455 during his siege of Threave Castle, next to nothing remains; only a rounded arch in the north wall of the old parish church, itself in a pretty bad state. It was founded in 1218 by Alan of Galloway, for the Premonstratensian Order. In its day, it was the equal of any other abbey in Galloway – indeed, it was said to have the tallest spire of them all and was still standing in 1684. I don't have to tell you what happened to all the stone, but I shall anyway. It went into the construction of the old Tongland Bridge, the paper and grain mills, and the manse.

The first abbot was Caducan, the son of Lord Fergus. He died not long after the Battle of Largs, and was buried before the high altar in the abbey. The most interesting abbot was an Italian named John Damian who was appointed by James IV in 1504. In 1507, he proudly boasted that he could fly to France and be there before the king's messengers, who had recently departed. His bluff was called. He had a pair of wings made and jumped off the walls of Stirling Castle, only to break a leg. He was lucky he landed in a dung heap, or it could have been much worse. He blamed the makers of the wings for using the wrong kind of feathers: *some hen fedderis in the wingis quhilk yarnit for and covet the mydding not the skyis.* How appropriate, therefore, that he landed where he did. The Scots *makar*, William Dunbar, satirised the event in his poem *The Fenyeit [False] Friar of Tungland.*

It sounds a tall tale, but it is true nevertheless. Similarly, you may think it rather far-fetched when I tell you this little place, in the depths of the Galloway countryside, produced a brand of motorcar from 1921-23.

The driving force behind this remarkable factory was Dorothée Pullinger. She was born in 1894, near Dieppe in Normandy, the eldest of eleven children to Thomas, the managing director of Arrol-Johnston, Scotland's first and largest maker of automobiles.

The family came to England when she was eight. After she left school, she got a job as a draughtsperson at the Paisley works of Arrol-Johnston. In 1914, she applied to become a member of the Institute of Automobile Engineers but was rejected on the grounds that "the word person means a man, not a woman". After the outbreak of WWI, she was appointed the Lady Supervisor of the 7,000-strong women workforce at the Vickers munition works at Barrow-in-Furness.

The factory at Tongland originally made aero engines during the war and after it was over, Dorothée persuaded her father to keep the factory open to provide employment for the local women. Indeed, the workforce did consist mainly of women, hence their slogan "built by ladies for those of their own sex". They wore a company badge in the suffragette colours of green and purple.

It had an engineering college and an apprenticeship course. And get this – the course lasted three years instead of the usual five at the parent company, because the weaker sex were found to be quicker on the uptake than the male of the species. So put that in your pipe and smoke it, boys!

Dorothée designed and adapted an existing Arrol-Johnston car to create a "female" version, which they called the "Galloway 10/20". Lighter and smaller than the "male", it included a rear-view mirror (the first on any car); better storage (very important for the shopping); a better line of vision (achieved by simply raising the height of the driver's seat so the lady could look *over* the steering wheel rather that through it); and finally moving the handbrake from where it was situated, practically under the dashboard in the male version, to where it is in most cars today.

About 406 cars were produced in Tongland until 1923 when the manufacture was transferred to Heathhall in Dumfries. Not surprisingly, Dorothée was a keen motorist. In 1924, she won the Cup in the Scottish Six-Day Motor Trials driving one of her Galloways.

In 1925, a larger version, the Galloway 12, was introduced. It remained in production until 1928. They retailed between £325-£360 depending on body style – expensive compared to an Austin or Morris. In total, it's estimated 4,000

Galloways were built before the Depression of 1929 took effect and there wasn't enough demand to make it viable.

So much for the rise and fall of the Galloway car. But what about Dorothée? What happened to her?

In 1919, she founded the Women's Engineering Society. The following year, she was awarded a MBE for her war work, and in 1923 she was finally accepted as a member of the Institute of Automobile Engineers. Better late than never.

She married in 1924 and had two children who were born in 1926 and 1931, respectively. In 1928, she moved to Croydon with her husband and set up a steam laundry business using machinery imported from the United States. The business grew to seventeen shops.

During WWII, she was the only woman appointed to the Industrial Panel of the Ministry of Production, whose remit was to recruit women for the munitions factories. The Panel produced a report in 1944 – *Looking Ahead: Work and the Future of British Industry.*

In 1947, she moved to Guernsey and three years later, she set up *Normandie Laundries.* She died on the island in 1986, aged 92. Apparently in her old age, she could be seen driving around Guernsey in one of her Galloways in the sort of style that David Coulthard would recognise from his racing days.

What a pioneering woman she was! In 2012, she was inducted into the Scottish Engineering Hall of Fame. Despite that, I don't think she is that famous. I confess I had never heard of her until now. She deserves to be much better known.

Let's hear it! Hip, hip, hooray for Dorothée!

Chapter Thirty-Two

Gatehouse of Fleet: The Artists, the Lost Kingdom and the Gardens

BACK in *our* car, we leave the A75 again and take the B727 to visit the picturesque town of Gatehouse of Fleet. You can certainly imagine artists hanging about here now that the A75, the major east-west artery to Ireland with its endless stream of juggernauts bound to and from Stranraer, bypasses it to the north, thus restoring a certain amount of peace and tranquillity.

Not only did the artists flock here but Gatehouse also grew its own. This is the birthplace of the remarkable Faed family: John (1819-1902), James (1821-1911), and Thomas (1826-1900).

John was prolific, producing about 280 paintings of religious, literary and historical scenes, the bulk of which were hung in the Royal Scottish Academy and the Royal Academy in London. He was also very popular in the United States.

James, as a boy, showed talent as an engineer. After their father's death in 1864, however, he joined his brothers in Edinburgh and began painting landscapes, miniatures and portraits in both oils and watercolours. They were received with great acclaim. After an introduction to the mezzotinter John Bonnar, the engineering side of his talents came to the fore again and he took up engraving for the next fifty years, accepting his last commission at eighty years old.

As for Thomas, he was elected an Associate of the Royal Scottish Academy in 1849. He went to London in 1852 and was elected an Associate of the Royal Academy in 1861 and became a full-blown Academian in 1864.

What a talented family! In the Old Mill on the Fleet Visitor Centre, a room is named after them. As well as featuring a huge painting executed by John, the room tells the life and times of Gatehouse. The first thing you see when you enter the centre is a massive model of the town shortly after it came into being. It was a planned town with a wide, straight main street with very long, narrow back gardens looking very much like that former system of subsistence farming known as "run rigs". Compare that with the pocket handkerchief sort of "garden" that modern builders allocate to houses today.

The roots of the town go back to the 1760s when John Murray of Broughton built a village to house the workers on his Cally estate. The old inn or "gait-house" (from the Old Norse *gait* meaning "road") that had been there since the building of a wooden bridge across the Fleet was expanded and renamed the "Murray Arms". A tannery was built, as was a brewery, a foundry, a brick works, a boat yard and a port. In 1785, two water-powered cotton mills arrived, followed sometime later, by a third mill. Collectively, they employed 500 people – almost half of the town's population.

In 1825, Alexander of Broughton constructed a canal to facilitate river traffic along the Fleet with the result that Port McAdam near Cardoness Castle became pretty busy with as many as 150 ships docking annually. In fact, at its peak, during the first half of the 19th century, Gatehouse was such a hive of industry that it was dubbed the "Glasgow of the South". Not what you might have expected for such a small town in such a rural setting.

But the times they were a-changing. Because of its remoteness, Gatehouse could not compete with the industrial boom going in cities such as Glasgow. While their populations increased exponentially, that of Gatehouse declined. Between 1850 and 1900, its population dwindled from 1,750 to about a 1,000. That's a significant drop for a small place. The Portpatrick Railway, which was built in 1861, may have stemmed the flow, but the station was a six-mile, jolting horse-and-carriage journey away.

Over the years, the mills closed and re-opened, producing different products, but now there is only one, the lower one of the original two – a multi-purpose building with a café and deli on the ground floor, exhibition rooms on the middle and a second-hand bookshop on the top.

The lairds' "little" house in the country is now the Cally Palace Hotel, situated a little out of town to the south, while at the western end of the bridge, the Ship Inn is a reminder of the town's shipbuilding past. It was formerly known as the Anwoth Hotel and it was here that Dorothy Sayers wrote *The Five Red Herrings*, published in 1931. As a matter of fact, it is dedicated to mine host, Joe Dignam, "the kindest of landlords".

The murder victim, Campbell, the kind of person who was all the better for a good killing, lived in Gatehouse, but his body was found in a burn near Kirkcudbright. As the title suggests, there are five suspects, but of course, only one was the real killer. As I mentioned earlier, Gatehouse features prominently in the book, and also in the BBC TV adaption starring Ian Carmichael. A number of locations also appeared in *The Wicker Man*. If you are a film buff, you will know where they are.

Gatehouse of Fleet

The Five Red Herrings is of course, a made-up mystery and the solution to that I will leave you to find out for yourself, but on a hill not so far away called "Trusty's Hill" – just twenty minutes or so by foot from the town centre – clues were found which went towards solving a mystery which has baffled scholars for generations: just where exactly was the kingdom of Rheged, and where was its stronghold?

Traditionally, it was thought to have been centred in Cumbria, but now there is fresh evidence to show it was not – that it was in Galloway. A series of information boards in the Centre tell the story. But be warned. To quote Winston Churchill, "It's a riddle wrapped in a mystery inside an enigma."

At Trusty's Hill, archaelogists unearthed Pictish symbols – a double disc and z-rod and a Pictish sea-beast and sword. To me, the beast, or monster, looks like a cross between a seahorse and a shrimp. I suppose scale determines if it's a monster or not and we have nothing with which to compare it. And it's a funny sort of sword that doesn't have a handle. I think it's more likely to be another sea creature of some sort, or a brooch or a pin. But what do I know? There is a third carving which is really rather comical. It's like a cartoon caterpillar's face with spirally antennae. Actually, those who *do* know about such things, think it's a piece of graffiti added later.

The first recorded instance of these carvings appeared in the *Statistical Account of Scotland* in 1794, but they weren't recognised for what they were. Although we know *now* what they are, the question is: what are they doing here, far, far away from the Pictish heartland in the northeast – foreign territory in fact? This land belonged to the Britons. And what do they mean anyway? And just who was "Trusty", after whom the hill was named?

It's unlikely we will ever decipher what the Pictish carvings mean since they have defied interpretation for a millennium. The Picts moved in mysterious ways. As for "Trusty", it might come from "Tristram" but who *he* was, who knows?

Only two other instances of Pictish carved stones outwith Pictland have been found – one is Din Eidyn, better known as the volcanic plug that Edinburgh Castle sits on, formerly the capital of the Gododdin, the Britons of east Scotland. The other is Dunadd, the royal capital of Dalriada, in present-day Argyll and Bute.

Trusty's Hill and Dunadd have certain similarities. The carvings, in both cases, are carved into the living rock. In Dunadd, on one side of the entrance, the stone with the carving of a boar was where they crowned their kings. On the other side, there was a deep basin for the anointing of the crowned head. At Trusty's Hill, the same set-up applies, so it seems reasonable to conclude Trusty's Hill must likewise have been a royal stronghold.

The layout of both places was also similar. There was a fort at the top with a stone-and-timber rampart with lesser enclosures on the lower slopes following the natural defences of the crags. We also know from the animal bones that were found, the people who lived here ate beef (mainly), mutton and pork, as well as cereals. Clearly, they were having a wide and varied diet. Living off the fat of the land, might be another way to put it. More than that, they were skilled metalworkers.

The excavations of 2012 revealed jewellery that would have belonged to people of high rank, as well as decorations for horses' trappings. The pottery finds suggest these people were trading with the continent, probably through the funnel of Whithorn, and before they disappeared from the pages of history, were converted to Christianity by St Ninian's men.

So, if we add what we now know about Trusty's Hill to what we already knew about the Mote of Mark in Kippford, it looks increasingly likely that the stronghold of the long-lost kingdom of Rheged, like some other Camelot, has been found at last!

If that is one mystery solved, Gatehouse has another to offer – namely where was that anthem of Scottish nationalism, *Scots Wha Hae* written? The Murray Arms on the High Street boasts that not only did Burns sleep there in 1793, but also claims that this is where he composed it while on his tour of Galloway with his friend, John Syme. Syme's story, on the other hand, is that Burns composed it as they were riding from St Mary's Isle where they had been dining with Lord Selkirk (after whom the grace is named), to Kenmure. We know Burns was not unaccustomed to composing verses in his head while he was on horseback.

There is a third version as to the song's genesis. Burns was back in Dumfries on 2nd August and on, or about, 30th August, he sent a letter to Thomson with whom he was collaborating to write the words for the Scottish traditional songs Thomson was collecting. In it Burns tells him he had composed the verses during "yesternight's evening walk". The Murray Arms' claim therefore seems to be greatly exaggerated. But does it really matter? The song's the thing, as Hamlet didn't quite say.

There *is* something that Gatehouse can undisputedly lay claim to, however – the Cally Gardens. Its walled kitchen garden was created at enormous expense between 1765-70 to serve the *Big Hoose*. It's more than a hectare in size, and if that doesn't mean anything to you, just think bigger than the biggest football field permitted by FIFA, or slightly less than an international rugby football field. And if that *still* doesn't mean anything to you, then just think big.

A letter penned by the head gardener in 1848 gives a fascinating insight into the gardens in those days. Mr Pearson writes that nearly all the walls, fifteen feet high on average, were covered with neatly-trained fruit trees; two rows of vines 100 feet long and 20 broad; three peach houses 150 feet long; an orange and a camellia house 35 feet long and pineapple pits 100 feet long. Please remember where this is. This is Scotland, latitude a pip-squeak short of 55 degrees north. And that's not all. There were three acres of orchards and a large number of greenhouses. There would have to be in this climate.

Naturally such exoticism didn't come cheap. Just imagine how much it must have cost to build the walls alone! Then there were the wages of the gardeners. Six of them, six labourers earning about 10 shillings a week, and one boy on a third of that. And there were expenses too: seeds, coal, tools, nails, glass repairs and such like, not forgetting the garden horse that needed to be fed (although I suppose he did make a certain contribution towards his keep by way of fertiliser). It all amounted to £309 per annum. The dearest peaches in all of Scotland.

During WWII, 300 boys from Glasgow were evacuated here, where they "dug for victory" as the slogan of the time put it. When it was the turn of peace again, the rise and rise of mass production, made possible by mechanisation, plus imports from abroad, put the final nail in the coffin of the walled kitchen garden. It had had its day. Fresh fruit and vegetables were available for all in a way they had never been before.

The Gardens became a tree nursery for the Forestry Commission before being sold to a Mr Taylor, who produced cut flowers and fuschias. In 1987, enter Michael Wickenden who, after ten years' search, was on the lookout for the perfect location for his specialist nursery. The walled garden had a new lease of life.

Unfortunately, this was not to prove the case for Michael. He was many things: gardener, photographer, expert plant collector, explorer, traveller and trekker. What a man! Sadly, while trekking in Myanmar in October 2016, he was taken ill and died before he could be taken to hospital. He was only 61.

The nursery is a Grade II site, which means it will be preserved for others to enjoy for as long as the foreseeable future. Good luck to the new owner, Kevin Hughes.

Chapter Thirty-Three

Cardoness Castle and Anwoth Old Kirk: The Nasty Neighbours and the Rebel Reverend

WE stand in the carpark, looking up at it in awe. Cardoness Castle towers above us, a massive wall of stone. Once upon a time it would have looked even more impressive. The land we are standing on was reclaimed from the sea in 1824 when the mudflats were planted with grass. Half a century before that, the rocky outcrop on which the castle stands was a promontory jutting out into the bay.

The castle was built by the McCullochs towards the end of the 15th century. Gilbert McCulloch from the Machars of Wigtownshire acquired the estate by marrying the youngest daughter of the de Kerdenes family. A tragic tale attached to her is recounted by Sir Andrew Agnew in his *A History of the Hereditary Sheriffs of Galloway* (1864). She was his ninth daughter, and her charming father, in Henry VIII sort of style, told his wife that by God if she didn't produce a son this time, he'd drown her and their daughters and look for another wife.

That did the trick. She did produce a boy and great was the rejoicing. It was a cruel winter with a hard frost and the family went out onto the Black Loch for a bit of a knees-up. In a twist of fate that was even crueller, the ice gave way and the family were all drowned apart from the ninth daughter, who had stayed at home because she was too ill to attend the celebrations. She grew up to be the progenitor of the McCullochs of Cardoness, no strangers to dealing out cruelty themselves, as you shall see.

It was either Gilbert or his son, James, who built the castle. James was the neighbour from hell, especially as far as the Gordons were concerned. He was outlawed twice, in 1471 and 1481, and was involved in no fewer than five land-litigation disputes. He married his only daughter to Alexander MacLellan,

Cardoness Castle

who it was said, was a "natural idiot". No greater love hath a man's greed for land and a power than he giveth his only begotten daughter in marriage to a man like that. Alexander died in 1500.

The bad genes were passed on to his son, Ninian, who was tried for stealing "1,500 beasts" from his widowed stepmother. At least he kept this crime in the family. He died in 1509, possibly executed for his crimes, such as charging illegal rents from the local farmers.

He left behind a young son, Thomas. His uncle, Sir Alexander (Sande), became his guardian. He moved in high circles. A personal friend of James IV, he was keeper of Linlithgow Palace as well as keeper of the royal falcons. He once won the princely sum of 35 shillings from the king in an archery contest. He carried on the family tradition of being a nasty neighbour and was twice convicted for violence against them, only for the convictions to be quashed by the king. It's good to have friends with influence. They both got their comeuppances, however, in 1513 when they were killed at the Battle of Flodden.

Thomas died in 1516 and was succeeded by his brother Alexander, also known as the "Cutlar McCulloch". He led an attack on the Isle of Man as revenge for one made on Galloway by Lord Derby in 1507. He found this a very lucrative form of income, and raided the Isle many more times in the 1530s. From these raids arose the following prayer from the Manxmen. It comes trippingly off the tongue:

God keep the good corn, the sheep, and the bullock
From Satan, from sin, and from Cutlar McCullock.

During the time of tension between the neighbouring countries of England and Scotland, never mind the McCullochs' neighbours, at some time between 1563-65, Elizabeth I sent a spy to Cardoness to know what she would be up against should it come to an invasion. He reported: *Cardines Towre...is nyne foote thick of the wall, without bermeking, and withoute battling.* He means a *barmkin* and battlements respectively. (Actually he may not have been correct about the *barmkin*, the fortified wall around the tower.) He goes on: *At full sea, boates of eight tonnes may come under the wall.*

• • •

It was calculated that it would take a force of 200 men to take the castle and it would have to be taken from the landward side. Luckily for the McCullochs, who were supporters of Mary, Queen of Scots, the invasion never came and they could keep on harassing the neighbours – but not for much longer in the grand scheme of things.

These disputes, along with William McCulloch's financial mismanagement, drained the family's resources. In 1622, the estate was mortgaged, and in 1628, handed over to their enemy, John Gordon of Upper Ardwall, who continued to live in his more comfortable residence at Bush o' Bield, near Anwoth. But that wasn't the end of Cardoness and the McCullochs. Not quite. Not yet. They hated to see the castle lying empty, and less than forty years later, another Alexander McCulloch moved back in. In 1668, he was imprisoned for allegedly dragging Gordon's widow from her sickbed and flinging her on a dung heap.

In 1684, his son, Sir Godfrey McCulloch, shot William Gordon in the leg who died two days later from an infection. Godfrey fled to France but secretly returned in 1694, living under the alias of "Mr Johnstoun", but one day he was recognised as he attended a service in St Giles. Funny that. I wouldn't have put him down as a churchgoer. He was arrested and beheaded in 1697. He was one of the last to have the honour of losing his head to the "Maiden", but by no means the last man to lose his head over a maiden.

Three centuries before the French Revolution, which guillotined aristocrats left, right and centre, the Maiden was a guillotine commissioned in 1564 by the Provost and Magistrates of Edinburgh as a "humane" method of execution. Compared to the sword, which the executioner frequently messed up, it was. It was supposedly recommended to the Edinburgh authorities by James Douglas, 4th Earl of Morton, Regent of Scotland and mortal enemy of Mary, Queen of Scots. Ironically, he met his own death under the blade of the Maiden in 1581.

Two astonishing legends appertain to Godfrey's death. One, related by Sir Walter Scott, says he was saved by a gnome to whom he had earlier done a good turn and was spirited away, never to be seen again. Another story goes that after his decapitation, he ran 100 yards down the Royal Mile before he ran out off puff. You can't get too more differing stories than that, and both equally unbelievable.

His death marked the end of the road for Cardoness and the McCullochs. The Castle and the estate were forfeited and many of the family went to America. After that, it had several owners: Gordons, Maxwells, Stewarts,

Murrays and back to the Maxwells again, until it eventually passed into the care of the state in 1927. Now it's cared for by Historic Environment Scotland.

The castle is said to be haunted. Five sightings of ghostly apparitions have been reported, including a lady in the hall. Another story goes that someone was hanged in the vicinity of the prison and his ghost hangs about the place. Well, it would, wouldn't it?

The visitor centre is located in a converted cottage, where it's worth looking closely at a model which shows you what the castle was like in its prime. It is six storeys high and accessed by a massive stone ramp. The landward side – the weak side, to the north – is practically featureless. Note the inverted-keyhole gunholes. This is almost as good as a birth certificate in determining the date the castle was constructed. They were built to accommodate the latest weapon of man's destruction – the firearm. Some sixty years later it gave way to the horizontal letterbox type.

The interior of the castle, or tower house, if you prefer, follows the usual formula with some differences. The entrance is by a wooden door that once had a stout wooden beam behind it, then a little further in, a barred iron gate or *yett,* like a portcullis. And that's not all. An unwelcome visitor, should he get that far, would then be confronted with, above his head, the "murder hole" through which defenders could drop nasty things on them. This is not a common feature in Scottish castles and a sure sign that the McCulloch who built this was not merely building for show like Orchardton Tower or MacLellan Castle. He was expecting trouble. That said, the hole probably had another use – a handy way of lifting and lowering goods instead of lugging them up narrow and twisting spiral stairs.

The ground floor consists of a guardroom and a large stone-vaulted cellar with more storage space above. To the left is the guardroom. Note the two circular recesses which once would have contained grain. So says the notice, engraved in iron. So that must be true then. Frankly, I don't believe it. Why here and why so small a container? Another suggestion is that one held water or was a pickling tub while the other was a slop sink. Take your pick.

Cardoness Castle (Interior)

Ascending the spiral stair, we come to a small room. Look at the floor and you will see the trapdoor for the murder hole and the split-level prison. The upper one, with its small window and latrine, is luxurious compared to the pit below where prisoners were thrown into the pitch black and left to die of thirst and starvation with little ventilation. Horrible though the McCullochs were, they were not the inventors of this inhumane method of despatching their enemies by this slow-release to death, nor were they only ones to employ such evil punishments, it has to be said.

Straight ahead are two doorways, obviously two rooms once, but the dividing wall has gone long ago so it doesn't matter which you choose. They were only storage rooms; no point in exhausting your imagination by imagining what these rooms looked like in the past. Reserve that for the floor above.

This is the grand hall, one large room where more private functions took place, as opposed to the larger outer hall in the courtyard. We know it would have been very posh because of the massive fireplace (the mantelpiece is missing), with, on one side, the ornate buffet (a cupboard for the display of the best silverware), and on the other, the much plainer and functional *sautbox* built into the wall. The best place to keep salt dry – near the fire, naturally.

Now is the time to use your imagination. Imagine these cold, bare, stone walls covered in plaster, bedecked with tapestries. Note how deep the window seats are, reflecting just how thick the walls are, and now imagine the blank windows with wooden shutters on the bottom half and glazed on the top. Then lift your eyes to where no ceiling exists now and imagine one of painted wood. Now come back down to the hearth again and imagine that fireplace burning merrily with logs, from which the sweet smell of wood smoke fills the room. Lastly, imagine the room filled with the sound of mirth and laughter and the chatter of lively conversation from the guests dining around the board, the seating arranged like wedding meals today, according to your status.

Above that floor was the lairds' bedchamber with a fireplace, naturally; the twin of the one below, only smaller and with the mantelpiece still in place. Originally one large room, it was later divided into two. Part of that dividing wall remains.

The roof affords a good view of the surrounding countryside and Fleet Bay, as well as the outlines of the outbuildings far below. In the distance is the Rutherford Tower – a pencil pointing to the sky which you can just make out, as long as know in which direction to look and keep a sharp lookout. Below it is the little village of Anwoth.

It is another *Wicker Man* location, at least the churchyard of the Old Kirk was, but that's not its claim to fame. A plaque on the wall explains that Samuel Rutherford (1600-61) was the incumbent here from 1626-36 and it is in his memory that the obelisk on the hill was erected in 1842. Fifty-five feet high and constructed of granite, they must have thought a great deal of him to erect such a monument in such a conspicuous place, instead of just planting it in the village somewhere.

So what did he do to deserve such an honour? He wasn't even a local lad: he was born in Roxburghshire. Before we get to why he was so highly thought of, first an interesting tale from his boyhood. Apparently, one day, while playing with his pals, he fell down a well, like the poor pussy in the nursery rhyme. In the absence of little Tommy Stout, who was to get him out? You can imagine how frantic his parents must have been, but when they arrived at the well, they found him cold and wet, but otherwise unharmed.

But how did he get out? Quite calmly, he told them: "A bonnie white man drew me forth and set me down."

In *Tam o' Shanter*, the narrator tells us: *A child might understand/The Deil had business on his hand.* From this tale, you might conclude that God had something in His mind for Samuel Rutherford.

To cut a long story short, he was a theologian, author and not least, a dedicated minister. In his *Letters* (1863), published 200 years after his death, Rutherford's editor, the Rev. Andrew Bonar, describes his parishioners as saying about him: "He is always praying, always preaching, always visiting the sick, always catechising, always writing and studying." To squeeze in all these things, he got up at 3am every day.

They were troublesome times, polarised around religion, the time of the Covenanters. Presbyterians against Episcopalians, and Sam the man and minister was very definitely on the side of the Covenanters. He was a committed non-conformist.

He wrote a book criticising Archbishop Laud, Charles I's principal advisor and policy maker, which enraged Thomas Sydserff, the Bishop of Galloway. For his pains, Rutherford was called before an ecclesiastical court in Wigton as a prelude to being tried in Edinburgh. He was removed from his post in Anwoth on 27th August 1636, forbidden to preach, and exiled to Aberdeen.

He may have been sent to what was in those days, a remote part of Scotland, but he would not be gagged. During his exile, he wrote something like 220 letters. His writing desk has been described by Andrew Thomson (1841-1901), that biographer of the lives of eminent ministers, as being the "most effective and widely resounding pulpit then in Christendom".

Two years after his removal from Anwoth, in 1638, our hero was reinstated by the General Assembly and promoted to Professor of Divinity at St Andrews.

In 1644 he published his most famous work, *Lex, Rex.* Catchy title. I like it. The subtitle was *The Law and the Prince: A Disputation for the Just Prerogative of King and People.* In it he argued: "The law is not the king's own but is given to him in trust. Power is a birthright of the people..."

Anwoth Old Kirk

After the Restoration in 1660, it was obvious that Rutherford and Charles II, who believed he was appointed by God to be the supreme ruler, would never get on, to put it mildly. The *Lex Rex* was burned at the Mercat Cross in Edinburgh by the public hangman. It was also burned at the gates of New College in St Andrews. Rutherford was charged with treason, along with the framers of the National Covenant, and condemned to death.

Summoned to face his accusers, the so-called *Drunken Parliament* which was dedicated to making the king an absolute monarch, he replied: "I have a summons already before a superior Judge and judiciary and I behove to answer my first summons and 'ere your day come, I will be where few kings and great folks come." You've got to admit it's a pretty piece of prose. Knowing the summons from his temporal masters would soon be coming, I can imagine him going over and over it again in his head to make sure he could trot it out, just right. Anyway, last laugh to him. He cheated his exectioners by dying peacefully in his bed on 29th March 1661 and was buried in St Andrews.

His body may not be in Anwoth but there is a very interesting Covenanter's grave, a victim of the "Killing Time" which, fortunately for Rutherford, he did not live to see. It's a pink sandstone slab on which is carved: *Here lyes John Bell of Whitesyde who was barbourously shot to death in the Paroch of Tongland at the command of Grier of Lag, 1685.* There follows a tirade against "cruel Lag", which goes on and on for a good many lines, the letters all very much crammed together. It wouldn't surprise me if the hand that held the chisel that chipped out these words belonged to Old Mortality.

Inside the roofless church there is an even more interesting grave. It occupies almost the entire width of the church. What is striking is the sheer amount of text on the tomb, just as crowded as the Covenanter's grave, if not more so. Clearly, meeting the mason's bill was not an issue. Chillingly, at one end, in high relief, is a skull and crossbones with *Memento Mori* inscribed around the skull.

It commemorates the lives of *Christen Makcaddam, Lady Crdynes, depairted 16th Ivny 1628* aged 33; *Margrat Makclellan depairted this life 2 Apprile 162- aged 31*; and *Marioune Muir depairted this life anno 1612*. Apart from the quaintness of the spelling, each one is interesting in different ways.

In the case of Christen, *now in earthis wombe, lived long a virgine, now a spotles wife... Heaven hir saule does gaine*. I think there is a certain poetry in the idea being returned to earth's womb to be born again in heaven. Margrat's inscription mocks death: *thou gaines nothing bot some few lifeles bones, hir choysest pairt, hir soule, triumphis for ay*. Marioune's inscription appears to be written by herself: *my bodie sal not heir remain but to ful glorie sal suirlie ryse againe*.

They don't write them like that any more.

It's clear the ladies had an unshakeable belief in their faith and resurrection, and it's a reminder that they took their religion very seriously indeed – for what was at stake was their immortal soul. No wonder the people in those days went to war and were prepared to die for their beliefs. An eternity in hell was too horrible to contemplate.

And by the way, the cemetery is yet another *Wicker Man* location.

Chapter Thirty-Four

Cairnholy and Carsluith: The Chambered Cairns and the House the Cairns Built

Y OU can drive up to Cairnholy chambered cairns but it's a very narrow track with very few places to pass should you meet another vehicle, and with a nasty drop on one side. So if you don't want to chance your luck or put your reversing skills to the test, it's better to stop at the bottom of the track with lots of room to park. It is a bit of a hike up to the cairns, though.

There are two, in two different sites, a matter of two-hundred yards or so apart on the top of Cairnharrow Hill overlooking Wigtown Bay. They are also known as "Clyde Cairns", as they are typical of tombs in the southwest of Scotland. What we see now is only a skeleton, a shadow of their former selves. Once upon a time they would have been covered with masses of stones like Camster Cairns in Caithness. If you want to know where the stones are now, you don't have to look far. Miles and miles of stone dykes. Fortunately, the monoliths were too big and heavy for the 18th century farmers to carry off. Did they know they were desecrating graves or did they just not care? It was all so very, very long ago.

The first one you come to is Cairn Holy I, funnily enough. It's immediately striking with its tall stones standing sentinel, like soldiers guarding the catafalque of some dead hero. There are eight of them, curved like a D, and the archaeologists tell us there was a forecourt in front of them. There was evidence of fires having been lit on them and from that they deduced that

Cairn Holy I

ceremonies would have been performed. But what sort of ceremonies? As far as we know, they did nor cremate their dead, so was it some sort of pagan worship? Or did it involve human sacrifice, like something out of *The Wicker Man*?

A stone, which once would have sealed the entrance, has toppled over and there is nothing to prevent us from peering inside to see that the tomb consisted of two chambers, completely closed-off from each other. The lid is missing so you can see inside. Lined with slabs, it is just big enough to take a body.

You will need to look very carefully, but if you do, you can just about see that two of the standing stones forming the second compartment (hint – look on the south side) bear cup-and-ring marks and lots and lots of little peck-marks. What can they mean?

They found very little in the way of human remains, which is not surprising after all this time. All flesh must come to dust, but pottery is far more durable. They did find some Beaker pottery, which tells us that this site was used by people long after the builders had erected these monuments to *their* dead.

On the forecourt they found a flake of pitchstone which came from Arran, and if it amazes you that these "primitive" people could travel such distances and across a substantial body of water then you will be stunned to know that that was just a hop and a jump, because they also found a ceremonial axe made of jadeite which had come all the way from the Italian Alps. It's now in the National Museum in Edinburgh.

Obviously the axe's owner must have been a person of some importance. But just how did it find its way all the way here? It's evidence they must have been trading with other groups. What was given in exchange, I wonder?

Cairn Holy II is a good deal smaller, more compact, but I think looks more interesting. It is said to be the tomb of the mythical Scottish king, Galdus, who defeated the Romans. In reality, it must have been the resting place of a really important person, like the owner of the axe for example.

The entrance to the tomb is through an impressive pair of standing stones. In front of them is a narrow V-shaped forecourt. The one on the right is tapered towards the top and looks just like an obelisk. It's hard to believe it has weathered like that and had not been fashioned by the hand of man. It would have collapsed had it not been for its broken, smaller partner which is doing a great job in its supporting role, literally. I christen it the *Leaning Stone of Cairnholy.*

Inside are two chambers, the inner roofed with a capstone, now balanced on its two or three supporting stones. That said, it doesn't look in any danger of collapsing anytime soon, but if it should, even with all the lifting tackle available to modern man, it would still require a good deal of effort to get it back in place again. Which begs the question: just how did these "primitives" do it? One thing is for certain: it must have been a huge co-operative effort, what training courses call today a "bonding exercise". And

Cairn Holy II

they must have revered their dead very much to have gone to such a lot of trouble.

Because of the missing supporting stones you can peer inside. Nothing to see now of course except bare earth, but the archaeologists laid bare a flint knife and an arrowhead, whilst in the outer chamber – like at Cairn Holy I – they found four or five Beaker pots.

We leave behind a whole lot of mysteries there and skip forward about four thousand years to the mid-fifteenth century and Carsluith Castle. We don't know a great deal about it either, but considerably more than we do about the people who built Cairnholy.

It's far more tower house than castle, and like the other tower houses we have seen, it's a roofless shell – though from the outside, it looks remarkably well preserved with the crow-stepped gable ends still standing to their full height of 30 metres. Even the tall chimney stacks are intact.

It was originally built by the Cairns family and, in 1422, Alexander de Cairns presented it to his nephew, John Cairns of Orchardton. About 1460, it came into the possession of James Lindsay of Fairgirth, Chamberlain of Galloway. His son, Sir Herbert, was killed at Flodden and the castle passed to his son-in-law, Richard Broun, who was married to Elizabeth, one of Lindsay's daughters.

The Brouns, who originally came from Cumbria, had a long pedigree, going back to the reign of David I in the 12th century. By the 16th century and as staunch Catholics, they were no friends of the Protestant McCullochs, their neighbours. As a matter of fact, this is the same family of Brouns from which the last abbot of Sweetheart Abbey came from – Gilbert. You will remember he

● ● ●

continued to practice his "papistrie" long after the Reformation of 1560. Just to remind you, for this unshakeable dedication to the Old Religion he was imprisoned, exiled and ended his days in Paris in 1612.

Not surprisingly, Carsluith was suspected of being a refuge for Catholic priests. There is no evidence to prove this was the case, but that probably only means the Brouns got away with it. In a panel above the door, you can just about make out their coat of arms, but the date is illegible. Look to your right as you go in and you will see a fragment from a red sandstone cross-slab. It's the same old story of old stones being recycled.

It's obvious the castle was not designed to withstand any serious siege; just enough to deter an attacker from breaking and entering. There are no windows on the ground floor, while those on the first are larger than you would expect, built more for admitting light than keeping out the slings and arrows of outraged enemies. As for the walls, they are a mere three-and-a-half feet thick. There are a number of gun ports but the Brouns must have felt relatively safe because at some later stage, a little oblong window was inserted above the single gunport for light and ventilation.

The only entrance, in the sheltered right angle of the L, similarly pays some sort of lip service to defence. Any attacker could march straight up to it, the only defence being a single gun port to the left of the door. It looks as if the worst the Brouns were expecting was some nasty neighbour such as one of that tribe of hellish McCullochs.

The Brouns set about expanding and improving the place, adding a stair tower in 1568. And why not? Do we not add extensions to our much more humble dwellings? Those who know their architecture have come to the conclusion that it was a later addition because of the way it doesn't quite properly meet an upper window of what was the original oblong tower.

When the extension was built, that window became a door, the entrance to a feature that made the castle really special – a projecting exterior wooden balcony, now gone, but you can still see the corbels that once supported it. From this lofty vantage point, the family could look down in comfort on the

Carsluith Castle

courtyard below and beyond. Obviously you only built an exposed feature like that if you expected to be able to enjoy it without the neighbourhood tearaways coming along and making a pest of themselves.

They were not without fault themselves, the Brouns. In 1579, John Broun, the son of Richard (who was the brother of Gilbert the abbot, and the grandson of John the builder), was implicated in the murder of John McCulloch of Barholm. Richard was fined £40 for his son's non-appearance. The grief your kids can cause you! You knew when you had them they would be an expense, but you never expected they'd cost you a fortune, which £40 was in those days.

Incidentally, Barholm Castle, just two miles away, has been much restored and is a private residence today, a fairy-tale sort of place which has been linked with the fictional Ellangowan in *Guy Mannering*. It is said that John Knox, that scourge of Catholics and Mary, Queen of Scots in particular, slept there in 1566. Even if it's not true, even the suggestion that he might have done, is enough to show how poles apart the Brouns and McCullochs were in matters of religion. Neighbours who saw eye to eye they were not.

The minute you enter the hall of Carsluith, you can see there is none of the ornate stonework that graced Cardoness but there is a mod con in the form of a sink for the washing of hands. There would have been a table beside it where a water jug would have stood. A drain leads outside to where a pop-eyed gargoyle still looks surprised to see the chute of dirty water that once spewed from its mouth. There is also a "buffet", or recess, which was probably shelved, to display the family silver. Inside the fireplace, to the left, is a receptacle for that precious commodity, salt.

On the floor above, where now there is no floor, you can see where there were a couple of latrines, side by side, like a "Ladies" and "Gentlemen". Another notice indicates where the bedchamber was. If you do not suffer from vertigo, a walkway lets you look down into the giddy depths below, but if you look straight ahead of you, in one direction you will see the lush, green, forested Galloway countryside and in the other, the blue of Wigtown Bay or the grey, or golden sands, depending on the weather and tides.

The castle stayed with the Brouns until 1748 when James, a London merchant, sold it and the lands to Alistair Johnson. With the proceeds, James was heading for a new life in India. The Johnsons never occupied it, only using it as a farm outbuilding. How insulting is that! And talking of outbuildings, the castle would have been supported by the usual suspects – the bakehouse, the brewery and the stables. They and the *barmkin* wall have disappeared without trace.

Marrbury Smokehouse

Over the next century or so, the castle changed hands a number of times, beginning with the Hannays from nearby Kirkdale House. It's all part and parcel of the ebb and flow of family fortunes. They come and they go. Nothing is forever. The castle came into State care in 1913. Now it is in the care of Historic Environment Scotland.

As you return to your car, and if you hadn't already done so when you arrived, you might wonder what those two pristine white-washed buildings are doing by the roadside, blocking off the view of the castle. What on earth, you might wonder, was Dumfries and Galloway Council doing when they granted planning permission for these incongruous buildings to be built, right in front of the castle?

As a matter of fact, both buildings have been around long, long before the regional council was as much as a glimmer in the bureaucrats' eyes. It's worth casting your own eye over them. Standing on the site of earlier farm buildings, these date from the early 19th century. The easily-identifiable Marrbury smokehouse is where, as long as you are a carnivore, you can treat yourself to salmon smoked in a variety of ways from the nearby River Cree.

You would never have guessed it was the former cart shed and stable.

● ● ●

Chapter Thirty-Five

Creetown: The Town that Rocks

W E'RE heading towards Creetown now. Towards the end of the 17th century, the huddle of houses on the banks of the river came to be known as "Ferrytown of Cree" where, in the 16th century, pilgrims were ferried across the river to visit the shrine of St Ninian at Whithorn. We'll be going there ourselves eventually, but not yet. "Cree" comes from the Scots Gaelic *crioch*, meaning a boundary.

According to legend, a hawthorn bush marks the spot where the pilgrims are said to have departed. It is still there today, amazingly. If it's the original bush it must be older than Methuselah when he died – incredibly ancient, even for a tree. It is said to bring good luck to lovers who touch it. No doubt the idea is that their love will last as long as the bush. If you want to try it out, you will find it on the bridleway near the Moneypool Burn.

Like other villages to the east, it benefitted from the military road from Bridge of Sark to Portpatrick in the 1760s, just as it – and they – benefit from its successor today, the A75 which now gives it a heavy-traffic bypass. In 1790, a turnpike road was built along the coast.

The present town was founded in 1785 by the laird, James McCulloch. Modestly, he named the planned town after the river and not himself. However, it seems an odd decision to name the main street after St John, while a smaller street to the north was designated the High Street. But then, Kirkcudbright's High Street also departs from the norm. Galloway is not a foreign country, at least for residents of the United Kingdom, but they do things differently there.

Everyone loves an eccentric, don't they? They do things differently too. One such was a certain worthy called James Connell, aka *Beardie*, who had a novel way of crossing the Cree. He built a pair of sheepskin wings stretched over a wooden framework with which he hoped to flap his way across the river. He was lucky to end up with only a broken ankle. The bridge across the Balloch Burn on St John Street is called the *Beardie Bridge* in his honour.

Most of us of a certain age remember the old tongue twister *She sells seashells by the seashore.* If you are not of that age then this is how it goes:

She sells seashells by the seashore.
The shells she sells are surely seashells.
So if she sells shells on the seashore,
I'm sure she sells seashore shells.

Try saying it, let alone spraying, it aloud. I challenge you to get through it, even past the second line without a stumble.

But just why am I bringing this up? Well, the answer is that is how Creetown made its living in the olden days. They were exported from here in their thousands to be turned into fertiliser.

In 1766, a grain mill was built, driven by the Balloch burn and unbelievably, the grinders continued to turn until 1950. After lead was found in the area in 1763, a lead-shot mill was built in 1770. The mines shut in 1890 but had a second lease of life during the First World War, which is more than can be said for the poor soldiers who had to fire the bullets they made. A tannery followed in 1781 and lasted until 1845. In 1790, that jolly-good laird aforesaid, James McCulloch – with employment for his tenants in mind – built a three-storey cotton mill that employed thirty-five women. It operated until 1800 before reinventing itself as a carpet factory and going on to last for another hundred years.

In 1792, the laird managed to elevate the town to the very posh-sounding Burgh of the Barony of Creetown. This gave McCulloch certain benefits, such as the ownership of heritable lands and certain rights, such as patronage of the parish church and the ferry crossing, not to mention dues from the mill and the harbour (such as it was). It also entitled the burghers to hold courts and fairs, for the trading of horses and selling of goods. Alas, under the Police (Scotland) Act of 1892, it was stripped of its burgh status and became plain old Creetown again.

Creetown

Its bread and butter came from granite. It had been a low-level sort of occupation from the 18th century, but it became a major player in the village's economy when the Kirmabreck Quarry was established in 1830 by the Liverpool Dock Trustees. It supplied the granite for the Liverpool docks.

"Hold on a minute!" I hear you say! "You said Dalbeattie did that!" Quite right, and well remembered. It's true; Craignair Quarry in Dalbeattie *did* supply the stone between 1826 and 1832, as did the quarries here at the Barr and Glebe in the parish of Kirmabreck. However, by 1830 the company decided it was easier (and more economical) to transport the stone from Creetown rather than Dalbeattie. A fleet of eleven schooners was on hand to do the necessary, which gives you some idea of just how much granite was excavated from them thar quarries – as many as 289 voyages in one year. By 1834, the quarries were employing 450 men.

Quarries are dangerous places, and so is the transporting of the excavated stone. Three schooners were lost at sea between 1830 and 1844, unfortunately two with the loss of all life. You can imagine, should any misadventure occur, given the cargo, the ship would literally sink like a stone.

It isn't just Liverpool that can claim a little bit of Creetown. Nearer to home, the docks at Greenock and Leith can also boast Creetown granite, as can Birkenhead, Newport and Swansea. St Andrews House in Edinburgh is also built from the same stuff, as is Bowater House in London and Dundee's Town House.

As a result of this industry, during the mid-nineteenth century Creetown expanded like the waist of a middle-aged man. According to the census of 1881, the population had reached 1,834 – more than twice what it is today. From this, you will be able to deduce that the quarry is no longer in operation, save twice a year when some of that special stone is chiselled out and sent to Dalbeattie for working and polishing. Can you guess for what purpose?

Well, people are always dying and there is always a need for headstones, though there is not so much demand these days since most people are burned rather than buried. However, if you or your ashes are interred, there's a good possibility that the stone that marks the spot comes from here.

The railway came in 1861, a lot closer than it did to Gatehouse; a sort of railway by-pass, but only by one mile, as opposed to six at Gatehouse. The A75 by-pass is undoubtedly a good idea, but I'm not so sure about the railway. In any case, it was a victim of one of Dr Beeching's cuts in 1965.

The granite past lives on however, most notably in the imposing Ellangowan Hotel whose bar doubled as the *Green Man* in *The Wicker Man,* and the clock tower which was erected the previous year, in 1897, to mark Queen Victoria's Diamond Jubilee. Very fitting. One of the hardest stones meets one of the most precious: granite is rated 6th in the Mohs scale of hardness, with diamonds coming top of the class at 10th. In the square, you will see a remarkable sight – a globe of pure white granite sculpted by local artist, Hideo Furuta. It looks so perfectly round, you feel all that it would take is a little poke of finger to set it off rolling down the street like a bowling ball, scattering pedestrians or knocking them over like ten-pins.

From a distance, it looks perfectly smooth, but closer inspection reveals that its surface is engraved with features pertinent to Creetown such as the river estuary, stake nets and of course, granite. It was the idea of the Scottish Arts Council and partly funded by £98,000 of National Lottery money.

As it happens, this small place is home to two museums: the Creetown Heritage Museum on St John Street and the Gem Rock Museum on Chain Street which is housed in the former school. It was the brainchild of a couple of enthusiasts, Jim and Kate Stephenson, whose hobby became their livelihood when they began the venture in 1981. If you can turn your hobby into your livelihood, that's what I would call cracking it.

It's one of the most unusual museums you are ever likely to see – a world-class one at that – and it's in a little place like this. Who would have thought it? In the main room, in glass cases, there are shelves upon shelves containing crystals from the British Isles and around the world, some of them very rare. So many cases, so many shelves – where to begin?

Each specimen has a label telling you what you are looking at. It's astonishing, it really is, the brilliant colours and the shapes. What appeals to me especially are the amethysts. Seen from the outside, just an unremarkable grey boulder, but split it open and what *an unco sicht!* Talk about an inner beauty, both in the colours and the intricacy of the shapes! Breathtaking! I have always thought that to chip open a rock and find a fossil nestled inside must be immensely thrilling, but to chip open one of these rocks and find this glorious sight inside must be like winning the lottery.

Amidst so many wonderful things, it's invidious to choose a star, but a couple of contenders must surely be the 4.5 billion-year-old, 3kg meteorite and the "Maverick'" gold nugget, one of the largest natural nuggets that can be seen in the entire UK. What is more likely to appeal to the kids, though, is the fossilised egg and poo of a dinosaur.

Another attraction is not a gem, but the skeleton of a cave bear called Olga. She's 50,000 years old. Just a baby, compared to all these other exhibits.

The variety and colour of the crystals dazzle. There is at least one example from every stone on the planet, from alexandrite to zircon. The only letter of the alphabet not represented is X. That gem prefers to remain anonymous. The diamonds are replicas, by the way, though I am sure it was never on your mind to put one in your pocket as a souvenir.

There's a lot more to the museum than this jeweller's shop display of gems. To enter the crystal cave is to enter a wonderland. It's our planet, but not as we know it, Jim – or whatever your name may be. Here, beneath the earth, the crystals are shown in their natural habitat, where florescent lighting brings out the natural colours of the crystals. As Wordsworth put it, beneath our feet, though we never see it: *Earth has not anything to show more fair.*

In the Professor's Study, with its leather armchairs, you are transported back to Victorian times. You can almost see Sherlock Holmes sitting there, researching some abstruse point, the solution to a mystery, in one of the many geological magazines and books in the library.

And you, too, can spend some time here if you have a mind to, even if it's not as prodigous as his – and you have the time to spare. If you haven't, but do have a burning question, the owner, Tim, a Fellow of the Gemmologists Association of Great Britain, will be more than happy to enlighten you.

A good place to start your tour is with the *Fire in the Stones* audio-visual presentation in the study, which demonstrates how the earth's tremendous forces created the crystals in the first place and brought them to the surface. It also informs you about the pioneering geologists and their findings, and how man has "improved" on nature by cutting them and polishing them, creating works of art for which men everywhere are grateful, so they can buy them for their wives or intendeds.

The Lapidarist's Workshop shows how the gems are polished before being put in their settings. Move into the Gift Shop and you will find an Aladdin's Cave of delights. Gems of every shape and colour, stones carved into bowls, and many more artefacts. The lady you love is sure to see something you can buy for her.

I leave this gem of a place (sorry!) a wiser man, about rocks and crystals and precious stones. But one thing puzzles me. How did they know the bear's name was Olga?

Chapter Thirty-Six

Kirroughtree to Loch Ken: Through the Forest to the Castle of the Gordons

THE SWC300 was never intended to be followed slavishly, and just before you come to Creebridge and Newton Stewart, another deviation offers itself which will be of particular interest to walkers and cyclists. Even if you are one of those who are not much addicted to exercise (like someone I know well), it's well-worth taking it and letting the scenery come to you by taking the forest drive through the Galloway Forest Park to New Galloway. Its common name is the A712, but since 1977, it has also been known as the "Queen's Way" to mark Her Majesty's Silver Jubilee.

The Forestry Commission was founded in 1919 to replenish the country's forests after their depletion during the First World War. It's now the UK's largest landowner. The Galloway Forest Park was created in 1947 and covers 300 square miles.

At Panure, just before the junction with the Queen's Way, is the first of three recreation areas in the Park. Kirroughtree visitor centre provides lots of information on the walks, cycle routes and activities that can be done here, such as watching the birds from a hide or letting the kids get rid of their energy in the adventure playpark. Then there is the Wild Goat Park, and the Red Deer Range, which was also established in 1977.

Clatteringshaws Loch sounds a noisy sort of place but nothing could be further from the truth. It's

Kirroughtree House Hotel

Loch Ken

a reservoir actually, one of the chain that forms part of the Galloway Hydro-Electric Scheme, which I mentioned in the Tongland chapter. In this part of the forest, you are miles from anywhere, which is why this is the best place to come at night to gaze at the stars and wonder at the mystery of the heavens.

The Park was given dark-sky preserve (DSP) status in November 2009, the only such place in mainland Scotland. During the day, you can follow the trails with the rolling Galloway Hills forming the backdrop. Look to the northwest, and on a clear day, you should be able to pick out Merrick, at 2746 feet, the highest hill in the Southern Uplands.

If you follow the trail round the loch, you will join the historical trail again when you come to a big boulder where, it is said, Bruce "rested" after defeating the English in 1307. And just how do they know that, do you suppose? (By the way, this mighty rock should not be confused with the other, and more impressive, Bruce stone in Glen Trool, the so-called *Cradle of Independence*.)

No, you'd be best to think of it more as a memorial, or reminder, that it was amongst these hills that Bruce, with his guerrilla band – outlawed after his slaying of the Red Comyn, and his defeat at the Battle of Methven in 1306 by Edward I – survived to fight another day and came out to harry the English before melting away into the hills.

Back in your car, if it please you, you can take the old Drovers' Road, rechristened the *Raiders' Road*, a ten-mile forest road which features in Samuel Rutherford Crockett's tale *The Raiders*. Of course, you don't have to have to do it the easy way: you can hike it, or bike it, or take to another sort of saddle, should you have an equine quadruped to strap it on.

And so, in the fullness of time, we come to New Galloway at the head of Loch Ken. This is Gordon territory. The Gordons of Lochinvar, from the Scots Gaelic *loch a' bharra* meaning "loch on the summit", came from Berwickshire in 1297. They were a cadet branch of the Gordons of Aberdeenshire. (My ancestors' lords and masters, by the way.) And in case you were wondering, a cadet branch is the line that is descended from the younger sons, the oldest having inherited the land and titles, according to the law of primogeniture. To the first-born goes all, except of course, should he be a she.

Their castle stood on a mound on an island in the loch which had been occupied since the Middle Ages. Unfortunately, if you want to see it, you will need to don a diving suit as it was drowned in the 20th century to form a reservoir.

Before that drowning day, it was possible to see, beneath the water, one causeway to the east bank of the loch, and another to the west. We also know the castle had five-foot-thick walls and a circular tower 10 feet in diameter on the northern side. Long before the drowning, there was not a lot left to see, so it's no great loss that it has disappeared forever, I suppose. It has been suggested that this was the birthplace John Balliol in 1249. If that is the case, it's a pity it has not survived. It might have lived in infamy.

New Galloway is yet another charming old village. It was founded in the early 16th century by the 1st Viscount Kenmure (1599-1634), aka Sir John Gordon of Lochninvar. He is not to be confused with the young Lochnivar who *came out of the west* in Scott's 1808 epic poem *Marmion*. For a start, the one referred to in the poem was Sir William de Gordon who died two centuries earlier, circa 1455. Not only that, and I'm sorry to disappoint the romantics amongst you, but the events in the poem are entirely the product of Scott's imagination.

As a matter of fact, it was Sir John Gordon who appointed Samuel Rutherford to the charge of Anwoth. He later was reported as saying: "It was the most meritorious action of my life." From which you will understand he was a staunch Presbyterian.

Rutherford was later to repay the compliment when he attended Kenmure on his deathbed and wrote a tract entitled: *The Last and heavenly Speeches and glorious Departure of John, Viscount Kenmure.* Faint praise, I don't think. It was printed in Edinburgh in 1649. It was a bit of a slow-burner, despite its riveting title. It did not go into a second edition until 1827. Far too late for poor Sam to collect his royalties.

In what seems a surprising conflict of interest, Kenmure was also a supporter of the Stuarts. It was at the coronation of Charles I in Edinburgh in May 1633, eight years after his coronation in London, that he was raised from a humble Sir to a Viscount. The following year, he attended the meeting of Parliament, but absented himself from the debate on "matters relevant to the church" and bolted to his hidey-hole in Kenmure Castle. He later explained he did not wish to "upset" his monarch.

Kenmure Castle

As you will have surmised, he appears to have been a bit of a ducker and diver. It was thanks to his friendship with the king that, in 1630, New Galloway became a Royal Burgh. You will remember that this status entitled it to hold fairs and markets. Unfortunately for New Galloway, it fell under the shadow of Kircudbright, twenty miles to the south, and it never prospered in the same way. To this day, it remains Scotland's smallest burgh. Small comfort in that little honour, I suspect.

Sir John's father, Sir Robert (c.1565-1628), along with his second son, Robert of Gelston, were among two of the first to establish the colonisation of North America when, in 1621, they founded the Barony of Galloway in Nova Scotia. In 1625, to encourage settlers to the new country, Robert Senior published a book entitled: *Encouragements for such as shall have intention to bee Vundertakers in the new plantation of Cape Breton, now New Galloway by mee Lochinvar.* The following year (despite his failure to be able to spell words of one syllable), he was appointed as one of the members of the Council of War for Scotland and Commissioner for the Middle Shires.

Their castle is just a mile to the south of the village. Alas, it is in ruins, and worse, in a perilous state of collapse. Two wings diverge at right angles from the square central tower. Above the doorway, decorated by a loop of rope moulding, is the Gordon coat of arms. And that is just as far as you should venture, should you decide to pay a visit. Through it, you can see piles of fallen masonry. The last thing you would want is your head breaking the fall of one of those.

In 1950, it was gutted by fire – not for the first time. It was set on fire during Mary's retreat from Langside in 1568, and again by Cromwell, in 1650. Things tend to happen in threes, as I've pointed out before.

About fifty cannonballs from Cromwell's knocking-about of the castle were dug up from the bottom of the mound. One thing that did survive from those desperate times was a slate sundial from 1623. It was presented to the Dumfries Museum in 1967.

In 1715, the 6th Viscount took part in the Jacobite Rebellion and for his pains, was executed at Tower Hill in February 1716. His lands were forfeited. In 1790, Francis Grose, in his *Antiquities of Scotland*, described two of the towers of the castle as being "in ruins". He made a drawing of it, and apart from some vegetation growing on top of the curtain wall, it still looks in

New Galloway Main Street

pretty-good nick. To this day, you can see the steps that lead up the mound and to the door in the curtain wall.

Time passes. In 1824, Captain John Gordon (1750-1840), became the 10th Viscount. During the 19th and 20th Centuries, the castle was remodelled out of all recognition from the one Grose knew. In what sounds more like enemy action, rather than reconstructive-surgery, a tower was demolished, as were the walls of the courtyard and much of the outer defences.

Fans of the *Outlander* TV series might like to know that Sam Heughan used to live in the converted stables when he was attending primary School in New Galloway.

Chapter Thirty-Seven

Balmaclennan and Barscobe Castle: The Rising and Retribution

WE cross the River Ken by means of the granite bridge built in 1821 by John Rennie (1761-1821). Amongst his impressive list of achievements are the Waterloo Bridge in London and London Bridge (built after his death), the latter now happily enjoying retirement in Lake Havasu City in Arizona. Reports that it was bought by mistake instead of Tower Bridge are greatly exaggerated.

We have arrived in Balmaclennan (literally farm of the MacLennans) which, you might remember me pointing out earlier, was a hotbed of Covenanters. It was here that Robert Paterson (1715-1801), aka *Old Mortality,* called home although he was hardly ever there. You know why and that's why his wife moved here, to be nearer the centre of his operations. She was never a widow in life, but it would be true to say she was a stonemason's widow long before she died. A mother to five children and with an absent husband, she carved out a living for herself by running a little school. After life's weary fit, here she lies. The inscription on her stone, erected by Thomas Paterson in 1855 reads:

> *In memory of Robert Paterson, stone engraver, well known as 'Old Mortality,' who died at Bankend of Carlaverock, 14th February 1800, aged 88; also of Elizabeth Gray, his spouse, who died at Balmaclellan village, 5th May 1785, aged 59; also of Robert, their son, who died 30th April 1846, aged 90; also of Agnes McKnight, his spouse, who died 5th August 1818; and their three sons, John, Alexander, and Robert.*

You can see an example of Old Mortality's handiwork on a nearby stone, if I am not very much mistaken, because of the way so many letters are squeezed into every space available. It tells us: *Here lyeth Robert Grierson, who was shot to death by command of Colonel James Douglas, at Ingleston, in the Parish of Glencairn, 1685.* It's too long to repeat in its entirety here, but this gives a flavour of it and the hated Episcopalianism that was being thrust upon the people:

> *Here's one of five at once were laid in dust*
> *To gratify Rome's execrable lust.*

If this were not enough to delight any taphophile, let me tell you that this hallowed ground also claims the honour of having the oldest civic war memorial in Scotland. It's a spiral column like a stick of barley sugar and commemorates the death of five local men who died in the Crimean War. A sixth, who died at Sebastapol, is mentioned on a gravestone but not on the memorial. Why that should be so, I confess I do not know.

Just outside the cemetery is another pillar, plain this time, about five feet high and made of whinstone. On first sight it might be mistaken for an ancient monument of some sort, but it's much more recent than that. It is reputed to be the grave of Elspeth McEwan, burned to death in 1698 for being a witch. She admitted as much herself, which begs the question – what did they do to her first?

A mile from here is Barscobe Castle, an L-shaped tower house which was built in 1648 by William McClennan from stones nicked from Threave Castle, if you please. A bit of a haul admittedly, but how could you resist all that dressed stone? Better by far than quarrying out the raw stone yourself. You can see his initials and coat of arms (a pair of chevrons), along with those of his wife (three boars' heads), set into the angle of the L. The "M" stands for Mary or Margaret, while the "G" stands for "Gordon" as you will have deduced if you are up on your heraldry. She was the illegitimate daughter of the 4th Viscount of Kenmure, Sir Robert Gordon, naughty boy, who died in 1663.

William the builder died in 1654 and his eldest son, Robert, inherited the lands and the castle. He was a fervent Covenanter, and the castle became the HQ for like-minded folks. They held what was called "Conventicles", secret meetings – because they were illegal – at the Holy Linn in the nearby woods. It has a waterfall and the water has carved the rocks into interesting and weird shapes, one of which is said to have been the pulpit and a hollow in another made a convenient font for the baptising of babies, hence the name "Holy Linn". The ousted minister of Balmaclennan, the Rev. Verner, is said to have baptised thirty-six children here at one go.

In November 1666, Robert McClennan was responsible for starting what became known as the "Pentland Uprising". It should really be called the "Glenkens Rising"; the Pentlands is where the rebellion came to grief only two weeks later. It all began in St John's Town of Dalry (Dalry for short), just up the River Ken a wee way. The story is that he and three others were in the Clachan Inn when they heard a commotion and, rushing out, found four soldiers beating up a defenceless old farmer because he had failed to pay a fine for not attending the Episcopalian service as prescribed by the government. McClennan and friends intervened – wouldn't you if you saw such a thing, if you were brave enough to tackle armed men? The villagers joined in, and the soldiers were disarmed. One soldier, Corporal Deanes by name, was shot in the leg with fragments from a clay pipe. It was the best the rescuer could think of, as he had no lead shot.

Barscobe Castle

The following day, McClennan and sixteen others attacked the hated dragoons at their garrison, killing one. Word got out about the insurrection and people flocked to the cause. McClennan led two hundred men to Dumfries where the hated commander of the dragoons, General James Turner, was billeted. They arrived at 5.30 in the morning, dragged him out of bed and kept him hostage, with Neilson of Corsock charged with being his minder-in-chief.

The rebels next went on a recruiting drive, gathering more men in Ayrshire and Lanarkshire. In Ayr, Colonel James Wallace of Auchens was appointed their leader. The army swelled to about a thousand. So far, so good. At Lanark they split, one part heading towards Glasgow, the other to Edinburgh where they planned to hand in a petition, pointing out they were only acting to protect their freedom of worship according to the National Covenant which the king had agreed to and signed in 1638 with his own fair hand.

During this whole venture, the weather had been dreadful. It was November after all. By the time the Edinburgh faction had reached there, half the troops had deserted. They found the city barricaded against them, and all hopes they had of their petition receiving a fair hearing were in tatters. It was worse than that, actually. They had been declared traitors, for which the penalty was hanging – if they were lucky. If they were unlucky, they would be drawn and quartered for good measure. Not surprisingly, even more of the motley troop melted away. There was nothing else for it but to head for the Galloway Hills but, before they did so, it was decided to hold a parade and a review by Col. Wallace at Rullion Green.

Big mistake. General Tam Dalyell (1599-1685) of the Binns, near Blackness, cut through the Pentland Hills with more than two thousand men and caught up with them there. He was known as *Bluidy Tam* or the *Muscovy Brute* because he allegedly introduced thumbscrews to Scotland from Russia. According to legend, he once played cards with the Devil and won by cheating. The Devil was furious and picked up the marble table they had been using and threw it at Tam's head. Tam ducked in time and the table flew out the window and landed in what's called the "Sergeant's Pond", so-called because it's where his regiment watered their horses.

It was no contest as far as the rag-tag rebels' army versus Dalyell's well-drilled troops was concerned. The Covenanters were easily routed and shown no mercy. Figures on the casualties vary, but it's estimated that on the Royal Army's side casualties were very few, while on the Rebel side more than fifty were killed and another 150 captured and sent to Edinburgh Castle. *Pour encourager les autres*, Corsock was "given the boot", a fiendish form of torture whereby both legs were placed in an iron contraption shaped like a massive boot, then a wedge was driven in until both legs were shattered against its side. If it's true about Dalyell and the thumbscrews, you can see it is just the sort of thing he would have employed.

McClennan somehow made his escape from the field of battle and continued fighting for the cause. After the battle of Bothwell Bridge in 1679, he was sentenced to be hanged, drawn and quartered (when they caught him) and his lands were forfeit. Dogged by ill-health, his luck ran out when he was finally captured by Claverhouse's men in 1682. Claverhouse (1648-89), the 1st Viscount Dundee, was known as *Bluidy Clavers* by the Covenanters and *Bonnie Dundee* by the Jacobites. So much for a rose by any other name!

However, McClennan's sentence was commuted when he took what was known as the "Test" and swore allegiance to the Crown. He was desperate to see Barscobe again. He didn't have long to enjoy it, however. Only a year later, he was murdered by William Grierson, brother of Robert Grierson of Mylnemark (he whose grave lies in the cemetery in Balmaclellan), because he thought that McClellan had betrayed the cause. Both Grierson brothers were arrested and jailed but, in what seems a miscarriage of justice, they were released shortly afterwards. I suppose some would say they had a point, but McClellan had endured sixteen years of hardship in the name of Covenanting.

Barscobe remained in the family until 1775 and then changed hands several times. In 1961, it came into the possession of the hotelier and politician Sir Hugh Wontner, who leased it to Dame Bridget D'Oyly Carte in the 1970s. That is a very fine handle, and she *is* related to the D'Oyly Cartes of Gilbert and Sullivan fame. She spent a great deal of time here – and, I would think, Sir Hugh's money (though she had plenty of her own) – on modernising and redesigning the interior. She had previous experience. Her father, Rupert, owned the Savoy, and she was in charge of the interior design and furnishings. She died in 1985, aged 77.

I'm sure it's much-changed since Bridget's day, but here's the good news. You can see the inside of the castle for yourself. It's now a prestigious B&B.

Chapter Thirty-Eight

Dalry and Laurieston: A Cautionary Tale and the New Teller of Tales

WE are going now to see where the Glenkens Rising began and it's immensely pleasing to see, as we come into St John's Town of Dalry, to give it its full name, that The Clachan is still there. Mind you, I doubt if Robert McClellan would recognise it if he came back today.

The inn stands at the junction of the A762 and the A713. From here you can either retrace your steps and take the A713 down the east side of Loch Ken, or take the A762 down the west side. If you choose the former, you will come to Parton Parish Church. The village is so quaint it's worth going to for its own sake, but in the churchyard, taphophiles and admirers alike will be delighted to find the gravestone of James Clerk Maxwell who is buried in the family plot. It's a small grey granite stone set against the wall. Very unpretentious. The inscription reads:

> *John Clerk Maxwell, died 3 April 1856. Frances Cay, his wife, died 6 December 1839. James Clerk Maxwell, died 5 November 1879. Katherine Mary Dewar, widow of James Clerk Maxwell, died 12 December 1886.*

You will note it does not even give his date of birth (13th June 1831) or his age at time of death (48). He died of abdominal cancer, just as his mother did and at the same age. One of life's tragic cases of deja-vu; it seems unfair that he died thereafter. Who knows what else he might have achieved, had he been spared?

A bronze memorial plaque, unveiled in 1989, gives a précis of his achievements. He was a mathematical physicist, two words which make my eyes glaze over. He is regarded as the father of modern physics, laying down the foundations of special relativity and quantum mechanics, whatever they are. In an end-of-the-millennium poll, a hundred of those who do understand such arcane matters, placed Einstein top of the heap, Newton second, and Maxwell third. On the centenary of Maxwell's birth, Einstein – or the horse's mouth – said Maxwell's work was the "most profound and the most fruitful that physics has experienced since the time of Newton".

What the memorial doesn't tell you is that as early as 1861, Maxwell demonstrated the first colour photograph, but what it *does* say is that he "prepared the way for radio communication and television". Now *that* I do understand and am grateful.

Everything he did was way above my head and now he would be below my feet if we paid him a visit, but on this occasion we are not. Instead, we are going to follow what comes more naturally to me – the artistic trail which lies down the other side of the loch. It begins here in Dalry, a lovely little place, much beloved by artists, in the broadest sense of the word.

Donald Watson (1918-2005), painter of birds and book illustrator, including *The Oxford Book of Birds*, lived here for fifty years. (David) Cowan Dobson (1894-1980), who painted the great and the good, also made this his home. As a matter of fact, his father was born here. The film composer Cedric Thorpe Davie (1913-83), first came to Dalry on holiday and came back as often as he could. He retired here in 1977 and this is where he died. Finally, Neil Gunn (1891-1973) lived here with his married sister from 1940-47.

We have another famous writer in our sights and we're on the way now, a pleasant drive, with Loch Ken on our left and trees on our right. Before long, Woodhall Loch appears on our right with Slogarie Hill rising behind it. An ancient folktale pertains to this area.

The story goes that the Laird of Slogarie, who was known as the "Earl of Hell" because of his addiction to drinking, gambling and swearing. He had a wife and two sons who were even more wicked than their old man. His good lady expired before him and, like the good sons they were, they tried to take their father's mind off his loss by indulging in that sinful habit of playing cards. Not only that, they had a wee drinky-poo – or more than a few libations, to put it another way – to make the evening even more convivial. Well, you know how it is when you are in your cups, the wee sweary-word is likely to slip out, despite your best intentions, when the cards just don't fall right.

You also don't notice time passing when you are enjoying yourself. The midnight hour struck, announcing the Sabbath day, but oh dearie me, the trio kept on casting the cards. Meanwhile, outside, a storm was brewing. Feeling rather chilly and the good wife having no need of it any more, they put her well-thumbed Bible on the dying embers for a bit of warmth.

They got much more heat than they bargained for. All at once the thunder bellowed, lightning struck and soon the house was all-ablaze. One's instinct, of course, is to abandon the conflagration but the laird had second thoughts. He wanted to save his money. He re-entered the burning building through a window, only for a beam to fall on top of him. He was trapped and burned to death.

Meanwhile his sons rode off, post haste, to get help. Alas, one fell over a crag, while the other ran into a tree and broke his neck. Reader, take note. That's what you get for burning Bibles and playing cards on a Sunday.

And so we arrive in Laurieston. Named after an 18th century landowner, it was formerly called the unlovely-sounding Clachanpluck. (Be careful how you pronounce it. Best not uttered when under the influence of alcohol.) It was here that Samuel Rutherford Crockett (1859-1914), and better known by his initials, went to school when he was living at the farm of Duchrae (just at the other side of the loch from Slogarie) with his mother, grandparents, and three uncles. He never knew his father, who died soon after he was born.

In an article written in 1895, Crockett tells us his grandparents were staunch Cameronians (a radical and zealous branch of the Covenanters), where most books were disapproved of, apart from improving books about the lives and the deaths (especially) of the Covenanters. It's not hard to work out where he got his middle name from, and perhaps the first too. It's ironic that in a house that had so few books, Crockett should grow up to be such a prolific writer of them. Grandfather would certainly not have approved. He once reprimanded the boy for picking a flower on a Sunday. (Good grief!)

We've stopped to see the monument that has been erected to Crockett's memory. It was paid for by public subscription and unveiled by his widow, Ruth, in 1932. Made of granite blocks, it stands on a grassy mound and bears an inscription by Robert Louis Stevenson:

Blows the wind today, and the sun and the rain are flying,
Blows the wind on the moors today and now,
Where about the graves of the martyrs the whaups are crying
My heart remembers Now!

It was in 1886, while Crockett was the minister in the Free Church at Penicuik, that under an alias, he published his first book – a collection of verse which he named *Dulce Cor,* which you remember means "Sweetheart", like the abbey. His collection of short stories, which included *The Stickit Minister,*

S.R. Crockett Memorial

appeared in 1893. He dedicated it to R.L.S. who responded by writing him a poem. That's where the excerpt that appears on the monument comes from.

The following year, he published his most famous novel, *The Raiders*, along with *Mad Sir Uchtred of the Hills*, *The Playactress* and *The Lilac Sunbonnet.* Four books in one year! Fancy that! They were so successful, it wasn't a financial risk he took when he decided to give up the day job. You can imagine what grandfather thought of that! For the rest of his life, he was as prolific as 1894 had promised. He produced sixty-seven novels in total, half of which are set in Galloway.

Incidentally, 1894 was also the year that Stevenson died in far-off Samoa, and it could be said that S.R.C. picked up the mantle as the new *Tusitala* or Teller of Tales, as the Samoans called R.L.S. There is no mistaking the influence of his mentor in *The Raiders*, written in the best *Kidnapped* and *Catriona* tradition.

Although he was extremely popular in his day, Crockett's novels have somewhat fallen out of favour today, considered to be too sentimental and nostalgic for modern tastes. He travelled widely and had the misfortune to die in France when the Great War broke out, which meant it took some time before his body could be repatriated. He is buried in the village of Balmaghie, where he was born. It's fitting that he who wrote so much about Galloway should be returned, not only to the land of his birth, but the precise place where his life began. I'm sure he would have been very happy with that – and flattered by the memorial.

Laurieston lies at a crossroads and if birds of prey fly your kite, as the saying has it, and if you take the B795, and your timing is right, you can see the forky-tailed raptors of the sky being fed at the Red Kite Feeding Centre at the unlovely-sounding Bellymack Farm.

Travel a little further and you will come to Balmaghie where the Parish Church which was built in 1794, is worth paying a visit because of its unusual octagonal tower. In the cemetery lie the remains of S.R.C.

Sleep well, Sam. I'll say it again, Sam. Sleep well.

• • •

Chapter Thirty-Nine

Newton Stewart, Minnigaff and Torhouse: A Brief Interlude

THE A75 has taken us swiftly back to where we abandoned it to follow the Queen's Way, and like a capricious lover, we are just about to abandon it again. At the roundabout, the SWC300 follows the A714 south to Wigtown but, just a little to the north, are Newton Stewart and the much smaller Minnigaff which lies on the other side of the river.

It's an unusual name that has been spelled variously ever since records began on the little settlement in 1694. "Monnygoof" makes it sound like it was inhabited by lots of idiots, while "Minnigoff" makes it sound like it was the centre for a silly game. The present spelling was standardised in 1737. It probably comes from the Scots Gaelic *muilin an ath* – mill by the ford, at that time the lowest crossing over the Cree. It was hereabouts that Robert the Bruce and many others would have forded the river on their way to the shrine of St Ninian.

Lead was discovered nearby in 1763 and was mined until 1839, but the town never grew in the same way as its more illustrious neighbour across the river. Before regionalisation it was in the Stewartry of Kirkcudbright, while Newton Stewart was in Wigtownshire. Now they are all part of the same happy family.

Sir James Mirrilees, the winner of the Nobel Prize for Economic Sciences, was born in Minnigaff in 1936. Yet another example of a tiny place in Scotland which has produced a great man. (If you haven't already noticed, for its size, Scotland has produced an extraordinary number of great men and women, punching far above its population for producing geniuses.) Mirrilees was knighted in 1998 after being awarded the Nobel Prize in 1996, along with William Vickery (1914-96), for their "fundamental contributions to the economic theory of incentives under asymmetric information". Naturally, I could explain it to you if I wished, dear reader, but space does not permit, unfortunately. However, you might be interested to know that the announcement of the Prize was only made three days before poor Vickery's death. I'm glad he knew of his achievement, at least I hope he did. It was collected posthumously, only the third time this has ever happened.

It is thought that there would have been tiny settlements on both sides of the river since the 13th century but, in 1677, the Stewarts of Castle Stewart began building what they called "Newton Stewart". It was granted burgh status by Charles II which entitled it to all the usual perks – a weekly market and two annual fairs. It also benefitted from the Old Military Road which arrived in the 1670s and along which Irish cattle were driven across the ford to market in Dumfries. Suffice it to say, by 1685, the upwardly mobile town had dwarfed its sibling across the river which, by contrast, was suffering from a case of stunted growth.

After he bought the Stewart Estates in 1792, the industrialist, Sir William Douglas, 1st Baronet, the fourth and youngest son of the 2nd Earl of Galloway, introduced cotton mills to the town and it was briefly named "Newton Douglas" in his honour. You may remember that he did the same in Castle Douglas and, just as that venture failed, so did this, unable to compete with the new-fangled power looms. When he died in 1805, I'm sure he must have been a very disappointed man.

The ford was replaced by a bridge in 1745, but it was washed away by floods in 1806. It was replaced in 1814 by the present bridge which was built by John Rennie who, I am sure you will recall, was also responsible for the one across the Ken at New Galloway.

Newton Stewart is a bustling little town with a museum housed in a former church. The cinema on Victoria Street is a very striking art deco building, and that was where *The Wicker Man* had its première in 1972.

Taking our leave, we head south towards Wigtown but are waylaid by a sign on a minor road directing us to the either the Neolithic or Bronze Age Torhouse Stone Circle. It is very conveniently located on the B733 after Spittal. It's a very rare structure for Southern Scotland and, what's even better, very well preserved. Such arrangements are normally found in the northeast of Scotland and in Ireland, which must surely be evidence of migration. Alas, the site

Torhouse Stone Circle

has not been excavated yet, so our knowledge of it is limited to what we can see of it today.

Standing atop a little mound, the circle is about 65 feet in circumference. It is composed of nineteen large granite boulders varying in height from 2 to 4.9 feet, with the larger stones being on the southeastern side. In the centre, three stones are aligned northeast/southwest with the smallest stone in the centre. From 1648, it was known as the tomb of King Galdus. You may remember that he was supposedly buried at Cairnholy. I suppose if you never lived in the first place, your tomb can be wherever people want it to be.

Outside the circle, to the southeast, there are two more standing stones – one large and one small – while to the east, there is another row of stones known as the "Torhousekie Stone Row". What can it all mean? We don't know, but it must have meant something significant to the builders. Whatever it meant, it did involve a good deal of hard work. You don't move these boulders about willy-nilly and without a great deal of communal effort either. All hands to the shifting and lifting of stones. Besides, there wasn't much on the telly.

It would be surprising if there were not many more stones here which have since been removed for the building of dykes as at Cairnholy. Look carefully at the dyke to the south of the road and see if you can find a stone with a deep hole in it. According to local tradition, it is customary to deposit a pebble or a coin in order to pass in peace. Unfortunately I have no loose change on me so, bending down, I pick up a little stone and pop it in.

May the peace of the prehistoric people who lived here long ago go with me.

Chapter Forty

Wigtown: Martyrs and Myth

WIGTOWN, you would not suppose, even if I told you in jest, did not derive its name from the days when false hairpieces were all the rage. Several hypotheses have been put forward as to the real origins of the town's name. One is it could be from the Old English *wic-ton*, or like the other Wigtown in Cumbria, which in 1162 was spelled "Wiggeton", that is to say, "Wigca's farm." Look, don't take my word for it, but the most likely derivation is the simplest – from the Norse *vik* meaning "bay". Like that advert in the Seventies about wearing a seat belt – you know it makes sense.

The nascent town was granted the status of royal burgh to Sir Malcolm Fleming by David II in 1341. Enter an old friend, Archibald the Grim, who bought the estate in 1372. The Douglases were no friends of the Stewarts, as you know, and the town was stripped of that status and did not become a royal burgh again until 1469.

If Kirkcudbright is known as the "Artists' Town" then Wigtown has justifiably earned the right to be known as "Scotland's National Book Town". In fact, it reinvented itself as such in 1997. After the closure of the town's two main employers, a distillery and a creamery (the latter which came about as a consequence of the closure of the branch railway which ran from Newton Stewart to Whithorn in 1950) – something needed to be done. And so successful has the rebranding been that bookshops have overflowed to the nearby villages of Bladnoch and Kirkinner, just a little to the south, making more than thirty bookshops in all. Surely, you cannot fail to find a book to your taste out of that lot!

Even better news, if malt whisky is to your taste, is that Bladoch distillery – which was established in 1817, and mothballed between 1993 and 2000 – has now reopened with a visitor centre and guided tours. It has the distinction of being Scotland's most southerly distillery, so if you are looking for a souvenir of your trip, apart from a book, that is, you might find the very thing you are looking for there.

Wall-to-wall books and a distillery to boot – to which you can add a climate milder than most towns in Scotland, thanks to the Gulf Stream – and what is there not to like about Wigtown and its satellite villages?

Even the rosy-pink stone of the County Buildings and the Town Hall looked flushed with pride at the way the books have rejuvenated the town's economy. It would be invidious to choose one shop over the others, but I will mention in the passing, that *The Book Shop* on North Main Street claims to be Scotland's largest second-hand bookshop.

The ground floor of the Town Hall has a small museum and a library on the second (yes, even more books!), while on the third, the Wildlife Viewing Room offers a panoramic view of the Galloway Hills to the north and those of the Lake District rippling the horizon to the south. Ornithologists will be delighted to know that TV screens show live links to the nearby nest site of the ospreys which returned to the area in 2004 – the first pair in more than a century.

The town is unusual in that the Square is actually an isosceles triangle. It's also unusual in having two mercat crosses. The oldest one, which dates from 1457, has the distinction of probably being the only cross in Scotland to have been imprisoned. It stood in front of the Old Court House and was removed for safekeeping while the square was being constructed in the 18th century. A second cross was erected in the main street in 1816 and some time later, the old cross was released and placed to the west of the upstart. But that was not the end of its adventures. After a while, it was given a facelift and replaced in the centre of the square where it remains to this day.

When the cross was new, a ferry operated from here to Creetown, thereby cutting off miles for those pilgrims coming from the west and heading to St Ninian's Chapel on the Isle of Whithorn – which is not actually an island at all, but a peninsula.

The establishment of Wigtown as a port hit Kirkcudbright hard. The two towns became great rivals. In 1471, Wigtown exported £17.10 shillings of goods while Kirkcudbright exported almost half as much again. That said, they were like Siamese twins: each affected the other. As one declined, so did the other. What both failed to do, in the remainder of the 15th century, was to capitalise on the ubiquitous herring as the ports on the Ayrshire coast did. The records show that in 1500-01, only two ships docked at Wigtown and Kirkcudbright. That was a good year. In other years there was none at all.

Things didn't improve much in the 1600s and, by the mid 19th century, it was curtains for the harbour. The silting of the River Bladnoch which spills into the bay here, as well as the silting of the bay itself, meant the harbour was in deep trouble – or rather the opposite. The trouble was that the water just wasn't deep enough for shipping.

It was cleared out in the 1980s but you can't stop the power of Nature, as Canute knew very well, and today it is very much silted-up again. It, and the river, would be a sight to gladden the heart of the eponymous semi-aquatic mammals in Flanders and Swan's comic *Hippopotamus Song*: "Mud, mud, glorious mud".

The salt marshes at the river's estuary attract such a large number of birds that they have been designated a Local Nature Reserve (LNR). In fact, Wigtown Bay is the largest in the UK. Ornithologists, or the merely curious, can observe them from hides near here.

But there is something sinister down there among the marshes – a memorial to the most shameful event in Wigtown's past. It took place in 1685 during the "Killing Time" when three men and two women, now known as the *Wigtown Martyrs*, were executed for their beliefs. The men were hanged. The women were the 63 year-old Margaret McLachlan (her name is spelled in a variety of ways) and the eighteen year-old Margaret Wilson (or Willson) as it is spelled on her tombstone.

They spent a month in prison, along with Margaret's younger sister, Agnes, before appearing in a farcical trial in front of the Commissioners Sir Robert Grierson of Lag aka *Cruel Lag* and Sheriff-Depute David Graham, the younger brother of *Bluidy Claivers*, aka the Marquis of Montrose.

Also in attendance were Major Winram (alternatively spelled Windram), captain of the dragoons; Captain Strachan; and Provost Coltrane of Wigtown. The two Margarets were found guilty and their sentence was to be *tyed to palisadoes and fixed in the sand, within the flood mark, at the mouth of the Blednoch stream, and there to stand till the flood*

Wigtown Martyrs Monument

● ● ●

over flowed them and [[they]] drowned.

The way the execution was carried out was brutal. As the sentence decreed, the two Margarets were tied to stakes in the tidal channel of the River Bladnoch to face the incoming tide, where they could see the cause of their deaths coming inexorably closer. But that's not all. The older Margaret was placed further out, the intention being that, as the younger woman watched her die, she would reflect on her fate, see the error of her ways, and repent before she disappeared under the water. In charge of operations were the dragoons under the command of Winram.

In 1708, the Church of Scotland decided to make a record of all the persecutions inflicted upon the Covenanters and commissioned Robert Wodrow to undertake the task. The result was his *History of the Sufferings of the Church of Scotland from the Restoration to the Revolution*, which was published in 1721.

In his graphic account, Wodrow tells us how stoically Margaret Wilson met her death. According to him, she sang the 25th Psalm from the 7th verse, then read the 8th chapter of Romans "with a great deal of cheerfulness" and then prayed. Before she was quite dead, they held her head out of the water and, on Winram's orders, she was asked if she would pray for the king. She replied she "wished the salvation of all men and the damnation of none". One of the horrified onlookers pleaded with her: "Say 'God save the King'. Say, 'God save the King.'" Margaret coolly responded: "God save him, if He will, for it is his salvation I desire." That was good enough for her supporters, who shouted to Winram in excitement: "She said it! She said it!"

Winram came up, mounted on his horse, and offered her the Oath of Abjuration of 1685 or a return to the water. The Oath was a response to the *Apologetical Declaration and Admonitory Vinication Against Intelligencers and Informers* by those radical Covenanters, the Cameronians, aka *The Society People.* In an action reminiscent of Martin Luther's burning of Pope Leo X's Papal Bull in 1520, it was nailed to the door of certain churches. It was, in short, a declaration of war against their oppressors.

The Oath was offered to any person over fourteen who was suspected of being a traitor. If they refused to take it, they could be put to death on the spot, without trial, in the presence of anyone holding a commission from the Privy Council and two witnesses. No wonder that the years that followed were known as the "Killing Time". They killed them in the hills; they killed them in the fields; they killed them in their homes.

By offering her the Oath, Winram was throwing young Margaret a lifeline. She refused to clutch at the proffered straw. "I will not," she said, obstinately. "I am one of Christ's children, let me go." She was thrust down into the water again and according to Wodrow, "finished her course with joy".

Well, maybe she did, but I'd be surprised if that were the case because the body's natural instinct to survive takes over. In fact, one wonders just how much of the details of the above can be trusted, especially when you realise Wodrow's work was published thirty-six years after the event.

With the best will in the world, memories tend to become foggy over the years. And there's just one other slight difficulty – remember, Wodrow's stance was hardly impartial. His remit was to collect evidence on how cruelly the Covenanters were persecuted. From his point of his view, what happened to the Margarets was a bit like finding a seam of gold.

It is one thing to be sceptical about the details, not to say the possible over-egging of the pudding as far as the deaths of the two unfortunate women are concerned, as recorded by Wodrow, but it is another thing entirely to maintain that the executions never took place at all.

That's what Mark Naper in his three-volume tome *Memorials of Graham of Claverhouse, Viscount Dundee* (1859-62) claims. As I mentioned above, Dundee's brother, David, was one of those who condemned the Margarets to death. You can imagine the outrage and furore Naper's book caused at the time. He responded to this criticism with *The Case for the Crown in re the Wigtown Martys proved to be Myths versus Wodrow and Lord Macauley* (1863). When that failed to slay the mythical beast, as he saw it, he followed that up with another book in 1870 entitled *History Rescued* which was written in response to the Rev. Archibald Stewart's *History Vindicated.*

Myth or not, it is a matter of fact that on 30th April, after the intervention of young Margaret's father, the Privy Council recommended that the women be reprieved and the thirteen-year old Agnes be granted freedom on a bond of £100 to be paid by her father. He was a wealthy farmer, but in those days such a sum was not insubstantial. Wouldn't any father pay such a price to let his daughter live? He would, we suppose, have done the same for his older daughter, but he couldn't, because at eighteen, she was old enough to know her own mind and take the Oath.

At this point, the plot thickens. After the issuing of the pardon, it does not appear in any subsequent records – it disappears completely off the face of the earth. One smells a rat.

If the execution *did* take place, then *Cruel Lag* must have acted with unseemly haste to carry it out, only eleven days later. But would he have taken that responsibility upon his own shoulders, to dismiss the findings of the Council? Given his zeal for persecuting Covenanters, he might well have done so, his nose severely put out of joint at the reversal of his death sentence. Indeed, if he *did* know and ignored the decision of the Privy Council, it makes his actions all the more reprehensible. I couldn't disagree with Wodrow, who claimed *they* are the ones who should have been prosecuted.

In his *History*, Wodrow cites the testimony of eyewitnesses from the Penninghame and Kirkenner Parish Kirk Records. One of them, a certain Thomas Wilson, is recorded in the former as having lived to "certifie the truth of these things, with many others who knew them too weel". And if you were wondering, yes, Thomas was Margaret's brother and yes, he was recounting events twenty years after the event. My money is on Thomas: you wouldn't forget a death like that in a hurry.

Likewise, Margaret McLachlan testified that she had seen her mother drown, her head being held under the water by the halberd of one of the town's officials who had given her one last chance to swear the Oath. According to legend, just before he performed the deed, he told her: "Then tak' another drink o't, my hearty." He spent the rest of his life suffering from an unquenchable thirst, having to resort at times to drinking from ditches and other unsavoury sources. Serves him right!

Another legend is that an unsympathetic constable named Bell (undoubtedly an Episcopalian – he would never have got the job otherwise), when asked by some ghoulish person for details on how the women died, he replied: "O, they just clepped roun' the stobs like partans and prayed." The praying part of that, at least, chimes with Wodrow's account. The story continues that Bell's wife bore him three children, all with "clepped" or webbed fingers. They were known as the *Cleppie Bells*.

And if you are wondering what "partans" are, let me tell you they are crabs, which – I don't need to tell you – do not have webbed feet. And if you are also wondering why the eyewitnesses waited twenty *years* before giving their testimonies, then the answer is simple – no-one ever asked them before.

A stone pillar, known as the *Marytrs' Stake*, commemorates this barbarous event. It sticks out of a boulder like Excalibur and replaces an older wooden stake. Duckboards lead the way across the saltmarshes to where it stands, surrounded by a wooden platform. The sea is far away, the coastline having silted up. There is another memorial on nearby Windy Hill to all the martyrs – a towering slim pyramid with the names of the five martyrs inscribed on it, as well as a good many others who died for the cause.

The Margarets were buried in the cemetery of the Old Parish Church, now in ruins, on the north side – traditionally the place reserved for criminals.

They are ringed in by an iron fence and the tombstones, which were erected in 1720, have been whitewashed.

Young Margaret's stone rests upon four pillars about a foot high. The first three lines of the fourteen-line inscription read:

LET EARTH AND STONE, STILL WITNESS BEARE
THEIR LYES A VIRGINE MARTYR HERE
MURTHR'D FOR OUNING CHRIST SUPREAME

Older Margaret lies next to her, her stone much smaller and upright, but inscribed on both sides, making best use of the space to praise her courage and condemn her murderers who are named and shamed.

Next to her are the graves of the three male martyrs. Their little stone reads:

Here lyes William Johnston, John Milroy, George Walker, who were without sentence of law hanged by Major Winram, for their adherence to Scotland's Reformation national and solemn league, 1685.

Of all the martyrs, Margaret Wilson is by far the best known, undoubtedly because of her youth and heroic death as described by Wodrow. John Everett Millais commemorated her in his 1871 painting *The Martyr of Solway*, where a very sad-looking Margaret, with her hands tied behind her back and a chain around her waist, stands side-on and averts her gaze from the incoming sea.

Margaret is also commemorated, along with her younger sister, Agnes, in a glass-enclosed memorial in the Old Town Cemetery in Stirling. They are depicted as reading the Bible with a guardian angel looking over their shoulders. The latter has a very sad expression on her face (it's definitely a she) – as well she might. It's as if she can see into the future, as you imagine angels can, and she knows as a guardian angel she wasn't much cop.

I, for one, wouldn't disagree with that.

Chapter Forty-One

Whithorn: The Cradle of Christianity

I T'S an ancient town, arguably the oldest continuously inhabited settlement in all of Scotland. It began in a small way, as I remember from my primary school days, as *Candida Casa*. The name comes from the Latin *candidus*, meaning "white", and has absolutely nothing to do with a fungal infection. Far less does it bear any resemblance in any shape or form, to that other famous White House in Washington DC. It was a tiny church founded by St Ninian in 397 and dedicated to St Martin, whom Ninian had met at Tours on his way back from Rome and who had died that year.

It would have stood out like a beacon, not just because of its whiteness but because it was built of stone where all else was built of wood. These "Christians", as they called themselves, meant business. They were here to stay.

There are no contemporary accounts of Ninian, Scotland's first saint. The first account we hear of him is in the Venerable Bede's *Historia Ecclesiastica Gentis Anglorum* written three centuries after "Nynia's" death in 432 AD. In it, he tells us precious little apart from what I've said above, and that he was a Briton and was a "revered bishop and a man of great sancity".

Much, much later, in the mid twelfth-century, St Aelred of Rievaulx wrote about the life of Ninian and the miracles attributed to him which he must have garnered from an 8th century poem. Firstly there was the punishment and cure of King Tudvael, a king of the Britons "as lustful as he was cruel". He was opposed to Ninian's proseletysing and threw him out of the kingdom. For his pains he was struck blind but cured by Ninian, whereupon the scales fell from his eyes and he became a believer.

Then there was the acquittal of a priest accused of fornication. (You will need to hang on to your hat for this one.) With the mob baying for the priest's blood, Ninian defended him but told them, "Don't take my word for it, ask the babe." Then turning to the one-day-old he addressed it thus: "Tell us by the most-high Thunderer's rule who is your begetter, and who is the author of this

Whithorn Priory

deed?" With pointed finger the infant replied, "See, this is my father – turn you all and look at him – for in marriage he begot me from my mother's body."

Then there was the miraculous growth of leeks which had only been planted that day, and which were urgently required for the brothers' dinner. Ninian sent the gardener monk out to pick them despite his protests, and lo! back he came with an armful of them, fully grown. If this tells you anything, it's that even in those far-off days, they knew about the importance of their having five-a-day. Then there was the case of the amazing umbrella (which hadn't been invented then) and miraculously appeared to save Aelred's book from the rain. You know how ink runs when it is exposed to moisture.

Then there are cures without number of the afflicted – the blind, the lepers, the malformed and the nearly dead who were restored to full health. What a man! What a saint! But death was not the end for Ninian. Most of us stop working after we retire. No such luck for poor old Ninian. He had to keep on working long after he was dead. A visit to his grave was equally efficacious, so it was reported.

But the church and settlement that grew up around the cult of St Ninian was by no means the first settlement in this area, dear me no, not by a long way. Two centuries before St Ninian's time, this was the land of the Novantae who lived here at the time of the Roman invasion.

In an exciting new development, the Whithorn Trust has reconstructed an Iron Age roundhouse based on excavations at Black Loch of Myreton near Montreith, just a few miles to the west. They were discovered when a farmer was laying drains. It's unique in Scotland, a wetland settlement consisting of eight houses and built on land, as opposed to crannogs, which, as you know, were built on stilts out in the loch. The wet boggy conditions did a great job in preserving the foundations of the houses, which have been dated to about 450 BC. Still around after all this time! Isn't that an amazing thing!

Oak planks formed the walls; posts were made of alder; woven hazel hurdles formed the floor and were covered with leaf litter. The houses seem to have been occupied by a series of families, the hearth being built up over time to form a mound. A quern was found, as well as some stone tools, including the iron part of an ard, or plough. Excavations are still ongoing but the reconstruction was opened to the public in the Spring of 2017. It's 43 feet in diameter and 30 feet high above the central hearth, which is made of layers of pebbles and clay.

When the Romans came, they drew a line in the sand, so to speak, when they built Hadrian's Wall. To the south, civilisation; to the north, the land of barbarians. But before that was built, they tried to civilise the natives by trading with them. It wasn't all about beating them over the head with a blunt instrument, and it seems they did establish links with the Novantae before they retreated behind the Wall.

In the 5th century, the later settlers, the Anglo-Saxons, called this place *Hwit Ærne* and not beyond your wit, I'm sure, dear reader, to see how the present-day "Whithorn" got its name.

Fast forward three centuries and this land became part of the kingdom of the Bernicians who lived in present-day Northumbria. They built a monastery in the 8th century, then along came the Vikings. But not the Vikings who were famous for raiding, raping and pillaging. These were Christian Norsemen. We know they were, because they buried their dead near the saint's shrine and placed carved crosses at their head. That said, and cat lovers should look away now – there is evidence that they farmed cats, presumably for the turning of kittens into mittens. They also produced fine combs made from antlers, so they weren't completely bad.

Nothing lasts forever, and their day ended about 1107 when Alexander I ascended the throne of Scotland. The feudal lords were the masters of Galloway now. Alexander was succeeded by his younger brother, David I, and it was during his reign (1124-53), that Fergus, the Lord of Galloway, built a priory and appointed Gilla-Aldan as bishop. The religious tradition of Whithorn was safe and well – for the time being. However, it seems that the Augustinian house that Fergus built only lasted for about fifty years before they were replaced by the Premonstratensians about 1175.

They get their name from the abbey of Premontre in northeastern France which was founded by Norbert of Xanten in 1121, hence they were also called "Norbertines". (You may recall I mentioned him before when we are at the Dumfries Museum.) They were also known as the "white canons" because of their white robes. Norbert was a follower of St Bernard of Clairvaux who advocated the Cistercian way of life, even more austere than the Augustinian.

They built a great cathedral on the site of the earlier church with a crypt and cloisters, and so the priory became a cathedral priory which was visited by the great and the good, as well as the not-so-good. Edward II was here in 1302 before he was king, helping his dad hammer the Scots. But the monks played a trick on him. They removed a famous painting of the saint to Sweetheart Abbey for safekeeping and strange to relate, once Edward had gone, back came the painting – all by itself!

As I mentioned earlier, Robert the Bruce came here in 1329, seeking a cure for whatever was ailing him. He died three months later. His son, David II, also paid a visit. At the Battle of Neville's Cross in 1346, he was shot by two arrows which lodged in his body. One arrowhead was removed, but the other stubbornly refused to come out until someone had the bright idea of his visiting Ninian's shrine. Maybe it was the king himself who thought of it. Anyway, out it came.

Margaret, Queen of James III, was another visitor, as was James IV. He came many, many times, at least once a year, doing the last part of the journey barefoot, so it is said. He had a guilty conscience about rebelling against his father and which resulted in his death at the battle of Sauchieburn in 1488. In penance, James wore an iron belt next to his skin, adding a link each year. He also came here when his Queen, Margaret, was pregnant in order to pray for the safe delivery of the baby, and afterwards, to give thanks – as well he might. He had six legitimate children (we won't mention the others), two daughters who were both stillborn, and four sons, of whom only the third, the future James V, survived past infancy. During his reign, in about 1500, another chapel was added at Whithorn but it was to be the last grand hurrah for the cathedral. Troubled times were just around the corner.

Other royal visitors followed: James V, and his daughter, Mary, Queen of Scots, as of course did folk of the lesser and common sort. Many did it the easy way, by sea, landing at the Isle of Whithorn and making the three-mile journey north on foot. And they didn't just come from Scotland – they came from England, Ireland and the Isle of Man.

Thanks to the offerings the rich royals left behind, the priory became fabulously wealthy, and it didn't do any harm to the local economy either. Pilgrims need to be housed, fed and watered, don't they? You need butchers and bakers, and let's not forget the candlemakers so you can light a candle at the shrine. And you also need cobblers and blacksmiths, for the pilgrims have come many miles and have many miles to go 'ere they return from whence they came. Oh, and there's bound to have been a gauntlet of gift shops where you could take home a nice little souvenir of your visit – a miniature plaster of St Ninian or *Candida Casa*, or how about a new crucifix?

The tradition of royal visitors has continued in our own times. The present Queen was here in 1951 when she was Princess Elizabeth, the first royal to come since Mary, Queen of Scots. Prince Charles came in 2000. Meanwhile, we plebs continue to come in our droves, following in the footsteps of all those pilgrims of the past: soldiers, sailors, beggarmen and thieves. We know there were criminals because they could be sentenced, as part of their punishment, to come here and pray for forgiveness.

The Priory made hay for four centuries, but them, in 1560, along came the Reformation and the shrine was destroyed. But even before then, the writing was on the wall. When prior Henry Madowell died in 1514, he was replaced with a commendator or a secular administrator. The last Catholic prior was Malcolm Fleming, who was imprisoned in 1563 for saying Mass. Worse times were to follow. In 1581, the government issued a ban on pilgrimages and in 1587 the cathedral was annexed by the Crown. Whithorn had had its day. Now all that remains are the ruined nave and the restored remains of the crypt to bear testimony to the glory that has passed from this place.

In 1800, archaeologists, digging at the east end of the crypt, discovered fragments of stone, dressed with a light-coloured plaster. Could this be from the original *Candida Casa* or "shining house", a beacon and a shining light to all those heathens out there?

The Pend is the present-day pilgrims' portal to the Parish Church of St Ninian and the Priory ruins. A *pend* is an arch pierced through a building to form a passageway. This one dates from medieval times and above the arch is the brightly-painted coat of arms of James IV, the priory's most dedicated patron. At either side of the arch, the pillars are capped with the coat of arms of Bishop Vaux (or Vaus), bishop from 1482-1508.

The Whithorn Story Visitor Centre is nearby. It does what it says above the door by displaying objects from major periods in the town's history. There is pottery and glass from the earliest days; coins from the Northumbrian era; antler combs from the Vikings (no mittens, mercifully); and a bishop's crozier from the 12th century.

The museum and visitor centre contains one of the best collections of carved stones in Scotland. The star of these is probably the four-foot tall "Peter" stone, which was found outside a chapel near Whithorn. The inscription on it reads *Loci Petri Apu Stoli* – the place of Peter the Apostle, the "place" likely being a cemetery with a small chapel. Now here's the interesting thing. The script style – the font if you like – is very rare in Scotland. It's from Merovingian Gaul; that's how they know it dates from the 7th century.

It may not be much to look at, but the oldest stone in the collection is the Latinus stone. Indeed, it is the oldest Christian stone in all of Scotland. It was rediscovered in 1890 in the walls of the medieval cathedral. Just another handy old stone lying about, from the builders' point of view. Being written in Latin, it makes it rather hard for me to read as I confess I've let my Latin slip somewhat since leaving school. Those who can understand it reliably inform us it says: *We praise you, the Lord! Latinus, descendant of Barravados, aged 35, and his daughter, aged 4, made a sign here.*

Clearly it is a gravemarker and dates from about 450AD. They can tell because there are faint traces of a six-armed Constantinian form of the Chi-Rho cross, the ancient secret symbol of the early Christians, a combined X and P, the first two letters of ΧΡΙΣΤΟΣ, *Christ* in Greek.

It's interesting that the name of the deceased has a Latin name (obviously) while his ancestor has a Celtic one. He has been Romanised, obviously. One would dearly love to know their story. Did he and the little one die together? Why so young? It's a mystery which will never be solved, alas.

What I like best are the pillar stones which have what look like human heads at the top. One has a boss in the centre with four studs, the top two of which look rather like eyes. My favourite is a fragment which has been grafted onto a plain sandstone pillar. It has two holes like eyes, while the crack left by the break looks rather like a lop-sided smile. It's rather comical really.

The present church of St Ninian dates from 1822 and was built over one of the transepts of the medieval church. The Pend is our portal back to the present.

Chapter Forty-Two

The Isle of Whithorn: The Catastrophe, the Chapel and the Cave

S O this is the Isle of Whithorn! And this is the harbour where St Ninian landed and all those countless other pilgrims who came in his wake. He, and they, certainly wouldn't recognise it now, a cluster of pretty and colourful buildings clustered around the harbour – and they would be mightily disorientated to find it's not even an island any more. The main street is actually a causeway, an umbilical cord linking it with the mainland.

At the far end of the harbour (where there is ample parking) are the remains of the roofless walls of the lifeboat station. Inside is the "Witness Cairn" which was started in 1997, one thousand and six-hundred years after the arrival of St Ninian. It's a pile of pebbles which visitors are encouraged to add to, preferably with something written thereon to make it more special.

The Lifeboat Station was set up in 1869 and operated for half-a-century. There were three lifeboats during that time, saving a total of thirty-eight lives. Well done, lads! Now the job is done by a lifeboat based in Kirkcudbright. Further away but much, much faster.

A sea of grass faces us now to where the ruined St Ninian's chapel has an abandoned sort of air, as if it has been washed up on the top of the cliffs. Next to the gate is a gleaming-white granite bench. It commemorates the tragic event of the *Solway Harvester* which went down off the Isle of Man in a force 9 gale on 11th January 2000 with the loss of seven local men. You can imagine the profound shock this had in such a small and tight-knit community. The skipper,

St Ninians Chapel, Isle of Whithorn

Craig Mills, his brother, Robin, and their cousin David, all came from the Isle. Three others came from Wigtown, while the remaining member of the crew came from the village of Garlieston, just up the coast a little. In the following months, divers recovered the bodies and an estimated 1,500 mourners attended the funeral service, far more than the little church could accommodate.

What exactly caused the scallop dredger to sink, apart from the atrocious weather, remains a mystery. There were theories that it was hit by a submarine or a container washed off another vessel. The UK government refused to fund the raising of the *Harvester*, but the Manx government stepped up to the plate and in June it was raised to the surface.

"The Isle", as it is known locally, is no stranger to tragedies of this nature – the *Solway Harvester* just happens to be the best known. In 1931, for example, during a sailing regatta, two men drowned when their boat capsized. No more regattas were held until after the War.

Talking of which, not a lot of people know that the coastline between here and Garlieston played a vital role in the Normandy landings. After an exhaustive search throughout the length and breadth of the land, the harbour here and Rigg and Portyerrock Bays to the north were used for the testing and development of temporary and portable structures known as "Mulberry harbours" to support the allied troops after D-Day.

The reason this area was chosen was because, apart from being sparsely populated, the beaches and the rise and fall of the tides best resembled the Normandy coast. Obviously the need for secrecy was paramount and the whole area was declared off-limits to all apart from local fishermen, and a security cordon was thrown around it. A military camp was constructed at Cairn Head on Portyerrock Bay to accommodate the army of sappers required for this vital role, whilst the village hall at Garlieston housed two hundred other workers.

It's a peaceful and quiet place, Garlieston, now. You would never guess it was once a frenetic hive of industry and how pivotal a part it played in the Allies' plans to liberate Europe. There *are* a couple of vestiges, however, if you know what to look for. Standing at the harbour, look to the north to the tip of the crab-like bay and you will see two wrecked "Beetles", or pontoons, stranded on the rocks; look to the south and you will see the remains of a "Hippo", a concrete caisson.

Still on a wartime theme, just out of town, stands a square, white, stumpy tower. It's a lighthouse actually, and during WWII, it was the site for anti-aircraft gunnery practice. Planes would fly past the headland and the guns would train their sights on them. It's also the site for a memorial to the *Solway Harvester* – an anchor in a granite block.

• • •

Back to the distant past and on the trail of St Ninian, the 13th century ruins of his chapel are hemmed in by a modern wire fence. It was built on the site of a smaller chapel built in the 1100s. This was the first stop for the pilgrims who came to the shrine by sea, giving thanks for their safe arrival, before they travelled on to Whithorn.

It was repaired and partly rebuilt by the Marquess of Bute in 1898. The reason for its ruinous state was not entirely due to the ravages of time. Sketches by MacGibbon and Ross for their 1894 *Ecclesiastical Architecture of Scotland* show what it was like then. It's a familiar tale. In 1864, the dressed stones were used as a quarry by an unnamed "retired sea captain" who used them to build his house. Is nothing sacred?

There is a large hole in the south wall where a doorway would have been and a large arched window in the east. There are other smaller windows and a square aumbry in the north wall, the cupboard where the sacramental vessels would have been stored. The remains of a broad stone wall show that the chapel would have been enclosed by something much more substantial that the flimsy fence that does so now.

Next on the St Ninian trail is the cave on Physgill beach. (Park near Physgill House.) Tradition has it that this is where St Ninian came to get away from it all and to have a bit of a pray in solitude. The roof has collapsed, but excavation in the 1880s uncovered 10th and 11th century carved crosses, pillar stones and an Anglian headstone bearing a runic inscription. They are now on display in the Priory Museum at Whithorn.

There are plenty more crosses to be seen in the outer cave, incised into the rock. They are now a part of history themselves. Seven small crosses to the left of the entrance are believed to have been carved by pilgrims in the eighth and ninth centuries. There is no question about when more recent pilgrims came. The dates are there for all to see: 1718, 1866, and 1871.

And still they come today to leave their mark: wooden crosses made from driftwood, pebbles bearing inscriptions, pushed into clefts into the rock. Whether Ninian himself was here is another matter. He *may* have come here for a bit of a pray, but why should he? If he wanted a secluded place to speak to his Creator, surely there was no need to trudge those weary miles to this remote place? It is remote enough now, God knows; in those days it must have seemed like the edge of the world. Surely, as a zealot, he would have wanted to get on with the job, not hang about a dark and draughty cave.

At some stage in its history, the entrance was walled up. The last traces of that were removed in 1950 and now you see it, more or less, as Ninian did – if he ever did.

● ● ●

It appears in *The Wicker Man,* as does Burrow Head, the second-most southerly point in Scotland. Because of its remoteness, it was a favourite haunt of smugglers in the 18th century. In 1973, it was the location of the film's climax, the bit that everyone remembers, where Sergeant Howie was burned to death alive inside the gigantic, eponymous wicker man.

Until quite recently, the remains of the legs of the structure were visible but they are gone now – gone, probably, to grace souvenir hunters' mantelpieces all over the land.

Chapter Forty-Three

From Rispain to Druchtag: Ancient Mysteries and Miracles

W E'RE practically back in Whithorn again. We've come to Rispain Camp, just a mile to the west of the town. You might be forgiven for thinking it is a Roman fort. About an acre in size, it's a square grassy area with rounded corners. Indeed, until the late 1970s, archaeologists thought so too – either that, or it was a medieval moated farmstead.

The truth is quite different. Radiocarbon dating has proved that it is much, much older. In fact, it harks back to the Iron Age, about 60 BC. Its name, Rispain, might come from the Welsh *rhwospen* meaning the "chief of the cultivated country". Archaeologists think it was occupied by the Novantae until about 200 AD. They kept cattle, sheep and pigs and grew wheat. They also grew barley, with which they brewed beer. How civilised! And to think the Romans thought they were barbarians!

The most notable feature is a ditch that was once twenty feet deep when it was first dug out, with the excavated material being thrown up to form banks all round. It runs right round the enclosure, apart from an access road twenty-feet wide. Excavations revealed a timber gateway which would have been joined to a timber stockade, which would have run around the top of the inner rampart. Very, very Roman!

A metalled road led to the interior, where three wooden roundhouses were identified. One, nearly forty-five feet in diameter, was excavated, and part of an enamelled bronze bracelet was found which was dated to about 100 AD. Thanks to our visit to the reconstructed roundhouse in Whithorn, we can imagine quite easily what the settlement would have looked like.

And so we arrive in Monreith, an extended village by the sea. Its origins go back to the Iron Age. In much more recent times, it used to be called "Milltown of Monreith", a bit of a mouthful to be sure, but so-named because of the grain mills that formerly employed the locals. There was also a tile works until the 1920s, the tiles being made out of the local clay.

Kirkmaiden church is our first place of call, the last resting place of the notorious McCullochs and the Maxwells, the landowners around these parts. According to local legend, when the pulpit and bell were being transported across Luce Bay to another church of the same name near the Mull of Galloway, a storm appeared out of nowhere and the ship sank. Now, so it is said, when one of the McCullochs of Myrton is about to die, you can hear the bell tolling from the depths of the bay. Very, very frightening if your name is McCulloch.

On the wall beside the entrance to the ruined church there is a plaque to François Thurot, a French navy officer whose body was washed ashore here after a battle between Britain and France on 28th February 1760. Who is he, you might ask, with some justification? Well, he was one of those larger-than-life characters whose adventures seem to step out from the pages of boys' adventure stories. He was born in Nuits-St-Georges (where the Burgundy comes from), in 1727. He was, in turn, a privateer, merchant-ship captain, smuggler and as far as his enemies were concerned, the terror of the seas.

The plaque, which was erected by a Swedish delegation of the Order of Coldin in 1960, says Thulot introduced the Order into Sweden. And what's that, you might also reasonably ask? Well, it's a masonic order connected with sailors. Thulot happened to be a senior member and, when he was in Gothenburg in 1757, he met a Friherr Björnberg who was a lowly member. Thulot promoted him, which meant Björnberg had the power to recruit new members. Now Sweden is the only country in the world where the Order still exists. No wonder they wanted to erect a plaque to Thulot.

The Maxwell mausoleum is in a much better condition than the roofless church. For one thing, it has a slate roof so raindrops don't keep falling on the

Kirkmaiden Church and Graveyard

heads of those sleeping the Big Sleep there. The red sandstone doorway is really impressive – a very fine imitation of Norman architecture, although it's actually late Victorian. The last person to be entombed there was Herbert Maxwell (1845-1937), 7th Baronet of Monreith, novelist, essayist and antiquarian. He was President of the Society of Antiquaries of Scotland from 1900-13 and

Chairman of the Commission on the Ancient and Historical Monuments of Scotland (RCAHMS) from its formation in 1908 to 1934. He was also Conservative MP for Wigtownshire from 1890-1906. A busy man. He was the grandfather of Gavin, author of *Ring of Bright Water*.

Overlooking the bay, on a rock, is Penny Wheatley's bronze statue of a rather cross-looking otter. Gavin Maxwell was born and raised at the nearby village of Elrig and used to be seen exercising his tame otter here when he came back on holiday.

Next to the church is St Medana's golf course. That's a new saint on me, although hagiography is not my specialist subject I have to admit. She was an 8th century beautiful Irish princess who, after becoming a convert to Christianity, fled her heathen native land with some of her handmaidens. They made landfall at East Tarbet on the Mull of Galloway and set up home in a cave there. Must have been a bit of a change from what she was accustomed to. Anyway, she set about converting the locals until one day, an admirer arrived out of the blue. She was not pleased to see him, to put it mildly, but heavenly help was at hand. She and her helpers stepped onto a rock, whereupon they were safely floated across Luce Bay to make landfall here.

The would-be lover was made of sterner stuff, however, and followed her. She was not in the least flattered and demanded to know what it was about her that he found so irresistibly attractive. "Your eyes," said he. "We'll see about that," quoth she, and plucking them out, threw them at his feet. At last he got the message that she didn't want to see him ever again, that and all she wanted to be was a bride of Christ, and so he hied himself back hence to Ireland.

But there is a happy ending, for Medana at least. She washed her bleeding face at a well now named after her, and you'll never guess – her eyesight was restored! She gave thanks by building a chapel there. Having set it up, though, she abandoned it and went travelling all over Scotland, founding more chapels until at last, she settled down as a governess to a Saxon princess.

The miraculous well, also known as the "Chincough", is supposed to be efficacious for the whooping cough apparently – an old name for that malady, apparently. You would have thought that a cure for blindness would have been more appropriate.

Behind the village is the Fell of Barhullion. Once the site of yet another prehistoric fort, one of the Maxwell lairds boasted that on a clear day, from its lofty height of 150 feet, he could see five kingdoms: Scotland, obviously, England, Ireland and the Isle of Man. And the fifth? The Kingdom of Heaven, of course! It *is* a heavenly view right enough.

This area is a pre-historian's dream. You can't help, when you are walking about, stumbling across some standing stone or other (or you would if they were lying flat), and cup-and-ring-marked rocks where Mr Iron-Age Man put his coffee mug down on the furniture despite his wife nagging him time and time again to use a coaster.

One such prehistoric site is the charmingly-named "Wren's Egg" at Blairbury Farm. It is said that on the shortest day of the year, if you clamber on top of the egg, about six feet high, you will see the sun set directly behind Big Scaur, an isolated rock out in Luce Bay. It has to be on that day, and only that day, for this phenomenon to happen.

In actual fact, the "egg" is a glacial erratic, remarkably round, and named ironically, because of its massive size. Two smaller stones, less than three feet high, are aligned nearby. It would be astonishing if the glacier had plonked them there, just like that. No, the hand of man has been at work here, but what it means, I have absolutely no idea, though if I were a betting man, I would have said it had something to do with the planets, or the sun and the moon, and Earth's relationship with them. The idea that they are all that remain of two stone circles has been discounted.

If you haven't the time to go hillwalking, or you think it's too energetic an activity by half, you might like to have a stroll along the beach. That's full of interest too. Monreith boasts a beautiful sandy beach, with caves perforating the cliffs. One is streaked red and known as the "Butcher's Cave". I can well see why. Never mind a butcher's shop – it looks as if a massacre has taken place here. Part of the wall is streaked with a lighter shade of red but in what looks like the epicentre, it's a deep, deep purple-red, the colour of raw liver. If the rock had been lying flat, I would have said it was a sacrificial table where generations of sacrificial blood had stained the rock this appalling colour. Thank goodness, it isn't; it must be porphyry. The Romans prized it highly and the sarcophagus of St Helena, the mother of Constantine, the first Christian Roman emperor, is made of the stuff. Poor Helena.

And at Black Rocks Bay, if you walk out to the point, you can see the remains of a flounder pool. If you remember the annual festival held in Palnackie, you will know what happened next to those members of the flatfish race.

Walk along a little way, round the bend, and you will come to Cairndoon shore, where, in a cave somewhere along here, a local hermit, an eccentric if you like, lived here in the 1960s.

Back in the car and heading west towards towards Port William, we stop at Barshalloch Point where there is another ancient fort, like Rispain, with a ditch thirty feet wide and ten deep. A steep flight of wooden steps leads to the top. This fort is D-shaped; the defence on the fourth side was the sea cliffs. Better by far than any man-made mound. The fort has not been excavated, but we know it would have had a cluster of roundhouses huddling behind wooden ramparts.

After that is little Port William, hemmed in between the shore and the steeply-rising ground behind it. It was formerly known as "Killantrae", from the Gaelic meaning "church on the beach". That settlement probably goes back as far as St Ninian's time. It changed its name in the 1770s when Sir William Maxwell of Monreith built a new town. He also improved the harbour and built a corn mill, which still stands today. The harbour was improved again in 1790, and yet again in 1848. Being the only harbour along this part of the coastline, it was a favourite place for smugglers to land their illicit goods from the Isle of Man and cache them amongst neighbourhood farms. Think of *Whisky Galore.*

It was known as the "Running Trade". The Lord of Man legally paid a small tax on items such as claret, rum and tea that he sold on to the smugglers, who avoided the exorbitant duties in Scotland and England by paying no tax at all. What they didn't consume themselves, they sold on. Business was brisk and profitable.

On the harbour green, a bronze statue of a man by local artist, Andrew Brown, stands leaning on a rail, hands clasped, staring out to sea, reflecting on the meaning of life.

We leave him to his contemplations and embark on another little detour. The B7021 takes us to Drumtrodden Standing Stones and the nearby Drumtrodden cup-and-ring marks. The former used to consist of three stones, ten-feet high, standing in line like soldiers on parade, but after three or four thousand years of standing to attention, two have decided to have a bit of a lie down – and who can blame them? Early records suggest there might have been four stones but, if so, there is no trace of the other one. Making a massive stone like that disappear like snow off a dyke is no easy matter. And maybe that *is* the answer – it was broken into pieces and used to form part of a dyke.

Nobody knows for sure, but it is thought they had something to do with observing the sun or moon. They are aligned northeast/southwest and I'm sure that must have some significance or other, like marking the summer and winter solstices. What is certain is it took a lot of effort to erect them and somehow some *high heid yin* must have persuaded the tribe to haul these massive stones up here from somewhere. And if that were not enough, persuade them to make these two-ton monsters stand upright.

Regardless of all the whys and wherefores, it certainly would have kept the men occupied. And were the monoliths once standing amidst a platform of smaller stones? And were they first transported to this hillside location all the way from the beach below? A heavy burden, God knows, and a trip they would have done many, many times. That would have been considered women's work, probably, but also would have given those teenagers who are always complaining about being bored, something to do. And I can just imagine how they would have moaned when they were told that's what they had to do!

A real community effort. And this at a time, mind, when the living wasn't easy, where finding something to put on the table must have been an occupation that took up a great deal of time and effort.

And if the reason for the erection of these stones makes the pre-historians (and us) scratch our collective heads in wonderment, then what on earth to make of the symbols on some stones a few hundred yards away with their mysterious cup-and-ring marks?

Those who know a bit more than us think these stones come from an even earlier period than the monoliths – probably from the Neolithic or early Bronze Age. There are three clusters of them, pretty-much worn and weathered – hardly surprising considering their age. There is no sign saying not to touch and, as I run my finger round one of the spirals, I am literally in touch with the very distant past. I can imagine the artist who once stood on this very spot, dressed in some animal skin or other, laboriously smiting his cutting stone with another to create this groove.

There are over 65 cup marks and at least 84 cup-and-ring marks, with the number varying between one and six on each stone. A good number of the rings have a groove running from the centre of the circle to the ground. Some circles are incomplete.

What can it all mean? It certainly meant something to the people who inhabited this early landscape and not just there – they are also found elsewhere in Scotland, northeast England, northwest Spain, Brittany and Ireland. They feature spirals, stars and straight lines as well as the occasional axe, but there are no animal or human figures like you see in prehistoric cave paintings.

We leave these tantalising mysteries behind and travel though space, but especially through time, to a structure a mere nine hundred to one thousand years old. We are at Druchtag Motte, and our first sight of it takes our breath away.

Mottes are two-a-penny hereabouts, but this is the best-preserved example I have ever seen. It stands over twenty feet high with a ditch 25-foot wide and 8-foot deep enclosing it. It would have been even deeper when it was first excavated. It looks like a sandcastle with a moat. It takes a matter of moments to build that on the beach, but think of the amount of men it must have taken to dig out that massive ditch and then build up all that spoil and soil, growing increasingly higher, then flattening it out at the top. Even with today's modern earthmovers it would be quite an undertaking.

And they weren't finished yet, not by a long way. On top of that, the vassals built their lord's keep into which he could retreat in times of danger. They would also have built a wooden palisade around the top of the mound. There is no evidence of a bailey or courtyard here, but normally there would have been such a thing, where the lord's hall would have stood, as well as the outbuildings to service it – the kitchens, bakehouse, brewery and chapel. That would have needed a protective ditch and a wooden palisade as well.

The motte hasn't been excavated, so there are no clues as to the name of the lord who had this built. Mottes such as this were all the rage in the reign of David I (1124-53). He encouraged the Normans to settle in Scotland, so this motte may have been built by one of these immigrants rather than a local landowner. A third, but less likely possibility, is it might have been thrown up during the Wars of Scottish Independence as protection from the dastardly English. But by that time, motte-and-bailey castles had just about had their day. Fire was a persistent hazard, to say nothing of the advances in the technology of warfare. Stone was the new material.

Because Druchtag was such an outstanding example of its kind, it was taken into State care in 1888. The summit is 66 feet across with some dimples in it but, say the archaeologists, they are not evidence of habitation. I suppose they should know. But if they are not, then just what are they?

You can't see it from here, but as the crow flies, is the village of Elrig, where, as I said, Gavin Maxwell was brought up. He wrote an account of his boyhood in *The House of Elrig* (1965). In the loch of the same name is a crannog, just barely visible above the water, while just on the northern shore, stands the Carlin stone, triangular-shaped and less than six feet high. Some say it might have formed part of a circle; it probably didn't, say the archaeologists.

We're not going to see it. To be honest, it's not worth going out of our way, not when we've already seen so many more examples that are better.

• • •

257

Chapter Forty-Four

St Finian's Chapel and Glenluce Abbey: Dire Deeds Concerning a Monastery

WE have not a gone a mile, a mile, a mile but barely three, back on the A747, when we stop at the ruins of St Finian's chapel, just a stone's throw from the seashore. It is thought to have been built sometime between 900 and 1000, a handy place to rest your feet along the well-trodden pilgrim way from Ireland to *Candida Casa* and later, to Whithorn Priory.

There's not a lot left of the chapel to see, the remaining walls mainly being about knee-high to a moderately-sized person such as me. Excavations revealed that the building was 22 feet by 13, with the door to the south and with a perimeter wall so reduced in height now that even a geriatric grasshopper could hop over it with ease. A stone bench encased in wood was found in the interior, but there was no trace of any other furniture.

Finian was born c.495 AD and came across the sea from Ireland to be educated at Whithorn, after which he went to Rome for seven years to complete his education. (He is not to be confused with St Finnian of Clonard, by the way.) Returning to Ireland, he founded a monastery at Movilla near Newtownards, County Down, in 540. Movilla is the anglicised version of *Magh Bhile* in Irish Gaelic, meaning "the plain of the sacred tree", indicating that the site was formerly used for pagan worship. Here he taught the lad that was to become St Columba. You would never have guessed that one day he would be elevated to the sainthood: he was a very naughty boy.

According to legend, Finian, the founder, expelled Columba from the abbey for secretly copying a psalter. Eventually, as everyone knows, he ended up in Iona and on his proselytising travels, famously had a close encounter with the Loch Ness monster. Parents should take heart from this little tale – their little monsters who are behaving badly both at home and at school, may surprise them one day by going on to greater things. As for Finian, he went on to higher things too when he died about 570.

But wait a minute! Some scholars have suggested that Finian and Ninian are the one and the same, both names being a corruption of "Uinniau". Hmm! I can see the similarity between Finian and Ninian especially. But there's more – there was a bishop Uinniau, alive and well fifty years after Ninian died in 432 and operating in this area, if "operating" is the right word. Could it possibly be, bearing in mind how difficult it is to date some births and deaths with accuracy in the distant past, that this Bishop Uinnian is the real St Ninian around whom the cult grew?

What is a fact is you can't go far without coming across evidence of pre- and-medieval history hereabouts. It's also true you can't go very far without stumbling across some religious edifice or other. A few miles later, we come to another one – Glenluce Abbey.

So unlike St Finian's chapel, in so many ways! Where that was confined to the strip of land between the sea and the hills rising behind, here the land broadens out to create a green and pleasant place. A perfect place to build a monastery, so thought Roland, Lord of Galloway, towards the end of the 12th century.

It began with an abbot and twelve monks dressed in their white robes because they were Cistercians, remember – a devil of a colour for showing up the dirt. First they cleared the land, then they began building the church as that is the most important part, naturally. Following good practice, they built it on the north side of the site, so its tall shadow would not be cast over the secular buildings. The complex was added to over the centuries, and like Topsy, it just grew, right up to a few years before its demise in fact.

Sadly, it's a shadow of its former self now. Two parts of the south transept wall remain standing, but there is little left of the rest. The best-preserved parts of the abbey are the buildings on the east side of the cloister, part of which has been restored. The star of the abbey today is the chapter house which was restored in 1515 and the windows with their wonderful traceries, some four hundred years later, in the 1900s! And how magnificent they are! If there is anything that gives you a window into the past and a glimpse of how wonderful this place must have looked then, then it is these.

Part of the original flooring remains, fenced off at the bottom of the central pillar, while above your head, some of the graceful vaulting still remains with their bosses. Around the walls are the restored stone benches which the monks' bums would have warmed. The abbot's stall stands in the centre of the east wall between the windows.

This is very helpful, as – however hard you try, despite the illustrations on the noticeboards you see in Historic Environment sites – there is nothing

· · ·

quite like being *in* the real thing or a restoration of it. Not only does it give you a feeling of what it was like, but you can actually *hear* what it sounded like in here when the monks got the rare chance to exercise their vocal chords. You are encouraged to test the acoustics. There is no-one else about. We do. Amazing!

Glenluce Abbey

Yes, the windows are very intricate indeed, but compare that with the simple, austere lives of the monks whose dormitory was on the storey above. That was a completely different story, if you pardon the pun. There, probably fifteen of them would have slept in an unheated dormitory, on a thin straw mattress and under thin blankets.

In the north transept of the church, a graveslab is wrongly attributed to Sir Robert Gordon of Lochinvar. In actual fact, it belongs to Robert Gordon of Muirfad, who died on 26th April 1548. He was a descendant of William Gordon, aka *Gay Lochinvar.*

On the south chancel is a late 17th century armorial panel impaled with the arms of Thomas Hay of Park and his wife, Janet Hamilton. Sounds very painful. In the museum you can see a fragment of an 11th century cross-slab that was found in the chapter house. It is inscribed with a Greek cross with, in the archaeologists' jargon, "expanded terminals to the arms and ringed armpits".

Another cross-slab with an incised cross and two holes cut through it was found, but now lost, sadly. How do you lose a massive stone like that? I bet I know. Recycled somewhere. No respect.

On the fourth side of the cloister, on the south side, was where the kitchens and the refectory stood. Further south, the foundations of other outbuildings can be seen. We all know the abbey's days were numbered with the Reformation in 1560, but before then, it did not have its troubles to seek. In 1544, the monks were expelled over a land dispute. Land was everything: it was the source of the monastery's wealth. On it, sheep could safely graze, giving the coats off their backs until their date with destiny and the butcher's knife. By 1400, the monastery had amassed 1,300 sheep.

After the Reformation, those monks willing to submit to the new Protestantism were allowed to stay on until they died. Commendator Thomas Hay and five monks were still there in 1575. The last commendator, Laurence

Gordon, died in 1602 and whether he went to meet his Maker in a great feeling of fear and trepidation, given his caving-in to the new orthodoxy, history does not record.

One interesting, if grisly, tale that *is* recorded concerning the abbey, revolves around Gilbert Kennedy, 4th Earl of Cassillis (c.1541-76) aka the *King of Carrick*. It's worth mentioning, however, before I get to him, that the 1st Earl fell at Flodden in 1513, the second was murdered in 1527 by the Sheriff of Ayr and the third was poisoned in Dieppe after helping to negotiate the marriage of the sixteen-year-old Mary to the fourteen-year old Francis, the Dauphin of France. Given that his forebears all came to sticky ends, one wonders if Gilbert pondered on the chances of his shuffling off the mortal coil following a similar pattern, like Peggoty's relations who were all "drowndead" in *David Copperfield*.

In December 1560, Kennedy was condemned by the General Assembly as an "idolator and a maintainer of idolatry". Five years later, he was still openly attending mass. But then, reader, he married Margaret Lyon, daughter of John Lyon, 7th Lord Glamis. His bride persuaded him to give up the Old Religion. See what the love of a good woman can do!

But Kennedy would not give up his Queen. He knew her well. He was one of those on the bench in that risible trial in which Boswell was found not guilty of playing any part in the murder of Mary's husband, Darnley. He also fought for her gallantly at Langside in 1568, and from her captivity, she wrote to him several times, expressing her gratitude. A noble, and a nobleman, loyal to his monarch, right up to the end. Her end maybe, but he became an utter monster.

The historian of the Kennedys, antiquarian, author, friend and collaborator of Sir Walter Scott, Robert Pitcairn (1793-1855), in his *Historical and Genealogical Account of the Principal Families of the Surname of Kennedy*, described him as a "werry greidy manne and cairitt nocht how he gatt land sa that he culd cum be the samin (come by the same)". That gives a flavour of Pitcairn's style and spelling. And so he chunters on for more than two hundred pages, including notes and appendices. It may be Scots, but it's like reading a foreign language. Fortunately, there is also a glossary.

Kennedy had his eye on the lands of Glenluce and entered into negotiations with the abbot to take over the abbey lands by feudal tenure. Very inconsiderately, the abbot died before the transactions were complete. Undeterred, Kennedy persuaded one of the monks to forge the signatures of the deceased abbot and his fellow monks on a deed which conveyed the lands to him and his heirs.

Then, lest the monk had a crisis of conscience, he paid an assassin to "stik him", and then, to make sure his tracks were well and truly covered, he got his uncle, Hugh of Bargany to hang the assassin on a false charge of theft. Charming. But he wasn't finished yet. What he did next is a tale I'll reserve for its proper place and time.

As for the abbey, over the centuries, weather and time played their parts in its deterioration but the greatest of all was in 1590, when its nicely-dressed stone was quarried for the construction of a four-storey tower house called the "Castle of Park" for Thomas Hay, the son of the commendator. Above the door is this quaint inscription:

BLISSIT.[BE].THE. NA[ME].OF.[THE]LORD.THIS
WERK.WAS.BEGUN.T[H]E.F[IR]ST.DAY.O[F].MARCH
15[90].BE.THOMAS.HAY.OF.PARK.AND
JONET.MAK.DOVEL.HIS.SPOVS

I love the spelling of Janet's name – and how unusual, especially in those days, for a wife to be given equal status as her husband!

The house was extended in the 18th century and occupied until 1830, when they abandoned it and moved to Dunragit House. It was taken over by the Ministry of Works in 1949. It was subsequently restored by Historic Scotland who leased it to the Landmark Trust, who in turn, let it out to visitors. If you have a penchant for staying in unusual places with a bit of history attached, then the Landmark Trust is the place to look for properties. This particular one comes with a couple of previous residents – a monk who was walled up in one of the rooms, and a green lady who became pregnant while working at the castle. We don't know by whose hand, so to speak, but she does, and I bet she's haunting the place looking for the father – and some maintenance money.

In 1933, what was left of the abbey passed into the care of the State and now is in the good hands of Historic Environment Scotland. During the restoration, decorated clay tiles from the floor of the church were found, as well as some pottery, and something unique in the history of monasteries – clay and lead water pipes which brought in water from the Water of Luce as there was not a well on the site. You can see some of them in the small museum and some others *in situ*. Normally there not being a well on the site would have been a very big setback to Roland's dream of establishing a monastery here, but thanks to these pipes, his dream became reality.

It was no pipe dream. Or maybe actually it was.

Chapter Forty-Five

To the Mull of Galloway: Stones and Stories

GLENLUCE, the village, was originally named "Ballinclach" or "stone village" and grew up on the back of the monastery's wealth. It became a burgh in 1496. Its name was changed to Glenluce, literally "valley of light", in 1705. Lying equidistant between the Machars and Rhins of Galloway and situated on the Old Military Road between Dumfries and Portpatrick, it became an important cattle tryst with junctions north to Ayr and southeast to Wigtown.

We're on the way to Dunragit now, where the Hays went after they left Castle of Park. The name comes from *Din Rheged* meaning "Fort of Rheged". It has been suggested that this was one of the royal sites – even King Arthur's *Pen Rhionydd* as recorded in the medieval Welsh Triads. As the name suggests, "triads", in the Welsh tradition, consist of three inter-related texts.

The house that the Hays built, Dunragit House, has been turned into flats. Posh, mind you – but how the mighty has fallen!

Actually, Dunragit is a Neolithic complex. Aerial photography revealed a cursus monument – a ditch-like structure consisting of two parallel lines. They vary in length from a matter of yards to miles, with no set width and blocked off at the ends. What on earth were they for? Suggestions include: astronomical alignments; processional routes; an area reserved for ceremonial use as opposed to habitation, perhaps for the veneration of the ancestors; or a proving ground for young men about to embark on adulthood. They were built between 3,400 and 3,000 BC – the oldest structures in the British Isles.

Three later timber concentric circles dating to about 2,500 BC were also discovered. These can only be seen from the air, but you can't miss, 400 yards away, the mound of Droughduil, which, in another case of mistaken identity was once believed to be a medieval motte. Archaeologists' suspicions were aroused that it was not a motte by the mound's alignment with the entrance to one of the timber circles. They were right to be suspicious.

Excavation in 2002 revealed it to be contemporaneous with the circles. Nowadays, nature is reclaiming its territory as one side is covered with gorse, but it still retains that neat conical shape as if some inhabitant of Brobdignag had upended his pail and flattened out the top to build a castle for the kids.

Another motte was found in the grounds of Dunragit House, but that has nothing to do with this Neolithic complex. It's known as "Round Dunan" and a mere youngster, dating from the 5th or 6th century AD.

Most people, I suppose, would regard the A75 as a blessing, as it bypasses the towns and villages along the former route. In fact, given the volume of present-day traffic, it's hard not to see that without it, there would be one gigantic vehicular snake stretching from Stranraer to Dumfries.

Apart from the slower pace of life the bypass brought to this village, there was one other unexpected benefit. As it was being built, digging revealed hidden treasures. I suppose, given the amount of historical evidence to be seen above ground here, it would be surprising if nothing *had* been found below ground. What they found spanned centuries: Mesolithic stone tools and flints by the thousands; Neolithic arrowheads; Bronze Age cemetery urns, cist burials and grave goods, including two bead necklaces, one made up of 130 pieces of Whitby jet; and six Iron Age roundhouses, pottery and a brooch. That's what I would call a find!

Nearby are the 12-acre Glenwhan Gardens which were created, or should I say transformed from the hillside where gorse and bracken once grew, into some other Eden. Would you buy a 103-acre farm and farmhouse over the phone, sight unseen? No, neither would I, but that's exactly what Tessa Knott and her husband did in 1979. After a visit to nearby Logan Botanic Garden, they were inspired. Thanks to the help of the mild Gulf Stream and the protective shelter of trees and the turning of boggy ground into ponds, the greater miracle of kidding plants that normally flourish in the southern hemisphere was accomplished, and they are perfectly at home in southern Scotland. And, by the way, while some miracles sometimes happen instantaneously, this took decades of hard, backbreaking physical work as well as planning to provide colour throughout each season of the year.

A Tree Trail takes you past more than 150 different species of trees. You do not go alone, as a handy leaflet accompanies you so you know what you are looking at. Meanwhile, the Wildflower Walk with its mown-grass paths take you through more than 120 species of ferns, grasses and flowers, each in their season of course.

A new addition, for the millennium, is the "Peace Pinnacle", an eye-catching sculpture of stone balls of diminishing size, balanced on top of each other. In real life, it would be the sort of thing you would only see in a circus and you would hold your breath lest they all fell down. I am sure these won't, but I get the message – peace is difficult to achieve and precarious to keep.

At the appropriately-named Sandhead, we say goodbye to the B7804 and join the A716. Here, Luce Sands extend for seven miles around the curve of the bay, all the way to Stairhaven, south of Glenluce. It was declared a Special Site of Scientific Interest (SSSI) in 1981. About midway along, south of Dunragit, are the dunes of Torrs Warren, the largest acidic dune system in southern Scotland. It's home to over 220 plants, some of them very rare, as well as invertebrates and amphibians who live in the saltmarshes. Then there are the overwintering birds such as white-fronted geese from Greenland and waders who dip their webbed feet in the waters. And in the distant past, humankind also made their home here. Tools from the Mesolithic Age have been uncovered, dating from between 5000 to 3500 BC.

On the way into Sandhead, another motte pops up like a gigantic molehill. This is Balgreggan Motte, which would have supported a wooden keep in the 12th or 13th century. It stands thirty feet high, on top of a ridge. During WWII, the Royal Observer Corps used it as lookout point. (They knew not how useful they would be in the future, the ancient builders.) After the keep burned down, the McDoualls built a stone castle a little to the west. In its turn, it was replaced by Balgreggan House which was reduced to dust in 1966. As I've said before, nothing lasts forever, but some things last longer than others.

Further along the road, we follow the sign up the single-track road to Kirkmadrine Church which boasts the second-best collection of Christian stones after Whithorn. The name "Kirkmadrine" is derived from the Norse *kirkya* meaning "church", while the second part is the name of a long-forgotten saint. The inhabitants of this area, the Gail-Ghaidheil (literally foreign Gaels) were Gaelic speakers influenced

Kirkmadrine Church

Gravestone at Kirkmadrine Church

by the Norse invaders. Very likely they settled in this region after the Norse were expelled from Dublin in 902.

A tall Celtic-style cross on a mound dominates the churchyard. It is dedicated to the McTaggart family, beginning with John who died in 1810. The church was built in 1889 on the site of an earlier medieval church. Some of its stones were used by Lady McTaggart-Stewart to build a mortuary chapel for the family. And why not? It's good to see life in the old stones yet, being put to good use to celebrate the lives of those who went before. It's not possible to get inside, but a peek through one of the windows not boarded up reveals a goodly number of gravestones set in the floor.

In 1860, Dr Arthur Mitchell recognised two pillar stones serving as gateposts for what they really were – gravemarkers. One has a six-line Latin inscription commemorating two "chief priests": Viventius and Mavorius. The other is in honour of Florentius and another individual whose name, sadly, is illegible. Do not be deceived, as many still are, by what appears to be another name, IDES. It's actually *id est,* Latin for "that is" with the "T" missing. In 1861, at the behest of James Young Simpson (yes, the discoverer of chloroform as an anaesthetic), plastercasts of the stones were made for the National Museum of Antiquities.

Dr Mitchell continued his search of the cemetery and found two more stones bearing crosses. It was not the archaeological equivalent of buried treasure, since the stones were in plain view for all to see – if only they knew what were looking at. And what they had been looking at unknowingly all this time was really something very special. The former gateposts were dated to about 450, making them the oldest Christian inscribed stones in Scotland – with the exception of the Latinus Stone in Whithorn. The implication of this is it was the site of a daughter church of Whithorn, or even a monastery.

The locals remembered seeing another stone, but where it was now no-one knew. A local antiquarian, William Todd, had made a sketch of it in 1822. Like the other two stones, it had the Chi-Rho monogram and the words *INITIUM ET FINIS.* It was finally rediscovered in 1916 by a stonemason repairing the gate of the nearby United Free manse Stoneykirk (appropriately enough) – but not before he had smashed it into pieces. It was only when he turned a piece over and then another, that he saw the writing on the stone and saw what he had done. No matter. It was expertly put together and you would never know it once had been split asunder. It dates from about 600 and the inscription is of course, a quotation from *Revelations.* There's no denying the truth of that statement. We are born and we die.

The McTaggart Monument

Another stone is dedicated to Ventidius who, it seems, was a sub-deacon, the only other word that could be deciphered. There are other stones besides, including five cross-fragments dated from between 700 and 1100, evidence that this place saw continuous Christian worship from the Dark Ages through to medieval times.

The stones can only be seen through a glass porch, but there are some pretty-interesting gravestones of a more modern vintage to be seen in the churchyard. By "modern" I mean about seven centuries old. They are illegible but bear some pretty interesting carvings. They are easy to find.

Retracing our steps and then joining the A716 again, we carry on ever more southerly to Ardwell (from the Gaelic *Àrd Bhaile*, meaning "high town") where its palm trees wave a welcome in a pretty stiff breeze.

Before too long the road takes a jink to the east to hug the shore along Kilstay and Drummore Bays. The former has an interesting legend attached to it. A long, long time ago, when sailors were more at the mercy of the seas and the vagaries of the weather than they are today, before they embarked on a crossing of the vast Luce Bay, and in order to ensure a safe passage, they would place offerings at the mouth of a cave which was said to be inhabited by fairies. This cave, the entrance to which is gone now, used to run right across the peninsula, end to end, emerging at the other side at Clanyard Bay.

The sailors, frightened to meet a fairy face to face, did not hang about to see if their offering was acceptable or not. One day however, one bold boy decided he would investigate the cave accompanied by his pipes and his dog. No doubt he thought the skirl of the pipes would be enough to scare the pants off the fairy folk and right enough, in that confined space it must have sounded truly terrible.

It was the dog which turned out to be the one who was scared. It emerged from the cave terrified and hairless. As for the piper, he was never seen again, but it is said that on a still and windless night, if you listen very carefully, from deep underground, you can hear the faint sound of a piper playing...

Chapter Forty-Six

The Mull of Galloway: Scotland's Most Southerly Point

THE A716 comes to a stop at Drummore, Scotland's most southerly village. It owes its name to the Gaelic *druim mòr*, meaning "great ridge". Believe it or not (and it's hard to accept I know), but at this point you are further south than Carlisle in the west of England and Durham in the east. It was near here that the stone attributed to Ventidius was found, proof that this was an ancient seat of Christianity.

In the early 19th century, a harbour was built. Lime out; coal in. Nowadays you will find the harbour filled with pleasure craft. It's a great place for mucking about in boats. But sometimes you may see a more sinister vessel belonging to the military. You see, that vast expanse of sand that I told you about before, the SSSI, is actually a practice bombing range. Look at the OS map and you will see "Danger Area" written in red all over it. But please, don't let me put you off. I am sure it's all perfectly safe really.

Now on the B7041, we are heading to Scotland's most southerly point – the Mull of Galloway. On our right is yet another motte – High Drummore. You're probably suffering from a surfeit of mottes by now but this is different in that the remains of the bailey can still be seen to the east, eight-foot high and twenty-three-foot wide. The western side was protected by a ditch and a rampart. If you are interested in statistics and even if you are not, I'm going to tell you that the top of the motte is forty feet in diameter and the hollows in the ground where excavations took place can still be seen. A gold torc was discovered, now in the National Museum in Edinburgh.

At the splendidly-named Drumnaglaur ("bloody muddy place"), must surely be the translation), the B7065 meets the B7041 before it thins out into a single-lane road which threads its way through Auchie Glen. Off to the left, and out of sight, is the site of Kirkmaiden Church, the one intended to receive the pulpit and bell from its namesake on the other side of the bay at Monreith.

The road stops at the Mull of Galloway and it's where Scotland stops too – a bleak, windy sort of place. The promontory is practically a presque-isle, pinched by the twin bays of West and East Tarbert. A few millennia from now it will be a fully-fledged island, and mainland Scotland will stop a little bit further north. In the late Bronze Age or early Iron Age, the inhabitants constructed a system of ditches and earthworks across this narrow waist to keep out undesirables. Traces of their earth-moving efforts can still be made out.

Later, this was the fortress of the Southern Picts, who, when they were not doing battle with the Romans, brewed heather ale from a secret recipe, handed down from generation to generation. Its fame grew far and wide, as far as what is now Northern Ireland. King Niall decided he had to have that recipe and launched an invasion. Battle raged until there were only two Picts left – an old man and his son. Niall said he would spare one if the other would cough up the recipe.

Knowing that his son was mortally wounded, the old man volunteered to divulge the secret but only to a druid who had turned traitor in return for being appointed the brewmaster. He watched in horror as his son was thrown over the cliffs. There are many deaths, and that must be one of the worst. The grieving father led the druid to the highest point of the cliffs (you would have thought that the traitor might have suspected the old man was up to something) and grabbing his arm, the old man launched them both into the void.

There are other versions of the tale. Robert Louis Stevenson wrote one in verse which begins:

From the bonny bells of heather
They brewed a drink long-syne,
Was sweeter far than honey,
Was stronger far than wine.

Fortunately the recipe has not been lost entirely. It may not be the same exactly, but it tastes good enough to me. Try it and see.

These days the Mull is inhabited by those who take to the air and those whose domain is in the sea. In the RSPB visitor centre, information boards tell you all you need know about the wildlife: seabirds, dolphins, porpoises and basking sharks.

The most noticeable feature is the eighty-foot high lighthouse built by Robert Stevenson in 1830. It took two years to build and, at £9,000, an absolute snip. It would cost £9 million to build today. The tower is eighty-five feet high, making the light 325 feet above sea level. It has a range of 28 nautical miles. It became fully automatic in 1988, and of course is lit by electricity – but only from 1971! Before that it was powered by paraffin which was landed at the bay at East Tarbet, as were the keepers' provisions. It's astonishing to think that this simple lamp, the sort of thing that needed to be pumped to be primed, was used in Victorian houses up and down the land, but thanks to the prisms that surrounded it, it was magnified to the power of 29,000 candles. Blimey, imagine having to light all of those! Thank God for prisms!

It was manned by a head lightkeeper and two assistants and they all lived here along with their families. They grew their own vegetables and kept chickens and sheep, as well as a horse for hauling provisions from the beach at East Tarbet. At night, they worked in shifts to watch the light, to check it was flashing the way it should. During the day, they were engaged in keeping the premises spick and span. Today they have been converted into three holiday cottages with sleeping accommodation for six and four guests.

A short circular walk leads to the lighthouse. At the start of the walk, or the end, depending on whether you choose to go clockwise or anticlockwise, a noticeboard gives an account of a tragic accident. On 8th June 1944, in fog, a Bristol Beaufighter piloted by Claudius Echalier of the British Air Transport Auxiliary (ATA), accompanied by Flight Engineer Royston Edwin Staniford, hit the boundary wall, then the roof of the stores building (now the RSPB visitor centre), before plunging over the edge of the cliff into the sea.

The men were based at Prestwick. Echalier was one of five French nationals serving with the ATA. During the war, 1,320 civilian pilots from 28 countries ferried planes from the factories, assembly plants and maintenance units to wherever they were needed, thus freeing up RAF pilots for combat. 168 were women and, from 1943, they were paid the same as men. Depending on their level of experience, the pilots could be required to fly any one of 147 different types of planes. 174 pilots lost their lives providing this indispensible service, including the pioneering aviator, Amy Johnson.

Another noticeboard near the cliff edge overlooks Gallie Craig, literally "craggy rock". It juts out into the sea to the west, truly *the* most southerly point in Scotland. One of these days, a million years or more from now, it

The Lighthouse, Mull of Galloway

Gallie Craig

will become an isolated rock as there is a massive big cave where the sea has been gnawing away at it for centuries like sugar at a molar. The photograph on the noticeboard must have been taken on a good day, for the sea is calm and blue. Today it is grey and gurly except where it foams white at the foot of the cliffs.

The cliff we are standing on is known as "Foxes Rattle" which explains why there is a picture of a fox on the noticeboard. Apparently this cliff is home to a family of the aforesaid, who are grateful for the daily eggs the birds have kindly laid for them. In this quest, they dislodge stones and send them rattling down the cliff. They won't be trying that today, not in these winds. We are battling them to keep on our feet, not a little fearful that a sudden gust and change in direction might pluck us up and tip us over the edge.

You can follow in the footsteps of the keepers for a bird's-eye view of the landscape by climbing the 114 steps to the top of the lighthouse, as long as it is open of course. On a clear day, it offers a commanding view straight to the bottom of the white-fringed cliffs, with Luce Bay and the Machars to the east, and to the southwest, the Isle of Man.

The Exhibition Centre is housed in the former fuel store and engine room next to the lighthouse. It was closed at the time of our visit but through the window, as well as three diesel engines, I could see a Fresnel Lens, like a multi-faceted diamond. It came from McArthur's Head Lighthouse on Islay.

In the early 1900s, a foghorn was placed near the top of the cliff. A path leads down 127 steps to a viewing platform where you can see it at close quarters, as well as the sea beneath your feet and the birds that wheel and gyre overhead. Originally it too had a paraffin engine to blow the air into it, until it was replaced by the diesel engines above in 1955. Three to do what one did before, that's progress! They still sound the horn from time to time for nostalgia's sake.

On the way back to the car park, we blow into the Gallie Craig Coffee House, erected in 2004, for a bowl of hot soup. On the terrace, an iron railing prevents visitors from dropping into the abyss yawning beneath their feet. There can be few, if any, coffee houses in the land that offer such a view. Its glass frontage gives an uninterrupted view of acres of sea and sky, while its turf roof is designed to blend into the contours of the land to make it as inconspicuous as possible. Despite this camouflage, you cannot miss it.

Further to the west, a path leads to Kennedy's Cairn. Who is or was, Kennedy? Details are sketchy, but it seems he was a postie who died in a snowstorm whilst carrying out his duties. An iron staircase corkscrews round the cairn inviting you to climb to the top. It seems rude not to.

This will be the closest I'll ever get to being put on a pedestal. Keeping a firm grip of my hat, I mount the stairs and, like Keats's *stout Cortez*, gaze solemnly out to sea, only not the Pacific of course.

Chapter Forty-Seven

Kirkmaiden to Dunskey: Films, Fish and Gardens

THE Mull marks a turning point. It's a long and winding road, but from now on, we are heading back to Dumfries to complete the circle. This time, we are taking the middle way back up the peninsula on the B7065 to Kirkmaiden, where, just to the south of the village, the summit of Core Hill marks the site of an Iron Age fort where archaeologists unearthed a stone axe.

It's confusing having all these Kirkmaiden churches. The one here is not to be confused in any way with the remains of that at Portankill near the tip of the peninsula, far less the one in the Machars which has the memorial to François Thulot and which Wikipedia wrongly attributes to here. We all know that the things you're liable to read on the Internet bible are not necessarily true.

This church dates from 1638 and is the resting place of the McDouall family. It has a Treacle Bible which, although not quite as famous as the Breeches Bible of 1579, which as I am sure you remember, gets its name from Genesis III:7 where it is written that Adam and Eve *sewed figge tree leaves and made themselves breeches.* The Treacle Bible is so-named because in the 1594 edition of the Good Book, Jeremiah VIII:22 poses the question: *Is there no tryacle in Gilead?* At the time of publication, "tryacle" meant a "cure-all", as well as the molasses that we think of today. The name stuck.

We're on our way to Port Logan now, on the B7065. The original settlement dates back to 1682 and was originally called "Port Nessock", the Gaelic *neasaig* meaning "nose" because of the way the mull stuck out into the sea. From here they exported kelp and samphire – a salt-tolerant plant that is good for you. So I am told.

Round about 1810, Lt. Colonel Andrew McDouall commissioned a harbour. The celebrated engineer, John Rennie (1761-1821) of London Bridge and the Bell Rock Lighthouse fame, to name but two, submitted proposals in

Kirkmaiden Church, with Core Hill Iron Age fort in background

1813. His vision of a breakwater protecting the entire bay was rejected due to cost. Thomas Telford (1757-1834), submitted a much more modest plan and work finally got underway in 1818 and was completed in 1820. Which just goes to show you that even back then, the wheels of bureaucracy grind exceeding slow.

It is not one of Telford's greatest erections, if I can put it that way, more famous for other projects such as the Caledonian Canal, but it is his most westerly in mainland Britain. This lighthouse is just a little stone affair that almost looks as if you could pick it up between finger and thumb and ring for the maid. It's actually 25 feet high and 10 feet in diameter.

Alas, after all that time and effort, the harbour never really took off. It was only used to land cattle from Ireland and never competed with Portpatrick as McDouall had intended. Alas, the best-laid plans o' lairds *gang aft agley* just as much as those *o' mice an' men.*

Recently, the harbour appeared in the film *Keepers* (2018) starring Gerard Butler and Peter Mullan. (The film was released in the UK the following year with the alternative title of *The Vanishing.*) It's a psychological thriller based on real-life events that took place on Flannan Isle in the Outer Hebrides. In a sort of *Marie Celeste* scenario, when the relief keepers arrived on Boxing Day 1900, they found no flag on the flagpole, no empty provision boxes ready for restocking, the clocks wound down, no keepers and no bodies. The lamps were filled and cleaned and a set of oilskins was hanging on a peg.

The mystery deepened in W.W. Gibson's narrative poem written twelve years later. He refers to an un-eaten meal and an *over-toppled chair,* as if the keepers had left in a hurry. The chair is a fact; the uneaten meal is the poet's embellishment. What really happened, we may never know, but the most likely solution is some sort of tsunami, or a freak wave, which the third keeper saw coming and rushed out to warn his mates – only for him to be swept away by it too. The film has an alternative solution to the mystery, but the filmmakers would never forgive me if I told you what it was.

Actually, it's a bit of a film star in itself, Port Logan. The BBC drama *Two Thousand Acres of Sky* was also filmed here. The series ran from 2001 to

• • •

2003, the village standing in for a village on the fictional island of Ronansay off the coast of Skye.

At the harbour, you will also find the former lifeboat station which was established in 1866 and funded by R.M. Ballantyne, the famous author of boys' adventure stories which I devoured in my short-trousered days. I dare say they are not read much now. Similarly, the lifeboat station is now the village hall,

Port Logan Harbour

but in its lifetime 71 lives were saved. That's no small achievement; something to be proud of.

Part of the harbour development involved building a causewayed road past the Laigh Row, or Lower Road, blocking off the residents' view of the sea. The laird expected them to move to a new Upper Road which he was going to generously construct for them as compensation. Thanks, but no thanks, said the villagers. They found the shelter from the winds that the causeway provided more than compensated for loss of the sea view and preferred to stay where they were. And should they get homesick for the sight of the sea, then the solution was simple – add another storey. And that's exactly what they did. Now it looks the sort of thing you see on the Dutch coast, with the houses cowering for shelter well below the level of the land.

Port Logan may have lost out to Portpatrick in the cattle trade but it has something the bigger port doesn't – the world's oldest, so it is claimed, natural marine aquarium. It's an Ice-Age blowhole, a natural fissure in the slated, slanted rock, which created a shallow pool that was used as a fish larder for Logan House. Anything nature can do, the improving laird aforesaid could make better. He blasted it wider, deeper and rounder with gunpowder and built a keeper's cottage and stone bathing hut while he was at it. Completed around 1800, the intention was it would provide a never-ending supply of fish, caught at sea, and kept here until needed. As easy as shooting them in a barrel. The water was changed with the tide, but the fish were trapped behind a grille. Nowadays, the water is controlled by a valve.

You can visit the pool today at the Logan Fish Pond and Marine Life Centre on the north side of the bay. Entry is by the former keeper's cottage gussied up to look like a castle with two towers, one round, one square, castellations, and two crosses which you can fantasise as being arrow-slits. And if the cottage is a pretend castle, then you can imagine that the pond, which looks like a massive flooded quarry, is actually the pretend bailey protected by castellated ramparts. It's really quite extraordinary.

It's no longer a fresh-fish larder but an unusual sort of aquarium where you can observe the denizens of the deep swimming about and see them swimming about in a place where they are fed instead of being fodder. How lucky they are! Better be gawped at than face a date with a plate. Alas, when we called, a notice told us it was closed due to illness. It's an ill wind...

It's a disappointment, but hardly a tragedy. Sadly, this idyllic spot has seen its share of that. I'm sorry to say, it's yet another aircraft disaster and it came little more than a month after the crash on the Mull of Galloway. On 27th July 1944, two USAF Douglas C-47 Dakotas took off from Filton, Gloucestershire, bound for the USA, via Prestwick.

The weather was bad, and too late, the leading pilot saw the cliffs looming up. He tried to gain altitude but smacked straight into the cliffs at a height of four hundred feet. On board was a crew of five and seventeen wounded soldiers. I can imagine the latter were looking forward to being repatriated, reunited with family and friends, out of harm's way, hopeful that by the time they were fighting-fit again, the bloody war would be over. Sad to say, there were no survivors.

More recently, in May 2017, two men were drowned when they set out from here for Stranraer, in a speedboat. Their bodies were taken from the sea near the west coast of Ireland. It seems they were part of a puppy-smuggling ring bringing designer puppies from Ireland to Scotland. Their supplier had previously been convicted of causing unnecessary suffering to animals. Sitting low in the water, the speedboat was totally inappropriate for such a journey. It's conjectured that it was swamped by waves. Incidentally, I think it's relevant to mention, just to indicate what a charming bunch of customers these were, that one of them was about to face trial for causing the deaths of two pensioners by dangerous driving and driving without insurance.

Logan Fish Pond and Marine Life Centre, Port Logan

A little to the north are the famed Logan Botanic Gardens, one of three run under the aegis of Edinburgh's Royal Botanic Gardens. An avenue of palm trees leads you there, a harbinger of what lies ahead. It features plants from Central and South America, Southern Africa and Australasia. This miracle of standing nature on its head is achieved, as you already know, by the Gulf Stream which allows plants and trees from the southern hemisphere to not only survive here, but flourish.

It contains over 1,800 species of plants of which about 120 are endangered. It's good to know that as long as this place exists, or as long as there are no exceptionally severe winters, these plants will survive. Top of the rare charts must go to the Wollemi Pine. The species was only discovered in 1994 in the Blue Mountains of New South Wales.

The Logan House Gardens are adjacent. The house was built in 1702. In 1800, a walled kitchen garden was built to grow vegetables for the house, incorporating the only part of Castle Balzieland left standing after it burned down in 1500.

If the palms and the eucalyptus trees are special to the Logan Botanic Gardens, then the avenue created by the hundred-year old "Monkey Puzzle" trees (*araucaria araucana*) must be one of the main attractions here, as are the rhododendrons, including the giant *rhododendron russellianum.* There are also seven UK champion trees (the biggest or oldest of their kind) and fourteen Scottish champions, one of which is the big-leaf *rhododendron sinograndе.* Isn't that an amazing thing!

Here's another! Believe it or not, there is an octopus's garden – and if that doesn't intrigue you to pay a visit, then I don't know what will.

But that's not all. There is something else to stretch the elastic of your credibility to the breaking point. It's yet another garden – Dunskey Gardens which you will find to the north of Portpatrick. (Dunskey, from *dun* meaning "hill" and *key* meaning "quay".) The snag is, it's only open for groups and by prior appointment. There is a way around that, however. Fork out for a stay at the castle and the gardens come free. For romantics it's a must, and I must do it some day.

Port Logan

The gardens boast three

restored glasshouses from the 19th century, built by Mackenzie and Moncur, the hottest hothouse designers of their day, by royal appointment to Queen Victoria and the Prince of Wales, no less. In addition to the exotic plants, there are grapes, peaches and nectarines. It seems incredibly easy here, in Southern Scotland, to kid plant life on that this is their natural habitat.

The other main attraction here is the Hedge Maze where you can lose the kids for a while. There is a method of getting to the centre and out again, but what is it? It was only built in 2003, the first and only in southwest Scotland. A scaled-down version of the Hampton Court Maze, it was created by using homegrown *griselinia littoralis* which is native to New Zealand.

The castle, now a hotel, is an amazing Edwardian pile built in 1900 and retains many of the original features: Doric columns in the drawing room; a stone Baronial fireplace in the grand hall; Delft blue tiles in the Dutch kitchen. The whole thing is sumptuous and not to be confused with the other, older 16th century Dunskey Castle, not that you are likely to, since it is a roofless ruin.

It was built by the Adairs of Kilhilt and stands on the site of an earlier fortification that was burned to the ground by the dastardly McCullochs of Myrton and Cardoness. It stands on a rocky promontory to the south of Portpatrick. The only side where it needed an artificial defence was to the northeast. Accordingly, a ditch 49 feet wide and 8 feet deep was cut out of the rock. More easily said than done. It stands four storeys high with a vaulted basement in which there were three cellars, one of which they think was reserved for wine. How astonishing! I always thought that was the prime purpose of a cellar.

It is said to be haunted by the ghost of a nursemaid. Apparently, she somehow managed to drop a baby from one of the upper windows where it dashed its brains out on the rocks below. She can't rest in peace, probably, out of remorse. I can picture her wringing her hands like Lady Macbeth, bemoaning the fact that she was so butter-fingered.

The castle is also said to have its very own brownie. They are supposed to be helpful little people, and in the past, every well-regulated household had one. Should you decide to visit the castle and should you happen to see him, do not be afraid, he will not harm you, but beware – brownies are hideously ugly. They are small, wizened creatures with short, curly, brown hair. There are regional variations, but in these parts, are said to have no noses, just a hole in their faces. They wear a brown hood and like to go about naked – yes even in a draughty Scottish castle. Hardy fellows.

For all these reasons, you might get a bit of a shock should you surprise the resident brownie here, just as much as he might be taken aback too, being unaccustomed to visitors. As a race, they prefer not to be seen (which is understandable, given their appearance), and that is why they work at night doing household tasks, such as a bit of dusting and sweeping, whilst you are tucked up in bed. All they ask in return are pieces of food, to be left in the corners of the rooms.

The castle was the location for the film *Hunted* (1952), starring Dirk Bogarde. You are probably unfamiliar with it, so let me tell you, briefly, that it's a crime drama, revolving around the police chasing Dirk Bogarde's character who has murdered his wife's lover. An orphaned six-year old boy, who is running away from his adoptive parents, is a witness to the crime, and Bogarde flees to Scotland taking the boy with him. I will not give the denouement away, but should you see it, I advise you to have your hankie at the ready.

It was also the location for another film, the 1948 version of *Kidnapped,* the plot of which, of course, needs no introduction. Interestingly, David Balfour was played by Roddy McDowall who was born in London, but whose father was a merchant seaman of Scottish descent. The McDoualls became the local lairds when they were granted lands by John Balliol in 1295. Their seat was Castle Balzieland, which as I said earlier, burned down in 1500, along with the family records.

Wouldn't it be fitting if this is where Roddy's ancestors came from, that he was coming back to his roots when this part of the film was shot here? But of course such coincidences normally only belong in the movies.

Chapter Forty-Eight

Portpatrick to Kirkcolm: The Local Hero, The Romantic Ministers and the Explorer

PORTPATRICK. It's a place well known and beloved by holiday-makers from around the globe. To get there, we took the B7042 from Sandhead because it cuts off two sides of a triangle. That said, there's nothing in particular to see there, so it's probably better to ignore the short cut and take the long way round via the A77.

It doesn't take too much a leap of the imagination to presume that this place has something to do with the patron saint of Ireland just across the water. Andrew Agnew in his *The Agnews of Lochnaw* (1864) tells the miraculous tale of how, when trying to convert the heathens of Ayrshire, they beheaded him in Glenapp. Keeping a cool head, Patrick picked it up and walked back to Portpatrick. Finding there were no boats about to leave, Patrick swam back to Ireland with it. You might wonder what he did with his head while he was doing that. Innumerable witnesses on the other side (by which I mean Ireland) testified that he held it between his teeth. I'm not saying they were telling porky pies, but there's something about that tale that just doesn't quite ring true...

Another tale relates that it was from here, with one giant stride for a man, he stepped over to Ireland leaving a footprint behind on a rock. Unfortunately, when the jetty was built, it was unwittingly destroyed, and so to was the evidence of the launchpad for this amazing feat.

Some of *Kidnapped* was also shot here (better by far than being beheaded), but – long, long before it became a film star – the village was a fishing port, blessed by a natural crescent-shaped harbour. Like the Logan Fish Pond, anything nature has created, man can improve on and in 1770, John Smeaton, the leading engineer of his day, was entrusted with the task. He built

Portpatrick Harbour

breakwaters to enclose the crescent but Nature had the last laugh when the waves, driven by the relentless Westerlies, eventually broke the breakwaters and in 1821, John Rennie was hired to construct the new harbour. A combination of lack of money and bad weather meant that the weather won that one too.

During the 1830s there were frequent sailings to Ireland, as well as to Glasgow and the Isle of Man, and by 1863, a calm inner basin was constructed. Too little, too late. The government switched the mail service to Stranraer, which, despite involving a long sail up and down Loch Ryan, did have the benefit of being sheltered from those dastardly Westerlies by the Rhins peninsula. Besides, Portpatrick was not big enough to accommodate shipping of the bigger sort.

Nowadays, the harbour is owned by a community trust. It's a heart-warming story about how a small community can come together to achieve something against the odds. In 2007, after plans by the private owners, Portpatrick Harbour Ltd., to build a 57-berth marina were knocked back by the council, the community formed a trust to buy the harbour for £350,000. There was just a slight problem – where was the money going to come from?

Banks refused to lend as they regarded the harbour as vastly overvalued, nor was the Trust eligible for a government grant as the rules forbade financing a debt. Enter local hero, Callum Currie, an offshore oil technician. In January 2015, he organised an extraordinary general meeting of the Trust. 160 people showed up. Callum proposed they approach the Community Shares Scotland (CSS) – a scheme funded by the Big Lottery Fund (Scotland) and the Carnegie UK Trust.

The CSS advised the Trust to sell "Save the Harbour" shares. E-mails were sent; shops and stores advertised the share issue. The launch date was set for September when the annual folk festival takes place, swelling the population of the town. A share was fixed at £25. You could buy as many as you liked but were only entitled to one vote, thus preventing large investors from having an undue amount of influence.

Amazingly, in only three weeks enough money had been raised. The harbour was saved. Shareholders came from as far away as Bermuda and Canada. Callum was elected chairman of the Portpatrick Harbour Community Benefit Society, and quite rightly too!

Now the plan is to refurbish the village hall using the money earned from mooring fees. It's a win-win situation. Well done, Callum and the rest of the CBS; you are an example to us all.

But back in the heydays of the harbour, in the 1760s, it connected with (and you may remember me mentioning it before), the Old Military Road, which came from Bridge of Sark on the English border, via Dumfries. A blessing for the cattle drovers. Then in 1862, the railway from Castle Douglas arrived with a spur to the harbour, while yet another line went on to Stranraer. So far, so good. But all things must pass. The link to the harbour was removed in 1875 and the line to Stranraer in 1950, long before Baron Beeching wielded his axe.

If the harbour is Portpatrick's main attraction, the ruined Old Parish Church is worth a visit because of its unusual shape and its history. It dates from 1629 and was in use until 1842, when a successor was built. It probably stands on the site of an earlier chapel known as St Patrick's. It's unusual because of its circular tower which is actually older than the church, possibly as much as by a century. Before the church formed a close attachment to it, the tower was probably a lighthouse. It certainly looks very much like one.

From 1759-1826, the church formed attachments of another kind. It was a very popular wedding venue. So much so, it became known as the *Irish Gretna Green*. After the harbour at Donaghadee, eighteen miles east of Belfast on the Ards Peninsula, was deepened to accommodate packet boats, they found themselves carrying not just mail, but males and females fleeing Ireland to be joined in holy matrimony.

The boat left daily and it is said the ceremony could be conducted, done and dusted, and the newly-weds back in Donaghadee within the hour. Such a life-changing experience in such a short time! Their parents may have banned the match, but what about the publication of the banns and the period of residence as the law required, I hear you ask? Well, you have also heard that love is blind –

Portpatrick

and so were those old romantics, the ministers who married them regardless.

The cemetery contains monuments to the ships that foundered here: *Dasher* (1830), *Lion* (1835), SS *Orion* (1850) and *Eugenie* (1856). A very dangerous strip of coast, obviously.

In 1897, the Board of Trade sanctioned the building of a new lighthouse at Blackhead, just to the north of the town, at an estimated cost of £13,500. A foghorn was also requisitioned at £2,790. The lighthouse was designed by David Alan Stevenson (1854-1938). You would have thought that his predecessors and relations had hardly any lighthouses left to build, but astonishingly, this later Stevenson clocked up another twenty-six. They named this one *Killantringan* from "Ringan or Ninian's Cill" or cell. On 1st October, the light was switched on and the one at Portpatrick switched off.

Almost at once, the new lighthouse was called into action. On 26th November, the head lightkeeper noticed a fishing boat in distress and alerted the lifeboat station at Portpatrick by setting off a rocket. The crew was rescued and the stricken vessel was towed into harbour. That was the first, and there were many more over the years. Notably, on 26th February 1982, the 800-ton container ship *Craigantlet*, out of Belfast and bound for Liverpool, ran aground on the rocks at Port-a-Maggie, just below the lighthouse. The crew was airlifted to safety by helicopter. Some of the containers were bearing hazardous chemicals and, because of the danger of the ship breaking up and spillage, the area was declared unsafe. It took nearly seven weeks to remove the containers. The *Craigantlet* was left to the weather and the waves. What is left of the bow can be seen from the top of the cliff at low tide.

As far as the foghorn was concerned, it was shut off in 1987. Modern navigational aids rendered it and the others obsolete. Pity that. I used to like the sound of a good mournful foghorn. The keepers also became redundant in 1988 when the light became fully automated.

The north end of the harbour marks the start of the 212-mile Southern Upland Way. It ends at Cockburnspath, on the east coast near Berwick-upon-Tweed. Along the way, it goes past places of interest that we have already visited such as St John's Town of Dalry. It also goes near places we will be visiting later. I'll tell you about them when we get there.

But in the meantime and not for the first time, we find ourselves on a little bit of a detour, following the B738 on a loop round the northern part of the Rhins peninsula. "Rhins" by the way, comes from the Gaelic *Na Rannaibh* meaning "points" or "headlands".

Just before Portslogan (not to be confused with Port Logan) and just by the side of the road and the junction with the Southern Upland Way is the

• • •

intriguingly-named *Knock and Maize* standing stone. It's from the late Neolithic or Early Bronze Age and although it does have a couple of cup-marks on it, it's lucky to be so near the road, as you might have been disappointed if you'd trekked miles to see it – unless, of course, you are the sort of person who likes a good walk for its own sake. In support of my point, the first Ordnance Survey account, known as the "name book", rudely describes it as a "cattle-rubbing post". It stands perfectly straight, 5.6 foot-tall, or short if you prefer to look at it that way. It's thought it might be a cemetery marker. A suitable place for excavation, I would have thought.

After Portslogan, the road forks to the wonderfully-named Auchnotteroch (a splendid challenge for Sassenachs to pronounce) and Leswalt. As we are about to discover, all roads lead to Leswalt. We stick to the B738, where presently it divides again where the B7043 leads to Lochnaw Loch and Leswalt. A castle belonging to the Agnews used to stand in the loch. In 1390, it was attacked and sacked by our old friend, Archibald the Grim.

He granted the lands here to his illegitimate son, William, but Margaret, Duchess of Touraine, wife of his legitimate son, Archibald, the 4th Duke, and daughter of Robert III (yes, she whose tomb we visited in Lincluden Abbey), forced William to transfer his lands to Andrew Agnew. It was his descendant, the 5th sheriff of Lochnaw, who you may remember, was involved in the murder of Thomas McLennan of Bombie at the door of St Giles Cathedral.

Not long after Ervie, we spot a monument on the top of Craigengerroch Hill. It had been whitewashed once but now it's more grey than white. It's known as the *Marian Monument*. A stone plaque on one side bears the legend "Marian Hill 1818". Some say she was a local girl who was gored by a bull. Others say she was the wife of Admiral Sir John Ross (1777-1856), the polar explorer, who was born at Balsarroch House. It once stood at the bottom of the hill a little to the north, and she used to come up here looking for his ship returning. It's a nicer story than the other, so I hope that's the one that's true.

Ross's story is a remarkable one. He joined the Royal Navy at the tender age of nine. He led three expeditions to the Arctic in the search for the North West Passage and ended up as a rear admiral. He embarked on his third expedition there at the advanced age of 73. This was in search of the lost Sir John Franklin expedition. He found no trace of Franklin or his men, but did bring back news from the Inuit that Franklin and his crew of 129 men were all dead. This news did not please Lady Franklin, to put it mildly. She dismissed it completely, worried it would bring an end to future rescue attempts.

Unsurprisingly, given his age, Ross never went to sea again, and lived with his second wife at his house in Stranraer which he named *North West*

The Marian Hill Monument

Castle. Having hung up his sea boots, he picked up his pen and began writing pamphlets, a thorn in the side of the Admiralty. One of them was critical about their maps, while another found fault with their attempts to find, and rescue, Franklin. If he hoped this would curry favour with Lady Franklin, it didn't work.

And just for the record, the rumours of the death of Franklin and his men were not exaggerated. An expedition was sent out in 1857 at the behest of the persistent Lady Franklin and which uncovered the unpalatable truth that her husband had indeed died in 1847. But there was worse, much worse to come. There was disbelief from Lady Franklin and denial from a shocked nation when it emerged that in their desperation, in that white wilderness, the men had resorted to cannibalism. Englishmen would never resort to such a thing, the protesters denied, throwing up their hands in horror. There were no survivors.

As for Ross, he died while on a visit to London in 1856 and is buried in Kensal Green Cemetery.

Just after the site of the birthplace of the great man, the road takes a dogleg to the east, where for once, the road does not lead to Leswalt but to Corsewall Point. In 1815, the Lighthouse Board sanctioned the construction of a lighthouse there and another at the Point of Ayre on the Isle of Man. Robert Stevenson (1772-1850), was awarded the contract. Things went well. Stevenson made a voyage of inspection in December of that year and was pleased to see the tower had already grown to thirty feet and the keepers' cottages were under construction. Its finished height was 112 feet and had a range of 22 nautical miles. The light was switched on in 1817.

Then, scandal – the head lightkeeper fell asleep whilst on duty. He was demoted and sent to the infamous Bell Rock, immortalised in Robert Southey's poem *The Inchcape Rock*. It sounds almost as bad as being transported to Australia, only the weather is not nearly so good.

In 1970, on a test fight, Concorde flew over the lighthouse and the sonic boom not only smashed the speed record for a civil aircraft, but a goodly number of window-panes on the lighthouse too. It was automated in 1994 and the keepers' cottages have been converted into a hotel.

● ● ●

The 15th century Corsewell Castle, a little to the south, is ruined and ivy-clad, just a stump of its former towering self. It's really not worth mentioning – and I only do so because, according to legend, it had a spring of such power that by lifting the lid that covered it, they could flood the moat at will. The easiest way to take a castle is to cut off the water supply and just wait. Attackers would have a long wait here if they were to rely solely on that method.

A small cannon was discovered in 1791, while more interestingly, a cache of gold coins, silver-plate and jewellery was unearthed in 1802. And that is all I propose to say about Corsewall Castle. By the turn of the century, its owners, the Campbells, abandoned it in favour of a grand new house.

Continuing east towards Kirkcolm and coming to the crest of a brow, we come across a surprising sight. Stretching ahead of us, gently rolling hills rise out of a valley ahead of us. If we didn't know better, we might think ourselves in the middle of the Southern Uplands. How can this be? We know we are on a narrow peninsula. We know Loch Ryan lies below, but from this vantage point, it can't be seen at all.

And so we descend to Kirkcolm on the shore of the loch. Easy to see its derivation – the church of Columba. The church has a cross-slab that started off at Kilmorie Chapel which was next to a well, known as St Mary's Well, just a little to the south. In the 18th century, it was used as the lintel for a doorway of the old Kirkcolm church. When that was abandoned in 1821, it was moved to the grounds of Corsewall House. In the winter of 1987, a large tree fell on it. Fortunately it was not damaged, and the decision was taken to move it to its present position.

It's well worth preserving because of the fusion of Norse and Christian imagery in the designs. One side shows a stumpy, ornately-carved cross which sits above a Gordian knot of intertwined sea serpents. The other side depicts the same cross with a crucified figure. Another figure stands beneath the cross with an enormous pair of tongs at his side. A massive bird is perched on his right shoulder, and another stands by his feet. He is thought to represent Odin or Sigrud, or possibly even Thor, the blacksmith.

In Norse mythology, Odin was the god of everything from healing to death, but Sigrud's story has to do with being able to talk to

View from Corsewall Lighthouse

the birds, like St Francis. He was able to do this after he drank the blood of the dragon, Fafnir (actually his brother in disguise). The birds told him to roast Fafnir's heart and eat it, as that would bestow upon him the gift of prophecy. And what could be more useful that a pair of tongs to pluck out the heart from the dragon, and a couple of your feathered friends to give you a bit of moral support after you had committed fratricide?

Because of the bird and the tongs, I am convinced it's Sigrud who is depicted on the stone rather than Odin. But what do I know? People who really *do* know about such matters, regardless of whether it's Sigrud or Odin, suggest the whole scene could be interpreted as representing the triumph of Christianity over paganism. Yes, I can see that.

What I can also see is that the stone should be moved again, inside somewhere, and the sooner the better, before it deteriorates any further. It would be a pity to lose a stone of such historic significance.

● ● ●

Chapter Forty-Nine

Stranraer and Castle Kennedy Gardens: Ships and Planes

S O this is Stranraer! In Scots Gaelic *An t-Sròn Reamhar* means "The Fat Nose". It sounds a bit pejorative, but it could also be translated more kindly as "the broad headland".

In actual fact, it has probably got nothing to do with either of them at all but from the strand or burn that separates the row (pronounced *raw* in Scots) of houses on its banks. The burn has now gone to ground under the two Strand Streets, North and South. The town used to be called "Strandraw", spelled "Stranrawer", later modified to what it is today.

One of the first wars of Scottish Independence was fought near here on the 9th and 10th of January 1307. It did not go well for the freedom fighters who were led by Robert the Bruce's brothers, Alexander and Thomas, along with Malcolm McQuillan, Lord of Kintyre, and Sir Reginald de Crawford. With a force of 1,000 men aboard eighteen galleys, they landed near here but were quickly repulsed by the local forces led by Dungal MacDouall – a supporter of the Balliols, the Comyns and Edward I, naturally. Only two galleys managed to escape, but all the leaders were captured. McQuillan was executed on the spot. The others were sent to Carlisle for execution. McQuillan's head, along with those of two Irish chiefs, were sent to Edward. Charming. The moral is if you want to be the nominal head of Scotland, you mustn't mind others sending you the heads of others.

You can't miss the Castle of St John, built by the Adairs of Kilhilt. It stands at the town centre and has done since 1511 though you would never guess it's as old as that as it is amazingly well preserved. You might like to know that the Adair coat of arms, which used to be displayed above the fireplace, was composed of a severed head and three severed hands with the motto *Loyal au Mort* (Loyal unto Death). But maybe you'd rather not have been told that.

Castle of St John, Stranraer

It's a museum at present but its long life has gone through many transformations: family home, court, prison and a military garrison during the "Killing Time". Tradition has it that in 1678, it was the HQ of Graham of Claverhouse – aka *Bluidy Claivers* – when he was suppressing the Covenanters. The last time it was used as a prison was 1907. In the early 19th century, the gabled roof was dismantled and prisoners used the open space as an exercise yard. I suppose they had no great urge to attempt an escape by jumping from it.

Had you been a prisoner in 1830, however, you might have been able to just walk out the door. In that year, the jailers were dismissed for drunkenness and leaving the prison door open. Their replacements seem to have been little better. In 1833, they were found guilty of "gross negligence" and one of them, Robert Telford, was described as "much addicted to the habits of intemperance", which I think is rather a nice way of putting it.

When the castle was first built, there was nothing to see all around but sea, sand and sky. It attracted a settlement around it like a magnet. In 1595, James VI created Ninian Adair the governor of the burgh of Stranraer. It gave him an enormous raft of powers such as the right to appoint magistrates, bailiffs and other officials, as well as the town the right to hold weekly markets with two tax-free ones annually.

By the turn of the 17th century, the town had established itself as the market centre for the Rhins and, as you know, in 1760, the Old Military Road connected it with Portpatrick and Dumfries. It wasn't just for the importing of cattle. It was also for the exporting of people during the Plantation of Ulster. (Remember McCulloch of Kirkcudbright.)

The old town hall, built in 1776, is now home to the Stranraer Museum, featuring Victorian times and the adventures and misadventures of uncle and nephew polar explorers, Sir John Ross and Sir James Clark Ross (1800-62). The North West Castle, John Ross's home, has been turned into a hotel. He must have had a sense of theatre, for he had a life-size reconstruction of his cabin built in the house from where he delivered lectures on polar navigation. It now forms part of the bar. And here's something else. In 1970, the hotel was the first in the

• • •

world to have its very own indoor curling rink. How appropriate for the former home of a polar explorer!

In 1859, it became the retirement home of the Rev. Robert Cunningham, the former first headmaster at George Watson's College in Edinburgh and founder of the Edinburgh Institution for Language and Mathematics, later to be known as "Melville College". For those who don't know, these are two of Edinburgh's most prestigious schools. Another claim to fame is he was one of the founders of the Free Church of Scotland after the Disruption of 1843. He was born in Stranraer and here, on 10th August 1883, in this house, he took his leave of the world.

It was not until the mid 18th century that Stranraer's harbour was built. It was developed during the next, and that, together with the Old Military Road, contributed to the growth of the town. But the key player was the railway from Dumfries which arrived in 1861. The following year, a branch line connected it with the harbour and there was another to Portpatrick. Later still, another line connected it with Girvan. Now see how it has grown – the second-largest town in the region after Dumfries, with a population of 10,000 souls.

And the harbour grew too. It became the unrivalled port linking Scotland with Ireland. Roll-on, roll-off ferries appeared here long before anywhere else in the UK. Then tragedy struck on the afternoon of 31st January 1953. The ferry was on a routine crossing from Stranraer to Larne when it was swamped by heavy seas and sank off the coast of Northern Ireland. 132 people out of 174 passengers and crew aboard the British Railways ferry, the *Princess Victoria*, lost their lives, including all the women and children, when their lifeboat capsized as it was being launched. They were the first victims of the infamous "North Sea Surge" which swept down the east coast of Scotland and England and inundated the Netherlands. It was the greatest maritime disaster in UK waters since WWII. In 2003, on the 50th anniversary of the tragedy, a new memorial was unveiled in the town's Agnew Park.

Ironically, the *Princess Victoria*'s predecessor and namesake was sunk by a mine in the Humber estuary in 1940 with the loss of 36 lives. In a further irony, she had been converted from a ferry to a minelayer. In the eight months that she saw service, she laid 2,756 mines.

And whilst on the subject of the war, Stranraer has the honour of having a flying boat named after it: the *Supermarine Stranraer*. Fifty-seven of them were built and saw service between 1937 and 1957, their mission being to detect submarines and escort convoys. They were designed by R.J. Mitchell of Spitfire fame, but aircrew and ground crew alike considered it as not one of his finest creations. It was given several nicknames, of which the most derogatory was the *whistling shithouse.* This was because the toilet opened directly out into the air and when the lid was lifted, it made a whistling sound. I have to agree it does seem to be a design fault, but since the flights were mainly over water, maybe Mitchell thought there was no need for refinements.

Incidentally, it was from here, on 25th June 1942, that Winston Churchill left for Baltimore on a Boeing Flying Boat to have his second rendezvous with President Roosevelt.

Stranraer, which put paid to Portpatrick as a port, met its own nemesis a century-and-a-half later. In 1973, Townsend Thoresen (later P&O) moved to Cairnryan, nearer the mouth of the loch on the eastern side. It was only the start. In 2000, the SeaCat catamaran service moved their operations from Belfast to Troon; then to complete this hat-trick of decline, Stena began operating out of Cairnryan.

Has this resulted in Stranraer becoming a tranquil backwater like other towns and villages along the A75? There is no getting away from the fact that this is where the buck stops. The A75 goes through the east of the town before it meets the A77 to Cairnryan. There *is* by-pass of sorts, the A751, but do the juggernauts use it? I'm not so sure they do.

We are taking our leave of Stranraer, but just for a moment, we are heading east on the A75 to Castle Kennedy. It's a little village named after the castle which was built in 1607 by the Earl of Cassilis on the site of an earlier one. In 1677, it passed into the possession of Sir James Dalrymple, later the 1st Earl of Stair. He died in 1690 and was succeeded by his son, John. He went on to have an illustrious career as a soldier, eventually becoming a Field Marshal in March 1742 and the Governor of Menorca the following month.

From 1714-20, he was Ambassador to the French Court. The story goes that after he arrived unexpectedly from France in 1716, a servant was warming up his bedding before the fire when it caught ablaze. The earl wasn't the only one who was gutted: the whole castle was too. Instead of repairing it, they repaired to Culhorn near Stranraer instead and the 2nd Earl used it as the focal point of the gardens which he began laying out in the 1730s, impressed and influenced by the gardens of Versailles.

Castle Kennedy and Gardens

In October 1735, he was promoted to General and drafted his men to lay-out the gardens.

They moved earth to build the massive banks (one is called the Giant's Grave, which gives you an idea of how big they are) and although they knew not what they did, they also created a heaven on earth.

The gardens lie between two lochs – the Black Loch and the White Loch. The latter is a Site of Special Scientific Interest, (SSSI), while the former has the remains of a crannog. There are two walled gardens: the old castle garden and the walled kitchen garden, which were built about 1740. The ruins of two greenhouses can still be seen. They seem to do it in twos here, like Noah's animals entering the ark.

To the east of the gardens is what was Castle Kennedy Airfield. The first plane landed in 1913. During the First World War, it was used for delivering mail and other goods to Ireland, but it was during WWII that it came into its own. In 1941 it became a training ground, especially for air gunners. At its peak, in the summer of 1942, seventy-three aircraft were stationed here. In December, the gunnery school was moved to Wales and replaced by two torpedo training schools. The aircraft used were adapted Bristol Beaufighters. Unfortunately there were several accidents and one near miss, involving the castle. As a result the torpedo school was removed to Turnberry but, as a sort of compensation, they got the gunnery school back.

It stayed here until the end of the war, during which time it trained crews as far away as Iran, Iraq and even China, not to mention some Commonwealth countries. It was disbanded in June 1945 and used as a sub-depot for Wellingtons and Mosquitos until they were modified for resale or scrapped.

The airfield closed in November 1946 and a kart club began using the premises. One of its members was none other than David Coulthard. Now the airfield has returned to its original purpose, albeit on a much smaller scale. It is used by light aircraft and as a base for military helicopters.

As for us, we are heading back to our original purpose, to follow the SWC300.

Chapter Fifty

Cairnryan to Bennane Head: The Aviator, the Mercenary Monk and the Cannibal

WE'RE back on the A77 now, on the east side of Loch Ryan, heading towards Cairnryan.

Location is everything. Thanks to it being nearer Ireland (though not by far) than Stranraer, and more sheltered, it's not all that surprising, I suppose, that the ferry companies made this the natural choice for their roll-on, roll-off terminus. Seeing it now, it's hard to imagine it but there once was a settlement here in 1701 to house the estate workers who serviced Lochryan House.

During that century, the village was an important staging post on the route from Stranraer to Ayr. Driver, as you pass through, spare a moment's thought for the travellers of yesteryear. It was a route that was plagued with highwaymen who relieved the travellers of their valuables along the way.

In WWII times, in 1940 to be precise, Cairnryan played its part when three piers were built for the construction of the Mulberry harbours required for the D-Day landings. A railway line was also laid down to link it with Stranraer and dismantled twenty years later. The piers didn't last much longer. One was scrapped, one was blown up in an accidental ammunition explosion, whilst the third is a mouldering monument to the important part these waters played in the past.

It was in Loch Ryan between 30th November and 30th December 1945 that "Operation Deadlight" took place. 86 of the German Atlantic U-boat fleet were assembled before being towed out to be scuppered in the deep water of the channel that lies between Scotland and Ireland. Those travelling over it today might like to pause and reflect that beneath their ferry's hull a greater rust lies concealed.

Those rusting vessels of destruction are by no means the only post-war debris that lies beneath the waves. Up until 1958, the port used to receive, by rail and by sea, surplus and time-expired ammunition for disposal at sea. The railway carriages were labelled *Davy Jones' Locker, Cairnryan*. This was hazardous work: accidents happened and lives were lost, the war still claiming its toll long after peace was declared and long before we realised that the dumping of such materials out at sea was more a sort of sweeping stuff under the carpet rather than a long-term solution.

Between 1957-58, another Operation took place here – *Operation Hardrock*. It was a joint Army/RAF project to build a rocket-tracking station on St Kilda. The missiles themselves, known as *Corporal*, were launched from South Uist, but it was from here that the necessary equipment was sent. Yes, it was from this unlikely spot that Britain entered the space age.

In the late 1960s, the port became a breaker's yard. Amongst its most famous victims were the *Eagle* and its sister ship, the *Ark Royal*, which was broken up in 1980. It is said that some of the ex-crew, grown men, when they came to pay their last respects, wept when they saw the state to which the once mighty aircraft carrier was reduced.

In the 1970s, the era of the roll-on, roll-off ferries arrived, as you already know.

We roll on, on our pneumatic tyres, turning away from the loch, through Glen App towards Ballantrae, where – just to the south of the town – is Glen App Castle. It is a five-star hotel and restaurant now but, in the beginning, it was built in 1870 for James Hunter, the Depute Lord Lieutenant of Ayrshire.

In 1917, it became the home of Sir James Mackay, 1st Earl of Inchcape (1852-1932). Amongst many, many other things, he was Chairman of P&O. In 1944, it played a minor part in WWII when it was the venue for a meeting between Churchill and Eisenhower. It remained in the family until the 1980s.

The earl's daughter, Elsie Mackay (1893-1928), was an amazing woman. She was a film actress who appeared under the name of "Poppy Wyndham" in eight films between 1919 and 1920.

In 1923, she learned to fly and had a burning ambition to be the first woman to cross the Atlantic. She bought a Stinson Detroiter, a monoplane which she named *Endeavour*. It had a cruising speed of 84 mph. You can imagine how long it would take to cross 3,000 miles at that speed – or work it out, if you will – but it would have seemed like a snail's progress, practically endless.

Early on the morning of 13th March 1928, she took off from Cranwell with her one-eyed co-pilot, Captain Hinchliffe DFC, heading for

• • •

Newfoundland. He was a distinguished WWI fighter pilot who had been shot in the head and crashed in Nieppe Forest in Northern France. That's how he lost his left eye. He covered up the socket with a patch.

He had only told two friends about the intended flight, while Elsie told no-one at all, covering up her tracks by adopting the pseudonym "Gordon Sinclair". Five hours later, the lighthouse keeper at Mizen Head on the south west coast of Cork, saw their plane fly over the village of Crookhaven. Some time later, a French steamer spotted it still on course for Newfoundland. It was never seen again.

Eight months later, a wheel with a serial number on it was washed ashore in northwest Ireland, positively identifying it as the *Endeavour*. What happened, no-one knows, but we do know that in 1927 – flying west to east – an American pilot named Ruth Elder experienced oil-pressure problems with the same type of plane. Bizarrely, it was because of Ruth that Elsie picked that model. Despite her engine trouble, Ruth and her pilot, George Haldeman, ditched 360 miles short of land and survived to tell the tale.

A stained-glass window in the chancel of Glenapp Church is dedicated to her memory. Her father, the earl, set up a trust of £500,000 for fifty years which was to go towards the reduction of the national debt. He was buried in the churchyard in an ebony coffin with silver mountings. It seems an enormous waste of money, to say nothing about our present distaste for the ivory trade, but he had a long affinity with India as an administrator, which is why, I imagine, he wanted the ebony.

Ballantrae, from the Scottish Gaelic *Baile na Tràgha* means "town by the beach". It is well named, and famous as the setting for R.L. Stevenson's 1889 tale of brotherly conflict set in 1745. I keep an eye on my speed. The cops are red hot here. In 1961, during the Monte Carlo Rally, ten drivers were stopped and charged with speeding. The Rally has never come back. I can't understand why not.

Out at sea to our left, the volcanic plug of Ailsa Craig appears as a pimple. We'll see it emerge from the water as we travel north. Meanwhile, on a knoll to our right, are the very ruinous remains of Ardstinchar Castle. There is very little of it left today, just the gnarled finger of the keep pointing to the sky. The castle originally had four

Ardstinchar Castle

square towers but the west wall was so short it looked practically triangular, like Caerlaverock. The reason it was so short was because of the shape of the rocky outcrop it was built on.

The builder was Hew ⟦sic⟧ Kennedy, the third son of Gilbert Kennedy of Dunure. His grandfather, James, was married to Mary, daughter of Robert III, and thus royal blood flowed through his veins. He was a Dominican friar at Ayr who gave up the habit and set out for a more adventurous life, trying his hand at being a mercenary, fighting for the French against the English. He was known as *Freir Hew* and distinguished himself at the Battle of Baugé near Angers in 1421 during the Hundred Years War. He was present when Joan of Arc relieved the siege of Orléans in 1429. He had many other adventures which I won't trouble you with, apart from the *Battle of the Herrings* which has to do with the siege. To me, it conjures up a *Monty Pythonesque* image of the Scots and French hurling fish and insults at the English.

The unusual name for the battle involves Sir John Folstoff, the real-life inspiration for the beloved Shakespearean character with a very similar name. The cause of the confrontation was an attempt by the French to divert a convoy of supplies, led by Folstoff, to the English at Orléans. The convoy was composed of three hundred carts and wagons containing such items as cannons, cannon balls, crossbow shafts – and barrels of herring – because Lent was coming and meat was *Verboten*.

Charles VII of France was very grateful to Frier Hew for his services and rewarded him right royally by graciously allowing him to have two quarters of fleur-de-lys on his coat of arms. He also gave him the Chatelaine of Gournay-sur-Marne for his lifetime, and a job as Squire of the Stables in the Royal Household. In 1436, he was sent to Scotland to escort the eleven-year-old Margaret Stewart, daughter of James I, for her nuptials with the thirteen-year old Dauphin.

According to James Paterson in his *History of the County of Ayr* (1847), Hew, on hearing of the death of his brother, Alexander, "com to Scotland an bocht the ten pund land of Ardstensar and buildit the house thairof". He did not come empty-handed: he is credited with introducing to Scotland something he had seen in France during his sojourn there. It's something for which you might bless him or curse him – the prototype of the modern game of golf. In fact, the game had caught on so well by 1457 that James II banned it as being an unhealthy distraction from archery, a vital skill required for the defence of the realm. How was hitting an innocent little leather ball with a stupid bent stick going to save us from the English?

• • •

Anyway, arguably guilty of creating more golf widows throughout the length and breadth of the land than men he actually killed in combat, Hew returned to his former profession (old habits die hard), and he ended up as Archdeacon of St Andrews. We don't know when he died, but one presumes it was peacefully in his bed. God knows He had plenty of chances to take him to heaven when he was fighting the ungodly.

It probably won't surprise you to learn that in 1563, Mary, Queen of Scots stayed at Ardstinchar. She had been staying with the Kennedys' relatives in Dunure Castle, near Maybole. Her destination was Whithorn. It must be great to have all these castles dotted about the country where you can prey upon the owners for a bit of five-star B&B. From her bedroom here, she would have had a good view of her kingdom (if that's the right word for what a queen rules over) and the Kennedy lands, as far as the eyes could see, for they were mighty powerful in these parts.

By the way, if you were wondering where the name "Kennedy" comes from, you might like to know that it might be from *ceann* and *éidigh*, meaning "ugly head". Alternatively, it could be from *Ó Cinnéide* meaning "grandson of Cinnédidh". If you are one of that ilk, then I suspect I can guess which is your preferred derivation.

You know (and I hope not from personal experience) that it's not uncommon for there to be trouble between families. The Kennedys took that to excess. There was no love lost between the Kennedys of Ardstinchar and Balgray, and the Kennedys of Cassilis just up the coast a little. Gilbert, the last Baron of Ardstinchar and Bargany, was killed in an unequal battle between the warring families in December 1601 – an event which has been handed down to history as the *Maybole Stoneballing*.

As he frae Ayr, ae day did canter, Gilbert and his retinue were attacked by John Kennedy, the 5th Earl of Cassillis, with a force of two hundred men. Gilbert died of his wounds later. It was such an unequal and unprovoked attack that his death was seen as nothing short of murder. A thousand mounted men came to his funeral – it must have been a sight to behold.

In revenge, his brother, Thomas, slew another Thomas Kennedy, the uncle of the 5th Earl above. Gilbert was only twenty-five and left behind a four-year old son called Thomas. He died "without issue", as the saying has it, in 1631, and the estate was bought by Sir John Hamilton of Letterick, son of the 1st Marquis of Hamilton. And that was the last of the Kennedys to live in the house that Hew built.

By 1770, the castle had fallen into disrepair, a condition exacerbated when the stones, (in the age-old story) were used for the building of a bridge across the river Stinchar. They also built some cottages, and even better, a house for all – the inn at Ballantrae, now the King's Arms Hotel. And quite right too! What's the use of a castle mouldering away, only serving to remind you of past history (which becomes dimmer over the years), when the stones could be of much more practical use in helping to keep your feet dry and your throat wet? (There's another bridge now, which dates from 1964.)

Onwards and northwards. On the northern side of Bennane Head, halfway between Ballantrae and Girvan, there is – no, not another castle – but a cave that was inhabited by (Alexander) Sawney Bean.

He is thought to have been born towards the end of the 14th century to an agricultural labourer or ditch-digger in East Lothian. Sawney tried following in his father's footsteps but didn't care for it much. Too much like hard work. There must be an easier way to earn a living, so he thought. Bad boy, he ran away from home with a woman named "Black Agnes", reputed to be a witch.

After thieving and robbing their way through southern Scotland, this charming couple set up home in the cave aforesaid. A des res by no means, but beggars can't be choosers. They made a living by robbing and murdering passing travellers. Happily for the Beans, the entrance to their cave was cut off at high tide, which is why they escaped detection for their murderous misdeeds for so long. It was assumed no human beings would live in such a place. But then, the Beans were not really normal human beings.

And so they lived happily in their cave, and in due course along came a string of other little Beans – eight sons and six daughters. Well, to be fair to them, there wasn't much to do, stuck indoors waiting for the tide to go out.

Teenagers, as we know, tend to incline towards boredom. It's a stage they have to go though. For the want of something better to do, Sawney's teenagers turned to incest. Given their upbringing, they were hardly the sort who could be taken home to meet the intended in-laws for Sunday tea. Anyway, Agnes and Alexander eventually became proud grandparents of thirty-two grandchildren!

At more than 600 yards long, with side passages which served as "bedrooms", the cave was roomy enough for all. But there was a problem: there was an awfully large amount of mouths to feed and they could hardly pop down to the corner shop for provisions. In fact, their appearance in such a small community would be remarked upon. They needed to keep their heads down.

The solution was blindingly obvious: they turned the victims they robbed into protein. Indeed, they showed a measure of foresight too, as they pickled body parts of their victims against times when passing travellers were few.

• • •

The beginning of the end came when a young man and his wife, on their way back from a fair, were attacked by the Beans. She perished, but he was skilled in the art of self-defence and held them off until he was rescued by some people also returning from the fair. It was the first time anyone had seen who was responsible for these mysterious disappearances and the body parts which were occasionally washed ashore. The hunt was on to find their lair. It is said that James I personally took charge at the head of four hundred men.

Eventually the Beans were tracked down to the cave by bloodhounds, where the hunters found – amongst items of jewellery and other valuables – piles of human bones, dried body parts hanging from the ceiling and others picked in barrels. Never, in their wildest nightmares, did they expect to see that.

The entire family was put in chains and taken to Edinburgh. After the briefest of trials, they were sentenced to death. The men had their genitals, hands and feet cut off and were left to bleed to death. (At least the Beans killed their victims before they chopped them up.) The females were burned alive at the stake – apart from one who, it is said, at some time previously, had left the family cave and settled in Girvan. There, she planted a tree which came to be known as the *Hairy Tree* and from which she was hanged when the family, and her connection with it, was discovered. All I can say is, she must have left home at a pretty early age for it to be able to grow into a tree capable of hanging her.

But is the Sawney Bean story true or is just a macabre myth? In the quarter of a century that the Beans were operating in the area (pardon the expression), the body count must have amounted to hundreds, if not a thousand or more. As it happens, a similar tale exists from about the same time concerning a certain Christie Cleek who roamed the Grampians, robbing and killing travellers and eating them – and their horses. This would seem to suggest a rivalry between northern and southern Scotland similar to the way children boast of their fantastical accomplishments. "That's nothing! Christie Cleek ate their horses *as well*," you can just hear a proud Aberdonian scoff, hoping to trump what Sawney did.

That said, you know how the tallest stories often contain a kernel of truth...

There's another cave here which is worth mentioning – the Bennane Cave. At sometime in the 19th century, it was partially walled up, leaving a gap for access. Very curious. No-one knows who built it or why, but a couple of tramps lived in it.

In the 1920s, it was home to a "Snib" Scott, which is all we know about him. Later, in the Sixties, it was inhabited by Henry Ewing Torbet who lived in the cave until he died in 1983, aged seventy-one. Unlike the Beans, probably modern-day Bains (sorry folks, if that happens to be your name), Torbet was known to the community as an eccentric who would do odd jobs for payment in kind, but not cash. What need had he of money? He didn't even bother to lift his pension. He kept himself to himself, did not, at first, divulge his name, happy to be known by that of his predecessor.

It seems he was born in Dundee in 1912 and worked in a bank until his 48th birthday, then just up and walked away from it, as well as friends and family, to begin a new life as a tramp. I can see how the prospect of years ahead of adding up dreary figures would be enough to provoke a mid-life crisis. What's a chap with a spirit of adventure to do but kick over the traces and disappear?

An alternative and sadder story may lie behind this eccentric behaviour. He was invalided out of the War and came home to find that his fiancée had married another. I can see how he would have been a trifle upset at the time – but why should that be the reason for running away all those years later?

He emulated W.H. Davies (1871-1940), the poet and the author of *Autobiography of a Super-Tramp*, who only worked when he had to. He was well liked by the community and when he hadn't been seen for a few days, the local bobby called in at the cave and found him in a bad way. He had been hit by a car. He was taken to hospital and died there a week later.

A benevolent council paid for his funeral and the locals chipped in to erect a cairn in his memory. The plaque upon it reads: *Henry Ewing Torbet (Snib) of Bennane Cave 1912-1983. Respected and Independent.*

How much poorer would life's tapestry be without eccentrics like "Snib" and Henry Ewing Torbet! Sleep the good sleep, gents. You had a hard life, but you chose that path for yourselves. I hope you are having an easier time in the next – but I somehow suspect you prefer the rocky road. It makes life more interesting and eternity is a long, long time.

Happy tramping!

Chapter Fifty-One

Lendalfoot to Girvan: The Wreck, the Rebel Cleric, the Craig and the Fossil Collectors

I T'S an extraordinary part of the coast, this. It really is. Just after Sawney Bean's cave and that of the latter-day hermits, there is a cliff called "Games Loup".

Scots don't need to be told that *loup* means "leap", and it is indeed a mighty one from the top of the cliff to where the sea grinds away at the rocks far below. I don't know where the "Games" comes from, but a certain Sir John Cathcart of the nearby Carleton Castle certainly wasn't playing any when he threw his wives over the edge. He was a Scottish Bluebeard who maintained his lifestyle by marrying rich heiresses.

Eight met their deaths in this manner. More fool them for not getting a tad suspicious. You might have thought when he proposed a little romantic stroll along the cliff top, they would have said "Not on your Nellie", or words to that effect. He got his comeuppance one day when his latest bride, May Kennedy of Culzean, turned the tables on him. He had the nerve to tell her what he was going to do but would she first remove her jewellery and her fine clothes, thank you very much. Feigning coyness, she asked him to turn his back as she undressed, then shoved him over the cliff. And serves him right!

The story is told in the *Historical Ballad of May Culzean. Founded on fact.* (Printed by Macarter & Co., 1817.) The remains of the castle can be seen in the distance from the picnic area at Carleton Bay. It's another crumbling edifice, slightly better preserved than Ardstinchar, but not by much.

In actual fact, there *was* a historical John Cathcart who lived happily, as far as we know, with his wife, Helen Wallace, in Killochan Castle, three miles northeast of Girvan. How he became associated with the legend and Carleton castle, no-one knows.

Here, in the picnic area, this extraordinary coast has yet another offering – an impressive bronze memorial with a lot of Russian words engraved on it. It's dedicated to the Russian battle cruiser *Varyag* and depicts the vessel, four funnels smoking, full-steam ahead. What is particularly striking about it is the way it's not only cleaving the waves, but the shaft of the cross too, so the bow and the stern protrude on either side. But what on earth, the visitor happening upon this memorial for the first time must wonder, is such a thing doing on the Scottish coast? Listen, and I will tell you.

In the beginning, and it's unthinkable today, the *Varyag* was built in the United States for the imperial Russian Navy. During the Russo-Japanese War, it and the smaller gunboat *Koreets* found themselves trapped in the neutral Korean port of Chemulpo by fifteen Japanese warships. Rather than surrender, the Russians decided to fight their way out. As you would expect, they got a good thumping and when the *Varyag* could fight no more, both ships limped back into harbour where Rudenev, the captain of the *Varyag,* decided to scuttle her and blow up the *Koreets* rather than let them fall into enemy hands. Before that, the mariners were rescued by a number of neutral ships including HMS *Talbot.* Eventually the survivors returned to a heroes' welcome in Russia.

In 1905, the Japanese raised, repaired and renamed the sunken ship *Soya.* The wheel of history turned and, in WWI, Japan and Russia became allies and the Russians bought their boat back. Without further ado, the new owners restored its former name. When the Bolshevik Revolution broke out in 1917, the *Varyag* happened to be in a British port for a refit and was commandeered by the Royal Navy to stop it falling into the hands of the Bolsheviks.

In 1920, she was sold to Germany for scrap and was on her way there

The *Varyag* Monument

under tow when she ran aground on the rocks here. When the monument was unveiled in 2007, the event was covered on Russian TV. That's how special the ship is to all Russians, not just mariners. Into the seas of death sailed I don't know how many, but in this incident, thirty-one lost their lives and ninety-one were seriously wounded.

Just a stone's throw from here, due east, is Knockdow. It was here in 1673 that the celebrated Covenanter, the Rev. Alexander Peden (1626-86), aka *Prophet Peden*, was arrested by Major William Cockburn. After the Restoration, when he was ejected from his charge in New Luce, for ten years he wandered far and wide, preaching to the masses at Conventicles. Often, he only narrowly evaded capture and for a time, went to earth in Ireland. He adopted a disguise – a cloth mask with a red wig and beard and real teeth. It's in the National Museum of Scotland if you care to have a look, but beware, it's a fearsome thing – the sort of thing the kids wear at Hallowe'en – but I doubt if you could persuade them to go anywhere near such a hideous-looking object as this.

As far as a disguise is concerned, it must have been completely useless, so distinctive, that had one of Peden's parishioners of the great outdoors happened to chance upon him on some track or other through the heather, without a second glance he might have said in the passing, "Aye, aye, your Reverend. How's it gaen?"

After his arrest by Cockburn, Peden was sentenced by the Privy Council to four years and three months on the Bass Rock, a *de facto* prison colony, followed by another year and three months in the infamous Edinburgh Tolbooth prison. How they calculated what the tariff should be, I have absolutely no idea. But they weren't done with him yet. He was banished to the American plantations along with sixty others and transported, in the first instance, by ship to London. However, when the American captain heard the reason for his transportation, he set him ashore. Peden made his way back to Scotland. He ended his days, like a hermit, in a cave near his birthplace in Auchinleck in Ayrshire. And that, so you would have thought, was that. But like Oliver Cromwell's head, which famously went walkabout, Peden's body still had some legs to it.

He was buried in the cemetery at Auchinleck, but some six weeks later, some soldiers from Sorn – as the parish was known – thought it would be a lark to dig up the old preacher and hang him from the gallows in Cumnock. The plan was prevented at the last minute by the 2nd Earl of Dumfries, William Crichton. Foiled in their grisly plan, they had to bury poor Peden for a second time. They did so at the foot of the gallows to make the point that they regarded him as a common criminal. A badly-worn red sandstone slab says he was buried "in contempt". A more respectful white headstone was erected later, followed by an impressive granite memorial in 1991. Buried twice and with three gravestones to his name – that's another thing to be remembered for too.

To the west, rising out of the sea, much more noticeable now, is Ailsa Craig. Positioned approximately halfway between Glasgow and Ireland, it is about ten miles from Girvan as the seagull flies. It is two miles in diameter and

1,110 foot high. That makes it a Marilyn. Colloquially, it is known as *Paddy's Milestone*. Its actual name comes from the Gaelic *Aillse Creag*, meaning "fairy rock". Alternatively, it could come from *Creag Ealasaid*, meaning "Elizabeth's rock". Personally, I prefer the fairy tale from which you might well conclude I am an old romantic or completely away with the fairies.

Ailsa Craig, pictured from the HMS
Campbeltown

It's a bird sanctuary where gannets, razorbills, kittiwakes, shags, fulmars, guillemots and puffins, not forgetting the ubiquitous gulls, can clamour into the sky for all they are worth with impunity, but in the 18th century there used to be an annual cull of the gannets – for food. They don't appeal to me, I have to say, but they were said to be very tasty. That's precisely what the rats thought of the puffin eggs and the baby puffins. In fact, they thought them so delicious they ate them to extinction. Everybody loves the clown-faced birds, but only to look at. Another turn of Fortune's wheel and the rats were exterminated in 1991. Now there are about 130 pairs of puffins for whom Ailsa Craig is home when they are not out at sea.

Robert III granted the island to the monks of Crossraguel to "put food on their table". Hmm. I wonder if gannet was on the menu even back then. That indefatigable early traveller, Thomas Pennant, was here in 1772 and reported ruins of a chapel near the landing place. When the lighthouse was being constructed, four stone coffins were uncovered. Who the deceased were, we do not know, but they could well have been monks.

Like the Bass Rock, the Craig was a former prison in the 18th and 19th centuries, and you can see why – it looks extremely inhospitable and isolated. But in the 16th century, it was home to the Hamilton family. If you have the eyes of a hawk, or a pair of binoculars, you might be able to make out the forty-foot high remains of their tower house. It was built as part of a plan to protect the coast from Phillip of II of Spain. The Spanish Armada and all that. And we all know what happened to that!

In another turn of the wheel, during the Reformation, the rock became a place of refuge for Catholics. Hew [sic] Barclay of Ladyland, near Kilbirnie in

North Ayrshire, who had been imprisoned twice for practising his faith but had escaped to Spain, returned in 1597 and took possession of the castle and fortified it. His plan was to turn it into a provisioning post for another hoped-for Spanish invasion. That never came, of course, and neither did Hew's plans. The Protestant minister of Paisley, Andrew Knox, discovered the plot and Barclay drowned while trying to

Ailsa Craig (Detail)

escape his clutches. Either that or he committed suicide by drowning. He knew there would be no pardon this, the third time, and his dying would not be easy. Barclay's friends, on the other hand, claimed he had been personally dispatched by Knox and appealed to James VI. Some hope! In fact, His Majesty went further and forbade "any to molest Knox", and instructed magistrates to assist in protecting him.

On the south side of the island, forty feet above the shore, is a cave named after a smuggler called MacNall. In it, two stone coffins were discovered, both containing human remains. One skeleton might be MacNall's, but whose is the other? That's one mystery. The other is it must have taken a great deal of effort to get those stone sarcophagi all the way up there. Whodunnit and why? We shall never know, but there is one thing we *do* know – Ailsa Craig made a very handy place for the temporary storing of smuggled goods.

It has a lighthouse which was built by Thomas Stevenson (the father of Robert Louis), and it was completed in 1886. It was his last. He died the following year, aged 68. The lamp was originally lit by oil and then electricity. It became automated in 1990 using a combination of acetylene gas and solar power. Since 2001, it relies completely on solar power.

Rather quaintly, before a wireless connection was established with the mainland in 1935, the keepers used to communicate by carrier pigeon. When the birds couldn't fly because of bad weather, a system of lights was used. One fire to the north of the lighthouse meant "bring doctor"; one fire to the south meant "provisions needed".

Two foghorns were also erected on the north and south ends of the island. They were powered by gas until 1911, when they were replaced with oil. They were retired in 1966 and replaced with a Tyfon fog signal near the lighthouse until it too was discontinued in 1987. You can still see the remains of the gasworks which produced the coal gas which was needed to pump the air to the old foghorns. The remains of a cable-powered railway which was used to carry the coal wagons up to the gasworks from the landing stage can still be seen too. These wagons, by the way, were inadvertently also responsible for transporting the rats that ate the puffins. There was also another railway which took granite blocks from the quarry down to the crusher and from thence to another pier for shipping to the mainland.

The Ailsa Craig Granite Company produced kerbstones and railway sleepers until it closed in 1928. However, as many people know, and curling afficionados the world over certainly do, the granite from here is highly prized – the Common Green, and especially the Blue Hone, for curling stones the making of. The quarrying for that began in the mid-nineteenth century, and in 2004 it was estimated that 60-70% of all curling stones in current use came from here. (The others come from the Trefor Quarry in Wales.) Looks like the Celts have cornered the market.

The stones are made by Kays of Scotland, who have exclusive rights to the granite – granted by the Marquess of Ailsa, a title first granted to Archibald Kennedy, the 12th Earl of Cassillis, in 1831. In 2013, they quarried 2,000 tons which, it is estimated, will be enough to make all the curling stones the planet needs until 2020. But curlers of the future, do not fear – there's plenty more where that came from.

You can visit Ailsa Craig for yourself, if you have the time to spare. Day trips are available from Girvan aboard the MFV *Glorious*, or from Portpatrick, which – of course – is a much longer trip. It's your chance to get closer to the wildlife. On the voyage, you may see seals, porpoises, perhaps even a Minke whale or a basking shark, while on the island there are 40,000 pairs of gannets making guano on the cliffs when they are not flying all the way to West Africa for the winter. They all look identical – which poses another mystery. How, when it comes to feeding time, out of all that lot, do the mothers manage to recognise their own greedy little offspring?

On shore, here in Girvan (from the Scottish Gaelic *Inbhir Gharbhain* – mouth of the River Girvan), the records show that a much smaller hill once stood here above the harbour. It was a moot hill, an artificial mound like that at Scone where the kings of Scotland were crowned for generations. It was also where open-air parliaments were held. Since these moot hills were a Viking institution, this tells us that once upon a time, the place that became Givan was under their thrall. The Battle of Largs in 1263 put paid to their expansionist plans, but they left this legacy behind and it was where Robert the Bruce held court in 1328.

The village was granted burgh status by Charles II in 1668, which, as you know, entitled it to hold weekly markets and a yearly fair. At that time, Thomas Boyd the Younger of Penkil was granted permission for the construction of a harbour which, apart from its designated use for fishing and shipping, came in very handy for the smuggling business.

In time, the growing town became a centre for shoemaking and cotton weaving, with something like a hundred looms clacking away in the cottages. But it was the coming of the railway in 1860 that brought Girvan its main source of income – tourists. They came from Glasgow to be beside the seaside, for the clean fresh air and the beaches. Amongst them were the celebrated Gray family – Robert, his wife Elizabeth, and their daughters, Alice and Edith. (They had other children too, but you'll see why I single these out in a minute.)

Robert (1825-87), was a bank inspector and a famous amateur ornithologist. His day job gave him the opportunity to travel and keep his eye open for birds. By 1856 at the latest, he had spotted Elizabeth Anderson (1831-1925). Reader, he married her.

She was born in the Burns Arms in Alloway, where her father was the landlord before he moved down to the Girvan area to take up a new career in farming. His hobby was collecting fossils, an interest he passed on to Elizabeth. A form of trilobite is named after him. It's a great thing to have something named after you, even if it's just a form of low life. Most people have to resort to giving their sons or daughters their names. But that's not all. I bet he was chuffed to bits when a type of coral was also named after him. Well he must have thought it was OK, at least.

The Grays came to Girvan for their holidays from 1855 to 1941, spending many happy hours hunting for, and documenting, the fossils they found. When they were old enough, the girls joined in too. Theirs was a marriage made in heaven because Robert was more than happy to exhibit Elizabeth's finds at the Natural History Society he had founded.

Like her husband, Elizabeth has a couple of creatures named after her – a type of starfish *Hudsonaster grayae* and an echinoderm (that's a beastie with a spiny skin to you and me), *Archophiactis grayae.* And there you have it, the curse of taking your husband's name, not in vain, but in marriage.

In 1903, when she was 72, recognition at last for Elizabeth when she was awarded the Murchison Fund by the Geological Society of London for her lifelong contribution to Ordovician and Silurian stratigraphy. So there you go. All that combing the beaches, splitting open rocks was worth it in the end. But she wasn't nearly finished yet. She kept collecting fossils for another twenty years, until bronchitis carried her off in 1924.

Her daughters, Alice and Edith, picked up the hammer and went on collecting and documenting fossils. Eventually they sold their own and their mother's collection to the Natural History Museum. Their names will live for evermore.

Away from the beaches, in the town, arguably, the main point of interest is *Auld Stumpy* as the former tolbooth is affectionately known. It was built in 1827 – and just in the nick of time, so to speak, as it was used as a jail during the 1832 Reform Act riots. It sits like a rocket as if about to be launched into space. As a matter of fact, it *did* move, not into space, but expanded into space when it was grafted onto the MacMaster Hall which was built in 1911. However, it caught fire in 1939 and was left with *scarce a stump,* like Tam o' Shanter's trusty mare, Maggie.

Possibly a more eye-catching building is the red sandstone McKechnie Institute with its octagonal tower. Opened in 1889, it was the gift of a local benefactor, Thomas McKechnie. It used to be the library, but that has been moved to new premises and it's now an art gallery and a small museum, as well as being a venue for meetings, art classes and such like.

In 1963, William Grant & Sons built a distillery in a WWII munitions factory just out of town and, in the secular equivalent of turning swords into ploughshares, began making whisky, not weapons. I think even teetotallers would drink to that. In 2009, HRH Prince Charles opened the Ailsa Bay Distillery on the site, and in September 2018 it launched its Aerstone range of two different ten year-old expressions. The Sea Cask is "smooth and easy" like a Speyside; the Land Cask is "rich and smoky" and matured inland.

Another famous manufacturer produces something much more to my travelling companion and fellow mortal's taste – chocolate. Nestlé set up business here in 1979 and produces chocolate pellets to be turned into *Kit-Kat* and *Aero.* (Other chocolate bars are available.) So now you know where some of that milk produced by those famous Ayrshire dairy cows goes!

Chapter Fifty-Two

Turnberry to Maybole: The Saints, the Souter and the Gypsy Suitor

AT Turnberry, the A77 turns away from the coast to Kirkoswald and that's our way. We're on the Burns trail again. However, if you were to continue for a short distance on the A719 towards Ayr, you would come to a track that leads to Turnberry Point. There you will find the ruins of Turnberry Castle and a lighthouse. There is little point in going to see the castle, for very little of it remains.

That said, it is worthy of mention because it is the most likely birthplace of Robert the Bruce. It was built by the Earls of Carrick early in the 13th century and was the home of Marjorie, Countess of Carrick. Her husband, Adam of Kilconquhar, was killed at Acre when on crusade, and – as was the custom – his sword was brought back home. The bearer of that and the bad news was none other than Robert Bruce, 6th Lord of Annandale. The new widow was hardly devastated. She kidnapped Bruce and held him prisoner until he agreed to marry her. Reader, he did, in 1271, and to them was born a daughter, Christian, and in 1274, a son, Robert, who went on to become King of Scots. The rest you know.

Actually, part of the reason that so little of the castle remains is because, having recaptured it from the English in 1307, Bruce ordered its destruction three years later to prevent it falling into their hands again. It must have been a decision that broke his heart. It never was rebuilt.

A lighthouse is built on the site of the castle and was designed by brothers Thomas and David Stevenson. Although commissioned in 1869 by the Board of Trade, building only began in earnest in 1871 because of a dispute as to how big the lens should be, and believe it or, what kind of oil should be used to light the lamp. It was switched on in 1873 and became automated in 1986.

Next, Kirkoswald. Obviously the church of Saint Oswald. But just *who* was he?

Well, he was born about 604 AD. He was defeated, died and dismembered at the battle of Maserfield in 642. He was King of Northumbria and his enemy was Penda, King of Mercia – the present-day English Midlands. As a youth, he was exiled to Dál Riada, where he got religion. He converted to Christianity; became a bit of a zealot in fact. He was the future Saint Aidan's right-hand man and interpreter, granting him the island of Lindisfarne from where he converted pagans in their thousands.

Now be prepared to suspend your disbelief. According to Bede, after Oswald died, he was fast-tracked to sainthood. This might be because, according to Bede, people came along to the spot where he died and carted away the earth "to a man's height". Another legend says that a bird picked up his right arm, flew to a tree and dropped it. It was a bit more than a beakful after all. Now hear this. A spring sprang forth from where it fell, and both it and the tree brought forth miracles thereafter. Isn't that an incredible thing! And the people who live there don't need to be told this, but that is how the town of Oswestry got its name. Oswald's tree, you see!

Just a couple more of miraculous stories about St Oswald's bones. When they were being shifted to Bardney Abbey in Lincolnshire (saints' bones or parts thereof tend to be movable objects – quite often of their own accord), the monks were not, at first, happy to receive them, because when he was a mere king, he had conquered their lands. But then, lo! a pillar of light emanated from those rickle of bones in the cart, right up to the heavens. The monks saw and believed. If you don't believe me, believe Bede. A holy man like him wouldn't tell porkie pies, would he?

Oswald's head is claimed by Durham Cathedral, but four others in continental Europe assert they have the genuine article. That doesn't surprise me; there are enough bits of the true cross to create a forest. What does surprise me is how his cult spread so far and wide.

One of his arms (I imagine it was the left), and which miraculously had remained uncorrupted, ended up in Peterborough Abbey and not in a way you might expect. It seems a gang of monks from the abbey made their way to Bamburgh, where the arm was currently residing, and stole it. It was no mean journey to undertake in those days, which tells you how keen they must have been to get it.

They built a chapel to house the revered relic and, mindful of how they had procured it, built it into a narrow tower with an internal stair where a monk could stand guard over it. Literally. It was made in such a way that it was impossible to sit down. They were taking no chances that anyone would fall asleep on the job. It must have felt like being walled-up alive. I wonder if it occurred to the guards on duty that they were doing time for their crime.

What we seek here in Kirkoswald is a little cottage on Main Street with a thatched roof. It was the home of Souter Johnnie, who was immortalised by Burns in *Tam o' Shanter*. "Souter Johnnie" was John Davidson, who built this cottage with his own hands in 1785, and it's where he died in 1806 in his 78th year. He is buried in the churchyard just down the street, along with the real life Tam o' Shanter (Douglas Graham) and Kirkton Jean (Jean Kennedy). It's good to know they are all together again. I hope there is beer in heaven.

Tam, or Graham (c.1738-1811), leased the farm of Shanter near the village of Maidens. He was rather fond of alcoholic refreshment and owned a boat named *Tam o' Shanter* which, it was said, he used for smuggling. He was introduced to Burns by Davidson, who had a reputation for being a bit of a wit and all round jolly-good bloke. The tale of how Maggie, the mare, came to lose her tail was made up to protect Graham's drinking friends, who, while under the influence, had trimmed it for a laugh, as you do. His wife, Kate, was superstitious – as the poem tells us – and when Tam did eventually make it home, one hopes that after she had bludgeoned Tam with the rolling pin, she got a sort of satisfaction from saying, "I tellt ye!"

Jean Kennedy, along with her sister Anne, kept an inn in Kirkoswald. It was a respectable sort of establishment known as *The Leddies' House*, which, with some artistic licence, Burns called *The Lord's House* in the poem.

Souter Johnnie's cottage stayed in the Davidson family until 1920, and was handed over to the National Trust for Scotland in 1932. Despite building it himself, Johnnie was no more a builder by trade than Burns's father was when he built his family home in Alloway, the one in which Burns was born. We'll be heading there later, the most northerly point on the SWC300.

Johnnie was a shoemaker, a *souter* in Scots, and the cottage displays a good number of the tools of his trade – mysterious objects that would not look out of place in a medieval torture chamber – as well as some pieces of period furniture. This much Johnnie might recognise, but he would scratch his head to see his humble home transformed into an art gallery and gift shop and wonder if he had had a drop too much.

In the garden, a thatched alehouse features life-size statues of Tam and Johnnie *boozin' at the nappy* in the company of the landlord and his wife. They look happy enough. They were sculpted by James Thom in the 1830s and originally placed in the garden, but have been moved in here to preserve and protect them from the worst a Scottish climate can do.

* * *

Also resting after his labours in the graveyard is Hugh Rodger (1726-97), Burns's teacher when he came here in 1775, aged sixteen, to learn "Mensuration, Surveying, Dialling & etc". As well as being introduced to the smuggling industry in what Burns called the *smuggling coast,* these studies may have been useful to Burns in his later career as an exciseman, but he was distracted from his studies by the girl next door, Margaret (Peggy) Thomson. Her house is now Souter's Inn, where the southern gable-end once was part of the school.

Burns wrote a poem to Peggy, *Composed in August,* where he describes her as a *charming Filette.* Later in life, he presented her with a copy of the Kilmarnock Edition, which he inscribed *Once fondly lov'd and still remembered dear.* Aww!

Burns's mother, Agnes, had close connections with Kirkoswald. Her mother died when she was ten and after her father remarried, she was sent to live here with her Granny Rannie which I think has a very nice ring to it. The old lady was a fount of knowledge on old Scottish ballads and Covenanting songs, which she passed on to Agnes who passed it on to Burns. So you know that's where he got *that* from.

We're moving on to Crossraguel Abbey, named after an early Christian cross – the Cross of Riaghail – that was once said to have stood there. St Riaghail (Latin *Regulus*) was an Irish monk who came across with Columba in 563. He had a vision that he was to take the relics of St Andrew from Patras in Greece and move them as far west as he could. He was shipwrecked off the coast of Fife, and the precious relics were lost. Happily they were discovered later, and a great cathedral was built in the city. They named it St Andrews in his honour, and the country honoured him further when they made him its patron saint. Not only that, but the design of the national flag is based upon the type of cross on which he was said to have been crucified.

The abbey's story began about 1225 when Donnchadh (Duncan), Earl of Carrick, granted lands and churches to the Cluniac Abbey at Paisley, provided that a daughter abbey was founded at Crossraguel. (It's probably no accident that Crossraguel is equidistant from Paisley and Whithorn, along the pilgrim way.) The parent abbey was miserly and set up a small chapel instead, more intent on furthering its own interests at home. Nearly twenty years later, in 1244, the Episcopal Court in Glasgow ruled that a monastery should be built. And it was so. However, you don't build an abbey overnight, and it was not for another twenty years that the monastery was completed. In 1265, the abbot of Paisley appealed unsuccessfully to the Pope against a ruling that all Paisley's possessions in Carrick were to be handed over to Crossraguel.

The Lord giveth and the Lord taketh away. Along came the Wars of Independence and in 1307, it was badly damaged by Edward I. It was rebuilt, only bigger and better, and then of course, along came the Reformation and the abbey was again badly damaged in 1561. However, monks continued to live there until 1592.

Ruins of Crossraguel Abbey

A grim story is attached to the abbey. The time has come at last to reintroduce you to that *werry greidy manne*, Gilbert Kennedy, the 4th Earl of Cassilis (c.1541-76), whom we met at Glenluce Abbey and whose lands – you may remember – he acquired by foul means. He was also known as 6th Lord Kennedy and *King of Carrick*, on account of the power he wielded in the region.

After Glenluce, Kennedy turned his eye on Crossraguel Abbey. His uncle, Quintin Kennedy (1520-64), who turned out to be the last abbot before the Reformation, had been given a nineteen-year, rent-free lease on the abbey lands by Mary, Queen of Scots. In 1562, he had a three day debate with John Knox. Not surprisingly, neither failed to convert the other. The good abbot died in 1564, and our ruthless earl inherited. But there was a snag. There were three other legatees. Greedy Gilbert set about eliminating the opposition.

First of all, he seized Stewart, the first commendator of Crossraguel (1565-87), and imprisoned him in the "black vault" in his castle at Dunure, five miles south of Ayr, until he agreed to consent to the Earl's modest proposal of renouncing his entitlement to his share of the abbey lands. When Stewart refused, his toes were toasted over a fire. More than his toes actually. His legs were so badly burned he was never able to walk again.

In 1570, Stewart was rescued by his brother-in-law, Thomas Kennedy of Bargany. You should always choose your brother-in-law carefully – you never know when he might come in useful. He sent a small number of men into the castle, hoping, by subterfuge, to smuggle the commendator out without being noticed. Alas, they were spotted. Bargany's men had their man but couldn't make off with him, trapped inside the keep.

Gilbert laid siege to his own castle. In a somewhat drastic measure, his men set about undermining the base of the keep. In response, Stewart's rescuers began dismantling the battlements and sent blocks and stones raining down on their heads. The standoff was resolved when Bargany himself arrived with a large force. Gilbert surrendered, not just his castle, but his rights to the abbey's lands. You might say that served him right, but it also meant all the more of Crossraguel's lands for Bargany, who was not averse to making money out of the abbey himself.

It was the end of the friendship between the families, naturally. Nothing new in family feuds, as we have seen. Gilbert's end came about prematurely when his horse fell on him and he died of his injuries. Couldn't have happened to a nicer chap.

The last abbot of Crossraguel, long after the Reformation, was Peter Hewat in 1612. It was a sinecure given to him by James VI after an incident that took place at Gowrie House in Perth round about 1600. According to the king, he was lured there to be assassinated. According to the Gowries, it was quite the reverse. The king wanted to get rid of *them* because he owed them a vast amount of money. Their version is that the king's bodyguard killed Gowrie and his brother.

Well, who would *you* believe? The clergy took the Gowries' side and refused to ratify a charge of treason against them – all except for the lone voice of Peter Hewat, aforesaid. The king rewarded him by granting him the abbacy of Crossraguel, which entitled him to a seat in Parliament and to be a member of the Court of High Commission. There went a man who knew on which side his bread was buttered.

Now we are in Maybole. If anyone has bothered to compile a league table of Scotland's longest towns, then Maybole must be near the top, if not the very top. The name comes from the Scots Gaelic *Am Magh Baoghail,* anglicised into "Minnyboll" meaning "maidens' dwelling". It received a charter from Donnchadh, Earl of Carrick, in 1193.

There dwelled in the tower house that the 5th Earl of Cassilis built in 1560, not a maiden but a lady, Lady Jean Hamilton, the wife of the 6th Earl. She fell in love with Johnnie Faa, King of the gypsies, and ran away with him. The earl wasn't going to have his wife stolen from under his very nose like that. Faa and his mistress didn't get far. He caught up with them at the ford over the Doon, still known today as the "Gypsies' Steps". He hanged Faa and his followers on a *dule* tree in front of the castle gate at Cassilis. The word *dule* comes from the Scots word meaning "sorrow" or "grief". Usually sited at crossroads, it was where criminals came to grief, hanged and left hanging to rot, *pour encourager les autres.* He made his wife watch the proceedings from a window. She was locked up in a room at the top of the tower house in Maybole, and that is where she died. A Green Lady can sometimes be seen at the window of her prison chamber, so it is said.

● ● ●

An alternative version of the story is that her lover was not Faa at all, but an aristocrat whose gypsy companions had cast the "glamoureye" over her. The earl then went on to marry another lady, predating Jane Eyre's situation by three centuries. It's a tale that is highly suspect. In the first instance, it's unlikely that the earl would endanger his immortal soul by committing bigamy. More convincingly, after she died, he wrote a letter in which he referred to her as "my deir bedfellow".

In actual fact, both stories are probably apocryphal and stem from the ballad *Johnnie Faa*, which had been in circulation long before the events described above. As anyone who has played Chinese Whispers knows, stories can change immensely in the telling, thus the migration from *our good Lord's yett* in the original ballad through "the Castle yett" to "Lord Cassillis' yett" could easily be achieved.

The castle (on Castle Street, funnily enough) is a curious mixture of styles, with a couple of fairy-tale turrets at the top of an L-shaped four-storey tower with an attic on the top. A wing has been added on, making an ill-matched union, like Lady Jean and the 6th Earl's marriage.

The oldest building in Maybole is the Collegiate Church, just off the High Street, dedicated to the Virgin Mary. In 1371, Sir John Kennedy of Dunure built a chapel next to the parish kirk. No doubt he thought this act of generosity would do his immortal soul no harm at all, but he was taking no chances. In 1381, the Collegiate Church – consisting of a provost, two priests and a clerk – was founded to pray for Sir John and his family in perpetuity. You are dead for a long, long time. It was still in use in 1563 – three years after the Reformation, please note – when a mass was publicly celebrated for 200 people that Easter. The leaders were later arrested and fined, but escaped with their lives.

You can get to it by taking John Knox Street, which is no doubt making that Reverend gentleman revolve at a hundred miles an hour in his grave, to think that a street in his name should be in such close proximity to such an idolatrous institution.

The earls of Cassilis continued to be buried there until late in the 17th century, but by the next it was in a pretty ruinous state and that's the condition it is in now, though some of the tracery of the windows still remains. And you can just about make out the Cassilis coat of arms, if you look closely over the wall. If you want to get closer to the ruins, as the notice outside tells you, you have to get the key for the gate from Crossraguel Abbey. That means a drive there and a drive back to return it. I think not.

As we head out of Maybole, we are impressed by the spire of the disused Maybole Old Church, built in 1808 – and, by the looks of it, scheduled for demolition. I hope they keep the façade. I've never seen a church spire quite like it before, at least not in Scotland. It's built up in layers like a ziggurat. If I didn't know better, I would have thought the Aztecs had been here.

● ● ●

Chapter Fifty-Three

Culzean Castle: A Ghostly Encounter

OUT of little acorns, tall oaks grow, so runs the adage. It takes time of course – a great deal of it, in fact – and so it is with the immensely impressive Culzean Castle.

It all began in the 15th century with a tower house called "Coif Castle" or the "House of Cove", because it stands on a rocky headland overlooking what is now called Culzean Bay. That name and spelling first appeared in the 18th century, having been poshed up from "Cullean" as it was formerly written. What's in a spelling? The word sounds just the same.

According to legend, fairies lived in the caves below, and so – temporarily, it is said – did Robert the Bruce on his return from Arran, while he was gathering his forces around him. He was destined to spend a lot of his life as a troglodyte during his years as an outlaw.

In 1569, the 4th Earl of Cassillis (pronounced "Cassells") gave the castle and its estates to his brother, Sir Thomas Kennedy. (One should always choose one's brothers carefully.) As a matter of fact, we have met these two gents before, if that is not too kind a word to describe the 4th Earl. His name was Gilbert and he was the one who toasted the toes of the Commendator of Crossraguel, while Thomas was the one who died as a result of his injuries after the *Maybole Stoneballing* in 1601.

Thomas was also known as the *Tutor of Cassillis* as he brought up his nephew, John, the 5th Earl, who lost his dear papa when he was only two. Thomas was a loyal supporter of Mary, Queen of Scots, as was his sister, Jean, who had the dubious honour of blindfolding her on the scaffold, for which kindness she received her crucifix and other mementoes, in the possession of the Kennedy family to this day.

Thomas may have inherited the castle but he did not inherit the title. Nearly two centuries later, in 1759, John, the 8th Earl, handed in his dinner pail and the title passed to the Tutor's descendant, also named Thomas, who became the 9th Earl. It wasn't quite as easy as that, however. The title was contested by someone whose much-worn memorial we had seen in Dumfries – William Douglas, the future Duke of Queensberry, who claimed descent from the 8th Earl through the female line. That sounds complicated enough itself, and it took three years before the matter was resolved – going all the way to the House of Lords, who ruled in Thomas's favour.

But before we get to him and his descendants, and the castle as it appears today, I have to tell you about Sir Archibald the Wicked (c.1655-1710). You will notice that his lifetime fell within the "Killing Time" and, like his ancestors, the Wicked One was a fervent Catholic, which meant, of course, he was a rabid anti-Covenanter. You will not be surprised to learn, given his handle, that he was well versed in crime. Furthermore, it was said the older he got, the worse he got, like an addict needs more and more of their fix.

The story goes that in 1685, he and his men – scouring the landscape for Conventicles – came upon one being led by a Reverend Weir. Culzean set his armed men loose on the unarmed worshippers. One of them, Gilbert McAdam, armed only with a walking stick, tried to defend his aged mother from receiving a blow from the butt-end of a musket. It was knocked out of his grasp and, grabbing hold of his mother, he turned to flee. They were pursued by a horseman, who put a bullet through Gilbert's brain. The horseman was none other than Sir Archibald, as you will have guessed, but before he could ride away, the distraught mother grabbed hold of the bridle and uttered a curse:

When the hour of death approaches... no priest will be able to quench the ceaseless flames which burn in your bosom, and no words of affection soothe your dying pillow...

According to witnesses, Archibald was visibly shaken. Servants reported that on wintry nights, when the wind howled around the castle turrets, he

could be heard to cry in his anguish and his torment, "What woman was this who dared to scream so within the walls of Culzean castle?"

And so at last, the time came for Archibald to pass over to the other side. He was not a good patient. Like the Queen of Hearts, he threatened to knock off the doctors' heads because they could not cure him. The priests were not

Culzean Castle and Gardens

• • •

any more efficacious. He sent them away because they could not quench the fire in his breast. The sweat beaded his forehead, his eyes bulged in their sockets and he stared in horror, pointed at something he could see at the bottom of his bed, but which no-one else could, and gave vent to an unearthly laugh.

And so, eventually, he died. It was a fearsome night. Think of the storm that Tam o' Shanter rode through on his way home to face the wrath of Kate. The servants testified to hearing shrieks of laughter and groans of agony and fell to their knees and prayed, terrified out of their wits.

And then the day of the funeral dawned. Four white horses were attached to the hearse. One dropped dead on the spot, while the others kicked up such a fuss they had to be released. Four black ones were put in their place, but they refused to pull. The coffin was removed, the priest said some words over it, the coffin was replaced and at last the procession could proceed – but just as they set off, another fearsome storm broke out. The proceedings were just about to be abandoned when the storm stopped as suddenly as it started. However, the moment they reached the burial place, it started up again. Flashes of fire were seen to run along the length of the coffin, after which it felt much lighter. Some thought it was a lightning strike; others thought it was the Deil taking his faithful servant hame.

An event happened out at sea which would support the latter version. As a ship, passing through the bay, was being tossed about by mighty waves, the helmsman cried, "A boat! A boat!" It was not a day for being out at sea. Actually, it wasn't a boat at all, but the poor fellow could be forgiven for misinterpreting what he saw illuminated by flashes of lightning, through the driving rain. Incredibly, it turned out to be a coach pulled by four black horses.

The captain hailed the coachman with a question. "From whence to where?" he asked, as if a coach-and-four was the sort of thing you might expect to see upon the briny any day of the week. I admire his sang-froid, I really do.

"From hell to Culzean's burial," replied the spectral coachman.

And what the captain replied to that, history does not record. Maybe he was struck dumb.

Chapter Fifty-Four

Culzean Castle: The Kennedys of Cassilis and Culzean

SIR Thomas Kennedy, the 9th Earl (1726-75), came into the ownership of the castle unexpectedly when his brother, John, died in 1744. He had only been master of Culzean for two years. At the time of John's death, Thomas had embarked on an army career and had gone to fight in Flanders. Imagine, a castle-owner and only eighteen! In Jane Austen terms, that would have made him in want of a wife, or so one would have thought. But the estate he inherited was far removed from Darcy's. It was in a pretty bad way, so maybe he wasn't quite the eligible bachelor after all. He never married.

He was in no hurry to take up his inheritance. In 1745, he bought the rank of captain. (Imagine being able to do that!) He fought at the battle of Fontenoy, but gave up the army life the following year. He appointed a factor, Archibald Kennedy – no relation – to manage his estate and, like many young aristocrats of his day, he went on the Grand Tour. He lived in France and Italy for seven years.

As a result of his travels, he was much influenced by classical art and architecture. As well as bringing back ideas on how to improve his stately home, he also brought back works of art. On a later trip to Italy, in 1764, he had his portrait painted by Batoni who had captured the market in committing the faces of the aristocracy to canvas. You can see it in pride of place, hanging above the fireplace in the library.

In 1774, Thomas was elected by his fellow peers to represent them in the House of Lords in Westminster. Like the disciples, only twelve are chosen. It was a great honour. They serve for a period of five years. That put paid to his smuggling activities. Yes, truth to tell, the new master of Culzean was also a master smuggler. That is why he appointed the factor he did. He was also a wine merchant. The caves beneath the castle were a very handy temporary repository for the contraband from the Isle of Man. No, it just wouldn't do for someone in such a prestigious post to be caught engaging in such illegal practices.

What's the owner of a large estate to do to maintain it? Thomas concentrated on the slave trade instead. That was perfectly respectable (back then, at least). In fact, it appears he had been involved in that despicable business as early as 1767. That said, and to balance the record a little, he did provide a new house for a freed slave, Scipio, that cost him £90.

In the event, Thomas only served a year as a peer because he died in 1775. The castle, estate and title passed to his brother, David. What Thomas began, David raised to another level. His brother was hardly cold in clay before David hired the prestigious architect, Robert Adam (1725-92), to make improvements. He also emulated his brother in being elected as a Representative Peer and by resisting the allures of ladies who wanted to walk him down the aisle.

Money was no object – money he did not have. When he died in 1792, he left debts of £4 million in today's terms. What he also left was the castle pretty much as we see it today. Thank you for that, David. We are in *your* debt.

History repeated itself, when David controversially altered the terms of Thomas's will and left the estates of Culzean and Cassillis to a distant cousin – in both senses of the word – to a Captain Archibald Kennedy, from New York. It sparked off legal battles that were not settled until 1825, in the House of Lords. Archibald happened to be married to a wealthy American heiress, Catherine Schuyler. David's thinking was that he was the only member of the family rich enough to keep the estates afloat.

He may have had a rich wife, but Archibald was rich on his own account too. He had had a distinguished naval career in the Seven Years War (1756-63), making a fortune in prize money from capturing enemy ships. Captains were entitled to just less than half of the worth of a ship and its cargo, to say nothing of a per capita price, on prisoners. It's easy to see, under such winning ways, you could become wealthy pretty rapidly.

He had a very prestigious address – No. 1, Broadway. Unfortunately for Archibald, after the American War of Independence broke out in 1755 George Washington commandeered the house for himself, along with several other of his properties. Archibald went back to London and never again returned to the revolting former colony.

When you're down on your luck, you really are down. Inheriting Culzean was a bit of a white elephant. After having paid off the debts, he didn't have long to enjoy it. He paid a visit in 1793, ordered fabric and furnishings, only to die the following year aged about 76. The exact year of his birth is obscure.

• • •

His son, also Archibald, became the 12th Earl. He was an upwardly mobile sort of person. His ambition was to be more than just a Representative Peer like Thomas and David, but a real and permanent Peer in the House of Lords which would make him eligible for the high offices of state. To these ends, he courted the great and the good of the day, including Prime Ministers Lord

Culzean Castle, showing Clock Tower

Melville and Sir Robert Peel. He also courted, and married, Margaret Erskine in 1793, daughter of John Erskine of Dun. I am not suggesting he married her for her money; please don't think that.

In 1806, he became the first Baron of Ailsa which did entitle him to a seat in the Lords and, in 1820, George IV made him a Knight of the Order of the Thistle, the Scottish equivalent of the Order of the Garter. There are only sixteen of them at any one time, one of their duties being to represent the monarch whenever he, or she, can't be there in person.

Further advancement followed in 1832 when the Duke of Clarence became William IV and created him 1st Marquess of Ailsa. They had been boyhood friends in New York, and the relationship was cemented in 1827 when his second son, John Kennedy Erskine (who inherited his mother's estate of Dun, despite her not being dead yet), married Augusta Fitzclarence, the illegitimate daughter of the Duke and Mrs Jordan, an actress aka Dorothea Bland.

She wasn't really a Mrs, and Jordan wasn't her real name either. She styled herself a "Mrs" to lessen the shame of a having an illegitimate child, and "Jordan" because she likened crossing the sea from Ireland to England as being the equivalent of arriving in the Promised Land. I don't know about her face, but she was reputed to have the best legs in show business. She had four illegitimate children before she met the Duke, and went on to have no fewer than ten with him. She was his mistress for twenty years.

Can you imagine taking on nine grandchildren, one a babe in arms, when you are sixty-two! That's what the 1st Marquess of Ailsa did after his eldest son, Archibald, aka the Earl of Cassillis, died in August 1832 a month after his wife, Eleanor, had given birth to their tenth child. She died in November. The reason there were only nine to look after was because Alexander had died in

● ● ●

October, aged only fourteen. The Marquess must have thought his family was cursed. This terrible list of tragic deaths began with the death of his younger son, John, in 1831.

The 1st Marquess was a keen horseman, one of the founders of the Ayr Gold Cup which was inaugurated in 1804, originally for horses bred and trained in Scotland. He was the first-ever winner and also the second, on *Chancellor*. He was also interested in agricultural improvements and introduced new types of potato to the Culzean estate. He died in 1846, never having achieved the high office of state he desired. He chopped and changed his political opinions too often for that.

He was succeeded by his grandson, Archibald the 13th Earl, and 2nd Marquess. In 1859, he also was made a Knight of the Thistle and, like his grandfather, he was a keen horseman. He was not so lucky in the saddle, however. In 1870, when out on a hunting expedition, he was thrown from his horse and died a few days later of his injuries.

His son, Archibald (other names were available to his parents), became the 14th Earl and the 3rd Marquess. He was born in 1848 and died in 1939. It was a long life, and it was one that saw a lot of changes. He once collected a speeding fine for driving at 31 mph in a 20 mph area. His plea that he needed that speed to get up a hill did not wash. The law is the law. No matter, the fine was a trifling matter to him.

Sailing was his passion. He liked to race yachts; a rich man's sport, to be sure. He owned several, and was a member of no fewer than nine yacht clubs. He also took Culzean on a different tack when he set up a boat-building business. He had some prestigious customers such as the King of Belgium and the Vanderbilts. The boathouse and repair yard he built in Culzean grew into the Ailsa Shipbuilding Company based in Troon and which, incredibly, only shut down in 2000.

About halfway through his life, he suffered a mid-life crisis (as many do) and became addicted to golf. (Remember whose fault that was!) He oversaw the development of a championship course at Turnberry, with a purpose-built hotel to accommodate the golfers who were whisked there by rail.

He married twice. His first wife was Evelyn Stuart, an evangelical Christian and teetotaller whom he married in 1871. Not my cup of tea, but it suited him. He was devastated when she died in 1888. He shut up Culzean and took himself off to go a-travelling in Europe which is where he met Isabella MacMaster, whom he married in 1891.

But I get too far ahead of myself. During his tenure, he embarked on a programme of building and modernisation. Not since Robert Adam had

Culzean seen such changes. His first Marchioness thought the castle too uncomfortable and persuaded, or ordered, her husband to build a new wing. Amongst other changes, the brewhouse was transformed into a nursery to accommodate their five children. We already know what she didn't like; the brewhouse's change of function surely tells us what she *did* like. No wonder he was devastated when she donned her angels' wings and left him to meet her Maker in heaven.

The times they were a-changing and the Culzean estate found itself in financial trouble again, not this time through profligacy and gambling, but through punitive taxation and death duties. In 1933, a family summit was held and the decision was taken to entail the estate and form a limited company with the family members as directors. Entailment meant that the estate could only be passed on to the designated heir and could not be seized for non-payment of debt.

Archibald's eldest son (you'll never guess what his given name was) became the 4th Marquess of Ailsa in 1938. He died in 1943 and his brother Charles, who was also childless, became the 5th Marquess. He died in June 1956 and was succeeded by his brother Angus, the 6th Marquess, who died in the May of the following year. He never lived at Culzean.

Before he died, Archibald, the 4th Marquess, had entered into negotiations to hand over Culzean to the National Trust for Scotland. The discussions were continued by his widow, Lady Frances, who made it a condition that she should be allowed to live in the new west wing for the rest of her life (she died in 1949), and that the top floor of the castle should be reserved for the use of General Eisenhower in gratitude for his support during WWII. He had a particular fondness for the castle. He first visited it in 1946 and stayed there three more times, once when he was President. Thus the top floor of Culzean temporarily became the White House. Now it's a prestigious hotel and a popular wedding venue.

And so the story of the castle's connection with the Kennedys of Culzean and the Earls of Cassillis came to an end, bizarrely in the same way it began three centuries earlier – with three brothers. There's a symmetry in that which rather appeals to me.

That's the history. Now for the visit, in time present.

As all visitors must, we enter by the porch, one of the 1877 additions, and find ourselves in the armoury. Never having seen anything remotely like it before, I get an overwhelming *Alice in Wonderland* sort of feeling. Each and every wall is crammed with pistols and swords, arranged neatly in circles, ovals and criss-crosses, so that there is scarcely an inch of bare wall left. Only the armoury at Windsor Castle has a bigger collection of weapons.

They are for show now, but once upon a time the pistols were fired in anger. The collection was begun by the 12th Earl (and the 1st Marquess of Ailsa), who obtained the obsolete weapons from the Office of Ordinance at the Tower of London.

In a corner is a very curious object. It's an alligator doing a handstand. His fearsome jaws are opened in a wide grin as if to proudly boast, "Hey, look at me! See what I can do!" Not so clever of him to be caught and killed and have his back slit open as a repository for walking sticks and umbrellas. It's rather grisly, to be honest. I wouldn't give it houseroom, and I can't understand why anyone would.

Accompanied by Bob, our guide, we set off on our tour. There are a goodly number of portraits and it's good to put faces to some of the names I've mentioned above. And talking of faces, please note the firescreens. Hamlet, far less Shakespeare, never said, *Vanity, thy name is woman.* But Hamlet *did* say, and Shakespeare *did* write, *Frailty, thy name is woman.* It's easy to see how the misquotation happened, but there is a darker connection between the words.

In the 18th century, where the whitest of faces was considered the epitome of beauty (and who decided that?), the society ladies' pursuit of a fair face actually led to their deaths. To achieve this desired whiteness, they clarted their faces with white lead and/or mercury water, then rouged their cheeks to appear less corpse-like. And there you have it – vanity and frailty come together in the face of a woman. How the owners of today's tanning salons must dread the day when someone decides a deathlike pallor is the new look! *And come it will for a' that* – for fashion is a fickle thing.

Hanging in the Blue Dining Room is a Papal Indulgence issued by Benedict XIV to Sir Thomas, the 9th Earl, when he was touring Italy in the 1750s. When in Rome, why not pop in to see the Pope and buy a little souvenir to take home for your soul's sake?

The Oval Staircase surely must be the *pièce de résistance* of the whole castle. Twelve pillars on each floor, and – in a departure from the normal order – Doric on the bottom, Corinthian in the middle, and Ionic at the top. I agree with that; I always think you should keep the best to last. Light floods in from an oculus in the roof. It is quite, quite perfect.

One portrait worthy of mention is that of Lord John Kennedy, aged five, the youngest son of the 2nd Marquess, in my Lady Ailsa's Boudoir. He's posing with a pony by the Swan Loch. The reason I mention it is because he is gussied up like a girl. They did that, Bob tells us, to protect the sons from being kidnapped and held hostage. Girls, apparently, were not worth kidnapping.

There are a lot of treasures here, to be sure, but whatever you do when you come here, you must look *up* and admire the Adam ceilings. The finest example, arguably, is that in the Round Drawing Room. It really is quite sublime. Not all the ceilings are decorated, however; only the public rooms. That was to show off to visitors how rich they were, even if we know now they were up to their ears in debt.

And while you are in the Round Drawing Room, don't forget to spare a glance at the carpet beneath your feet. One should always look down as well as up! Bob informs us it requires a team of people to give it a turn so that it is evenly exposed to sunlight and the tread of feet.

We make our way across the courtyard towards the castle exit, in full view of the front door – something that plebs like us could never have done when it was in the possession of the Kennedys. To our left is the servants' walkway that runs between the castle and the clock tower. In any other place, the complex of buildings around the clock tower would have been an impressive stately home in its own right. As for the walkway, it takes the meaning of "tradesmen's entrance" to a new level. It lies below the level of the courtyard so that they, and the servants, couldn't be seen approaching the castle by those inside. Heaven forfend!

The ruined arch, which visitors pass through as they approach and leave the castle, was deliberately built as a ruin by Adam to frame it. It comes from an age when it was thought there was not anything half so romantic as a ruin. It does indeed make a very fitting frame for the castle – and a good photograph.

But then I am a bit of an old romantic. Just ask my wife. She will tell you I certainly am one of those things.

Chapter Fifty-Five

Alloway: The Birthplace of a Poet

THERE is much more to Culzean than the castle – the gardens, the park, the beach and the caves, the former repositories for contraband. We simply do not have time enough.

I began this route in Dumfries where Scotland's national bard died. Now, as we draw towards the end of our SWC300 journey, we are heading to the place where he was born. You can't get away from Burns on this route, especially when you reach Ayrshire.

The way to Alloway on the A719 takes us to Electric, or Croy, Brae. It is famous for an optical illusion, where, due to the particular way the road is laid out, vehicles going downhill appear to be going uphill. A stone in a lay-by informs the traveller about this phenomenon. If it's written in stone, then you know it must be true.

A short distance later, the ruins of Dunure Castle appear far below on the coast. Even if I didn't know that this was where the charming Gilbert Kennedy toasted the toes of Alan Stewart, the Commendator of Crossraguel Abbey, the ruins do not appear remotely romantic, as in the way some poets seem to regard such things.

And so we arrive in Alloway and the £21 million Robert Burns Birthplace Museum which has replaced the unlamented Tam o' Shanter Experience. We find the way there very easily and scarcely a parking place to be had in the car park. But then it is a holiday week, the schools are closed and the kids have

The Electric Brae

been brought here to absorb some culture. If seeing weren't believing, then hearing is, as decibels of excited chatter assault our eardrums. We needn't have worried. There are plenty of interactive exhibits to absorb them.

You can't get away from the notion that this is Scotland's answer to William Shakespeare. Outside the entrance a noticeboard – it must be twenty feet long by six high – proclaims *Birthplace of a Genius* and is flanked on either side by his portrait set against a saltire background. You know you are really, really famous when you are recognised by your face alone. It's only at the very end of the board that you see his name written in much smaller letters. They are not really necessary.

Entrance for us is free, as usual, being members of the NTS and before we pass into the museum proper, there is an anteroom containing a bust of the great man and where a video presentation is in progress. There is also a desk and a chair belonging to Burns; a notice explaining why the interior of the museum is so dimly lit; and on a wall, surprisingly, this quotation from Hugh MacDiarmid's *A Drunk Man Looks at the Thistle*:

> *Mair nonsense has been uttered in his name*
> *Than in ony's, barrin' Liberty and Christ.*

Typical of Scotland and the Scots' psyche. With the exception of Holy Willie, who explained his *fleshly lust* as a peccadillo sent to him by God *lest he owre proud and high shou'd turn/that he's sae gifted,* Scots as a whole are a modest people who neither put themselves or their heroes on a pedestal. The exception is Burns where, in the town of his birth, they have gone to great lengths to show their pride in their local lad.

In the same poem, MacDiarmaid also complained: *Few kens a wurd Burns wrote.* Surely an exaggeration – sounds more like sour grapes to me – but one thing is certain: even if these kids did not know a single word before they came here, they will, at the very least, have been exposed to a great many before they leave, for they are written in huge letters everywhere you look in this vast hangar of a place.

One of the first, under the heading *Chapter and Verse* is a quotation from a letter by Burns to Dr John Moore, dated 2nd August 1787, in which he writes: "The earliest thing of Compositon that I recollect taking pleasure in was *The Vision of Mirza* and a hymn of Addison's." It is very gratifying to see my surname writ large like that but, more importantly, it surely must lay to rest the myth that Burns was an uneducated ploughman who turned his hand to writing poetry as a sort of hobby when he wasn't turning over the poor, unproductive soil behind the backside of a horse.

Another piece of text is emblazoned across the glass front of a display cabinet: *The face that launched a thousand shortbread tins.* Not Burns's words, but very true *for a' that.* And not just shortbread tins; a thousand other items of merchandise as well – some examples of which are on view in the dim interior of the cabinet. Articles such as a Tam o' Shanter tobacco tin, a Tam o' Shanter snuff-box, a Sweet Afton Virginia Tobacco packet, a Burns medallion, a souvenir tea-towel, a souvenir spoon, a fridge magnet, a faux banknote tray, and – perhaps most surprisingly – a poster with Burns's face in place of Che Guevera's in that iconic poster so familiar with students in the Sixties.

In short, never mind shortbread, the manufacturers of all things Scottish are not averse to stamping the face of the versifying Rabbie Burns upon it in the never-ending mission to drive up sales and increase profits. Too bad for Burns's descendants that his image is well out of copyright. They could have been gorging themselves on millionaire shortbread.

These images on the merchandise above may not be exact and faithful reproductions of the famous Nasmyth portrait, but they are still recognisably Burns. But what about this face in the glass cube that you can walk around and observe from every angle? How many would recognise *that* as the face of Burns? Damn few is my guess, and the ones that could, are *a' deid.* Which is ironic, as it is claimed this is the *real* face of Burns – not some romantic or idealised portrait.

In a separate cabinet is the plaster cast of the Bard's skull. It's pretty dark in there and it's pretty low down too, so it's very hard to see anything except for a white mound gleaming palely in the gloom like a moon a-rising. However, from what I can make out, it's only half a skull with nothing below the eye sockets. If that is all the reconstructing team had to go on, then it's no wonder the reconstructed face looks nothing like the Nasmyth portrait, universally accepted as being *the* face of Rabbie Burns.

However, as I explained in Chapter Three, the team did not build their face upon the skull alone. Just how true-to-life Nasmyth's portrait may or may not be, you can make up your own mind. That said, how about reading a clue in the last four letters of the painter's name?

No such problem in knowing what Burns's descendants looked like, or at least some of them, for in another cabinet are photographs of his son, William Nicol Burns, his grandson, Robert Burns, and his great-granddaughter, Jean Armour Burns Brown, which seems to cover all the family bases. In addition, there are two of his granddaughters taken in their old age – and very fierce they look, too. There are paintings of two more of Burns's sons, James Glencairn Burns and Robert Burns Junior, the latter looking very odd indeed, his head and his legs out of all proportion to his body. Maxwell, you remember, was born the day of his father's funeral and was buried with him, aged only two, which explains why there is no likeness of him, poor soul.

There are some line drawings of other relations too, including one of Jean. Like her portrait in the Burns House museum, she looks rather stern. I find it hard to believe that this is the face of *Bonnie Jean,* the Mauchline Belle, even allowing for what time and hard work wrought upon her features.

Nearby there's a contraption, where by placing your face, just so, and by pressing some buttons, a silhouette of your profile will be taken and e-mailed to you – all completely free. Perhaps if I see my face like this, as in the silhouettes of yesterday, it might give me some indication of just how possible it might be to reconstruct an accurate likeness of the full face. I'm remembering that Burns thought that the closest likeness he had ever seen of himself was the silhouette miniature made by Alexander Reid. Could this help to settle the matter of which is closer to the real face of Burns – Dundee University's reconstruction or Nasmyth's portrait? Alas, our silhouettes never arrived, I am sorry to say, so I am no closer to providing an answer.

What I didn't see, despite looking for them particularly, are the original panes of glass from *The Globe* where Burns scratched the lines to Polly Stewart. The girl at the desk suggested they might be out on loan but she didn't really know, nor could she tell me where the stylus is with which he did the damage. I did see, however, a pane from the window of the Cross Keys Inn in Falkirk where he stayed on 25th August 1787 on his tour with Willie Nicol. This is what he scratched:

Sound be his sleep and blythe his morn,
That never did a lassie wrang;
Who poverty ne'er held in scorn,
For misery ever tholed a pang.

He had recently been given his diamond-tipped stylus from the Earl of Glencairn and was trying it out. This was not his first, but it is the oldest surviving example of this type of his handiwork .

I won't tell you what else we saw. Suffice it to say, there are so many memorabilia, you really need to come and see them for yourself. As for us, we're off to see the next part of the Burns experience, taking the Poet's Path to the birth cottage. On the way, we encounter a giant mouse which towers over us. We pause for a photograph, the bold mouse cheekily posing with my hat.

We approach the whitewashed cottage from the rear, noting how it is slightly curved, and very attractive it looks too with its thatched roof and small windows. It looks chocolate-box material if ever I saw it, and I'd be surprised if someone, somewhere, is not using it to sell something.

As you know, it was built by Burns's father, with his bare hands. What William built, Burns described as *an auld cley biggin'*, a far cry from the romantic cabin of *clay and*

Burns *To a Mouse* Statue

wattles made in Yeats's *Lake Isle of Innisfree*, but not so different in construction, especially as far as its ability to withstand a storm was concerned.

As Burns himself tells us:

Our Monarch's hindmost year but ane
Was five-and-twenty days begun
'Twas then a blast o' Janwar win'
Blew hansel in on Robin...

The storm of 1759 was so severe, it damaged the cottage so badly that it had to be more or less completely rebuilt. And as I write these words, a £100,000 appeal has been launched to repair and re-thatch it.

After the family moved to Mount Oliphant in 1766, Mr Burnes let the house out until he sold it in 1781 for the princely sum of £14 to the Incorporation of Shoemakers in Ayr – a charitable organisation for retired shoemakers and their families. They turned it into an alehouse to fund their cause. After Burns's fame grew, they extended the building to cater for the growing number of visitors. One of them was John Keats, who came here in 1818.

In 1881, it was bought by the Burns Monument Trust for £4000 who proceeded to return it to more like the sort of place that Burns knew. After his father died on Friday, 13th February 1784, Burns – now twenty-five and head of the family – changed the spelling of the family name, and they moved to the farm of Mossgiel near Mauchline.

The Burns Birthplace Cottage

His father was a gardener to trade, and behind the house there were seven acres of land which he hoped to turn into a market garden. He never achieved his dream, but the NTS is in the process of creating vegetable plots, an orchard, a pond, a wildflower meadow and a woodland walk. If he were to come back and see it, I'm sure William would heartily approve.

As was common practice in those days, the cottage sheltered man and beast alike. Cattle up one end, people at the other. We enter the hallowed ground of the birthplace cottage the way the cattle would once have done.

To my surprise, there is no-one there to greet us or answer any questions we may have, such as: is this the original floor? It looks as if it could be, very cracked and worn smooth. Are these the same flags that the barefoot poet-to-be pattered across on baby feet and until he was seven? Am I literally treading in his footsteps?

By contrast, the floor of the byre is cobbled and looks new. I'd be surprised if cloven hoofs have ever trodden here. It is completely pristine and smells a lot sweeter than it would have done when occupied, not that I'm recommending that it could be improved by adding a fragrant cowpat or two. You can carry realism too far.

As the writing on the wall tells us, this is where the milking, the butter and cheese making – and not least, the mucking-out – would have taken place. Getting the butter to churn was hard work, and woman's work back then too. Sometimes the milk refused to churn, a sure sign that witches had put a spell on it – as the blackboard in the stall reminds us.

In the living room, the focus of attention is not the fireplace, as it is in most rooms, but the box-bed where, suspended above it, are four blindingly-white nighties looking like disembodied souls ascending to heaven. It's nonsense really, as it's the very place where the babies took their first breaths, not where they expired. Stitched on the front are their names and dates of birth. Robert was first. Everyone knows the date. What they may not know is that it was a Thursday. The rhyme has it that *Thursday's child has far to go.* How true that is! He did indeed go far in his short life.

Pride of place is given, beside the fireplace, to a spinning wheel and a chair with the shortest legs a chair ever had. It's hardly any height above the ground at all. It's hard to imagine anyone managing to lower themselves onto that, let alone struggle up again. On it is written an extract from *The Cotter's Saturday Night*:

The Mother wi' her needle and her shears
Gars auld claes look amaist as weel's the new.

The poem is a romantic picture of a rustic domestic scene and about as far removed from the harsh reality of the hardship of life and the struggle to survive as Burns's parents went through as it's possible to imagine.

We go round the side of the house to see the cottage from the front. It looks even more chocolate-boxy than ever, but then you probably knew that already – it's almost as famous as the face of he who was born here.

We are retracing our steps now to visit Alloway's Auld Kirk. It was built in the early 1500s on the site of a church dating back three centuries before that. Some parts of it are supposedly incorporated into the present building. It was abandoned in 1756, and it's pretty much as Burns would have known it – roofless and with its gable ends still intact and the bell still in its cote. Next to the exterior font, a shallow semi-circular bowl jutting out from the wall where people purified themselves before they entered the hallowed interior of the kirk, an old sycamore grows. It must have been a sapling when Burns was a lad – if it were even there then at all.

What definitely was not where it is now, is his father's grave, in a prominent position as soon as you enter the churchyard. It might well be, however, the grave of his sister, Isabella, and her daughters, Agnes and Isabella. Their stone is very much overgrown with moss and illegible. No-one has taken the trouble to clear it off. The plot of a famous dead poet's sister is not worth caring for, obviously.

The bones, or the dust, of William are not interred with them, despite the poem on the back of the stone written by Robert which states: *Here lie the loving husband's dear*

Alloway Auld Kirk

● ● ●
341

remains. The front says, *Sacred to the Memory of William Burns* and *Agnes Brown, who died on the 14*[th] *Jan' 1820 in the 88 year of her age.* And there you have it – that was not how he spelled his name at the time of his death, and for what it's worth, not how Agnes spelled her name either – *Broun.* This has to be, not even a replica, but a replacement.

No, sadly, the truth of the matter is that the original stone fell victim to souvenir hunters who sacrligeously carried it off, bit by bit, to put a fragment on their mantelpiece after his first-born became famous. He was not dead yet or they would have gone there instead, presumably. Where William was buried originally, no-one knows – so please, when you come here, tread softly.

What you will certainly tread on is a stone on the path that was laid by Burn's brother, Gilbert. This is what it says:

> *MY FATHER with two or three other neighbours, raised by subscription a sum for enclosing this ANCIENT CEMETERY with a wall, hence he came to consider it as his BURIAL PLACE.*

It is a safe bet to say that two iron mortsafes that can be seen in the interior of the church were not here in Burns's day. They were designed to protect the coffins from the so-called resurrectionists who supplied the anatomists with corpses for dissection in the 19th century. Usually the mortsafes were removed after the body would have decomposed so badly it was no longer of any use to them. This grisly practice came to an end with the Anatomy Act of 1832, when it became legal to cut up bodies in the interests of medical research.

Another thing Burns would never have seen is the splendid Grecian mausoleum to the Hughes family which is tucked in in a corner of the churchyard. By contrast, what he must have seen are the much older but fascinating headstones on the left of the entrance of the church. He would have seen them in much better condition than they are today, and more of them too as they are very much sunken into the ground.

Brig o' Doon

One is the grave of a blacksmith, shown shoeing a horse along with the tools of his trade, and – above them – an hour-glass timer showing the sands of time have run out for him. Had the timer been shown lying on its side, it would have indicated he had died an unnatural death, before his allotted timespan.

Another fascinating stone belongs to a farmer, while another is a miller's. Their names we do not know. I can't help thinking if this were my stone, it would feature the Book of Knowledge, and the tool of my trade – the *tawse*, or leather belt – for back in those days, I was both a recipient and the administrator of that form of corporal punishment.

View from Brig o' Doon

From personal experience, I can tell you it really is better to give than receive.

We're moving on to the Brig o' Doon now. It was probably built in the 1400s and rebuilt in the 1700s, fortunately surviving a stay of execution after the new bridge was built upstream in 1816 (and which makes a great vantage point from which to admire it). Even if it weren't famous as the place where poor Maggie lost her tail, it's worth coming to see in its own right, for it is very picturesque with its weathered grey stone, cobbled high arch and not least, the view it offers both upstream and downstream from the *keystane* which Maggie's tale didn't quite reach.

We make our way back to the car park through the Memorial Gardens. Unfortunately the Burns Monument is completely shrouded in scaffolding and sheeting. Had we been able to see it, we would have seen a Grecian-style, seventy-foot rotunda composed of nine pillars standing on top of a triangular base. The nine pillars represent the nine muses, while the base represents, and points to each of the traditional regions of Ayrshire – Kyle, Carrick and Cunninghame.

It was completed in 1823 at a cost of £3,247, and was paid for by subscription. It was designed by Sir Thomas Hamilton. Inside is a circular room containing a bust of the poet, set into a niche in the far wall. Stairs lead to the top, where there is a walkway round the top where you get a bird's-eye view of the gardens and the river. But of course we can't see any of that.

We're off now to see what she shall see on the next stage of our SWC300 journey.

* * *

Chapter Fifty-Six

By the Banks o' Bonnie Doon: Doom-Laden Tales

WE have rejoined the A77 which is taking us south through Minishant where, shortly afterwards, we take the B7045 to Kirkmichael and continue straight on towards Straiton. (Pardon the pun.)

Before that comes Kirkmichael, an attractive little place whose origins date back to the 13th century when John de Gemmelsoun founded a church here dedicated to St. Michael. The present church goes back to 1787. The stone lych gate is earlier – from 1702. It was a weaving village, and traveller, as you pass through, you should know that the attractive white-washed cottages you see on either side were built in the late 18th century, and are still occupied.

Straiton's origins are marginally earlier, going back to 1760 when it was laid out by our old friend Thomas, 9th Earl of Cassillis, but rebuilt by Edward Hunter-Blair of Blairquhan Castle in 1900. It is quite a film star. It doubled as Balmoral Castle in the 2006 Oscar-winning movie *The Queen* starring Helen Mirren. Less prestigiously, it was also the setting for *Beauty and the Geek,* a reality TV programme where the premise is to pair a bimbo and a brainy bloke and see what each can learn from the other – something academic in her case and social skills in his. Good grief!

Nowadays it is a venue for weddings and corporate events, but the castle began with the McWhirters' tower house in 1346. It passed into the Hunter-Blair family in 1798. In 1820, Sir David of that ilk commissioned the architect, William Burn, to design a new house. It was completed in 1824 and remained in the family until 2012, when it was sold to a subsidiary of a Chinese company which bottles mineral water.

In the gardens is an incredibly old sycamore which dates back to the reign of James V in the first part of the 16th century. Even more interesting than that, it is thought to be a *dule,* or hanging tree. This specimen was heavily pruned in

1997 to preserve its life. The trunk, which is more than eighteen feet in diameter, is completely hollow.

In the churchyard lies the body of one who was put to death but who was not a criminal in the usual sense of the word. It's yet another Covenanter's grave. In January 1686, Thomas Machaffie – a young man who was suffering from a fever which he had caught from hiding in a damp cave – was being sheltered by some sympathetic friends when he was discovered by a Captain Bruce and his men. He was dragged from his sickbed, taken outside and shot dead on the spot.

From here we take the B741 to Dalmellington. It was also a weaving village until coal mining arrived in the mid-eighteenth century. They also discovered ironstone and the Dalmellington Iron Company was set up. In 1856 the railway connected it, and the collieries to the north, with Ayr. More pits were opened up in the 20th century, the last being in 1954. The last pit to stop working was Pennyvenie in 1978 after 97 years of operation.

Dunaskin, a little of town to the west, is where you will find the Scottish Industrial Railway Centre. Sadly, the Dunaskin Heritage Centre ceased to be in 2005 after local authority funding was withdrawn, but happily the Ayrshire Railway Preservation Group stepped into the breach and the story of Dalmellington's industrial past was preserved. It is home to industrial locomotives from the past, both steam and diesel (not to mention a splendid model railway).

The derelict Ardoon House was the ironworks manager's house, designed by that man again, William Burn. He, along with David Bryce of Glasgow, built it in the 1850s. It occupies an elevated position on the site. The office was built in 1871 and was extended in the 1940s by the National Coal Board, who turned it into its regional headquarters. Now it is the museum's visitor centre, shop, restaurant and best place to begin your visit by taking in the audio-visual presentations.

The pride of the centre is the Blowing Engine House. It's the last one from the mid-nineteenth century left standing in Europe. Isn't that an amazing thing! It's not known for sure who designed it, but very probably it was the usual suspect, Mr Burn. It may have been a functional building, but it's also a thing of beauty with a lot of classical embellishments.

It used to house the engine that powered the bellows, that blew the air, that breathed life into the flames of the furnaces that made the iron. In fact, the works were doing so well by 1864 that a second engine was required and the engine house had to be extended. However, the end came in 1921... but then, in

1928, the works had a new lease of life when they were converted to making bricks. When that stopped in 1978, that really was the end.

To accommodate the workforce, 900 houses were built, some in purpose-built hill-villages such as Lethanhill. They were demolished in the 1950s, as they had become unfit for human habitation. They had no running water, no baths and no toilets. Heating and cooking was provided by an open fire, rubbish was put on a midden, and water was collected from a communal well. Welcome to 18th century-living in the 20th century.

On the A713, Chapel Row at Waterside retains a cottage as it was in 1914. Compared with earlier times it was luxurious, consisting of a living room, a bedroom, a parlour and a washroom. That's for clothes, not people, by the way. One of the exhibits is a *whurlie-bed* – a double bed on wheels that was stored beneath the actual bed. Despite the cramped accommodation and the lack of facilities, large families were the rule rather than the exception which made the pressure on space even tighter.

From Scotland's industrial past we are going further back in the past to visit Scotland's only relocated castle. We're taking the little road down the west side of the *banks and braes o' bonnie Doon,* one of Burns's most famous songs, composed in 1791. The loch was dammed in 1935 as part of a hydroelectric scheme, which resulted in the level of the loch being raised by twenty-seven feet. The ruined castle, which once stood on an island in the loch, would have been submerged had it not been dismantled, stone by stone, and painstakingly reassembled on the brae.

Why, you might reasonably ask, would anyone go to the lengths of dismantling a ruined castle, transporting the stones across the river, hauling them up the bank (quite some distance, by the way), and reassembling them? If it proved an impossible task to put Humpty Dumpty together again, then rebuilding the castle could scarcely have been much less challenging. The walls are of a good height, but much lower than when first built. The keep, which stood inside them, was left to drown. But that was a later, 16th century addition, to these 13th century walls.

The reason they went to so much trouble is because of its associations with Robert the Bruce. A small plaque outside, and a larger one inside the walls, provides a potted history of the castle and an artist's impression shows what it would have looked like in its prime. Impressive! It was unusual, unique in fact. It was built in the late 13th century for an ancestor of Robert the Bruce, possibly even his father. With a high, eleven-sided curtain wall, it was one of the principal castles of the Earls of Carrick.

Doon Castle Broch

After Bruce had oh, so foully murdered the Red Comyn in Greyfriars in February 1306, Aymer de Valence, his brother-in-law, was sent to sort the Bruce out. And so he did, defeating the Scots at the Battle of Methven in June of the same year. Bruce's brother-in-law, Sir Christopher Seton, however, managed to flee from the battle and this is where he holed up. Despite its apparently impregnable position in the loch, it was captured, as was Seton, who was taken to Dumfries and hanged.

It was here, in his heartland, that Bruce began his guerrilla war against the English. You don't need me to tell you how that ended in 1314 when, at last, this castle was liberated.

In the 1330s however, Scotland was again under attack from the English. The luckless Scots were defeated at the Battle of Halidon Hill in 1333, and Doon Castle was only one of five castles to hold out against the English. They besieged it for two years before they gave up. Cutting off the water supply is the easiest way to bring a castle to its knees, but that was not an option here. All the besieged had to do was lower buckets into the loch. They knew, like the Ancient Mariner did not, they were surrounded on all sides by fresh water. In fact, Loch Doon is the largest inland fresh water loch in all of Scotland. But what I would really like to know is, what did they find to eat – unless it was fish? They must have been utterly sick of it.

The castle's troubles were not over, however. Having got rid of the English, there was more from those nearer to hand – the neighbours. Later in the century, the castle came into the power of the Kennedys, but they lost it in a siege to William Douglas in 1446. It was back in the hands of Gilbert Kennedy, 3rd Earl of Cassillis, by 1450, and it was he who probably built the tower house within the walls.

In 1511 William Crawford launched an unsuccessful attack on the castle, but in 1520 it did not get off so lightly. On the orders of James V, it was attacked and torched in an effort to subdue those who were getting above their station, becoming too high and mighty. One source says the portcullis, which defended the keep, lies at the bottom of the loch.

After that, the castle was abandoned and left alone until it became a handy source of stone for the building of a shooting lodge, and the greatest threat of all, as you know – the ten-metre rise in the level of the loch.

Before that happened, however, six dugout canoes were excavated from the bottom of the loch in 1823. One contained a Viking battle-axe, now in the Kirkcudbright museum, while two canoes are enjoying the fresh air and a new lease of life in the Hunterian Museum in Glasgow. They are thought to have been used in the construction of the castle. If so, they must have plied between the shore and the island many, many times with their cargo of stones.

That's not the only thing that has been dredged up from the bottom of Loch Doon. A Spitfire, would you believe? On 25th October 1941, on a routine training flight, eyewitnesses testified to seeing one of the wings graze the surface of the water and, the next minute, it cartwheeled into the air before plunging into the loch. The body of the pilot – Frantisek Hekl from the 312 (Czech) Squadron, based at Ayr – was never found, but the plane itself was recovered in 1982 by divers from the Dumfries and Galloway Sub Aqua Club, assisted by divers from the Blackpool Sub Aqua Club. It was restored and can be seen in the Dumfries and Galloway Aviation Museum.

Another routine training flight turned into disaster for Roswell Murray MacTavish of 439 Squadron, Royal Canadian Air Force, who crashed into the forest on 18th March 1944. He was killed and is buried in Ayr but the scattered remains of the aircraft, including its engine, were left to rust where they made this unscheduled and unexplained fall to earth.

Believe it or not, hundreds of miles from the killing fields of Flanders, this remote and peaceful place was identified as the perfect place to teach the new art of shooting down aircraft – as well as training new pilots and crew. The work began in September 1916 with, first of all, 15,000 construction workers, 1,300 POWs and 500 servicemen who were employed, before any of that training could begin, to build their accommodation, as well as all the necessary ancillary buildings and amenities such as sewers and the like. It was the equivalent of building a small town. In addition to that, in a harbinger of what was to come some thirty years later, the level of the loch was raised by six feet to make it suitable for seaplanes to land and take-off.

On the western side of the loch, where the target area was to be, hangars, piers, jetties and a slipway were built, while on the eastern side, an area of boggy land was identified as the site for an airfield. But try as they might, after miles and miles of drains were laid, the land refused to dry-out sufficiently. After six months of trying, the hangars were dismantled and rebuilt on a new aerodrome at Bogton Loch, five miles to the north, just to the east of

Dalmellington. And to make *it* suitable, the land had to be drained which they did by diverting the River Doon.

It all sounds like a labour such as Hercules might have undertaken, and it turned into a bit of a white elephant when the government decided to abandon the project on account of spiralling costs. No-one knows what the expense of this doomed Doon project was, but it's safe to say it would have run into many millions of pounds.

Doon and doom. So similar as to be synonymous.

Chapter Fifty-Seven

New Cumnock and the Afton Valley: The Mining Disaster and the Guerillas' Hideout

WE retrace our steps through Glen Ness, towards Dalmellington, and take the B741 to New Cumnock. Being Ayrshire, you can't go far before bumping into some association or other with Burns, and New Cumnock makes sure you don't miss him – his portrait is on the sign as you enter the village along with *Sweet Afton*. The village stands on the river and, as everybody knows, it is one of his most famous songs.

Various suggestions have been put forward as to the derivation of the name of the village. The most likely is from the Gaelic *comunn achadh* meaning "place of confluence" or "meeting place", and this indeed is where the Afton meets the Nith. Despite the "New", the village dates back to the 13th century when a castle was built at the confluence by the Earls of Dunbar and March. It was given the charming name of Black Bog Castle. Wouldn't you just love to live there! By the 16th century, it lay in ruins.

The reason for the "New" is because, by 1650, the parish had grown so large that the church was inadequate for its needs and a new one was built on the site of the castle where a settlement grew up around it. Time passes. That new church is now known as the *Auld Kirk*.

New Cumnock doesn't look like it today, but it used to be a mining village with no fewer than five pits, employing more than 1,500 miners. Now there is none. Knockshinnock Castle and Bank collieries closed in 1968 and 1969 respectively. On 7th September 1950, the former was the scene of the village's worst pit disaster when a liquefied volume of peat and moss sludge broke into the seam, trapping 129 men below ground. It had come from an underground glaciated lake (shouldn't that be loch?) beneath their feet, and which they had unwittingly liberated after so many millennia.

The rescue teams were engulfed by the sludge or overcome by bad air and gas. Fortunately, their phoneline to the surface remained intact and the trapped men could provide precise details as to their location. The rescuers, wearing breathing apparatus and digging through an abandoned pit only twenty feet away, managed, after three days, to recuse 116 men. Unfortunately, an unlucky thirteen were killed. The mine is not their tomb, however. Months later, their bodies were recovered. Another ghastly task for the rescue force.

Just two years after the tragedy – or heroic rescue, if you prefer – a film called *The Brave Don't Cry*, or alternatively, *Knockshinnock Story*, was released, starring John Gregson. It was his first big break. Also, in a grassy area near the main street, Castle Street, a memorial commemorates them and others who lost their lives digging for "king coal".

This is not just Burns country, but William Wallace country too. As far as the latter is concerned, we are indebted for our information to Blind Harry's 15th century epic work *The Actes and Deidis of the Illustre and Vallyeant Champioun Schir William Wallace*, otherwise simply known as *The Wallace*. Blind Harry, aka Hary, or Henry the Minstrel, was born c.1440 and died in 1492.

All the world knows that Burns was born in Alloway, but there is growing evidence that Wallace may not have been born in Elderslie, near Paisley, as Harry says, but in Cumnock. In 1999, in Lübeck, Northern Germany, Wallace's seal was found attached to a letter he wrote in 1297. In it, he describes himself as the son of Alan Wallace. Now here's the thing. The Ragman Roll of 1296 (which lists the names of the gentry and nobility of Scotland who swore allegiance to Edward I) mentions an Alan Wallace described as a *crown tenant in Ayrshire*. Also, to support the Cumnock connection, according to Harry: *And Wallace past in Cumno with blith will, At the Blak Rok, quhar he was wont to be, Apon that sted a ryall house held he.*

The poem, or ballad, was written about 1477, by which time Wallace had been dead for more than 170 years. Harry was a minstrel at the court of James IV and was probably blinded when he was serving in the army. He claimed his source for the poem was a book written by

New Cumnock

Wallace's boyhood friend, later his personal priest and confessor, Father John Blair. The difficulty is no such book has ever been found – may never have existed, in fact – which means Harry must have depended on oral history for his information, and we all know how stories can change and be embroidered in the space of two minutes, never mind two centuries. It looks as if the oral history is the most likely scenario, as some events Harry mentions are not recorded in any other sources. And just to add to the confusion, Harry himself may be more than one person, as *The Wallace* runs to twelve volumes. Historians tend to treat it more as a work of versified historical fiction rather than fact.

Burns was a fan, even paraphrasing Harry's couplet *A false usurper sinks in every foe/And liberty return in every blow* in his *Scots Wha Hae wi' Wallace Bled*, Bruce's rousing address to his army before Bannockburn. If you compare that with Burns's *Lay the proud usurpers low/Tyrants fall in every foe*, then I think you will agree that his version is an improvement.

Also according to Harry, it was here, in Cumnock, after he murdered the English sheriff of Lanark, where Wallace mustered his men. I couldn't put it better than the blind poet himself: *To the Blak Crag in Cumno past agayne/His household set with men of mekill mayne/Thre monethis thar he dwellyt in gud rest.*

This stronghold was situated a couple of miles down the Afton valley, beneath Blackcraig Hill. A little further upstream, on the other side of the river, is a rocky outcrop called "William's Castle". The "three months' rest" that Blind Harry refers to is the time after Wallace laid down his sword when he, along with Sir Andrew Murray, defeated the English at Stirling Bridge in September 1297.

After this magnificent victory, against overwhelming odds, Wallace was made a knight and the Guardian of Scotland. Now was a time for a period of recuperation and consolidation. Those swords were heavy, especially Sir William's, with a blade of four feet, four inches – another foot more if you include the hilt, and weighing in at just a fraction below six pounds. That's why it needed two hands to swirl about his head and sever those belonging to the necks of the enemy, like the *taps frae thistles*. And after he had chopped off a few of those, it provided a very handy prop to lean on whilst he got his breath back.

After Wallace exited the scene after the Battle of Falkirk in 1298, enter Scotland's next hero – Robert the Bruce. On his return from hiding in the Western Isles and Ireland, he clashed with Sir Aymer de Vallence in Glen Trool not so far from here and defeated him at the Battle of Loudon Hill in May 1307. Another poet, John Barbour (c.1320-1395), the *Father of Scots*

Poetry, in *his* epic poem *The Brus*, tells how, after those victories, the fugitive king went into hiding between the Blackcraig and Craigbraneoch Hills in the Afton valley.

Meanwhile, at Cumnock Castle, Vallence, smarting from his latest defeat, was waiting for reinforcements in the shape of John of Lorn with 800 men and two dogs. But no ordinary dogs these – they were Bruce's bloodhounds whose astounding noses, they hoped, would pick up the scent of their old master. Lorn was a cousin of the deceased John III Comyn, aka Lord of Badenoch, aka Guardian of Scotland, aka the Red, which colour Bruce saw when he slew him on holy ground. You can understand how Lorn was no lover of Bruce.

However, Bruce was warned of the impending danger by Sir James Douglas, and he and his four hundred followers melted away into the hills. It is said that the rock face on Craigbraneoch Hill was named *Stayamera* as a taunt to Aymer de Vallence, where the first syllable means "keep on looking".

Edward I was not amused with Vallence's failure to find and vanquish the Bruce. The old warrior put an army together and marched north to do the job himself. His health was not good. On the way north, he died near Carlisle. The old fox was dead. His less cunning son, now Edward II, took up the baton and marched his father's army north through Nithsdale, arriving at Cumnock Castle on 19th August 1307. But Bruce and his men weren't daft – they hid in the hills and would not come out and fight. Why should they, against such overwhelming odds?

Edward went home, leaving Bruce to resume his hit-and-run tactics, until seven years later, he and his men did stand and fight. The date was 23rd June 1314. The place was Bannockburn.

Burns was a frequent visitor here as he passed through on his way from Ellisland to Mauchline. There are several plaques dedicated to him dotted about the town, and a statue. There also used to be a mural featuring him and Wallace on the gable end of what was the Castle Inn, where he used to break his journey. Unfortunately, the mural had been painted over at time of writing.

During Burns's day, the incumbent minister was the Reverend James Young. He was a fervent Calvinist who refused to christen a child because of the "wickedness" of his father. In response, Burns wrote a satirical poem: *The Kirk's Alarm*, in which he referred to Young as *Jamie Goose*.

The satire didn't work. Young was the minister from 1758-95. They had to carry him out in a coffin.

Chapter Fifty-Eight

The Crawick Multiverse: A Different View of the Cosmos

PRESENTLY we arrive at Kirkconell on the A75. The village is named after St Conal. The son of a local shepherd, he was a disciple of Glasgow's saint and founder, St Kentigern, or St Mungo, from the Gaelic *Mo Choe* meaning "my dear". The ruins of his church, which date from the 6th century, lie to the north of the village. A Celtic cross, erected by the Duke of Buccleuch in 1880, is said to mark where his bones lie. The present church dates from 1729, with foundations dating back to the 12th and 13th centuries.

The Crawick pass on the B740 is the first of three roughly parallel routes which snake through the Lowther Hills. It is the shortest, lowest and flattest, ending at Crawfordjohn, some four miles away. We are not going that far, but there is something really remarkable to be seen just a mile or so from the junction – the Crawick Multiverse.

Funded by the Duke of Buccleuch, to the tune of a cool £1 million, it opened in 2015. It is the creation of Charles Jencks, the world-famous American landscape artist. The 55-acre site, laid out in a disused opencast coalmine, consists of a series of paths winding through 2,000 boulders and megaliths representing galaxies, comets and Black Holes. At its heart is the massive Sun Amphitheatre capable of holding 5,000 people. Thus a wasteland has painstakingly been transformed into a place for the use of the community and an attraction which will intrigue and enthral visitors.

The site is bisected by a 440-yard-long, boulder-lined path aligned north/south, with "intersection" boulders marking the start of other paths running east/west. The sun is seen in eclipse, an effect created by a pair of hemispherical lagoons at its southern pole. In 2016, the artist added a new feature to the amphitheatre – a mosaic named *Sun Flare/Earth Shield* which represents the "dance of life and death" between the solar flares and the Earth's protective electromagnetic shield.

The Crawick Multiverse

There are two main walks, the Low Road and the Comet Walk. At the end of the former, arising out of a desert landscape, are the spiralling emerald-green mounds of the Andromeda and Milky Way galaxies, 80 and 50-foot high respectively. They are crowned with standing stones which represent other cosmological events, with water-filled hollows at the centre representing Black Holes. Well, maybe they do, but what they make me think of are the ruins of some pagan temple erected in prehistoric times.

While other galaxies are moving away from us, the Andromeda and Milky Way galaxies are moving together, and at their present speed, are on course to collide 4 billion years from now. Well not exactly collide, but unravel, stretching each other into long lines of planets and stars, represented here by the red sandstone standing stones at the bases of the mounds. That really will be the end of life on Earth as we know it. But perhaps we will have bailed out and moved to another galaxy far, far away, by then. Anyway, I'm not going to lose any sleep worrying about it.

Near the colliding galaxies at Crawick is the Supercluster, a sort of zooming-out to show the wider picture, triangular shapes representing a cluster of galaxies of which our galaxy and Andromeda are only two. Zooming-out further still, is the Multiverse, the mind-boggling, mind-blowing fact that our universe is but one of many billions. Here, a corkscrew path leads to where a cluster of standing stones, with a variety of lines carved on them, symbolise different types of universe and how their fates will be many and various.

If that is an outward-looking view of the cosmos, going back to the Big Bang, then there is also the possibility for a bit of navel-gazing too. To the east is the Omphalos, the navel of the Earth in Greek mythology. A V-shape on the roof seems to be sticking up two fingers to the heavens above. A padlocked iron gate prevents access to the interior where there are some "special stones".

At the northern point of the site are the Belvedere and the Void. The former consists of a monolith finger pointing to the Pole Star, while the Void below is its mirror image, set into the ground. It is surrounded by water, with the finger reached by a short grassy path. From its elevated position, the Belvedere offers a panoramic view of the site and surrounding countryside. I can't help but think how like Avebury the former is, while the central, boulder-lined path looks extraordinarily like the Ménec alignment in Carnac. Surely Jencks must have had the ancient inhabitants of this place in mind when he designed this? Whether you believe that some immortal hand and eye created our world and every living creature in it, or that the whole thing is just one monumental mysterious accident – I refuse to believe that the artist was not influenced by the Stone Age peoples when he landscaped this place.

Nearby is one of three shelters, looking, for all the world, like a prehistoric burial monument. There are collapsed stones all around, symbolising the effects of when comets and asteroids collide.

The start of the Comet Walk is marked by the largest stones on the whole site and leads the visitor along a scalloped ridge. Four of the stones have white-and-yellow streaks in them, representing comets' tails. They are laid out in such a way as if being pulled into an elliptical trajectory by the gravity of the sun/amphitheatre.

This place really is out of this world.

Chapter Fifty-Nine

Sanquhar and Crawick: Religious Rebels, Dreadful Deaths and Wicked Witches

ESCAPING the pull of the Multiverse, we rejoin the A76 where, in a few moments, we come to Sanquhar, from the Scots Gaelic *Seann Cathair*, meaning "old fort" – not named after the old castle to the south of the town, but a much older one, from neolithic times.

There was a third castle that belonged to the Douglases. It has a fascinating (if not a trifle far-fetched), tale attached to it.

In 1297, the English seized it from the possession of Sir William Douglas, aka *le Hardi*, or Bold, son of William Longlegs, Lord of Douglas. He devised a cunning plan to recapture the castle. Somehow he prevailed upon his brother-in-law, Thomas Dickson, to undertake the plan, which on the face of it, looked like a suicide mission.

Whilst most of the English were tucked up in bed, Dickson blocked the castle gates with a woodcart, slew the porter with his dagger and hacked down another three guards with his axe. Douglas's men swept in and, before the English knew what had hit them, the castle was in Douglas hands again. Three thousand English soldiers responded by laying siege to the castle, but the intrepid Dickson sneaked out by a secret passage and alerted William Wallace. He rode to the rescue with as many men as he could muster (it would be amazing if he could match the English numbers in such a short time) and vanquished the English, who lost five hundred men.

The present Sanquhar Castle (such as it is) was built by the Crichtons about 1400 in a stronger location than the Douglas stronghold, which apparently wasn't very strong at all as it was captured several times. It was built on rising ground with the Nith at the bottom to the west, the Townfoot burn to the north, and ditches to the east and south. It was about this time that the village began to grow, eventually becoming a royal burgh in 1598. Over the next two centuries, the castle similarly evolved and grew.

In 1617, James VI – and by now James I of England too – on his progress to Glasgow, lodged for the night. Of course, the monarch does not travel alone and it's the royal retinue that really costs the money. The Crichtons pulled out all the stops and put on a lavish party which included the king being lighted to bed with £30,000 worth of bonds that he owed Crichton. It's a lot of money today; it must have run into millions then.

I bet the king slept well that night, but I very much doubt if Lord Crichton did. I can just see his good Lady bending his ear, reminding him that they may be rich, but they didn't have money to burn. Very true. The royal visit practically bankrupted them.

They staggered on for another twelve years until, in 1639, they sold the castle to the 3rd Earl of Queensberry, Sir William Douglas. He moved up through the titled gears, becoming a marquess in 1682 and the 1st Duke of Queensberry in 1684. Between 1675 and 1697, he built the much grander Drumlanrig Castle. This timespan might give you an idea that it wasn't just a little place in the country. Indeed, it practically bankrupted *him*. The irony is, after spending all that money on it, he didn't like it and, after spending only one night in it, he returned to Sanquhar. After he had no more need for it, having gone to the castle in the sky, James, the 2nd Duke – having no such scruples about Drumlanrig – moved in, and Sanquhar Castle that was, was allowed to go into decline.

In 1895, John Crichton-Stewart, the Marquis of Bute, began restoring it but that ceased on his death in 1900 and that is how it appears today, apart from another century of decay and the generous contributions of the graffiti artists.

As far as the town is concerned, it earned its living by coal and wool. In fact, by the 18th century, Sanquhar had become a market centre for wool. The Wool Fair, held in July, regulated the price of wool for the whole of southern Scotland. It wasn't a bad job when you think about it, being a weaver. What would you rather be – a miner delving in the deep, dark bowels of the earth, or in your own house, banging away at your loom, although the hours were hideously long? But then, at the end of the 18th century, along came the Industrial Revolution and machines could do what a mere man could do, much faster and for much longer.

Although the hand-weaver's job was consigned to history in Sanquhar, the wool tradition still survives in its distinctive form of black-and-white knitting known as "Sanquhar Knitting", in the form of gloves especially. It was mainly women's work in those days (unsurprisingly) and supplemented the income of subsistence crofters. It provided cash for goods they could not provide for themselves, and in times of hardship when there was crop failure it could mean the difference between famine and survival.

Another household industry of a similar nature was "flowering". It was developed by Mrs Jamieson, the wife of an Ayrshire cotton agent. It has a lacy sort of look, satin stitches being sewn on muslin and then holes cut out. In the 1830s, more than 300 women in the parish of Sanquhar made their living by this *Ayrshire embroidery*. The muslin came with the pattern already traced on it in a soluble

Sanquhar Post Office

blue dye. They were sewn onto garments to decorate collars, cuffs and baby's gowns, especially. Fashions come and go, and by the 1860s it was all over.

But there is something else Sanquhar has which it never lost and can never be taken away. It may come as a surprise to you, being in such an out-of-the-way sort of place, but it has the oldest surviving post office, not just in Scotland, not just in the UK, but in the world! It has been operating continuously since 1712. That's long before the penny post in 1840. Isn't that an amazing thing!

Not a lot older than the Post Office, is the tollbooth which was built by the 3rd Duke of Queensbury; he whose fading memorial stone and column we had seen in the High Street of Dumfries. It was designed by William Adam in 1731, and very fine it looks too with its matching flights of stairs leading to the top floor. That has been made into museum, while the ground floor has been used to recreate one of the Tolbooth's original uses – the jail.

There were two jails, actually. The one on the second storey, below the clock tower, had a skylight that afforded an easy route of escape. One such escapee, William Stitt of Durisdeer, was imprisoned for debt. He had gone out to fetch some blankets because he was cold. The snag was that the bundle on his back was too bulky to allow him to get back in, so he settled down at the door to wait for the jailer to turn up for work in the morning.

The skylight had another use. A string lowered from it allowed friends of the prisoners to attach some creature comforts. Normally these were bottle-shaped. The cells on the ground floor were much more secure, and there was precious little comfort in them as a mock-up of one with a mannequin languishing in one of them shows.

One occupant of these cells was Henry Wright, a professional beggar, who traipsed around the country knocking on people's doors. The householder would normally stump up to get rid of him. He was not always successful, however, and one day he was arrested for stealing. Presumably, like Mr Stitt, he must have felt a tad cold because he set fire to some straw in his cell. Unfortunately, the fire spread, and he narrowly escaped with his life. Because of the fright he had given himself, when he came to trial he was given a light sentence. He died in Dumfries in 1888.

On the wall outside are the *jougs*, a medieval form of punishment where the wrongdoer was chained by the neck to face the mockery of passers-by who not only hurled insults at him but all things rotten that came to hand. Its last recorded use was in 1820, when a housebreaker had to stand on a stone as he was too short for his neck to reach the iron collar. Here he stood for two hours a day for three days, one of which happened to be market day. You can imagine the fun the market-goers had. And if that didn't teach the housebreaker a lesson, then I don't know what would.

One woman, instead of having to stand in the jougs was made to parade round the town with a halter round her neck and a placard on her back which read: "This is a thief." Oh, the shame of it!

Also on the theme of crime and punishment, leading off the High Street is the so-called "Gallows Close" where you can follow the last footsteps of those on their way to meet their end on the Muir. An old oak tree is said to mark the

spot where the gallows stood. In the close, there used to be a well where the condemned had their last drink on earth. The lucky ones had it fortified with something to help them through the ordeal they were just about to face.

Another close is where, in 1812, two French prisoners-of-war are said to have fought a duel over a local girl. The loser, Lt. Arnaud, is buried in the churchyard.

A blue plaque, No. 2 on the town trail, tells us that near this place stood the town house of Lord

Sanquhar Town House and Jail

Sanquhar and it's where Mary, Queen of Scots spent her second-last night in Scotland following her defeat at the Battle of Langside in May 1568. If you have been keeping up, you already know where she spent her last night. Later that year, Lord Sanquhar paid the price for his hospitality. Mary's enemies besieged and took the castle. Royal guests are nothing but trouble.

Another famous person who passed the night here, and on more than one occasion, you will not be surprised to hear, was Burns, passing through to see his *Bonnie Jean* when he was preparing a place for her at Ellisland and she was living at Mossgiel. He stopped at the Queensberry Arms Inn, a mail-staging inn, also called "Whigham's Inn" after the landlord. Through the close is where the stables used to be. Other famous lodgers were Prince Louis Napoleon, General Booth and Sir Walter Scott.

Burns came to know it better when he was here on duty as an exciseman. He described it as the only "tolerable" inn in the place. He wouldn't think so now. It's in a very sorry state of disrepair indeed, and looks as it it's been closed for years. One night, he had to vacate it to make room for the funeral cortège of a Mrs Oswald. Being Burns, he wrote a poem about it. He also did his usual vandal thing and inscribed a complimentary verse on a windowpane.

Another poem inspired by Sanquhar was the 1789 political ballad *The Five Carlins*, where the Dumfriesshire burghs were portrayed as characters discussing whom they should choose to be their MP – the Whig, Patrick Miller, the son of Burns's landlord, or the Tory incumbent, Sir James Johnston. The town of Sanquhar was portrayed as *Black Joan*, "a carlin stoor (stern) and grim". (A *carlin* is a wizened old woman.) Just for the record, Miller was elected.

Sanquhar's most famous son is undoubtedly James Crichton (1560-82), aka *The Admirable Crichton*. He is not to be confused with the eponymous hero of Barrie's play, though Barrie did borrow the soubriquet. To be honest, the sources disagree as to where Crichton was born but the most likely suspect is Eliok House near Sanquhar so, not surprisingly, they claim him. His father was Robert, Lord Advocate of Scotland, the highest lawyer in the land, and his mother was Elizabeth Stewart who claimed royal descent.

He was a real brainbox. At ten-years old, he went to St Andrews University, graduating with his masters when he was only fourteen. By the time he was twenty, he could speak no fewer than twelve languages fluently. It is supposed he had the gift of perfect recall. He was more than just a brainbox, however. Good looking, so refined, he was an expert horseman, fencer, singer, musician, orator and debater. It's just not fair for one man to have so many talents – but it didn't do him any good in the long run, as you shall see.

His party-piece was to challenge professors and other men of learning to throw any questions in the arts and sciences at him. A bit of a show-off, really. They failed to stump him. He joined the French army for a couple of years and in 1582, he so impressed the Duke of Mantua after he defeated and killed a professional duellist who had challenged him, that he engaged him as his principal adviser. It was an appointment that was to cost him his life, but brainy though he was, not even he could have foreseen that.

The Duke had a headstrong son called Vincenzo who had a mistress, until Crichton came along and the lady bestowed her favours upon him instead. One night, as Crichton was leaving her house, he was attacked by three masked ruffians. He defended himself admirably, killed one and ripped off the mask of another to reveal the face of Vincenzo himself. It was more than his life was worth to run his employer's son through with his sword, so getting down on one knee, he presented it, hilt first, to Vincenzo who gladly accepted it and drove the blade through Crichton's heart. He was only twenty-two.

But just how true is the tale? The writer, eccentric and no intellectual slouch in his own right, Sir Thomas Urquhart (1611-60), wrote an account of Crichton's life in *The Discovery of a Most Exquisite Jewel* (1652). It is a work very much given to hyperbole, and so the reader of Crichton's exploits might well be advised to take them with a good dose of salt. Still, they make a good story.

And speaking of far-fetched tales, Sanquhar produced its very own Baron Munchausen or teller-of-tall tales, who lived in the early part of the 19th century. His name was Willie Dalyell, and he once wheeled his ailing mother in a wheelbarrow over the Mennock Pass to Moffat for her to take the waters. That at least, appears to be a true story, despite it being quite a remarkable feat. A feat much less credible, is how he singlehandedly saved Glasgow from being burned down, and how, when out duck-hunting one day, he managed to skewer three ducks at once by firing his ramrod at them. Amazingly, the ducks then fell obligingly dead at his feet.

Another local worthy was Rob Allison, aka the *Doctor* because of his knack of curing pigs who were poorly, as opposed to curing them when they were dead. He had a peculiar hobby, you might even say it was a profession, as an attender of funerals. He went to each and every one, even to those of people he didn't know, not to mourn, but to partake of the refreshments, particularly the liquid sort in which he indulged liberally. Things got to such a sorry state that a public meeting was held where it was agreed the libations would be limited to two drams.

When he heard the news, Mr Allison was not impressed. "Wha the deil do ye think's gaun to change their claes for only twae glass o' whisky?" he retorted. He never attended another funeral again. One presumes that when he was safely laid in earth, the limit on the number of libations at funerals was lifted.

Undoubtedly Sanquhar's greatest claim to fame is as a hotbed of the Covenanting movement. On the site of the ancient mercat cross, a monument in the shape of an obelisk bears this inscription: *In commemoration of the two famous SANQUHAR DECLARATIONS which were*

Covenanting Monument, Sanquhar

published on this spot, where stood the ancient Cross of the Burgh; the one by the Rev. Richard Cameron, on 22 June 1680; the other by the Rev. James Renwick, on 25 May 1685, the killing time.

I've mentioned the "Killing Time" many times before, and Cameron several times. You will remember he was the one who gave his name to that extreme brand of Covenanters and it was here, on this very spot, that after his exile in Holland, he relaunched his campaign in 1680. He was accompanied by twenty armed men including his brother, and a certain David Hackston who was wanted for his part in the murder of Archbishop Sharp of St Andrews the previous year.

The monument isn't quite accurate as one of its sides tells you itself. To accommodate the demands of modern traffic, it was moved back a bit on the High Street. The Declaration wasn't really published either. It was read aloud by Cameron's brother, who then hung it on the mercat cross.

It was tantamount to a declaration of war, denouncing Charles II as a "tyrant" to whom they could not, and would not, swear allegiance – a monarch who had reneged on his previous oaths to ban bishops and accept Presbyterianism. You can certainly see the Cameronians' point.

The Privy Council's response was swift. A week and a day later, on 30th June, they condemned the Declaration as an *execrable paper* and declared the participants as *notorious traitors and rebels.* Cameron had a price of 5,000 merks placed on his head, an enormous temptation to any of the ungodly who did not give a fig whether the church had bishops or not, but were not averse to accepting that life-changing sum of money.

As it happens, no-one was led into temptation because less than a month later, on 22nd July, Cameron and about sixty followers were descended upon at Airds Moss near Cumnock by dragoons commanded by Andrew Bruce of Earlshall, aka *Bluidy Bruce.* Being completely outnumbered and taken by surprise, it was all over in fifteen brief minutes. Lucky Cameron was dispatched on the spot. Hackston had the misfortune to be captured and what happened to him next I will now go on to reveal, but if you are of a sensitive nature, I advise you to skip the next paragraph or three.

A scaffold was erected at the mercat cross in Edinburgh where, first of all, they cut off his right hand, then a bit later, his left. That was just the start. After that, they strung him up, but cut him down before he expired, his bowels were disgorged and his heart was shown to the crowd before it, and his entrails, were burned in a brazier on the scaffold. Gruesome.

The religious zealots weren't finished yet, though; not by a long chalk. Hackston's head was hacked off and paraded at the end of a long pole through the streets, to the Tolbooth. There they presented it, and his hands, to his father who was languishing in jail there. He kissed his son's head and allegedly said, "Good is the will of the Lord who cannot wrong me or mine, but has made goodness and mercy follow us all our days." (I don't know what beggars belief more – the barbarity, or that little speech.)

After that, his head was put on display at the Netherbow. One quarter of his body and his hands were taken to St Andrews; another quarter was taken to Glasgow; a third quarter was taken to Leith; the last was taken to Burntisland on the north shore of the Forth. That's what you get for being a traitor. The message is, loud and clear: think twice if you want to keep your head connected to your shoulders.

Cameron's head was treated in a similar manner. It, and his hands, were also displayed at the Netherbow. He, at least, had the advantage of being dead first when the parts were separated from his body.

Things got worse for the Covenanting cause when Charles died in 1685 and was succeeded by his brother, James, Duke of York, who was even more openly committed to Catholicism than he was. The king is dead; long live Catholicism.

As the writing on the obelisk points out, Renwick was in Sanquhar on 28th May 1685 to make *his* declaration. He was accompanied by an army of two hundred men, which put the residents into a great state of fear and alarm as they thought a battle was just about to begin on their doorstep – but they had no need to worry. It was merely a declaration of intent.

With 500 merks on his head, and after five years' preaching in conventicles, Renwick was eventually captured in Edinburgh and executed on 17th February 1688. His head and hands were displayed on the city gates afterwards, but he was not tortured first. There's some humanity in that. He was even allowed to speak first to the bloodthirsty crowd who had come to see him die. Freedom of speech is one thing, but the ability to be heard is another thing entirely. The crowd couldn't hear what he said because the incessant banging of drums drowned out his words.

He died bravely, or as his biographer John Howie put it, "With great cheerfulness, as if in transport of joy". He sang the 103rd Psalm, read the 19th Chapter from the Book of Revelations and prayed aloud. Then turning his face to the heavens, he uttered these words: "By and by, I shall be above these clouds; then I shall enjoy Thee and glorify Thee without intermission for ever."

It's a great thing to have a faith like that. Even if it turns out in the end that the Covenanters never find everlasting life in heaven, at least it made the dying easier. Renwick was the last, the very last, of the Covenanting martyrs.

The village of Crawick, just to the northwest, was once home to a carpet factory in the 1830s. It began, as the weaving industry did, in the family homes, before it morphed into an industrial process in factories. At its height, Crawick had fifty-four looms in operation and they exported their carpets worldwide, especially to South America, where Valparaiso, in Chile, was the receiving port.

But the real reason I want to mention Crawick is because of its being the meeting place for a coven of witches, though you wouldn't think so if you were to read James Brown's *History of Sanquhar* who sweeps them under the carpet, so to speak. He paints an idyllic picture of village life, the sort of place where weavers could leave off the weaving for a while, wives could let the tongues wag as they sort-of-watched the bairns playing and paddling in the babbling burn, the sort of place where it never rained, where the sun arose the following morn for much of the same.

The witches used to meet at the *Witches' Stairs,* a huge rock in the Linns of Crawick, where they would plan their evil deeds and pick their victims. One was the servant girl of the local minister who just could not get the milk to churn. "No worries," quoth the parson aforesaid, "just pass it under running water." No result. They tried tying a sprig of rowan over the doorway of the local witch's house. (Rowan trees are well known for driving away evil spirits.) No dice. They tried nailing a horseshoe to the cowshed door. That didn't work either. Then the minister's wife had a bright idea. It takes a woman to know how to sort out a witch problem. She suggested giving the *carlin* wife a roll of butter and a pitcher of milk. That they did. Problem solved. Wouldn't it have saved a lot of trouble if the old harpy had just asked nicely at the manse?

A similar story involves the miller, one Robert Stitt, who refused one of the witches a peck of meal. "You'll rue that 'ere mony days pass," she threatened him. A week later, the river was in spate and the miller went to open the sluice of the lade, missed his footing, fell in, and was drowned.

A third tale concerns a young man who had words with another witch as he was leaving the village. "Ye're gaun briskly awa', my lad," she retorted to his back, "but ye'll come ridin' hame the nicht." And sure he enough, he did, in a cart. He had broken a leg. It could have been worse, I suppose. It might have been his neck.

The moral of these stories is clear. Do not mess with any old ladies you should happen to encounter while you are in Sanquhar. They may look like harmless old biddies, but beneath that wizened, wrinkly old skin, dark forces may lurk. By all means help them across the street, but only if they want to go – or you may get more than you bargained for.

Chapter Sixty

Wanlockhead: Monmouth, Miners and Jenny Miller

AT Mennock we take the B797 into the Lowther Hills, the second of the three passes through them and where, nestling amongst them, at the meeting point of three valleys, is Wanlockhead. At 1,531 feet, it has the distinction of being Scotland's highest village. Until 1566, it was known as "Winlocke", from the Scottish Gaelic *Cuingealach* meaning "narrow pass". It's a scattered community, with a great deal of open space between the clusters of houses which were built to be near the mine seams, wherever they were found.

We've come to visit the lead-mining museum. Lead had been mined here since Roman times but it was not until 1680 that it became a serious enterprise when the Duke of Buccleuch built a smelting plant and cottages for the workers.

An interesting chap, the Duke. He was born in Rotterdam in 1649, the oldest illegitimate son of Charles II, and also the 1st Duke of Monmouth. In 1685, he led the unsuccessful Monmouth rebellion, a plot to depose his uncle, James VII. Being the son of a king, and a Protestant especially, he hoped he would be swept to the throne on a tide of popular support. He landed at Lyme Regis in June 1685, declaring himself king at the towns he passed through along the route to London.

Just because he said so, does not necessarily make it true. He did not attract the support he expected and James VII's forces of 4,000 men defeated his 3,000 at the Battle of Sedgemoor on 6th July 1685 in what turned out to be the last major battle on English soil. He was captured and taken before the king he sought to depose. He pleaded for mercy, even promised to turn Catholic if it would save his neck. It didn't. 15th July saw him standing on the scaffold at Tower Hill with the notorious Jack Ketch as his executioner. Ketch's aim was incredibly bad, or incredibly skilful if – as was claimed – his aim was to inflict the maximum amount of suffering possible on his victim.

Monmouth gave him some gold pieces and asked him to make a clean job of it, with one blow. It is said that after the first couple of blows, Monmouth lifted his head off the block and reproached Ketch, drawing forth groans of horror from a crowd not unaccustomed to bloody spectacles. Sources vary as to the number of blows that were struck – between five and eight. The official records of the Tower of London state the lesser number. Another source says the job was finished with a knife, the head being sawn off from the twitching body. I hope that is just a bloodthirsty embellishment.

Here's another grisly tale, if your stomach is up to it. According to legend, after Monmouth was buried, it was discovered there was no official portrait of him, so his body was exhumed, the head stitched back on and he was made to sit for his portrait. A likely tale. There are two portraits of him thought to have been painted prior to his execution, and one of another individual, said to be Monmouth, lying sleeping, or dead. However peculiar that may be, it is probably the latter that gave rise to the story of Monmouth's amazing resurrection.

Another (unlikely) tale is that Monmouth was the *Man in the Iron Mask*, a story made famous by Alexandre Dumas. The thinking is the king would not have executed his nephew, despite his being a rebellious knave, and some other poor sod was made to take his place. Some support for this theory is that traditionally, if the king granted the accused an audience, it did not necessarily mean a pardon, but it did at least mean his life would be spared.

Monmouth was smuggled to France, so the story goes, and put under the custody of his cousin, Louis XIV. There is just one *slight* problem concerning this theory, however – the mystery prisoner in the Bastille had been under arrest since 1670, fifteen years before the failed coup. And one more thing. The sacrificial victim may have been gussied up to look like Monmouth, but had nothing to lose, apart from his head, which he was going to lose anyway, by yelling out to the crowd at the last minute, "Ah'm no him!"

Wanlockhead

As I said above, in a former life, as the Duke of Buccleuch, he began to exploit the lead in these hills. Bountiful they were: also producing zinc, copper, silver and gold. In fact, some of the world's purest gold was found here – 22.8 out of a possible 24 carats – according to the system of fineness at the time.

• • •

There were many mines in Wanlockhead throughout the 18th and 19th centuries. They came and went as seams dried up and others were opened. At its peak, in 1876, 274 men and boys were employed in the mines.

The visitor centre is housed in the old smiddy. It also houses the museum which gives the visitor an insight into the mining process, as well as the lives of the

Museum of Lead Mining, Wanlockhead

miners through the centuries. A tongue-in-cheek advertisement offers "healthy outdoor employment to boys aged between 8 and 11." Wages are 2d a day for a ten-hour day and a six-day week. Unpaid holidays were available at New Year, fast day and payday. And at the age of 12, you had the chance of becoming a fully-fledged miner. A hard life could only get harder.

Miners worked in a gang of ten or a dozen and appointed a headman who negotiated with the mine's agent the price they would get for the lead, the weight of the smelted stuff, please note, not the weight of the galena or lead ore. This meant that different gangs were paid different rates. No union rules here and not a recipe for village harmony, you imagine, when, in such a small community, the truth will out as to how much more your neighbour is earning for the same work. And get this: they were paid once a year, in arrears, after the lead had been sold, and after deductions for the purchase of provisions they had made from the company store. This also included the candles and the tools they needed for their work. A miner could use 18 candles in a week, making a considerable dent in his wages.

As soon as you enter the museum, you can't help but notice the figure of a one-armed man seated at a desk. James Crawford by name, he was a mine owner's son who had his arm blown off by a musket ball at Culloden. In a sort of way, he was lucky as the heat from the wound cauterised the wound, preventing him from bleeding to death. In less than 45 seconds, the army surgeon cut back the remaining stump of bone to create a flap of skin and sewed him up. To help him through the ordeal, he was given a tot of brandy. No longer fit for army service, he was given a job behind a desk in the weighing room – so you see, he was a lucky fellow after all.

Another exhibit, notable for its sound effects, depicts the smelting process. The fuel was peat and coal, the blast provided by a massive pair of bellows. The molten metal ran into a pot which was then poured into a mould of ingots named "pigs" because they resembled a litter of piglets feeding from a sow. The heat must have been enormous, but the toxic fumes were a worse thing to have to cope with. Listen to the coughing wheeze of the smelter as he huffed and puffed at the bellows. In fact, you can't help but listen to him. It follows you around.

There is a great deal more to see but I'll leave that for you to discover for yourself. Accompanied by Bob, our guide for the day, we are off to visit the Lochnell Mine which was worked from 1710 to 1860. Conveniently, it does not go downwards; if anything it slopes slightly upwards as it burrows back into the hillside. I exchange my felt hat for a hard one which gives me a miner-sort of feeling, though in actual fact, my soft one is nearer the sort of thing the miners wore.

They make it so easy for visitors nowadays, with the floor of the tunnel smoothed out and illuminated by electric light, so you have to imagine the miners stumbling their way over the rocky floor of the tunnel, ill-lit by the flickering light of tallow candles, to reach the seam before the real work of the day began – pick, pick, picking away in that confined space. The men did that. The boys picked up the ore and carted it outside, where they washed it, having to haul it further and further each day.

A few hundred yards into the tunnel, it widens out into a gallery, actually the intersection of other tunnels, and there you can see three of the poor devils hard at work. Well, not actually – they are motionless, frozen in time because they are mannequins. From here, the tunnel extends into the distance. How far, I wonder? My God, pity those poor boys!

One miner, with a candle held in position by a lump of clay stuck to the front of his tricorn hat, holds a chisel against the rock face. His ragged trousers are tied just below the knee. That's not a fashion statement: it was to stop rats running up his legs. The next figure holds the hammer, about to strike the chisel. Imagine that, in that flickering light, you had to put your trust in your mate's aim being true. I suppose the worst that might happen in that scenario would be a broken finger or two, but the next figure is someone who literally held your life in his hands. He is the man, and a muscular man he had to be, who lowered you by a windlass to the level below while you stood in a leather bucket called a *kibble*. And if lowering you down at a controlled speed needed a good deal of strength, then think of how much was needed to haul you back out again.

Bob counted us all in and counts us all out again before padlocking the entrance to the mine. He is now leading us to a row of miners' cottages which have been converted to reflect what home life was like for the miners through the centuries – 1750, 1850 and 1910. There isn't one for 1950 because by that time the industry was over. Actually, it was all but finished in the 30s.

The first of these is really just a rude shelter with an earthen floor and a thatched roof of heather, which was good for letting the smoke out from the central hearth but not so good at keeping the rain out. There is no furniture. The family slept on heather mattresses (what a versatile material). Dear God, after a day working in those conditions, to have to come home to this!

A century later, home comforts have improved considerably. This is more of a house than a hovel and even boasts some rudimentary furniture. Although it doesn't belong to this humble dwelling, there is a very fine mahogany chest of drawers with barley-sugar pillars at the side and a curious set of deep drawers on the top level.

"Any idea of what was kept in these?" asks Bob.

No-one wants to make a fool of themselves by offering an opinion. They are extraordinarily deep. I can't imagine why you would need such a deep drawer.

"For your top hats," he explains, and of course the answer is obvious as soon as he tells us, only up till now I supposed people merely parked them on a peg somewhere and blew off the dust before putting them on.

Standing next to it is the mannequin of a slight young woman. It turns out she is not only there to give verisimilitude to the room. She has a name, and a story, and it's a sad one. It's also a ghost story, as you shall see.

Her name is Jenny Miller. She was born in Wanlockhead in 1858, and in 1877 she was working as a maid in a farm over the hills and not so far away that she couldn't walk to her sister's wedding. Although the weather was atrocious (it was January), Jenny did not want to miss the nuptials. She had a present to give – a teapot – and you can imagine on her wages, how many hours of work must have gone into buying that. A precious gift indeed. You can understand why she would want to see her sister's face when she saw it.

She never got there. According to one version, Jenny stumbled into the workings of a disused mine or just perished in a blizzard – or because of the blizzard, stumbled into the mine. The locals, moved by this tragedy, erected a cairn to her memory, and scratched upon a stone: *In Memoriam, Jenny Miller 1877.*

Exactly a century later, a man was walking in the Lowther Hills when out of a clear blue sky, a mist came down and out of the mist appeared a woman attired in old-fashioned clothes and carrying a wicker basket. "Look for the stone," she said. "Look for the stone," she repeated before being swallowed up by the mist.

The visitor, after having told the locals his strange tale, returned with some of them the following day and after searching through the cairn, they finally came upon Jenny's memorial stone which had been split in two. As Bob tells us the tale, I find myself standing right beside it. It makes it even more poignant.

Next to Jenny's stone are some iron rings. Bob explains they are quoits. It wasn't all hard work then; there was some fun, but for the children, hard work chucking these things at the target, I would have thought.

The third room looks much more homely, the epitome of late-Edwardian domesticity, with all mod cons, such as they were then. It even looks cluttered. In the corner, by the fire, sits grandpa, the massive family Bible at his elbow. He looks ineffably sad, as well he might. Too old and unfit to work any more, he is seeing out his days. With no pension and doctor's bills to pay, he feels a burden to his family and hopes God will call him soon.

In the field below the cottages stands a massive beam engine. These mighty machines, known as waterbucket pumps, were introduced to Wanlockhead in 1745. At the same time as a revolution was going on in the Highlands, another was going on down in the mines – not just here, but in others where flooding was a perpetual problem.

Before the invention of engines such as this, the mines were drained by hand-operated rag pumps – loops of rope with rags attached. It seems like spitting in the wind compared to this engine, built about 1870. It was capable of lifting out 1,600 gallons per hour, from 90 feet below ground, twenty-four hours a day. It emptied the water into a wooden-lined channel and then disgorged it

Wanlockhead Beam Engine

into a nearby burn. It was powered by water, which is very appropriate, don't you think? Gaze in wonder: this engine is the only ex-working machine that can be seen *in situ* in the entire British Isles.

In 1972, Historic Scotland took over its ownership and maintenance. It worked tirelessly until the early 1900s when the mine was exhausted, but not it. Give it water to drink and it could go on pumping the stuff forever. It hasn't done a day's work in a century and God knows, it deserves its retirement after all that time.

Nearby is a circular track. It is the site of the horse-engine, where the poor beasts walked round and round lifting ore and spoil out of the mine. An endless treadmill, it must have seemed like the first circle of hell, had they ever heard of such a thing. A dog's life rounding up sheep on the hills must have seemed like paradise.

Actually, for the workers, it wasn't all repetitive toil, day in, day out. There was some recreation – as we are just about to find out.

Chapter Sixty-One

Wanlockhead: A Centre of Culture

ARGUABLY, the most astonishing thing about the museum complex is the library. How enlightened for those times! Believe it or not, it's the second-oldest subscription library in Europe. And you don't have to go far to get to the first. It opened in nearby Leadhills in 1741. This one, emulating the other, was established on 1st November 1756, with thirty-two male members who were the main funders of the library. It was also supported by the 2nd Duke of Buccleuch, as well as the mining companies, who were keen to encourage self-improvement amongst the workforce. Subscription was four shillings annually, at a time when miners were earning nine or ten shillings a week. In 1784, there were forty-two members including a woman, Isabel Rutherford. That was a first. It was not until 1881 that Leadhills got around to allowing women to be members.

In the beginning, the library was housed in the school, but in 1787 it was transferred to a cottage. The books increased in number until they outgrew it. By 1851, there were more than 2,000 titles and the present purpose-built library, paid for by the members at a cost of £126, was built. Today it accommodates a thousand more titles. The oldest dates back to 1616, with another sixteen published before 1700. Naturally, the present-day visitor is not allowed to borrow them, and don't try putting your grubby little paws on them either.

In 1974, the Wanlockhead Museum Trust took over the running of the library and, in 2007, it became a Recognised Collection of National Significance.

Gail, the custodian, lets us see a facsimile of the oldest volume. The title is the "Whole-Armor of God or THE SPIRITVALL FVRNITVRE which GOD hath prouided to keepe ſafe euery CHRISTIAN SOLDIER from all the aſſaults of Satan" by William Gouge BD. A riveting read, I am sure it is not. An examination of the titles shows that a goodly number of the others are of a similar nature. They look in immaculate condition, as if they had never been touched. All of this is remarkable enough, but what gets me is that after a hard

Wanlockhead Museum and Library

day's graft down the mine, the miners were in the mood for reading anything, let alone books of such an improving nature.

Inside the cover of each book, a bookplate is pasted with its number and the coat of arms of the village featuring the miners' tools and the motto "GOD SEND GRACE".

What this library tells you is that the workforce was very far indeed from being the great, unwashed illiterate. I, for one, could not sink my teeth into the reading fare provided here. In 1803, Dorothy Wordsworth, passing near here with William and Coleridge, happened to come upon half-a-dozen or so shoeless boys. Dorothy engaged them in conversation and was astonished to find, as she wrote in her journal later, that they went to school where they "learned Latin, Homer, Virgil and some of them Greek". As a matter of fact, there had been a school in Wanlockhead since 1750 and it had an excellent reputation.

It produced some well-known alumni: Thomas Grierson Gracie (b.1861), brother to nine siblings, miner, musician and poet, author of *Songs and Rhymes of a Lead Miner* and *The Grey Glen*; William Hastie (b.1842), Professor of Divinity at Glasgow University; Robert Reid (b.1850), author of *Moorland Rhymes* and director of Henry Morgan's department store of Montreal. Just three more examples of that Scottish phenomenon known as the *lad o' pairts*.

In a corner of the long, book-lined room, a couple of incredibly clean miners are standing at an old-fashioned desk, the sort that teachers used to perch behind when I wore short trousers. One is examining a document of some sort while another looks on. Gail presses a button and the figures come to life, or at least their voices do.

The dapper man with the suit and trim little moustache and beard is inducting a miner, attired in sleeves and waistcoat, into the library. His tone is extremely patronising as he explains how it works, the rules and regulations. It's quite comical really. Wash your hands before touching the book; you'll be fined if you return it late and if, God forbid, you lose it, you will have to pay double its cover price.

In a display here, we learn that from 1777, the village also boasted a curling club, one of the first in Scotland, followed in 1883, by a boys' club. That was succeeded in 1902, by a bowling club. In addition to that, there was a football team, a drama group and a silver band whose instruments were bought by the 6th Duke of Buccleuch. Oh, wise and upright Duke! What a community! Who wouldn't like to be a part of it?

Still on a sporting theme, at Lowther Hills, above the village, is the only skiing area in the south of Scotland. Skiing began in the area in the 1920s, and was successively run by local residents and not-for-profit sports clubs. Since 1986, it has been operated and run by volunteers from the community-owned Lowther Hills Ski Club. There are two areas – a nursery slope for beginners, accessed from Leadhills, while intermediate skiers get on the slopes from here.

The railway came in 1900 via Leadhills, and the delightfully-named Elvanfoot. You won't be surprised to hear it is the highest railway in the land. It came a tad too late for Wanlockhead. By that time, the lead industry was beginning to tail off. Following the closure of most of the lead mines, the railway closed in 1938. By the 1950s, mining had stopped altogether.

Burns came here in December 1789 with Thomas Sloan, who was born here. Not the best of ideas to come to the country's highest village at that time of year, you would have thought. It was very icy and, a bit like putting chains on the tyres of your car, they decided to have their horses' hooves "frosted" or roughened up to give them a better grip. They weren't the only ones with the same idea, and there were many ahead of them. It is perhaps not to Burns's credit that he used his celebrity to prevail upon a local man, John Taylor, to use his influence to persuade the farrier to give Sloan and him priority. Whilst the job was being done at the smiddy (the present-day visitor centre), they waited at Ramage's Inn where, as a sort of quid pro quo to Taylor, Burns dashed off *Pegasus at Wanlockhead,* Pegasus being the name of his horse.

Ramage's is long since gone, but thirsty modern-day travellers will be pleased to know that they can refresh themselves at the Wanlockhead Inn, and yes, it *is* the highest pub in Scotland.

Burns was not put off by his experience. He was back again in January 1792, accompanied this time by Maria Riddell from Friar's Carse. You may remember that she and Burns fell out in 1794 as a result of his drunken behaviour there. They were reconciled the following year, and the year after that, Burns was dead, as you know. I'm all for reconciliation before it is too late. We only know about this visit thanks to a letter Maria wrote where she records they went some distance into the mine, but the bad air didn't suit Burns's bad chest and they came out. A second bad experience for Scotland's greatest poet, at Scotland's highest village.

Funnily enough, the village did not have its own cemetery until 1751. Prior to that, the dead had to be taken along what was known as the *corpse road* to Sanquhar, eight miles away. Sadly, the first occupant of the Meadowfoot cemetery was the ten-month old William Philip Minder, who died on 2nd April 1751.

Finally, Wanlockhead was the setting for a BBC TV series called *Hope Springs*. It was a comedy-drama about four (sexy) women ex-jail birds who went into hiding after they stole £3 million from one of the husbands. It was their intention to live a life of luxury in Barbados but after the money was mysteriously burned to ashes, they ended up in Hope Springs. We all know how that phrase ends and perhaps that's what the producers of the series hoped would happen when they bestowed that name on the series. Alas not. The programme only ran for eight episodes from 7th June 2009 to 26th July 2009, and was axed because it didn't attract big enough audiences.

They should have made a film about the village and the lives of the miners – and for sheer drama, what can compete with the tragic tale of Jenny Miller?

Real life is much more interesting, as I so often find these days.

Chapter Sixty-Two

Leadhills: More Tales from the Mine, Ramsay and a Railway

NOW we're going to the twin village of Leadhills, which, at 1,460 feet, is Scotland's second highest. Obviously there's lead in them thar hills, or they wouldn't have named it so. However, it used to be known as "Waterhead" – the source of the Glengonnar Water, one of the tributaries of the mighty Clyde.

They could also have called it "Goldhills". In the reign of James IV, it was known as *God's Treasure House in Scotland*. Between 1538 and 1542, £100,000 worth of gold was extracted at contemporary prices – about £500 million today. In fact, much of the gold coinage of James V and Mary, Queen of Scots came from here. There is 41oz of gold in his crown and only slightly less in his queen's – 35oz. No wonder it became known as *God's Treasure House*.

Commercial mining was over by 1620, but gold panning by the lead miners could sometimes be a profitable deployment of their free time. If you fancy your luck, you can try your hand too. Good luck. I did in Alaska for a laugh, and still have the specks somewhere. I can see them quite clearly if I put my own specs on.

The lead mines came into the possession of the Hope family of Hopetoun in 1637 when Sir James Hope (1614-61) married Anne, the daughter of Robert Foulis of Leadhills. His father, Thomas, an Edinburgh goldsmith, had originally bought the land in 1592. The Hopes went to the expense of building and improving the roads from here all the way to Leith, Edinburgh's port, fifty miles away. From there, the ore was exported for smelting in the Netherlands. Obviously there was money in lead, if he could afford to do that and still make a profit. Their own little gold mine, in fact.

A house, now named "Woodlands Hall", was built for the mine manager by the Scots Mining Company, founded by Sir John Erskine after the Rising of 1715. The house was probably built by William Adam and was first occupied by

James Stirling (1692-1770), in 1735. He was a celebrated mathematician and an associate of Isaac Newton. He was nicknamed *The Venetian* after he had to flee Venice in 1722 in fear of his life after he discovered the secrets of the glass-making trade. He also turned out to be an able administrator. When he was appointed, the company was practically bankrupt. A century later, it was the largest and most profitable of all the Leadhill mines.

Stirling was an enlightened man for his time who took the welfare of the miners seriously. He encouraged them to cultivate plots of land and obliged them to make contributions towards the maintenance of the sick and aged of the village. And he was the one who encouraged the miners to found the Reading Society for the betterment of their minds. It wasn't cheap, with a joining fee of three shillings and an annual subscription of two shillings.

When Stirling died, the Company erected the Curfew Bell in the village. It announced the call to work for the miners and the children to school. It was also used in the event of an accident in the mines or a walker lost in the hills. It stands on a sturdy timber frame, and can be heard once a year to usher in the New Year.

The library is also known as the "Allan Ramsay Library" or the "Leadhills Reading Society". Ramsay (1686-1758), is not to be confused with his son, also Allan (1713-1784), the portrait painter. Ramsay *père* was born in Leadhills, where his father was the manager of one of the mines. Sad to say, he never knew him. He died either just before, or just after he was born.

Despite lacking the guidance of a father figure, the lad made a name for himself. He started out as a wigmaker's apprentice in Edinburgh. Hair he fashioned, but poetry was his passion. He published his first collection by subscription in 1721. It was an enormous success. Before very long, he gave up the wig business and turned his premises into a bookshop.

He is credited with beginning the first rental library in 1726 (also misleadingly known as a "circulating" library), charging those who couldn't afford the price of a book a nominal sum to borrow it. Yes, it was a profit-orientated business, but remember there were no public libraries then. He operated this service (and business) from larger premises in Edinburgh's Luckenbooth, into which he had moved the previous year.

Like Burns, but long before him of course (Ramsay died the year before Burns was born), he was a collector, as well as a composer of songs. Between 1723 and 1737 he issued the *Tea-Table Miscellany*, a collection of his own verse, his friends' and well-known ballads. He got the idea for the name from my famous namesake, Joseph Addison, who devoted the time "for tea and bread and butter" to thinking about the next essay he was going to write for his newspaper, *The Spectator.* Thus, likewise, Ramsay set aside that time for his songs – only he put it like this: "e'en while the tea's fill'd reeking round".

Ramsay was born here and left at an early age; others came, and merely passed through. Their comments were not favourable. Writing in 1772, the naturalist and travel writer, Thomas Pennant, found the area "barren and gloomy", while the artist and author, William Gilpin, writing in 1776, commented upon the "infirm frame and squalid looks in most of the inhabitants". The Rev. William Peterkin, minister here from 1785 until his death in 1792, described Leadhills as "ugly beyond description".

Worse than being an eyesore was the threat to health, however. The Reverend Peterkin describes how the water below the smelting mills was poisonous, containing arsenic, sulphur, zinc and other harmful substances. Wild birds didn't last long. Dogs, cats and cattle fell into convulsions and died or had to be put down. He called it "lead-brash". Nor were the miners immune. Pennant called it "mill-reek" which brought on "palsies and sometimes madness, terminating in death in about ten days".

The American and Napoleonic Wars were in full swing; there was an insatiable hunger for lead and prices were high. So was the cost to miners' lives. James Braid (1795-1860), the mine's surgeon (who went on to pioneer hypnotism and hypnotherapy, and to become known as the *Father of Modern Hypnotism*), wrote about the noxious air in which the miners' candles could scarcely burn and which brought on pneumonia in the young and hydrothorax (serious flooding of the pleural cavity) in the old. Funnily enough, Braid reported that it did not seem to affect middle-aged men so badly, and that's why he recommended they should be the ones at the head of the seam.

As with the miners at Wanlockhead, they too had to provide their own tools and maintain them. While the men delved in the depths of the mine and the women span at home, the boys washed the impurities from the ore prior to smelting, aided often by the rain because the washing platform was outside and exposed to the elements. But there's a bright side. The cottages were rent-free.

Also like their neighbours up the road, the miners were paid collectively, not by the hour, but on the basis of a contract or "bargain" struck between them and the mining company. There were two types – "fathom work" which involved sinking shafts, excavating and such like, for which they were paid an agreed amount for the length or depth of "fathoms" dug; and "tribute work" where they were paid according to either the weight of raw ore or smelted lead.

They worked in groups of up to a dozen men, known as "partnerships". They were their own bosses, deciding how long they worked, their own working practices and what risks they took with regard to safety. The snag was, with such a degree of autonomy, the structure of the whole mine was compromised and very often one partnership's workings would get in the way of another's.

At 7am on 1st March 1817, tragedy struck. Two miners entered the mine before 4am and two more followed soon after. When they reached their work area at 25 fathoms, they encountered bad air but thought it was just a patch they could make their way through. They were wrong. They were overcome by the fumes and suffocated. The same fate happened to the next pair. Their bodies were discovered at 6am when the usual shift began.

They too began to be badly affected, and a trapdoor was opened to help clear the air. Unfortunately, the poisonous air made its way down to the 80-fathom level and three more men suffocated down there. The others were able to make it back to the surface where they were treated by Braid. It turned out that fumes from a faulty underground steam engine had combined with a thick fog that was enveloping the area and the mixture was lethal.

At the peak, during the 18th century, there were as many as forty mines operating here and the village had a population of 1,500. The decline began about 1830 and in 1861, the Scots Mining Company lost a twenty-year old legal battle with the Leadhills Mining Company over water rights to drive the machinery. The once mighty company gave up its lease and to the victor fell the spoils – the only company left to be able to heap up those enormous piles of waste ore. However, by 1920, the seams were beginning to peter out and by 1929, it was all over – a decade earlier than at Wanlockhead.

Leadhills can boast Scotland's highest golf course, and lovers of the game would surely like to boast they have played it. It also has its very own station, which of course, is the highest in the land. It is where you board the 2ft narrow-gauge Leadhills & Wanlockhead Railway which follows the original railway

track of the line that ran from Wanlockhead to the mainline at Elvanfoot from 1901 to 1938. It was built by the Caledonian Railway Company to transport the iron ore from the mines to Leith Docks. Before that, the ore went a hundred miles by road and took four days.

The award-winning Leadhills and Wanlockhead Heritage Railway Society was formed in 1986. The 2ft narrow-gauge railway is driven by

Leadhills and Wanlockhead Railway

the friction of its wheels on the track, and for that reason, is called an "adhesion" railway. It's only three-quarters-of-a mile long and at its highest point, it reaches 1,500 feet. It stops at Glengonnar Halt, just half-a-mile short of Wanlockhead, but plans are afoot to extend it all the way.

As we arrive, a train is just about to pull out. It's utterly quaint and charming, like something out of Toytown. The ticket office is

The Track at Leadhills and Wanlockhead Railway

formed out of two box vans fused together and also contains a small gift shop and museum. It is there we meet Martin Hollingworth, who gives us a guided tour of the engine sheds and signal box.

The latter was built using bricks from the eight-arch Rispin Cleuch Viaduct which once carried the track over the Glengonnar Water, and which was demolished in 1993. The signals come from the West Highland Line between Fort William and Mallaig. Martin invites me to pull one of the levers. I'm surprised at just how much effort it requires, but sure enough, away up the track, the signal responds to my command. Just what message I am sending to the driver, I haven't a clue, but before he has a chance to see it, Martin tells me to release the lever again.

There are seven locomotives, named after rivers mainly, and now in semi-retirement after having worked in various places around the UK: in collieries, at Leith Docks, the Mersey Road Tunnel and dykes in East Anglia. Clyde, more prosaically known as "Engine No.6", was built in Leeds in 1975 by Hunslet Locomotives and went to work at Eppleton Colliery in County Durham before coming here in 1990. He is the main workhorse, hauling passengers to and from Glengonnar Halt.

In addition to that, there is a tamping machine for track maintenance which, ever since it arrived in 2016, saves the enthusiasts a great deal of time and effort. It can do in five minutes what used to take an hour by hand. In addition, there are a couple of steam engines, one unnamed and another called "Charlotte" or "Engine No.9". She was made in Germany in 1913 and one of these days, hopefully, will be restored to full working order. I'm sure she'll be a great attraction, but imagine being put to work long after your 100th birthday. And it's uphill work too, at least half the time.

If, and when, Charlotte is restored, she will not be the only one to have worked long past retirement age. John Taylor was a miner here and still working at 117 – and, what's more, had twenty years of retirement ahead of him when he gave up work in 1751. He died in 1770 and was buried in the local cemetery. The grave is a sandstone tablet. No dates are given for the old-timer, but it tells us that his son, Robert, who died in 1791, aged 67, was buried alongside him. Apparently he had only nine children, so honour restored!

You may well take his age with a pinch of salt. It is based upon a memory of his of coming out of the mine to see an eclipse of the sun in 1652, at a time when he would had to have been old enough to work underground. It seems to be a fact that he died in 1770 and if you accept his age of death for a moment, that gives us a birthdate of 1633, making him nineteen at the time of the eclipse, otherwise known as *Mirk Monday*. It would appear his ever-loving family may have thought that he had lived too long because a story goes that when he was a comparative youngster, a mere centenarian, he was put outside the house "in case God had forgotten him". It seems God hadn't, since he called him thirty-seven years later.

If you have a mind to visit the cemetery, you will find it at the end of Ramsay Road. Depsite this being a small place, it's not easy to find, so better ask a local. Just outside it is a memorial obelisk erected by public subscription in 1891, to the famous engineer William Symington (1764-1831), who was born here. He was buried at St Botoloph without Aldgate, Greater London. In 1790, he built an engine for one of the mines at Wanlockhead and another for a mine in Sanquhar. Many more for pumping water and lifting coal to the surface followed. I'll spare you the details of how it works. All you need to know is what Symington did was to take the simplicity of the Newcomen engine and the efficiency of the Watt engine to create a new and improved engine. Actually, Watt was not amused and took out an injunction against him – to no avail. Interestingly, Watt was a grandson of John Taylor, deceased (at long last).

There is a Burns connection with Symington too. His landlord at Ellisland, Patrick Miller, commissioned Symington to build an engine for a pleasure boat that was tested out on nearby Dalwinston Loch in October 1788. It was the first-ever, practical, mechanically-powered method of transportation in the world. It ultimately led to the *Charlotte Dundas*, the world's first successful steamship, named after the daughter of Lord Dundas, Governor of the Forth and Clyde Canal Company. In March 1803, she towed two 70-ton barges nineteen miles along the Forth and Clyde Canal to Glasgow in the face of a stiff breeze. Steam had arrived; sail was heading into the sunset.

Actually, what happened next to *Charlotte* is a bit of a sad tale. She was never employed on the canal for fear of erosion to the banks caused by the paddles, and a plan to use her on the Bridgewater Canal foundered when the Duke died just before trials were to begin. Poor Charlotte was parked in a backwater of the Forth and Clyde and left to moulder until she was broken up in 1861.

As for Symington, he was broken-hearted. He was never paid back all of his investment. What a shameful end to such a historic vessel and a pioneering engineer.

Chapter Sixty-Three

Drumlanrig and Morton Castles: Scandalous Things Going On

W E'RE on another slight detour now. From here, the SWC300 follows the B7040 to Elvanfoot where it picks up the B7076 towards Moffat, but we're heading back on the A76 towards, in the first instance, the tiny village of Enterkinfoot. The name has gone through a variety of metamorphoses since its inception, but probably derives from the Scots Gaelic *eanach t'uircein* or *t'arcoin* meaning "sow's" or "bloodhound's marsh".

It grew around a late-16th century mill. Once overlooking it was Coshogle Castle (probably derived from the Celtic "red height"). It has long since gone, but, you will not be surprised to hear, is enjoying a new lease of life, like a transplant patient, some of its stones having been incorporated into the cottages in the village. If you want to get out and stretch your legs, you can amuse yourself by looking for a marriage stone, carved upon it, two coats of arms, the date 1576, and the initials RD and NI. We know his name was Robert Douglas, but who his bride was, alas, we do not know.

This is the pass the Romans used from their fortlet at Durisdeer. An old packhorse route also used to thread its way through here from Wanlockhead to Edinburgh. No presemt-day route runs through it, but as walkers probably already know, there is a track that leads into the centre of the hills. In his *Tour through the Whole Island of Great Britain* (1726), Daniel Defoe describes it thus: "Enterkin, the frightfullest pass, and most dangerous that I met with, between that and Penmenmuir in North Wales".

He should be thankful he wasn't there on 29th July 1684, during the "Killing Time" – a day that has come down in history as the *Enterkin Raid*. Nine Covenanters were being taken, under armed escort, from Dumfries to Edinburgh, via Thornhill, their ultimate destination being the slave plantations in the Americas. The detail was ambushed by a band of Covenanters led by James Harkness and his brother, Thomas. The officer in charge of the dragoons was shot through the head. His men fired a single volley in reply. It is not known how many died in the skirmish, but seven of the nine prisoners were rescued. However, in the aftermath, five Covenanters, including Thomas Harkness, were later arrested and put to death in the Grassmarket in Edinburgh.

James escaped to Ulster, only returning when the "Killing Time" was over. He died in 1723, aged 72 – a ripe old age, considering the time and times, he lived in. He is buried in Dalgarnock cemetery near Thornhill where there is a martyrs' cross bearing the names of fifty-four martyrs with the places and dates of their deaths, including Thomas. The cemetery is all that remains of the once-sizable village. By 1790, according to the Statistical Account, not a single cottage remained.

From Enterkinfoot, it is hardly any distance for us down the beautiful Nith valley to our next destination, Drumlanrig Castle (from "drum" meaning "hill" and "rig" meaning "ridge". In his *Tour*, Defoe writes: "We could not pass Dumfries without going out of the way, upwards of a day, to see the castle of Drumlanrig, the fine palace of the Duke of Queensberry." However much he may have admired the castle, the founder of the English novel was not impressed with its setting. He went on: "It is environed with mountains, and that of the wildest and most hideous aspect in all the south of Scotland". No comment.

The first stronghold on the site occupied by the present castle was built some time after 1357 and held by the Earls of Mar. James Douglas, 2nd Earl of Mar and Douglas, was killed at the Battle of Otterburn in 1388 and his son, William, succeeded him. Given its location in the Borders, it would be surprising if it were not in the wars – and it was. In 1549, it was sacked by the English during the *Rough Wooing*, Henry VIII's scheme to force the marriage between the infant Mary, Queen of Scots and his son, the future King Edward VI.

Drumlanrig Castle and Gardens

You won't be surprised to hear this is one of the places where Mary slept. That was in 1563, four years before she hastily married the Earl of Bothwell, widely believed to have murdered her husband, Darnley – an event that turned many of the Scots nobility against her.

Sometime after that, a posher castle was built and ready in time to accommodate Mary's son, James VI, in 1617, and in 1650, less welcome visitors – Cromwell's men. The present pile, which is distinctly pink, was built between 1675 and 1697, by William Douglas, 3rd Earl of Queensberry and from 1684, the 1st Duke of Queensberry, as I said earlier. You just have to have to take one look at its immense size to see why it nearly bankrupted him. The east wing was incorporated into the existing castle (not that you would notice), while the rest was demolished to become a very handy quarry for the building of the new one. And if you want to get some idea of just how long it took to grow, then you can, to some extent, by looking at the windows in the towers in the courtyard where, above them, the date they were constructed is inscribed.

The relationship between the Douglases and the Stewarts (later styled "Stuart" by Mary, Queen of Scots, because she thought the "w" in "Stewart" would be too difficult for the French to pronounce), was not always easy, to put it mildly. James, 7th Laird of Drumlanrig, aka *Old Drumlanrig*, marched against Mary at Carberry Hill near Musselburgh in 1567. What happened next you know – her forced abdication, her escape from Lochleven, her defeat at Langside, flight to England, and subsequent execution. But before that fatal day, it provoked a civil war as Mary's supporters kept up the struggle to repatriate and reinstate her.

As for *Old Drumlanrig*, he went on to fight alongside James VI's Regent, Earl of Morton and Mary's half-brother. The fact that he visited Mary's archenemy, John Knox, as he lay on his deathbed in 1572, is testimony to how bitterly he was opposed to her. He had two wives, and God knows how many mistresses, who provided him with twenty children of whom only one was born in wedlock. He died in 1578 and was succeeded by his grandson, James, 8th Baron of Drumlanrig. His son, William, 9th Baron, entertained Mary's son, James VI, in 1617, and in 1633, he was made the 1st Earl of Queensberry. His grandson, William 3rd Earl, became a Marquess in 1682 and the 1st Duke of Queensberry in 1684.

And so we arrive at the 2nd Duke, James (1662-1711), who built the present castle over two decades. In 1706, he was appointed Lord High Commissioner and, as such, was responsible for steering The Act of Union through Parliament in 1707. According to legend, at the very time he was putting his pen to the document, his mad son, James, was roasting a servant boy over a spit. He had been called an "idiot" since birth but, after that little episode, he became known as the "cannibalistic idiot". The Duke wisely decided to pass on the dukedom to the idiot's younger brother, Charles.

I will not trouble you much with him, except to mention he was Lord of the Bedchamber under George 1st, Vice Admiral of Scotland, and Privy Councillor. I will, however, go into more detail, about William, the 4th Duke (1724-1810) aka *Old Q*, Lord Lieutenant of Dumfries from 1794 until his death, and Vice Admiral of Scotland from 1767 to 1776. "Vice" would appear to be the operative word, as he was a member of Sir Francis Dashwood's notorious Hell-Fire Club where all sorts of perversions took place, but *Old Q* focused on the sex, apparently being active right up to his death.

He never married and must have been very careful as he only produced one child, a daughter, by the Marchesa Fagnani. On his death, the Dukedom of Queensberry, as well as Drumlanrig Castle, passed to his second cousin once removed, the 3rd Duke of Buccleuch. The two noble families had been united in 1720 when Lady Jean Douglas, the daughter of the 2nd Duke of Queensberry, married Francis Scott, the 2nd Duke of Buccleuch.

In the passing, it's worth mentioning that John Douglas, 9th Marquess (the one after whom the boxing rules were named, although he did not write them), was the father of Lord Alfred Bruce Douglas, aka *Bosie* (1870-1945), the lover of Oscar Wilde. The marquess left a calling card at Wilde's club on which he addressed him as a "Somdomite" [[sic]]. Wilde sued for libel and, on the marquess being acquitted, he won a counterclaim to get back the money he had spent on his defence. Wilde was bankrupted, but Douglas wasn't finished yet. He handed over to the police the evidence his private detectives had amassed and Wilde was charged with gross indecency and sentenced to two years' hard labour. His reputation in tatters and his health badly affected by his imprisonment, poor Oscar died in Paris in 1900, three years after his release from prison. He was pardoned in 2017. Just a tad too late, alas.

So here we are at the home of the present 12th Duke of Queensberry and 10th of Buccleuch, but before we invade their privacy, let me tell you the derivation of that name. Back in the 10th century, the legend has it that one day, King Kenneth III was hunting in a *cleuch* or ravine, when he was attacked by a young buck. His life was saved by a young man, John Scott, who wrestled the deer to the ground by grabbing it by the antlers. As a result of this heroic act, he was nicknamed *Buck Cleuch*. The name stuck and was passed down through the generations.

Walter of that ilk was knighted by James VI in 1590 and was known as *Bold Buccleuch* because of his fearless actions in the Border raids. In 1606, he was created 1st Lord Scott of Buccleuch. His great-granddaughter, Anne, married James, Duke of Monmouth in 1663 and he duly became 1st Duke of Buccleuch. Nice move, but you know what happened to *him* in the end. And now you know how the Scotts and the Douglases became united. (I know – like many relationships today, it's complicated.)

The castle underwent further restoration in 1827 and if it were not already big enough, two service wings were added, you will not be surprised to hear, by the architect, William Burn. As well as being the family home, it is also home to the Buccleuch Art Collection which contains a goodly-number of family portraits by Gainsborough, Reynolds and Ramsay. The jewel in the crown is considered to be Rembrandt's *Old Woman Reading* (1665). It used to have Leonardo's *Madonna of the Yarnwinder*, but it was stolen in 2003. Thieves, posing as police, just walked out with it as cool as you like. Happily, they were caught when they demanded a ransom for its return four years later.

If you want to see it, you will have to go to the Scottish National Gallery where it is on loan. It depicts the Christ child, sitting on the Madonna's lap, holding a yarnwinder – a symbol of Mary's domesticity, as well as foreshadowing the Crucifixion. It came into the Buccleuch family after the 3rd Duke married Lady Elizabeth Montagu whose parents were art connoisseurs and collectors. Painted between 1500 and 1503, it is estimated to be worth around £30 million. A handy thing to have behind you, should you happen to fall upon hard times.

During WWI, the castle was used as an auxiliary hospital and during the Second World War, the girls from St Denis School were evacuated there. Now an endless procession of visitors make their way through the Duke and Duchesses' family home. The admission charge helps keep a roof over their heads. You can imagine the cost of maintaining the ancient pile must be colossal.

Take a look at the carpet in the hall where the tour begins. Note the winged heart and look for it wherever you go around the castle, inside and outside. The story behind this is well known. I referred to it earlier, but just to remind you, it was an ancestor of the Douglases – the "Black Douglas", as he was named by the English for his misdeeds (as they saw them) – and to the Scots, "Good Sir James", the very worthy knight who carried Robert the Bruce's embalmed heart on crusade in a silver casket.

According to legend, at the battle of Teba de Ardales near Granada, Douglas threw the heart into the midst of the Moors, crying, "Forward, brave heart, as ever thou were wont to do and Douglas will follow thee or die!" After the battle, Douglas's body was found surrounded by dead Moors, so it was said. It was repatriated and buried in his own turf, so to speak, in St Bride's Church in Douglas. Bruce's heart was recovered, taken back to Scotland, and buried in Melrose Abbey.

And that is why you will see winged hearts everywhere you go in the castle and why the family motto is "Forward". (Challenge: enliven the kids' visit by getting them to see see how many winged hearts they can spot.)

Apart from the hearts, there are countless other items of interest to be seen. In addition to the Rembrandt aforesaid, the serving room next to the dining room is lined with portraits of past servants, notably the chef, Joseph Lawrence, who cooked for three Dukes and who managed to avoid poisoning a single one.

Arguably, one of the most interesting rooms is the one where Bonnie Prince Charlie stayed on his retreat from Derby on December 22nd 1745 and his date with destiny at Culloden. Apparently he left in such a hurry, he left behind his money-box which had been screwed to the floor. Actually, when you see it, it looks so heavy you wonder why he bothered. Imagine having to cart that about everywhere you went.

In 1972, Neil Armstrong slept, not only in the same room, but in the very same bed, three years after his setting foot on the moon. I suppose if you can sleep in a space capsule, a three-hundred-year-old bed must be the last word in comfort.

The walls are festooned with tapestries, and it's a tapestry in the next room that is the next item of interest. It features what looks like three playful tigers, only they are not. It is meant to be a Scottish scene and the cats aforesaid are meant to be wildcats, only they are not like any wild cats ever seen in Scotland. To be fair, hardly anyone ever *does* see one, nor had the artist, so he just used his imagination. Unfortunately, he was more than a tad out in his guesstimation, but since no-one at the time knew any better, it didn't matter. They saw and they believed.

Another curiosity is a ceramic monkey orchestra dressed up in 17th century clothes.

And there's more than just the interior of the castle to see – there's an art gallery and a children's activity room. You will be relieved, and not surprised, to hear that there is a gift shop, but it does come as something of a surprise to find the Scottish Cycle Museum in the stable block. On reflection, it shouldn't really come as that much of a surprise. The inventor of the bicycle, Kirkpatrick Macmillan, came from Thornhill, just a couple of miles to the south. You might think: Cycle Museum, how could that possibly be interesting? Well, you may think so, but you would be making a mistake if you didn't pay it a visit.

Bikes, bikes everywhere – on the floor, on the walls, yea, even suspended from the rafters. There is a 1990 replica of Macmillan's bike (we saw a couple of actual ones in the museum in Dumfries) and much, much more. Here is a bit of nostalgia, though it comes from long after my boyhood – the "Chopper" with its trendy design of seat and gears – but what I find particularly interesting is Mark Beaumont's machine which in 2017, he rode 18,000 miles around the world in 79 days, one less than Phileas Fogg's circumnavigation.

Also interesting, for its curiosity value, is a tandem with a sidecar for your child (or dog). But for my money, more interesting still, is a farthing penny. Yes, I did get that right. What else would you call a bicycle that has a teeny-weeny wheel at the front and a much, much bigger wheel at the back?

Every grand house deserves great gardens, and Drumlanrig does not disappoint. In fact, a bike from the museum would be handy to get around, so extensive are they. This truth is immediately evident to the visitor as he approaches the castle along the tree-lined Great Avenue at the end of which vista stands the colossal castle, all 120 rooms of it. It is quite breathtaking. I am proud to say I have never seen *Star Wars* nor have I seen *Outlander*, but those who have seen the latter, will recognise it as Bellhurst Manor. The avenue was created especially for Queen Victoria's grand approach for the visit, tons of food were bought for a banquet, and at the last moment – she called off. The Duke was not amused, and I don't blame him.

The gardens were laid out at the same time as the present castle, but allowed to fall into decline. They were restored in the Victorian era with thirty gardeners on the job. During the Second World War, they were abandoned again. They have been restored – in fact, they are so neat and tidy you would never have guessed they were once a wilderness. And would you care to guess how many gardeners it takes to keep them looking like this? Four!

I don't propose to say much about the gardens, except to mention the Red Oak planted by Neil Armstrong during his visit. And the reason why he was here, by the way, is because he was invited to visit Langholm, the home of his Scottish ancestors, the Armstrongs. No-one was more surprised than they when he accepted.

It's very fitting that the very first Douglas Fir ever to be planted in Britain should be here. That was in 1829. And you mustn't miss the Drumlanrig Sycamore, not that you are likely to, since it is the largest in Britain and more than three hundred years old.

There is a bog garden, a sand garden, a rose garden, a rock garden and three parterres. The other attractions I haven't mentioned in this Scottish country garden, I'm sure you will surely pardon.

What you probably *don't* want to see but which I would, rather perversely, I must confess, are the three ghosts that are said to haunt the castle. One is said to be Lady Anne Douglas with her head under her arm in the best ghostly tradition. She married Robert Douglas, 8th Earl of Morton in 1627, and died in 1654 of a fever. Why that entitles her to wander about the castle with her head tucked under her head scaring poor folks is a mystery.

She was born Anne Villiers about 1610. One of her nieces, Elizabeth Villiers, was one of the mistresses of William III, aka *William of Orange*, while another niece, Barbara Villiers, was the mistress of Charles II, or should I say one of seven, of whom Nell Gwyn is probably the most famous. Seems to have been a bit of a family profession amongst the Villiers ladies.

A second ghost is that of a young woman in a flowing dress, while the third is a monkey or some such creature. If true, it must surely be proof there is life after death in the animal kingdom too – great news for them and animal lovers of every sort, everywhere. Rover can romp about in heaven chasing bunny rabbits, who, if they are ever caught by the scruff of the neck, will never die.

Straight across the A76, and on the other side of the railway tracks is Morton Castle. Good luck in finding it. Perversely, it is only signposted as you get nearer.

Its origins are somewhat sketchy. There may have been an earlier castle on the site. Some say it had been built by 1260, while others say it was erected in the mid 1400s by the Earls of Morton, replacing an earlier castle that was destroyed in 1372. The archaeological evidence would suggest it probably *was* built about 1300, not by the Mortons but by Sir Thomas Randolph, Earl of Moray, nephew and loyal supporter of Robert the Bruce.

It was rendered defenceless in 1357, one of thirteen, as part of the deal between England and Scotland at the Treaty of Berwick in that year, in order to secure the release of David II after his capture at Neville's Cross near Durham in 1346. Fast forward in the castle's history to the mid 15th century, when James II granted the lands to James Douglas of Dalkeith, the 1st Earl of Morton.

In 1581, James Douglas, the 4th Earl, was executed (by his own guillotine,

Morton Castle

remember), for his complicity in the murder of Darnley, and his title and estates passed to John, 7th Lord Maxwell of Caer-laverock, the grandson of the 3rd Earl. But not for long. In 1588, the castle was captured and burned by James VI.

It was repaired and reoccupied, and in 1608, sold to

William Douglas of Coshogle who sold it ten years later to William Douglas of Dumlanrig. Parts of the castle remained habitable until 1715 when it was abandoned, and as is the fate of all abandoned castles, reborn as a lowly dyke or farm buildings or possibily incorporated into a newer, grander castle or mansion.

Towards the end of that century, the river was dammed to flood the marshes. A century later, William, 8th Duke of Queensbury, carried out repairs on the ruins and stamped the date, 1877, upon them as if it were a new-build. Thus you see the castle as it stands today, apart from what the ravages of time have done since. It passed into the care of Historic Scotland in 1975.

There is enough of the castle remaining to require not much imagination to see how impressive it would have been in its prime. It would have had a Caerlaverock sort-of-look, being built on a triangular piece of land, surrounded by the river and marshland on three sides, with a ditch being dug out on the remaining landward side.

Part of the tower, still standing, formed part of the entrance gateway – two D-shaped towers that stood back-to-back. (Look for the slot for the portcullis in the walls.) Inside, if you look up, you can make out the corbels that once would have supported the floor of the great hall. And it's probably in there that the clock, presently displayed in the anteroom of Drumlanrig Castle, would originally have stood, measuring the Mortons' lives away. Yes, astonishingly, posh people had clocks as early as the 16th century. Isn't that an amazing thing!

Going further back in time, some 13th century floor tiles from here are displayed in the museum in Dumfries. You may have clocked them when you were there. I hope you did.

Chapter Sixty-Four

Tibbers Castle and Thornhill: The Explorer, the Hero and the Angels

IF you go down to the woods today, south from Drumlanrig, you will come to Tibbers, a motte-and-bailey castle possibly dating from the 12th century. It appears in documents for the first time in 1298 when Edward I paid a visit. Sir Richard Siward, Sheriff of Dumfries, was the keeper, and had sworn fealty to Edward. It was one of the first to be targeted by Robert the Bruce in 1306, but recaptured shortly afterwards by the English. The keeper at that time was John de Seton, who had been one of the witnesses at the murder of the Red Comyn. He was captured and taken to Newcastle where he was hanged, drawn and quartered. It's a dangerous thing to witness a crime such as that. In 1313, however, the castle was back in the hands of the Scots.

It stayed in the hands of the Earls of Moray until the 3rd Earl was killed at the Battle of Neville's Cross in 1346, at which point it was given to Patrick de Dunbar, the 9th Earl. It stayed in the family until 1435 when James I disinherited the 11th Earl because of his father's defection to Henry VI of England. The Earl had paid a large dowry to marry his daughter to the seven-year old James, son and heir to the throne. The king kept the money but never submitted the hand of the daughter, the rotter. He was by no means the only noble James offended. No wonder he was assassinated – a king in a jolly-good need of a killing.

In 1450 (or 1451), James II granted the castle to George Crichton, Lord High Admiral of Scotland. When he died, it came under the control of the Crown again. We know it was attacked by Sir Alexander

The Motte at Tibbers Castle

Stewart, 5th Laird of Garlies, in 1547, after which it disappears from the records and, over the centuries, disappeared altogether, leaving behind only a grassy mound. In the 18th century, it was thought to be a Roman fort. It actually comes from the Gaelic *tiobar*, meaning a "well".

If "Tibbers" seems an unlikely name for a castle, "Thornhill" sounds a prickly sort of name for a village. It was built in 1717 by the 3rd Earl of Queensberry, who originally named it "New Dalgarnock" after the practically-deserted older village. It didn't catch on.

At the centre of the village stands a tall sandstone cross, on the top of which is the winged horse, Pegasus, made of Leadhills lead and not erected in honour of Burns's horse. It is the symbol of the Queensberrys. Both were high-flyers, after all.

As you already know, Thornhill was the birthplace of that bicycle pioneer, Kirpatrick Macmillan (1812-78). Well, actually it wasn't. He came from Keir Mill, one mile south of Penpont, two miles west of Thornhill. Close enough for Thornhill to claim him. And that's not all. Believe it or not, Penpont produced a great son of its own. It's astonishing, it really is, how these tiny communities churn out famous men. Yet considering how often we have come across this phenomenon on our travels, both here and on the NC500, I really shouldn't be as surprised as I am.

There is a monument to him near the school, a bronze bust on a sandstone plinth. Who am I talking about? The African explorer, Joseph Thomson (1858-95), that's who. On his first expedition for the National Geographical Society in 1878, he unexpectedly found himself promoted to leader when Alexander Keith Johnston died. The expedition lasted fourteen months and covered 3,000 miles. His second expedition in 1883 was to explore a route from the east coast of Africa to the northern shores of Lake Victoria. He tried, and failed, to climb Mt Kilimanjaro in a day (just a wee challenge to set yourself) but did succeed in being gored by a buffalo – and if that were not enough, he caught malaria and dysentery. Who would an explorer be!

In 1885, he wrote a book about his experiences, *Through Masai Land*, which became a bestseller. One of the many who read it was H. Rider Haggard, and which inspired him to write *King Solomon's Mines*. Far from being flattered, Thomson was not amused (like the reigning monarch at the time was not, on another matter), when Haggard's character, Captain Good, emulated what he had done to the Masai – took out his false teeth, aweing the natives with his magical powers. He wrote his own novel, *Ulu: An African Romance*. It was a flop. He should have stuck to the travel writing.

• • •

I will not trouble you with the details of his further expeditions. Suffice it to say it was part and parcel of the *Scramble for Africa*. In 1890 he was hired by Cecil Rhodes to conclude treaties and gain mining concessions from the tribal chiefs. Twenty years before this expedition, only 10% of Africa was under European control; twenty or so years later, by the outbreak of the First World War, it was close to an amazing 90%. The British weren't the only ones involved in this carving-up of Africa. The Germans, for one, were too. Think of C.S. Forester's *African Queen*.

The great explorer's health was never robust, and in 1892 he contracted pneumonia. He scoured England, France, Italy and South Africa in the search of the ideal climate for his chesty complaint. In the end, he died in London in 1895. He was only thirty-seven (but please note, in possession of full set of falsers from the age of twenty-five at least). In his short life, however, he achieved much, much more than we humble mortals can ever dream of. He had a gazelle named after him, a 243-foot waterfall in Kenya, and perhaps less gloriously, two types of snail. Last and least, a freshwater bi-valve.

Before we take our leave of him, I would like to leave this thought with you. Thomson was a very competent manager of men, and a diplomat, never killing a native in all of his expeditions or losing a man through violence. His motto, his *modus vivendi*, was: *He who goes gently, goes safely; he who goes safely, goes far.*

On the same memorial is a plaque to Samuel Wallace VC (1892-1968). Not at all possible for him to go safely, unfortunately, thanks to the times in which he was born. It is a dangerous thing to be born. You have absolutely no control of the time, place or to whom.

Wallace gained this distinction in November 1917 at Gonnelieu in France. His battery, surrounded by the enemy, was reduced to five, having lost five sergeants and their commander. As a temporary lieutenant (and it looked as if it was going to be very temporary indeed), for eight hours, he and his men ran from gun to gun, keeping up a constant fire on the enemy and inflicting heavy casualties. Thankfully, he and the wounded were able to leave when infantry support finally arrived.

And believe it or not, this little-out-of-the-way place in Scotland is the global HQ of the HALO Trust. It has offices in Washington DC and San Francisco, but here, in tiny Thornhill, are the headquarters. Isn't that an amazing thing!

What *is* the HALO Trust? That's a good question. I'd never heard of it either until I came here. It's a non-political, non-profit, non-religious, British charity and American organisation. It is dedicated to removing debris from battle-sites, particularly land mines.

It was the brainchild, in 1988, of Guy Willoughby and Sue and Colin Campbell Mitchell MP, former Lt. Colonel in the British army, aka *Mad Mitch.* He died in 1996, aged 70.

A charity it may be, but it also receives £25 million annually from the UK government and others around the world. There are about 6,000 people risking life and limb to remove these ghastly items that can, and do, kill and maim innocent kids at play while their parents try to rebuild their houses and their lives after the guns have fallen silent.

Currently HALO employs more than 7,000 people in 17 countries. Its achievements are awesome. It's a word that is overused these days, but I use it advisedly here. More than 1.5 million landmines, 11 million pieces of heavy weaponry and 200,000 cluster munitions – evil little monsters, specifically designed to kill people and vehicles, who unwittingly come into contact with them. In addition to that, 10,800 minefields have been cleared, amounting to more than 87,000 acres, not to mention another 362,000 acres made safe from other unexploded ordnance.

If you are wondering what HALO stands for, apart from sounding rather saintly, it stands for "Hazardous Areas Life-support Organisation". It may sound a tad contrived, but surely an appropriate name for the angels who go where others fear to tread, or do so unwaringly.

Chapter Sixty-Five

Durisdeer and the Devil's Beef Tub: Death and Some Gruesome Murders

BRANCHING a little way off the A702 is the picturesque little village of Durisdeer, from the Gaelic *dubhros* "a dark wood" and *doire* "an oak copse". It appeared in the 1978 film of *The Thirty-Nine Steps* starring Robert Powell.

If you go up the Well or Wald Path, you will come to a Roman fortlet where the ditch and ramparts are still pretty-well preserved. And if you do so, you will be following in the path of James IV who stopped at Durisdeer in 1497 on his way to St Ninian's Church at Whithorn. And if you had the wings of an eagle, you might be able to spot the remains of two temporary Roman camps that can't be seen at ground level.

The most notable feature of Durisdeer is the church, much bigger that you would expect to see in such a small settlement. It was designed by James Smith, and built by the 3rd Duke of Queensberry in the 1720s using stone from the abandoned Durisdeer Castle. The reason for its hugeness is that, attached to it is the two-storey session house and ducal apartments which, at the 3rd Duke's behest, were later used as the parish school. After being restored in 1968, they are presently being used as a tearoom, amongst other things. The clock in the tower was the gift of the 11th Duke to commemorate the millennium and the tercentenary of the church.

The church itself is an atmospheric place with box pews and galleries running round three sides, but most interesting of all, at least to my mind, is the *Queensberry Aisle* which ajoins the only wall of the medieval church left standing after it was demolished to make way for the new church.

Access to the Aisle is gained by a separate door. The white-marble baldacchino with barley-sugar pillars hits you in the eye. It was carved by the Flemish sculptor, John van Nost, in 1711. The floor consists of black-and-white chequered marble tiles like a Vermeer interior. A black slab denotes the

Durisdeer Church

entrance to the mausoleum, built between 1695 and 1708 for the 1st Duke of Queensberry.

On the wall behind the baldacchino is a baroque memorial to the 2nd Duke and his wife, Mary. It's actually *her* tomb, as the Latin inscription beneath the figures explains. She is lying on her back, her neck and head resting on a cushion as if having forty winks on a couch. Such portrayals are common-place, as if to say death is just a long sleep. But it's the figure of the Duke that's interesting. He is lying by her side, propped up on his right elbow, his head resting on his hand, his ankles crossed, a picture of insouciance as if he has just been telling her a bedtime story and she had drifted off to asleep. Above his head, a quartet of cherubs has just unrolled a scroll announcing the date of his decease two years later. Fortunately he hasn't noticed it. Who amongst us would like to know their date of death? It's better to die in ignorance.

Outside the church is the war memorial. It bears the names of thirty-three men who lost their lives in that other killing time, the First World War. In the cemetery is the grave of yet another Covenanter, Daniel McMaster, who was shot at Dalveen in 1685.

Also in the cemetery are the graves of the ballet dancer and actress, Moira Shearer (1926-2006), and her husband, the investigative journalist Sir Ludovic Kennedy (1919-2009). They met when he asked her to dance at a ball. She accepted but warned him: "I'm not a very good dancer." She was serious. Ballroom dancing was not her forte.

Most famously, Kennedy contested the conviction of Timothy Evans for the murder of his baby daughter, arguing that John Christie was the real murderer. Three years after Evans was hanged, when six more bodies were uncovered at 10 Rillington Place, Christie paid the ultimate penalty for his serial killings. Kennedy's book was made into a famous film, both bearing the same title. It's arguably the most infamous address in Britain after 10 Downing Street. Largely as a result of this celebrated case, the death penalty was abolished in this country in 1965 and the following year Evans was given a posthumous pardon.

● ● ●

Kennedy followed that up twenty years later with his *The Airman and the Carpenter* in which he contended that Richard Hauptman, who was executed in 1936, was not the kidnapper and killer of Charles Lindberg's baby. That too was made into a HBO film, *Crime of the Century*, starring Stephen Rea and Isabella Rossellini.

We rejoin the A702 at Durisdeer Mill, where the mill aforesaid is a B-listed building and shortly afterwards enter the Dalveen Pass, the third through the Lowthers and the highest at 1,148 feet. It's a wild sort of place; would be a terrible place to get lost in. If you didn't know any better, you could easily imagine you were in some remote valley miles from anywhere. That's what I like about it.

We run parallel for a while with the Roman road and after crossing the Southern Upland Way, we actually join it, not that you woud know it, before we arrive in Elvanfoot. The origin of the name is obscure but probably means "bright" or "shining water". It is situated at the confluence of the Elvan Water and the Clyde and thus Elvanfoot becomes the first and last village on the Clyde.

Just to the north of the village, we join the B7076, part of the National Cycle Network and which runs parallel with the A74 (M). We have been on it before, you remember, when we went to Lockerbie, amongst other places, and if there is an easier road to drive along throughout the length and breadth of the UK then I'd like to know what it is.

It's not long before we come to Beattock Summit, 1,016 feet above sea level and 53 miles to Glasgow Central and 349 to London, Euston, so the sign says on the West Coast Main Line. Actually it is 1,033 feet, but who's to know? In the days of steam, the gradient was so steep, coming from the north especially, that "banking" locomotives were kept on stand-by down in the village of Beattock to give the engines who were running out of puff a bit of a shove.

The summit is immortalised in *The Night Mail*, a 24-minute film made for the GPO. It is a wonderful collaborative effort using the skills of the directors Harry Watt and Basil Wright, the voices of Stuart Legg and John Grierson, the music of Benjamin

The Dalveen Pass

Britten and the rhythmical verse of W.H. Auden, and not least, the huff and puff of the engine itself, No.6155, the *Scots Guardsman*. Auden's image of the hills hereabouts resembling "slaughtered horses" was wisely cut.

The part of the poem that is relevant here is: *Pulling up Beattock, a steady climb:/The gradient's against her, but she's on time.* No need of a shove then – you can hear from the rhythm that she is clattering along, *shovelling steam over her shoulder* as if Beattock were a mere molehill.

The black-and-white film adds enormously to the atmosphere, and there is something terribly nostalgic about the poem's opening lines: *This is the Night Mail crossing the border/Bringing the cheque and postal order* – and something ineffably sad about the coda, spoken by Grierson: *And none will hear the postman's knock/Without a quickening of the heart,/For who can bear to feel himself forgotten?*

Whilst the primary purpose was to inform the general public about how much work went into delivering a letter (and the sooner the better), this mini-masterpiece far transcends mere propaganda and enters the realms of art in many ways. At the end, I am left imagining all those people coming down in the morning hoping to see the expected letter on the doormat, only to find it *still* has not come.

As we travel south, we pay particular attention to the plantation on the right. The saying "Every man should plant a tree, have a child and write a book" is attributed to various sources, the favourites being the Talmud and the Cuban poet and revolutionary, José Martí. Done that. Two kids, a dozen books, and trees without number. How tall they've grown! When I was a student, one summer I got a job planting them with the Countess of Seafield Estates. We slept in sleeping bags on the hard wooden floor at Nether Howcleuch Farm. Despite these Spartan conditions, it was such backbreaking work that we did indeed sleep. I don't know about the others, but I didn't count sheep – I counted trees.

When the trees stop and before the next plantation begins, we cross the motorway and join the B719 in the direction of Moffat – only we are not going there, not yet. We are heading for the Devil's Beef Tub on the A701, where, according to legend, Wallace met with the Border Clans before his first attack against the English in 1297.

This evocatively-named five-hundred foot natural hollow is formed by four hills. It was given the nickname because the enemies of those notorious Border Reivers, the Earls of Annandale, referred to them as "devils", and this is where they used to hide their stolen cattle. The Reivers operated on both sides of the border from the late 13th century to the early 17th century and were such a nuisance, to put it mildly, that after the death of Elizabeth I, the English seriously thought of fortifying Hadrian's Wall again.

In his novel, *Redgauntlet,* Sir Walter Scott described the Beef Tub thus: "It looks as if four hills were laying their heads together, to shut out daylight from the dark hollow space between them. A damned deep, black, blackguard-looking abyss of a hole it is." Defoe would whole-heartedly agree, and perhaps Auden. In the novel, Scott recounts the story of a Highlander who, in the aftermath of the Jacobite Rebellion of 1745, manages to escape the enemy's gunfire by rolling down one of the hills that form the Beef Tub like an Easter egg. Good for him!

Not so fortunate is the real-life story of John Hunter, a Covenanter, who, on 12th August 1685, was fleeing from Col. James Douglas's dragoons by climbing out of the Beef Tub. Alas, a speeding bullet travels a lot faster than he or they could run. A monument on the south-west rim marks where he fell. If you do not have the time or the inclination to make the climb, a replica monument has thoughtfully been placed by the roadside, where all you need to do is raise your eyes to the hills to see the spot of bloody execution. The stone tells you what I have said above, with the addition of where he is buried, namely Tweedsmuir Kirkyard. Home is that Hunter, home from the hills.

Taken from their home round about September 14th 1935 and left on this bare hillside, were the dismembered body parts of two women. On 29th September, a motorist stopped her car near the bridge over the Gardenholme Linn, a tributary of the River Annan, to admire the scenery. Looking down into the ravine, she saw a package with something that looked suspiciously like a human arm sticking out of it. She fetched her brother from Moffat and got him to go down into the ravine and look at the parcel at closer quarters. Her suspicions were confirmed.

Two hours later, the police found more than thirty parcels containing the body parts. One clue as to who had done this dreadful thing was that the bodies had been expertly dismembered. The killer had to be someone with medical knowledge and was taking care to ensure the bodies could not be identified. Some teeth had been extracted, the hands lacerated, the fingertips, ears, noses, lips and eyes removed. Even the blood had been drained.

There was another vital clue – one of the newspapers used to wrap up the bloody parcels (as butchers used to do in those days), was the *Sunday Graphic,* which was only sold in the Lancaster and Morecombe area. Not only that – it had a small subscription list. An elementary mistake by the murderer after all the careful precautions he had taken to ensure the bodies could not be identified. The search for his identity had been considerably narrowed down.

Dr Buck Ruxton, born in Bombay, was charged with the murder of his common-law wife, Isabelle Kerr – the estranged wife of a Dutchman – and Mary Rogerson, their maid. They had both been reported as missing, but, significantly, not by Ruxton. Another thing that counted against him was that on his way back from dumping the body-parts, he knocked a cyclist off his bike and didn't stop. The cyclist noted the registration number of the car and reported the incident to the police. It turned out to belong to Ruxton's Austin 12.

Buxton had told the neighbours the ladies had gone to visit his wife's sister in Edinburgh. Although the bones found at the Devils' Beef Tub were of the same age and build as the two missing women, that was not enough to positively identify them.

Ruxton changed his story to the police that his wife had left him and that Mary had run away somewhere to have an abortion. Meanwhile, Professors Glaister and Brash, and the renowned pathologist, Sidney Smith, of Edinburgh University, forensically examined the body parts. Meanwhile, Dr Alexander Mearns of Glasgow University, by examining the maggots on them, was able to ascertain how long they had been lying in the locus. They also superimposed an X-ray of the skull on a photograph of Mrs Ruxton's face taken from the same distance. They matched.

Ruxton was arrested two weeks later and then he did a very strange thing. He asked to see a newspaper reporter and handed him a sealed envelope to be opened after his death, or returned unopened, should he be acquitted. With the £3,000 the newspaper gave him for this, he financed his defence.

A fat lot of good it did him. The jury took only an hour to find him guilty. This was one of the first cases where the medical and forensic evidence played a large part in securing the conviction of a criminal. When the letter was opened, it contained a full confession in which Ruxton said he had killed his wife because he suspected she was having an affair. (He was paranoid about that and insanely jealous, without any good reason to be.) He was caught in the act of killing her by the maid, so she had to die too. If ever there was a time to be in the wrong place at the wrong time, then that was it.

Ironically, I can imagine she was overjoyed when she was engaged as nanny and general housemaid to the respected Ruxton household, where the good doctor, in the decade before the NHS, would treat poor patients for free. A jolly-good bloke. No wonder, there were 10,000 signatures pleading for clemency.

A children's rhyme at the time put it rather more unsympathetically:

Bloodstains on the carpet,
Bloodstains on your knife
Oh, Dr Buck Ruxton,
You murdered your wife.
Then Mary, she saw you,
You thought she would tell,
So, Dr Buck Ruxton,
You killed her as well.

He was executed on 12th May 1936 at Strangeways prison in Manchester. He was not tried for the murder of the twenty-year old Mary.

But then, after all, you can only be hanged once.

Chapter Sixty-Six

Moffat and Heathhall: Taking the Waters and to the Air

IN 1633, a mineral spring was found near Auldton of Moffat (from the Scots Gaelic *Am Magh Fada*), which boasted a church as early as 1177. The sulphurous and saline water was said to be very good for skin conditions, gout, rheumatism, and stomach complaints. It was refurbished in the 1990s and you can still go there today. Follow the street named "Well" in modern-day Moffat and you will come to it, you may be unsurprised to learn.

When a second spring containing iron was discovered in 1748, Moffat's reputation as a spa town was assured. The spring was called "Larchhill Well". The Victorians piped the water to a tank in the appropriately named "Tank Wood", and from there it was piped to a bathhouse in the town centre. Don't bother looking for it. It's gone.

Hotels sprung up to accommodate the visitors who were coming there for the good of their health, as well as travellers breaking their journey to and from Carlisle. The Black Bull was the first in 1683, and the Annandale Arms and Buccleuch Arms followed in 1760. Another spa was built in the town centre in 1827, later converted to the Town Hall. The impressive St Andrew's Parish Church was built in 1887.

The railway came to Beattock, two miles away, in 1848, but it was not until 1883 that a branch line was extended to Moffat. It brought passengers to the extensive Hydropathic Hotel which had opened in 1878. Sad to say, it burned down in 1921 and that, more or less, put an end to Moffat as a spa town. The branch line closed in 1954 and the station at Beattock in 1972. Moffat could settle down to getting back to sleep again. Or so it thought.

Because of its location, plentiful hotels, numerous B&Bs, self-catering cottages and ample (free) car parking, Moffat is as busy as ever. The Star Hotel – with a frontage of 20 feet – makes the Guinness Book of records as the narrowest hotel in Britain, while the Moffat House Hotel was originally built in

1767 for the 2nd Earl of Hoptoun by one of that famous family of Scottish architects, John Adam (1721-92).

A seven-minute video in the town museum, originally the old bakehouse, takes the visitor on a journey through the town's history from the Romans, the Reivers, the sulphurous spa times and right up to the present day. The museum was extended in 2013, and notably contains a Neolithic bow and a Roman brooch. The former was found in 1990 by a hill-walker in a peat bog known as "Rotten Bottom". (Sounds nasty. I wonder if taking the spa waters would affect a cure.) It was carbon-dated to being over 6,000 years old – the oldest ever found in the UK and Ireland. Take a bow that bow! Sorry to tell you, however, that what you see is an imitation. The real bow is in the National Museum of Scotland in Edinburgh.

Arguably the most absorbing thing about the square (which is rectangular) is the statue of a ram at the top of a tall sandstone fountain which, thoughtfully, incorporates a bowl lower down so animals may partake of the waters also. It was a gift to the town by businessman William Colville and celebrates Moffat's association with wool.

Various legends appertain to it. It was said that the sculptor committed suicide when it was pointed out that the statue had no ears. In actual fact, there is no truth to the legend whatsover as the ram was completed in 1875 and the sculptor, William Brodie, handed in his dinner pail in 1881. Tapping noises from inside the statue are said to emanate from the ghost of the sculptor, but what on

earth it is doing in there, apart from apparently wanting to get out, I have no idea. By the way, he also sculpted the statue of Greyfriar's Bobby in Edinburgh in 1872, though he was more of a bust man, if you see what I mean, responsible for many of the busts on the Scott Monument which were sculpted two years later.

As well as having a famous ram, Moffat also has a famous son – Air Chief Marshal Hugh Dowding (1882-1970). He was born at St Ninian's Boys' Preparatory School in the town, where his father was the *heidie* and founder. Young Hugh went on to Winchester College and the Royal Military Academy, Woolwich.

The Moffat Ram

He transferred to the RFC in 1914,

and I will skip his path to greatness after he gained his wings. He would have retired after a very successful career in June 1939, but then a certain little difficulty with Germany arose and he was asked to stay on. During the time he was in charge of RAF Fighter Command, he did not always see eye to eye with Churchill, preferring to keep his precious planes for the defence of the realm rather than risk them for the Battle of France. When that battle was lost, however, they did provide cover for the evacuation of Dunkirk.

Through the summer and autumn of 1940, Dowding's Fighter Command was all that stood between Britain and invasion. He developed an integrated system of air defence, while at the same time ensuring there was a supply of replacement aircraft and pilots. They say the sign of a good leader is that he knows when to delegate, and Dowding did that – he left the details of how to fight the actual battles to his commanders. They also say, "cometh the hour, cometh the man" and although it is applied to Churchill, it could fairly be said to apply to Dowding and the Battle of Britain – what Churchill called "Britain's darkest hours".

Then there was the problem with night-time bombing and the Blitz, where Dowding again found himself at odds with the powers-that-be on the subject of what was to be done about it. For Dowding, air-borne radar was the answer.

In the end, Dowding fell from grace. He had his enemies in the RAF, notably those like Douglas Bader who advocated a "Big Wing" strategy – basically a large offensive as a means of defence against the Luftwaffe – as opposed to Dowding's "Fabian" or hit-and-run tactics. (Robert the Bruce might have had an opinion on that.)

To this day, it is a matter of hot dispute whether or not the former would have been more effective, but then, after the Battle of Britain was won, the question became largely academic as Britain went on the offensive anyway and attacked Germany.

In what looks like a paving of the way for things to come, in October 1940 Dowding was given the rather Lilliputian-sounding honour of the Knight Grand Cross of the Order of the Bath. The following month, Churchill asked him to relinquish his command. It was not an offer he could refuse. He was replaced by Sholto Douglas, an advocate of the "Big Wing" theory. I think we can infer from that on which side of the divide Churchill stood.

Dowding died at Tunbridge Wells in 1970. It's amazing, when you think about it, the changes in technology that occurred during his lifetime. Born in 1882, the Wright brothers' first powered flight was nearly two decades in the future, and yet he lived to see men land on the moon. Isn't that an amazing thing!

His hometown has not forgotten him. A massive red sandstone memorial stands in the cemetery. It features a bronze portrait with some words below, but much more eye-catching is the black lettering on the top, those remarkably poetic words by Churchill: *Never, in the field of human conflict, was so much owed by so many to so few.* And beneath all that, just in case someone seeing this memorial should wonder what it is doing here, it supplies the answer: *Born in Moffat.*

Moffat also has a famous daughter. Well not really, but she could be an adopted one – D.E. Stevenson, the daughter of David Alan Stevenson, lighthouse designer and builder, the uncle of Robert Louis, who needs no introduction. She was a prolific and bestselling novelist who wrote most of her books in Moffat. She was born in 1892, two years before Robert Louis died in far-off Samoa. She died here in 1973. Obviously lighthouses weren't the only things that ran in the family – a way with words did too.

After paying our respects to Dorothy (my photographer and travelling companion became a big fan about the time poor Dorothy Emily was dying), we're on our way back to Dumfries and our last stop on this cultural heritage tour – the aviation museum at Heathhall.

Its origins began with a tragedy. On the night of the 3rd/4th June 1943, a Vickers Wellington Type 440 B Mk.X bomber from Leighton Buzzard suffered engine failure and crashed only a mile-and-a-half short of the runway in Dumfries. Three of the crew were killed and two were seriously injured. Thirty years later, local enthusiasts retrieved the engines, but – having done so – the question was what to do with them next. The solution was a pilot's flight hut remaining on the base and, from this humble beginning, the Dumfries and Galloway Aviation Museum was born in 1977. It is run and operated by volunteers under the leadership of David Reid. Hats off to him and them.

In another crash, on 7th April 1940, a Blackburn B-20 V8914, an experimental flying boat with a retractable lower hull, suffered what is known as "aileron flutter" and crashed into the sea. Three were killed and two were rescued by HMS *Transylvania.* (It didn't survive much longer itself – sunk by a U-boat on 10th August the same year.) The plane still lies at the bottom of the sea and is a designated war grave. However, in 1998 one of the engines was caught in a fishing boat's nets and dragged away from the wreckage. And that is why you see it here today.

Another unwitting and unwilling contribution to the museum was a General Dynamics F-111 swing-wing bomber which crashed off the Lincolnshire coast on 5th November 1975 when a bird penetrated the windshield. Ghastly! When I was a boy, a hen flew from its perch into my face, giving me a life-long fear of birds, in particular the wings that flap. Small beer compared to what happened to the pilot and the plane. He suffered severe head injuries but survived, as did his co-pilot. The kamikaze bird did not, nor did the plane. Where most military jets have ejection seats, in this model, the entire cockpit is ejected and that is what is on display here.

Finally, on the vexed matter of exhibits acquired by misfortune, you can see one of the engines of a Heinkel He 1114H-4. The aircraft was based at Soesterberg in the Netherlands and, on 8th August 1940, it hit the summit of Cairnsmore of Fleet on its way to lay mines off Belfast. They exploded, killing all four aircrew. Their remains are buried in Channock Chase German war cemetery in Staffordshire.

These tragic accidents augmented the museum's collection where there was plenty of space to accommodate them. When an American F-100 Super Sabre, a Lockheed T-33 Shooting Star aka *Little Miss Laura* (which saw service with the Belgian Air Force), and a French Dassault Mystère were acquired, larger premises were required and the museum moved to its present premises. It used to be RAF Dumfries which operated from 1940 until the surprisingly late date of 1957. Actually it never really closed at all, at least not for long. After a while it morphed into the Dumfries Gliding Club.

After a lot of hard work, the three-storey control tower, which had been used as a cowshed in the interim, became the focal point for the new museum. It was in a bit of a state, as you can imagine. There are a good number of plane engines on the ground floor with models hanging from the ceiling and everywhere else you care to look.

The middle floor features memorabilia from over a century of aviation history, too numerous to mention, but what catches my eye is the battered helmet of one of the pilots killed in a crash, while the upper floor takes you back in time to a wartime control and operations room. The hands on the clock on the wall stand still; the radio controllers with their headphones are motionless; the typists' fingers are suspended over their machines; an off-duty pilot stands gazing

Control and Operations Room, Dumfries and Galloway Aviation Museum

pensively out the window. I wonder what he's thinking. Possibly what the chances are of him surviving his next sortie.

As we leave the control tower, a plane appears to be beckoning us with a fistful of propellers sticking into the air. It's such an unusual sight, we have to investigate it right away. It turns out to be a Fairey Gannet AEW.3 XL497 with eight propeller blades. "AEW" stands for "airborne early warning", but the Gannet was originally conceived as an anti-submarine aeroplane. It operated from aircraft carriers between 1959 and 1978. It is powered by Mamba engines, placed side by side, like conjoined twins, sharing a common gearbox, in place of a heart. For a good reason, which I won't go into, the propellers spin in opposite directions. One engine could be shut down to save fuel and extend the range. Only 44 were ever built and only five are displayed in the UK so it's really a rather special addition to the collection here.

Nearby is a Hawker Siddeley Trident, retired from service with British Airways in 1985. There are not many museums that let you place as much as a fingertip on the exhibits, but here you can actually go inside the cabin and even sit in the pilots' seats. If you let your imagine soar, you can imagine you are flying the plane. It requires a great leap of the aforesaid, as you will not have failed to notice before you boarded, that it has neither wings nor engines.

The English Electric Lightning F.53, ZF584 is a relic from the Cold War. It made its appearance less than ten years after WWII ended, and yet the advance in technology was amazing. "Lightning" was its name, and it climbed into the air at lightning speed. The trouble was that it rapidly ran out of puff. Its fuel tanks were too small for long forays and if it intercepted a Russian plane over the North Sea, for example, it needed to be refuelled in mid-air before it could return to its base in Leuchars in Fife or Binbrook in Lincolnshire.

This specimen is no stranger to being an exhibit. It saw service with the Saudi Air Force from 1968 to 1986, after which it returned to the UK. It was mothballed for a number of years before being presented to Ferranti, who displayed it outside its Edinburgh factory until it closed in 2000.

I won't trouble you with a list of all the aircraft or parts thereof that you can see here. I will mention, however, a Gloster Meteor T7, Britain's first jet-powered fighter, and a Wessex helicopter which saw service in the Falklands War. Keeping it company in the rotor brigade is a Bristol Sycamore, the first British-designed helicopter to enter service with the RAF. It first clattered into the sky in 1950. Amazing to think that Leonardo da Vinci first conceived of the idea five centuries before that!

There is much, much more to the museum than aircraft and their engines. One building is dedicated to the Airborne Forces – in particular, the Parachute

Regiment. As well as parachutes, there are uniforms and weapons (non-serviceable, as a notice points out to terrorists who might think they had stumbled upon a treasure trove), as well as the restored part of the fuselage of an Airspeed Horsa Glider that was used by the Parachute Regiment at Arnhem and the Normandy Landings.

Spitfire exhibit on display at Dumfries and Galloway Aviation Museum

Meanwhile, on the Home Front – in something I dare say provides a piece of nostalgia for many visitors (like me) – a shop and a kitchen from the 1940s has been recreated. The shopkeeper in the former is rather comical. With his bowler hat and toothbrush moustache, he is the very image of Charlie Chaplin but that said, there was nothing funny about wartime rationing. To tell you the truth, I never found Chaplin in the least funny either.

There is also a corrugated Anderson shelter in which families sought protection from the bombs – if they were lucky enough to have a garden in which they could build one of course. If they didn't, there were communal shelters and Londoners famously used the Underground.

Made of six curved sheets of corrugated iron with steel plates at either end, and half-buried in the ground with earth heaped upon the top, they could accommodate up to six people. They measured six feet by four-and-a-half. Dark and damp, a bucket in a corner served as a toilet. They were issued free to householders with an income of less than £250, whilst those earning more than that were charged a nominal £7. You were expected to take important documents with you such as your birth and marriage certificates, and – whatever you did – you must not forget your gas mask. They were not universally popular, and a lot of people preferred just to take their chance rather than endure those Spartan conditions for the duration of an air raid. And who can blame them?

There is so much to see here, you could spend hours and not see everything. I've kept the best to last. It's arguably the star of the museum – the Spitfire that was *deep drown'd in Doon* like Tam o' Shanter's wife predicted would be the death of *him*. You will remember that the museum acquired it through tragic circumstances when the pilot made an error of judgement, when as he was banking, a wing clipped the water and it summersaulted into the air before plummeting into the depths below.

There is also an engine from another stricken Spitfire, paid for by the patriotic people of Newmarket, as part of the war effort. They named it *Blue Peter* after the winner of the 1939 Derby. The pilot was nineteen-year old David Gaspard Hunter Blair. On 23rd May 1942, he was flying out of Ayr, his mission being to provide air cover for the RMS *Queen Mary*. She had been requisitioned as a troopship, but – on the way – Blair was ordered to intercept an enemy plane inland. Something happened and he was forced to eject. Unfortunately his parachute failed to open and the plane crashed near the summit of the 2,615 foot-high Cairnsmore of Carsphairn. He was the third son of Sir John Hunter Blair, 7th Baronet of Blairquhan Castle.

The engine was recovered in 1993 with the help of a Royal Navy Sea King from HMS *Gannet*, and now it is in the museum in precisely the same state as it was when it was recovered. The story featured in the children's TV programme *Blue Peter*. In an odd coincidence, the founder of that programme was a man named John Hunter Blair. It's not exactly a common name.

Occupying the same hangar as the Spitfire, are an army jeep and a Morris 8. Its headlights are equipped with masked headlights – a narrow slit with a projecting shroud. Somehow it reminds me of a coquettish female with fluttering false eyelashes. It's an absurdly stupid thought. Nothing sexy at all about driving at night during the war. You would only do so if you had to – and at a snail's pace.

Hanging on the wall, framed, is a yellowing newspaper cutting about Archie McKellar, DSO, DFC & Bar (1912-40). Born in Paisley and a plasterer to trade, he joined the RAF in 1936.

He had an extremely distinguished career. On 16th October 1939, the Luftwaffe launched its first attack on Britain. They were targeting HMS *Hood*. She happened to be in dry dock, but they successfully attacked other ships. Archie, as he was known for short – or "Shrimp" affectionately, because he was so vertically challenged at only 5 foot 3 inches tall – was accredited with the shooting-down over the Forth, of the first enemy plane, a Junkers Ju 88, during the period known as the *Phoney War*.

Then, on 28th October, he shot down a Heinkel He 111, the first German plane to be shot down over land. Over water and land, the first two kills went to Archie. That was some start to his war.

Dowding was delighted. He sent a message of congratulations to Archie's Squadron 602: "Well done, first blood to the auxiliaries". For their part, the German pilots dubbed the Firth of Forth "Suicide alley".

He was transferred to Squadron 605, and it was there that his real claim to fame began. On 15th August 1940, he shot down 3 Heinkels 111. On 9th September, he repeated the performance by downing three more Heinkels and a Messerchmitt Bf 109. That was followed on 15th September, the day that was to be designated "Battle of Britain Day", with two more Messerschmitts and a Dornier Do 17. That same night, in the early hours of the next day, he upped his total to four by shooting down a Heinkel.

On 7th October, he surpassed himself by shooting down no fewer than five Messerschmitts. That made him an *Ace in a Day*. Three more kills followed on 20th, 26th and 27th October respectively. It's also possible he was responsible for another in the battle where he was shot down over Kent on 1st November at 08.20 hrs.

He had amassed a total of 21 kills, 22 if you count the last-mentioned. No-one else ever claimed it. With, or without it, that made him Top Gun during the Battle of Britain – yet you won't find his name on the roll of honour in the RAF Chapel in Westminster Abbey for those who laid down their lives during the Battle of Britain. In their wisdom, the powers-that-be decided that it took place from 10th July 1940 to 31st October. Poor Archie died eight hours too late for his name to be included.

Have you ever heard of anything more ridiculous?

Postscriptum

AND that was the last place we visited on our tour of the SWC300. It was rather a sad leave-taking we had of it, it has to be said. And just as poor Archie McKellar deserves to be better known, so does this scenically beautiful part of Scotland – what has been dubbed *Scotland's Secret Corner*.

As I say at the start of the adventure, we chose to begin our tour in Dumfries and travelled clockwise. In addition to that, we indulged in one or two detours, one of them in the opposite direction – east – as far as Gretna Green. I recommend you take it – and the others too, if time allows. It would be a pity to be so near and not explore the parts the SWC300 does not reach. Remember, it's a route – not a railroad.

Since it's circular, you can begin where you like, travel clockwise or anticlockwise, as the mood takes you.

And if you can't go just yet, why not read this book first – you will get a lot more out of your trip if you do. If you are interested in finding out the stories behind the many abbeys, castles, grand houses and tower houses that you encounter along the way, this book goes into depth about them in a way that the guidebooks and brochures never can.

Happy travelling!

Image Credits

The illustrations in this book are sourced from the personal photographic collection of the author, with the exception of the following images which are detailed below:

Page 34:   Image of Dumfries Museum and Camera Obscura is Copyright © FutureMuseumSW and is licensed under the Creative Commons Attribution-Share Alike 3.0 Unported license (https://creativecommons.org/licenses/by-sa/3.0/deed.en). Wikimedia Commons.

Page 65:   Image of the Savings Banks Museum in Ruthwell is Copyright © Professional Images (UK) Ltd./The Savings Bank, Ruthwell, all rights reserved, and is reproduced by kind permission of the owner.

Page 68:   Image of Annan is Copyright © Red Sunset and is licensed under the Creative Commons Attribution-Share Alike 3.0 Unported license (https://creativecommons.org/licenses/by-sa/3.0/deed.en). Wikimedia Commons.

Page 70:   Image of Eastriggs is Copyright © Red Sunset and is licensed under the Creative Commons Attribution-Share Alike 2.5 Generic license (https://creativecommons.org/licenses/by-sa/2.5/deed.en). Wikimedia Commons.

Page 76:   Image of the Old Blacksmith's Shop at Gretna Green is Copyright © Niki Odolphie from Frome, England and is licensed under the Creative Commons Attribution 2.0 Generic license (https://creativecommons.org/licenses/by/2.0/ deed.en). Wikimedia Commons.

Page 101:   Image of the Twelve Apostles stone circle is Copyright © August Schwerdfeger and is licensed under the Creative Commons Attribution 4.0 International license (https://creativecommons.org/ licenses/by/4.0/deed.en). Wikimedia Commons.

Page 116:   Image of Sweetheart Abbey in Dumfries by InspiredImages at Pixabay. Public Domain Image.

Page 153:   Image of Orchardtown Tower in Dumfries and Galloway is Copyright © Mike Palmer and is licensed under the Creative Commons Attribution-Share Alike 3.0 Unported license

About the Author

A native of Banff, Scotland, David M. Addison is a graduate of Aberdeen University. In addition to essays in various publications, he has written several books, mainly about his travels.

As well as a short spell teaching English as a foreign language in Poland when the Solidarity movement at its height, he spent a year (1978-79) as an exchange teacher in Montana.

He regards his decision to apply for the exchange as one of the best things he ever did, for not only did it give him the chance to travel extensively in the US and Canada but during the course of the year he made a number of enduring friendships. The third instalment in his *Innocent Abroad* series, entitled *Less Innocent Abroad*, is forthcoming from Extremis Publishing.

Since taking early retirement (he is not as old as he looks), he has more time but less money to indulge his unquenchable thirst for travel (and his wife would say for Cabernet Sauvignon and malt whisky). He is doing his best to spend the children's inheritance by travelling as far and wide and as often as he can.

Exploring the NC500

Travelling Scotland's Route 66

By David M. Addison

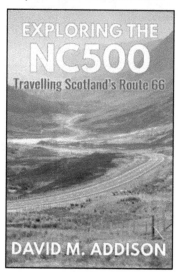

Travelling anti-clockwise, David M. Addison seeks his kicks on Scotland's equivalent of Route 66. Otherwise known as NC500, the route takes you through five hundred miles of some of Scotland's most spectacular scenery. No wonder it has been voted as one of the world's five most scenic road journeys.

There are many ways of exploring the NC500. You can drive it, cycle it, motorbike it or even walk it, even if you are not one of The Proclaimers! And there are as many activities, places of interest and sights to be seen along the way as there are miles.

This is a personal account of the author's exploration of the NC500 as well as some detours from it, such as to the Black Isle, Strathpeffer and Dingwall. Whatever your reason or reasons for exploring the NC500 may be, you should read this book before you go, or take it with you as a *vade mecum*. It will enhance your appreciation of the NC500 as you learn about the history behind the turbulent past of the many castles; hear folk tales, myths and legends connected with the area; become acquainted with the ancient peoples who once lived in this timeless landscape, and read about the lives of more recent heroes such as the good Hugh Miller who met a tragic end and villains such as the notorious Duke of Sutherland, who died in his bed (and may not be quite as bad as he is painted). There are a good number of other characters too of whom you may have never heard: some colourful, some eccentric, some *very* eccentric.

You may not necessarily wish to follow in the author's footsteps in all that he did, but if you read this book you will certainly see the landscape through more informed eyes as you do whatever you want to do *en route* NC500.

Sit in your car and enjoy the scenery for its own sake (and remember you get a different perspective from a different direction, so you may want to come back and do it again to get an alternative point of view!), or get out and explore it at closer quarters – the choice is yours, but this book will complement your experience, whatever you decide.

An Innocent Abroad

The Misadventures of an Exchange Teacher in Montana: Award-Winner's Edition

By David M. Addison

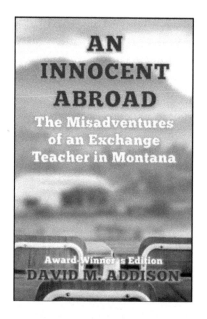

When, in 1978, taking a bold step into the unknown, the author, accompanied by his wife and young family, swapped his boring existence in Grangemouth in central Scotland for life in Missoula, Montana, in the western United States, he could never have foreseen just how much of a life-changing experience it would turn out to be.

As an exchange teacher, he was prepared for a less formal atmosphere in the classroom, while, for their part, his students had been warned that he would be "Mr Strict". It was not long before this clash of cultures reared its ugly head and the author found life far more "exciting" than he had bargained for. Within a matter of days of taking up his post, he found himself harangued in public by an irate parent, while another reported him to the principal for "corrupting" young minds.

Outwith the classroom, he found daily life just as shocking. Lulled by a common language into a false sense of a "lack of foreignness", he was totally unprepared for the series of culture shocks that awaited him from the moment he stepped into his home for the year – the house from *Psycho*.

There were times when he wished he had stayed at home in his boring but safe existence in Scotland, but mainly this is a heart-warming and humorous tale of how this Innocent abroad, reeling from one surprising event to the next, gradually begins to adapt to his new life. And thanks to a whole array of colourful personalities and kind people (hostile parents not withstanding), he finally comes to realise that this exchange was the best thing he had ever done.

This award-winning book, the opening volume of the *Innocent Abroad* series, charts the first months of the author's adventures and misadventures in a land which he finds surprisingly different.

Prize Writer
Competition
2015

WINNER

**An Award-Winning Book in the 2015 Bookbzz Prize Writer
Competition for Biography and Memoir**

For details of new and forthcoming books from
Extremis Publishing,
please visit our official website at:

www.extremispublishing.com

or follow us on social media at:

www.facebook.com/extremispublishing

www.linkedin.com/company/extremis-publishing-ltd-/

Lightning Source UK Ltd.
Milton Keynes UK
UKHW020627260421
382632UK00003B/222